BC

METHUEN'S MANUALS OF MODERN PSYCHOLOGY

EDITED BY C. A. MACE

THE PSYCHOLOGY OF JUNG

A Critical Interpretation

THE PSYCHOLOGY OF JUNG

A Critical Interpretation

———

Avis M. Dry

LONDON : METHUEN & CO LTD
NEW YORK : JOHN WILEY & SONS INC

First published in 1961
© 1961 by Avis M. Dry
Printed in Great Britain by
Hazell Watson & Viney Ltd
Aylesbury and Slough
Catalogue No. (Methuen) 2/6462/10

CONTENTS

ABBREVIATIONS

Works of Jung

Collected Papers	*Collected Papers on Analytical Psychology*
Contemp. Events	*Essays on Contemporary Events*
Contribs.	*Contributions to Analytical Psychology*
Integ. of Person.	*The Integration of the Personality*
Mod. Man	*Modern Man in Search of a Soul*
Psych. and Alchemy	*Psychology and Alchemy*
Psych. and Religion	*Psychology and Religion*
Psych. Types	*Psychological Types*
Psych. of the Unconsc.	*Psychology of the Unconscious*
Two Essays	*Two Essays on Analytical Psychology*

OTHER WORKS

Freud, S.

Introd. Lectures	*Introductory Lectures on Psycho-Analysis*
New Introd. Lectures	*New Introductory Lectures on Psycho-Analysis*

Horney, K.

New Ways	*New Ways in Psychoanalysis*

James, W.

Varieties	*Varieties of Religious Experience*

INTRODUCTION

Probably few writers in any field have been held in more varied esteem than C. G. Jung. His earliest contributions—the Word Association experiments and the monograph on Dementia Praecox, for example—have been universally recognized. But, as H. G. Baynes, a co-worker for many years, expressed it, in the allusions to this aspect of Jung's work 'there is a distinctly retrospective flavour which would be appropriate only to an author who has since died.'[1] Concerning the later work—that produced after about 1915—together with Psychology of the Unconscious (1912) no such agreement has been reached. Enthusiastic supporters can be found. Baynes, for instance, described the later ideas of Jung as 'psychological explosives which could affect human life as profoundly as the release of atomic energy.'[2] Another supporter, Dr. Jolan de Jacobi, states that Jung's 'far-reaching and powerful works . . . probe the remotest depths of the psyche. . . . No one who does not stand aside from real life will be able to avoid a coming to terms with Jung, whether his attitude be one of agreement or disagreement.'[3] A third, Dr. Erich Neumann, believes Jung's work to be 'the grandest attempt yet made to construct a theory of the psyche.'[4] Similarly, Dr. Joseph Goldbrunner considers that Jung has 'established his fame as a psychologist for whom Freud and Adler merely provided a few basic materials.'[5] Many members of Jung's school speak of a sense of enlargement which his writings bring. According to Goldbrunner again, the seeker after self-understanding 'feels something of the activity, emotions, experience and development of real life. The approach is dynamic, not academically static; the soul is not en-

[1] *Analytical Psychology and the English Mind*, p. 49. London: Methuen, 1950.
[2] Preface to *Two Essays on Analytical Psychology*, p. v. London: Ballière, Tindall & Cox, 1928.
[3] *Psychological Reflections*, pp. xxiii–iv. London: Routledge & Kegan Paul, 1953.
[4] 'The Significance of the Genetic Aspect for Analytical Psychology.' *J. Analyt. Psychol.*, Vol. IV, No. 2, 1959; pp. 125–37 (p. 126).
[5] *Individuation*, p. 61. London: Hollis & Carter, 1955.

meshed in a logically constructed system.'[1] Dr. Hans Schaer finds that 'The moment you start on Jung's psychology you have the feeling of entering into a spacious new world that contains wide tracts of unknown territory and many secrets, and that accordingly holds out all sorts of possibilities of discovery.'[2] Outside the ranks of the Jungian school itself, J. B. Priestley states that he has returned to Jung's books time after time, re-reading them with increasing pleasure and profit. 'He seems to me not only one of the great original thinkers of our time, but also one of its few liberators.'[3] Whereas many theorists cut down our horizons, giving a point of view at the expense of the size and complexity of life, Jung 'has opened roads along which the writer can travel hopefully.'[4] And one of the foremost Jungian practitioners in Britain, Dr. Michael Fordham, sees him as a reconciler of science and religion: 'His path has taken him into scientifically different situations, so that again and again many have supposed him lost to its disciplines, but in reality his scientific roots have always protected him from disaster, and after each new excursion he returns to his fundamental basis, greatly strengthened.'[5] He has made a contribution toward the spiritual crisis by providing 'a means of experiencing the reality of spiritual facts in such a way that they cannot be denied and at the same time their experience does not offend the scientific intellect, whose activity is enhanced and directed into a new and positive channel by a change in its use.'[6]

The attitude of the orthodox psychoanalytical school, on the other hand, has been almost uniformly hostile. Freud himself refers to some work done 'by C. G. Jung, at a time when this investigator was a mere psycho-analyst, and did not yet aspire to be a prophet.'[7] Edward Glover, in his *Freud or Jung*, describes the later Jungian psychology as 'a mish-mash of Oriental philosophy with a bowdlerised psychobiology',[8] and makes three major charges—that Jung's psychological theories are incoherent, that instead of going beyond Freud as his

---

[1] *Ibid.*, p. 12.
[2] *Religion and the Cure of Souls in Jung's Psychology*, p. 21. London: Routledge & Kegan Paul, 1951.
[3] Cited on flyleaf of *Essays on Contemporary Events*. London: Kegan Paul, 1947.
[4] *Times Literary Supplement*, p. iii. August 6, 1954.
[5] 'Professor C. G. Jung.' *Brit. J. Med. Psychol.*, Vol. XX, Pt. 3, 1945; pp. 221–35 (p. 221).   [6] *Ibid*, 232
[7] *Introductory Lectures on Psycho-Analysis*, p. 228. London: Allen & Unwin, 1922.
[8] *Freud or Jung*, p. 134. London: Allen & Unwin, 1950.

followers have claimed, he is a pre-Freudian and a psychologist of consciousness, and that he is a pedagogue more than a psychologist. Nor do writers have to be so strictly Freudian to be adverse in their judgment: 'so mysterious as to be almost undiscussable' is a recent academic verdict.[1]

In between the more extreme views lies a body of opinion ranging from indifference to a bewildered feeling that there may be something in Jung, though it's hard to see just what it is. Special reservations have sometimes been expressed about Jung's mode of presentation. It is always difficult to criticize Jung, writes J. E. Nicole, 'for he has a way peculiarly his own of urging his reader to keep hold of commonsense while all the time insidiously and persuasively sweeping him off his feet.'[2] It was said by one reviewer, as long ago as 1917, that 'There is in his work so much that is vital and suggestive that a re-interpretation in more scientific terms would be a real service'[3] and some twenty years afterwards H. A. Murray also spoke, rather more positively, of the value of Jung's writings as 'a hive of great suggestiveness.'[4] On the whole there seems in the last ten or fifteen years to have been an increased interest in Jung's contributions. A revised and much extended edition of his works is gradually being made available in English; articles written from the Jungian standpoint are not uncommon in the *British Journal of Medical Psychology*; the *Journal of Analytical Psychology* has been founded in Great Britain in addition to the older *Eranus Jahrbuch* in Switzerland, and while Jungian literature as yet is by no means so extensive as the Freudian, its quantity is becoming more formidable. Training schools have been established in Zürich, London, and the U.S.A., and the International Association for Analytical Psychology has been formed. However, although there are signs of closer co-operation in joint symposia with other schools,[5] the diverging attitudes continue: in the same year in which Erich Neumann spoke of Jung's work as the grandest attempt yet made to construct a theory of the psyche, Ernest Jones declared that after his great studies in Association and Dementia Praecox he

[1] Peters, R. S., *Brett's History of Psychology*, p. 695. London: Allen & Unwin, 1952.
[2] Review of Jung's 'Modern Man in Search of a Soul.' *J. Ment. Sci.*, Vol. LXXX, No. 331, 1934; pp. 718–20 (p. 720).
[3] Chase, H. W., 'Consciousness and the Unconscious.' *Psychol. Bull.*, 1917; pp. 7–10.
[4] *Explorations in Personality*, p. v. New York: Oxford University Press, 1938.
[5] See, for instance, the symposium on 'Counter-Transference.' *Brit. J. Med. Psychol.*, Vol. XXXIII, 1, 1960; pp. 1–31.

had descended 'into a pseudo-philosophy out of which he has never emerged.'[1]

Clearly, then, a field for investigation exists, and it is one in which investigation seems only just to have begun. Many of the works on Jung which are available—Jolande Jacobi's *Psychology of C. G. Jung*, Frieda Fordham's *Introduction to Jung's Psychology* or Gerhard Adler's essay on 'C. G. Jung's Contribution to Modern Consciousness'—have been written from an exclusively Jungian standpoint. Edward Glover's study, *Freud or Jung*, is written instead from an exclusively Freudian standpoint. As part of the recent expansion of activities and with the passage of two generations a new historical interest has grown up, expressed in a summary of the development of Jung's psychology by Dr. Michael Fordham,[2] a chapter on personal and historical background which Dr. Ira Progoff includes in an otherwise expository work,[3] and a pamphlet, 'Two Essays on Freud and Jung', by Dr. Jolande Jacobi, making available some portions of the correspondence between Freud and Jung during the years 1906–13. Jung's own autobiography, now apparently in preparation, will be eagerly awaited. On the side of discussion, it is from theologians that the most detailed critiques have come—H. L. Philp, with his *Jung and the Problem of Evil*, Father Raymond Hostie, who includes in his *Religion and the Psychology of Jung* an examination of Jung's postulates from the philosophical angle, Father Victor White, whose two books, *God and the Unconscious* and *Soul and Psyche*, are rather more sympathetic in their approach to Jung while taking essentially the same line as Philp and Hostie, and David Cox, who, in *Jung and St. Paul*, compares Jung's individuation process and the Christian way. To all these studies the present writer, a psychologist and in some measure an historian, is indebted in her survey of Jung's religious views. From the psychological standpoint, mention may be made of an unpublished thesis by Dr. Mahommad Azmal Makhdum, based on his experience of nine months' Freudian and nine

---

[1] *Free Associations*, p. 165. London: Hogarth Press, 1959. 'He cherished the notion,' Jones continues, 'that his descent owed something to one of Goethe's love affairs, and I feel sure his career was influenced by a medley of scientific, literary, and philosophical pretensions in which he tried to emulate his great ancestor.'

[2] 'The Evolution of Jung's Researches.' *Brit. J. Med. Psychol.*, Vol. XXIX, Pt. 1, 1956; pp. 3–8.

[3] *Jung's Psychology and its Social Meaning*. London: Routledge & Kegan Paul, 1953.

months' Jungian analysis, which contains some unusual comparisons,[1] a recent paper on the Archetype by Dr. Murray Jackson,[2] and a chapter more sympathetic than usual in Ruth Munroe's *Schools of Psychoanalytic Thought*.[3] In the main, however, psychologists outside his own school are still uninterested in the work of Jung. For instance, although similarities between Jung and some of the later psychoanalytical writers have been pointed out from time to time, they have not been taken up at any length, nor have many reasons been suggested for the changes in Jung's style of work or the contradictory opinions which the later writings have evoked. The aim of the present study, therefore, is to examine these problems, as well as the historical aspect, more closely, with a view, especially, to rendering the psychology of Jung more understandable to interested though uncommitted general readers.

The term uncommitted brings us to the question whether or not it is possible to write or apprehend anything at all useful about Jung from such a standpoint. In order to understand Jung, it has been said, one must experience his findings at first hand—his work must be 'at least partially lived through and validated existentially, before it can be thoroughly grasped on a conscious level.'[4] From the academic side, by contrast, comes the argument that a considerable amount of direct contact is likely to diminish objectivity. This, of course, is the old dilemma often set forth for depth psychology in general—either one remains outside and therefore insufficiently acquainted with the facts, or one moves inside and is cured of the desire to criticize. It may be less of a true dilemma than at first appears. On the one hand, the fact that Jung and others have put their work before the general public implies that it can be brought out of the consulting room to some extent, and that certain types of comment, concerning antecedents, development over a period of years, coherence or incoherence of formulation, or parallels with other writers, can reasonably be made. On the other hand, the idea has gained ground in recent years that a sympathetic interest is not incompatible with objectivity but is indeed essential for exploring any

---

[1] 'A Comparative Study of Freudian and Jungian Methods of Analysis.' Ph.D. thesis presented in the University of London, 1952.
[2] 'Jung's "archetype": clarity or confusion?' *Brit. J. Med. Psychol.*, Vol. XXIII, Pt. 2; pp. 83–94.
[3] *Schools of Psychoanalytic Thought*, Ch. 13, pp. 539–74. London: Hutchinson Medical Publications, 1957.
[4] Progoff, I., *op. cit.*, p. ix.

subject. The standpoint of an interested though uncommitted observer does not therefore seem impossible. At the same time, one would look forward to a study from within the movement, in rather the same way that one would wish to have, in addition to the studies of our own anthropologists with their outside viewpoint, others by persons who had actually grown up within the cultures which they had recorded; two questions for which the knowledge of the inside worker should be particularly helpful are Jung's handling of mythological material, which does not normally form part of a psychologist's equipment, and his relation to the German-speaking background.

At the end of a project extending over a number of years there are many people one would wish to thank. I am indebted to Dr. John Gabriel, of the University of New England, Armidale, Australia, for drawing my attention to the work of Jung, to Professor Ernest Beaglehole, of Victoria University College (now Victoria University), New Zealand, whose personality-in-culture work gave more definite shape to an interest in cultural and sub-cultural differences, and to the College Council for the award of a Research Scholarship through which the study was begun; to Professor G. P. Meredith, the late Professor D. R. MacCalman and Dr. R. J. Still, of Leeds University, for their guidance when I came to England, and Professor D. W. Harding, of Bedford College, London, for his hospitality during the 1953-4 session; to Professor and Mrs. R. W. Pickford, and Mr. Paul Campbell of the Davidson Clinic, who read the manuscript as it then stood while I was an Assistant at Glasgow University; and to Professor C. A. Mace, of Birkbeck College, for his advice and encouragement concerning revision in book form. I should also like to thank the staff and students of the C. G. Jung Institute, Zürich, for their friendship during the 1959-60 session. Here it should be said that any views expressed are entirely my own as an independent student, and that while some changes of emphasis have taken place as a result of lectures and discussions, no such material has been directly used.

Leeds, 1960

Chapter I

THE HISTORICAL BACKGROUND

Jung's thought, says one of his leading Zürich disciples, Professor C. A. Meier, has had a close connection with his personal life.[1] These words may cause us to reflect how surprisingly little is in fact known generally about Jung's own development. Not only has there been no full-length biographical or autobiographical study— we do not for the most part gain from Jung's writings that picture of personal preoccupations, family relationships and social circle which can be pieced together from the works of Freud, even though he appears to have participated very fully in the therapeutic process. One suggestion has been that this reserve is connected with Jung's attitude to personality. A personality, as something which is put before the public, can only be developed, he feels, through exaggeration of certain special features, and since his concern is with the whole, with individuality, as he prefers to call it, he has chosen to withdraw from the public view as much as possible. Perhaps also his attitude is an expression of the outlook of the learned classes in his generation, who, normally speaking, went about their work, known outside their family circle mainly to colleagues and to students, and subjected to no publicity more glaring than that of the presentation of the *Festschrift* on their sixtieth birthday.

We do of course know that Jung was born in 1875, in a small Swiss village where his father was a clergyman. 'I am the son of a parson,' he tells us in one of the few passages that do refer to personal life, 'and my grandfather was a sort of bishop, and I had five uncles all parsons'.[2] They 'belonged to the later part of the Middle Ages . . . they had the convictions in which people have lived since eighteen

---

[1] *Jung and Analytical Psychology*, p. 6. Newton Centre, Mass., 1959.
[2] 'The Symbolic Life.' Guild of Pastoral Psychology. Guild Lecture No. 80, 1954; p. 6.

1

hundred years.'[1] There were also physicians in the family, one of whom, his namesake, Carl Gustav Jung, was appointed to the Chair of Surgery at Basel in 1822. It is said to have been the memory of this ancestor, together with the increasing emphasis on natural science during the second half of the nineteenth century, which turned Jung's thoughts toward medicine, though his background as a whole led him toward humanistic studies. In his final year as a medical student, after reading Krafft-Ebing's *Text Book*, he saw psychiatry as the field in which medicine and philosophy would come together, and decided to specialize in it. He chose a psychiatric subject for his M.D. thesis—published in 1902 under the title of 'Psychology and Pathology of So-called Occult Phenomena'—and in 1900, after graduating at Basel, entered the Burghöltzli, the Psychiatric Clinic of Zürich University, as assistant, later Chief Assistant, to the Director, Professor Eugen Bleuler.

Leaving in the meantime the question of the wider impact of Jung's social environment upon his work,[2] let us try to reconstruct some portion of the intellectual world in which as a young medical student and assistant he would naturally live.

First, psychiatry itself, though backward in comparison with many subjects, had made considerable advances. During the previous hundred years, owing partly to the increasing social conscience of the era and partly to advances in physiology and chemistry which made an attack on mental illness seem more practicable, the superstition which, in spite of individual efforts, had engulfed the mentally ill throughout the centuries gradually receded, at any rate so far as conscious medical attitudes were concerned, and to some extent in legal practice. It was the psychotic type of illness, the true 'mental hospital case,' usually in its more advanced stages, which first become the province of the medical practitioner, on account of its greater severity and the increased need for institutional care with the growth of city populations. The gathering of patients into institutions gave opportunities for detailed observation of many different conditions, and the German investigators, especially, set about the task of introducing order into this confusing field—indeed, says Zilboorg, 'to produce a well-ordered classification almost seems to have become

[1] Cited in Fordham, Frieda: 'Dr. Jung on Life and Death.' *The Listener*, Oct. 29, 1959; pp. 722–25.
[2] See Ch. X, pp. 253–97.

the unspoken ambition of every psychiatrist of industry and promise, as it is the ambition of a good tenor to strike a high C.'[1] Among these classifications the most influential was that by Emil Kraepelin, which appeared first in 1883 and was expanded in 1896; its outstanding feature was the differentiation of two main types of illness, the manic-depressive, following a cyclic course with normal interludes, and dementia praecox, which Kraepelin described as a condition of gradually increasing deterioration, having its onset in adolescence or early adult life. This classification gave fresh impetus to study; during Jung's period at the Burghöltzli Professor Bleuler was at work on his great study, *Dementia Praecox*, in which he successfully maintained that the essential and invariable features of Kraepelin's dementia praecox were not the terminal dementia or the early onset, but disorganization of thinking and failure of the usual co-ordination between thought and affect.

Although Bleuler himself was comparatively sympathetic to the psychological approach, the views of the German psychiatrists by this time were, in the main, strongly somatological in bias. During the early part of the century, it is true, there had been speculations concerning the relation between personality and mental illness; one writer, William Ideler, spoke of 'the action of the unsatisfied over-excessive longings' in producing such disease, another Friedrich Beneke, thought that there was some symbolic relationship between psychological states and bodily processes, a third, K. G. Neumann, suggested that psychotic delirium was a form of dreaming while one was awake. In 1846 the philosophically minded physician C. G. Carus postulated unconscious mental processes operating in sharp contrast to those of consciousness, i.e. whereas the realm of consciousness is individual and egocentric, the realm of unconsciousness is supra-individual; the unconscious is untiring and sleepless, unfettered by the categories of space and time, and although it can be known only through its effects as perceived by consciousness, it is the source of all power and possibility, including consciousness itself.[2] But in the later years of the century the discoveries of medical science presented a picture far more impressive than any which could be gained from these relatively unco-ordinated insights. The descrip-

[1] Zilboorg, G., *History of Medical Psychology*, p. 450. New York: Norton, 1941.
[2] See White, Victor, *God and the Unconscious*, p. 30. London: Harvill Press, 1952.

tion of the alcoholic psychoses, for example, and the establishing of a connection between syphylis and paresis, led to the expectation that a definite physiological cause would ultimately be found for all types of mental illness. As an adjunct to their increasingly exact observation, however, these later nineteenth-century workers would sometimes use psychological experiment, which in the hands of Wundt, Ebbinghaus and others had been yielding remarkable results in the study of normal mental functioning; Kraepelin himself, with his pupil Aschaffenburg, introduced word-association tests in the hope that they would prove valuable in diagnosis.

In France during the same period quite a different line of work had opened up, the beginnings of which go back to Anton Mesmer in the eighteenth century. Mesmer, while practising as a physician, had found that he could often cure paralyses, blindness, and other apparently physical symptoms, with the help, as it seemed, of a device of iron rods and magnetized filings, throwing the patients into a trancelike state from which they would awake, in many cases, free from their complaints; to account for these happenings he elaborated a theory of animal magnetism, derived from the sixteenth-century philosopher-physician Paracelsus, according to which a mysterious magnetic fluid, emanating originally from the stars, flowed from the filings through the iron rods and into the bodies of the patients, restoring the equilibrium of the fluids which protected them from illness. Patients flocked to him; the medical profession itself was less enthusiastic. A Paris committee of inquiry concluded in 1784 that although cures had taken place the magnetic fluid had no existence and results depended solely on imagination. Mesmer himself, they noted, would appear in dramatic circumstances, stroking the bodies of the patients and making suggestions of restored health; they also drew attention to disturbances and convulsions that were apt to occur, and felt that these could be harmful. A second committee set up in 1820 reported similarly; a third dismissed all the phenomena as hoaxes.

Mesmerism, therefore, led a stormy and on the whole disreputable existence for more than forty years, owing, probably, to difficulties on both sides—the investigating scientists and medical men being biased against accepting an inexplicable force, and Mesmer himself contributing an element of charlatanism in his management of the therapeutic sessions. Nevertheless, the work was carried on. In France his disciple Puyseger proceeded more cautiously, avoiding violent manifestations and stressing instead the states of quiet sleep; and a Portuguese priest, the Abbé de Faria, dispensed with magnetizing devices and relied on the giving of 'orders' or 'directions' only. Toward the middle of the nineteenth century, a few doctors, Elliotson, Esdaile and Braid, experimented with mesmerism—renamed hypnotism by Braid—as a means of inducing anaesthesia during surgical operations. Since more reliable anaesthetics—chloroform and ether —soon became available, the usefulness of hypnotism in physical medicine was limited, but the applications that were made at least helped to give the method better standing.

In psychological medicine a step forward was taken by the French doctor, Liébeault, and his pupil Bernheim, in the 1860's. Liébeault and Bernheim believed the hypnotic state to be simply a heightened form of the normal suggestibility through which new beliefs and attitudes are commonly accepted. Since commands or statements under hypnosis were accepted uncritically, they reasoned, previous suggestions concerning blindness, paralysis, etc., whether originating with the patient himself or someone else, could often be supplanted. These practitioners, too, reported many cures. From 1878 onwards Charcot at Paris used the same method. A controversy grew up—Charcot maintaining against the Nancy school that hypnotizability itself was a manifestation of hysteria, indicating a physiological weakness of the nervous system. Although subsequent workers have tended to support the Nancy school, Charcot's great prestige as head of French psychiatry enabled him to attract many pupils, among them Pierre Janet and the American psychiatrist Morton Prince. Not only the simpler hysterical symptoms but more complicated conditions were investigated, in which two or more personality systems appeared to exist within the one human organism, i.e. those conditions of dual or multiple personality which have attracted a good deal of attention outside psychiatry itself. The most famous, probably, is Morton Prince's Sally Beauchamp; Flournoy in Geneva reported a similar case, Helene Smith, and several examples were collected by William James in the United States. Charcot's French pupil, Janet, in particular, investigated other nervous states, to which he gave the name of psychasthenia—the present-day obsessional and anxiety neuroses, together, probably, with latent schizophrenias.

As a result of all this work the theory of unconsious mental processes was placed on a much firmer empirical foundation, for it was

evident that the hysterically blind or paralytic patient could remember neither the 'suggestions' or 'associations' believed to be connected with his illness, nor the hypnotic suggestion which dispelled it,
and there were considerable differences in the accessibility of memories in the cases of dual personality. At the same time there was not
yet a very clear or detailed psychological explanation of these states.
The splitting or dissociation of consciousness was attributed to
psychic shock, superimposed on a constitutional weakness of the
nervous system, or 'psychopathic defect,' and there was a tendency
to stress the purely automatic nature of such performances. Altogether,
the unconscious, or the subconscious or subliminal, as it was often
called, had gained ground as an hypothesis. For instance, William
James, with whom this work was a main interest, suggested that 'Our
intuitions, hypotheses, fancies, superstitions, persuasions, convictions,
and in general all our non-rational operations, come from it.'[1] But,
he admitted, just *how* anything operates in this region is still unexplained'.[2]

Now in the last five years of the nineteenth century a third factor
made its appearance in psychiatry, so obscurely that it can hardly be
regarded as part of the background of Jung's thinking, though
destined in the following decades to have a revolutionary influence,
viz. the work of Sigmund Freud. By 1900 the *Studies of Hysteria* and
the *Interpretation of Dreams* had been published, laying the foundations of psycho-analytical theory, and we know from Progoff's chapter and from references in his own work that Jung first read the *Interpretation of Dreams* in that year. He felt, however, that he did not
understand it. All he could do, Progoff says, was to set it aside and
continue with his experiments and studies—a reaction which contrasts rather strikingly with that of another and more permanent
member of the early Freudian group, Hanns Sachs, who states that
when he had finished the *Interpretation of Dreams* he had 'found the
one thing worthwhile for me to live for'.[3] For these reasons—the lack
of impact of Freudian psychology in the psychiatric world in general
at this time, and Jung's own difficulty at first in coming to grips with
it—Freud's early contributions will be taken in conjunction with the
early Jungian work in the chapter following.

[1] *Varieties of Religious Experience*, pp. 483–4. London: Longmans, Green &
Co., 1902.
[2] *Ibid.*, p. 270.
[3] *Freud, Master and Friend*, p. 1. London: Imago Publishing Co., 1945.

More widely known, especially perhaps in English-speaking countries, was a movement which might be described in part as an offshoot of the French or French-dominated psychiatry, but which was influenced also by the theological trends of the time and by the spread of Eastern religious literature. The aim, or hope, of this movement, led in Great Britain by such well-known figures as the Cambridge philosopher Henry Sidgwick and the independent worker F. W. H. Myers, and supported to a considerable extent in the United States by William James, was that by applying the empirical methods of the natural sciences to the mysterious and apparently supernatural phenomena of automatic writing, seeing or speaking with spirits, telepathy and clairvoyance, it would be possible to reinstate traditional religious beliefs—or a wider version of them—which had been threatened by the discoveries made in other fields. Many of these investigators, James and Myers, for example, recognized that in some way 'the unconscious' was involved, but conceived of the unconscious itself as a mediating agency between man and whatever higher powers there might be. It was these studies, rather than Freudian psychology, which at the turn of the century and for some time afterwards were evoking appreciable interest among educated people.

But it would be building our reconstruction on too narrow a basis to confine attention to psychiatry alone. The nineteenth century, says Theodor Merz, may 'be called with some propriety the scientific century'[1]—many of the basic discoveries of physics, chemistry and biology were made in the generations which it covered. Above all it may be called the biological century since, more than any other, the theory of evolution put forward by Charles Darwin in 1858 captured the imagination and influenced thinking in related fields. Darwin was not indeed without precursors—his own grandfather, Erasmus Darwin, had suggested that man's origins had more in common with those of other species than religious tradition had led him to believe, and his contemporary, Alfred Wallace, worked out simultaneously a theory like his own, that the diversity of biological species, including Man himself, was due to changes brought about in response to the need for adaptation to differing environments, i.e. to natural selection—those members of a species who possessed the qualities required for survival living longer and leaving proportionately more

[1] *History of European Thought in the Nineteenth Century*, Vol. I, p. 89. Blackwood, 1914.

offspring, who in turn would transmit such qualities, and so on. Nevertheless, it was the weight of evidence collected by Darwin from observation of many species which made the theory so overwhelmingly convincing. At the same time geologists were at work, classifying the layers of rock on and beneath the earth's surface, and coming upon fossilized remains of extinct species which gave further support to the Darwinian theory: these species had obviously died out because in some way they had been unable to meet the demands of the environment, and in many instances they could be shown to form connecting links between species now existing.

Although such evidence in the case of Man was less complete, some highly interesting finds were made. In 1857, a year before the publication of Darwin's *Origin of Species*, the remains of a human or humanoid skeleton had been unearthed in the Neanderthal, near Düsseldorf. Six years later Darwin's great ally, T. H. Huxley, comparing the Neanderthal skull with primitive modern types, declared it to be only the lowest extreme of a series which led gradually to the best developed. Other specimens of Neanderthal man, as he came to be called, were discovered during the next forty years, and about ten years after the discovery of the first remains, five specimens of a second prehistoric type were found at Cro-Magnon in France—more massive than the skeletons of living races, but closer to them than *Homo neanderthalis*.

These discoveries, and the strong impetus which evolutionary theory gave to explanation of phenomena in terms of origin, led to a great deal of interest not only in prehistoric man, but also in primitive man, found in the remoter areas of the globe, whose condition was expected to throw light on the primal state and the evolutionary stages of culture.

In their studies of social organization some early anthropologists, notably J. J. Bachofen and the less well-known British worker, K. McLennan, postulated three successive stages—promiscuity, mother-right, involving the worship of a physical principle embodied in the conception of an Earth Mother, and finally father-right, based on an abstract intellectual principle like that of legal contract. (In the same year as Bachofen proclaimed his *Mutterrecht* however—1861—Sir Henry Maine claimed from his study of Roman law that the primitive family was of patriarchal type.) Bachofen was also one of the first investigators to interest himself in myth and symbol, suggesting that the life of a society could be reconstructed from very limited records, provided one understood the meaning of the symbols in its myths, religious rituals and similar material. Another subject of inquiry was the evolution of religion. Here one of the earliest landmarks was Tylor's *Primitive Culture*, 1871, with its theory of animism. Taking as his minimum definition of religion 'a belief in spiritual beings', Tylor concluded that this belief developed from dream phenomena and observation of the difference between the living and the dead, and was then extended to nature, so that man came to believe in spirits of trees, rivers, animals, etc. Later, in 1899, his student, Marett, suggested in his own theory of animatism that primitive religion was a vaguer thing than Tylor had supposed, including nothing more definite than a feeling of the awe-ful, unconnected with any postulated being; Bishop Codrington, similarly, in his study of Melanesian peoples, 1891, had introduced the term *mana*, a powerful nonphysical force for good or evil, not necessarily connected with a spirit.

Other anthropological controversies covered the entire field. Many striking similarities were soon noted between the objects, beliefs and practices of tribes who were often widely separated, so that the question arose, were these similarities to be taken as indications of a universal similarity of the human mind, or were they to be accounted for by migration and cultural diffusion? The argument waged furiously—the proponents of psychic unity often failing to allow for the most obvious contacts, the diffusionist school at times hardly admitting that even the simplest inventions could have been discovered independently. One of the most moderate, as well as one of the earliest, formulations of the problem was that by P. W. A. Bastian, who had begun his work before the publication of the *Origin of Species*. Bastian postulated a relatively small number of concepts in philosophy, language, religion, law, art and social organization which were common to mankind—*Elementargedanken* as he called them—but added that the form in which these ideas were realized depended in the first instance on geographical conditions, imposing different types of economic organization, i.e. the *Elementargedanken* always found expression as *Völkergedanken*, or Folk-Ideas. At a later stage migration and other contacts made geographical conditions less important in determining the expression of the *Elementargedanken* and cultural diffusion more so. Or, as the present-day anthropologist might say, all institutions have universal and cultural components in varying degrees.

A second question, discussion of which has continued to our own day, was that of similarity or difference between the primitive and the civilized mentality. While Bastian believed that no fundamental differences existed, the great anthropologist Emil Durkheim, in the later years of the nineteenth century, impressed by the social solidarity of tribal life, made a distinction between collective and individual consciousness: to civilized man alone belonged the achievement of anything that could be described as individual consciousness, or reflection and self-determination—primitive man, even more bound up with the thinking of his group, was determined solely by 'collective representations,' or ideas having a prior reality within the group which reached him with coercive power from outside. Lévy-Bruhl, in the first half of Jung's own career, took up this hypothesis of Durkheim's and described primitive man as living in a state of *participation mystique*, which included marked illogicality—opinions such as 'I am a bear', and 'I am a man', being held with no appreciation of their contradictory nature—and inability to differentiate clearly between himself and the world around.

Two further controversies, though originating in biology, had special relevance for the study of human social life, namely, those centred around the Inheritance of Acquired Characters and the Recapitulation theory: both preceded Darwinism but derived fresh stimulus from association with it.

The first was highly relevant to evolutionary theory, since, once the hypothesis of natural selection had been put forward, attention began to be focused on the problem of the way in which adaptation to environment could be transmitted—was it simply that those who were inherently adapted could leave more offspring, or could experience gained during the lifetime of an organism be transmitted biologically to its descendants? Darwin himself, followed the French biologist, Lamarck at the beginning of the nineteenth century, inclined to the latter possibility, but in the second half of the century evidence against it was accumulating. In 1880 Weismann, failing to secure the transmission of an acquired character after twenty generations, proposed to differentiate between body cells, directly affected by environmental happenings, and germ cells—those that alone give rise to offspring—which are well protected from them; this theory gained further support from the rediscovery, some twenty years later, of Mendel's experiments on heredity. Naturally the theory of evolution has been far from static in the last two generations. In particular, the discovery by T. H. Morgan and others of mutations does not seem to have been foreshadowed by the earlier biologists, for this kind of change in the germ plasm, following direct physical action as bombardment by X-rays, is very different from change arising out of the learning experience of the individual. Up to the present time work which has appeared at first sight to prove or to suggest the Inheritance of Acquired Characters has later been found to be affected by some other factor—unconscious selection of animals on the part of an experimenter or, in the case of material derived from human beings, ordinary social learning. Essentially this position had been reached, at latest, by the second decade of the twentieth century.

The Recapitulation Theory has had a similar history—stemming from embryology it fitted well with the prevailing nineteenth-century endeavour to establish the stages through which species or cultures had passed before taking on their present forms. The evidence was clear that the higher animals, including man, passed in their embryonic state through the whole evolutionary series (ontogeny runs parallel to phylogeny); the problem lay in determining whether this recapitulation of the evolutionary ancestor was of the adult or the embryo form. Von Baer, working in the decade before Darwin, believed that since development in general proceeded from the undifferentiated to the differentiated, the embryo and not the adult forms of the simpler creatures were the ones which were passed through—that which the species had in common with other species before divergent growth set in. Ernst Haeckel, the great German populariser of Darwinism in the '70's and '80's, maintained that the biologically higher organisms passed through the adult stages of the lower organisms, and it was this version of the Recapitulation Theory which enjoyed great favour among workers in the sciences of man. An example familiar to psychologists is Stanley Hall's application of the theory to children's play: children in their games, he thought, re-lived the stages of psychological development which characterized the childhood of the race, being determined at one time by the hunting instinct, corresponding to the nomadic stage of tribal life, and later by the craving to collect and possess, corresponding to the stage of settled agricultural life. Neither the biological form of Haeckel's theory nor its application to psychology has been supported by subsequent investigations. On the biological side, not only has Von Baer been proved right, it even seems that neoteny, or introduction into the *adult* descendant of characters which had been *youthful* in the ancestor, has been important in the evolutionary process. Continuing Stanley Hall's work on children's play, later studies suggest no clear correspondence with the life of primitive man, but do suggest that social influences are far more important in determining behaviour than the early workers had imagined. While the details of these arguments will not concern us greatly, the two hypotheses, taken in broad outline, illustrate the importance, in the second half of the nineteenth century, of biological concepts according to which, as Irving Hallowell has said, 'mind, whether viewed individually or racially is primarily, if not solely, a function of organic structure, of inherited disposition and tendencies' and environmental forces are 'primarily stimuli which evoke, or only modify immaterially, developmental trends and patterns that unfold from within the organism itself',[1] together with the substantial amount of revision which had been carried out during, say, the ten years immediately following the First World War.

Not only primitive and prehistoric man was studied in the search for origins. The study of the remains of ancient civilizations also was largely opened up in this period. An interest in the Greek and Roman civilizations had of course been an essential part of European intellectual life for many centuries, but the first person to have the idea of testing literary tradition by direct exploration seems to have been Heinrich Schliemann, who, supported by the great physiologist Virchow, began excavations at the traditional site of Troy, and discovered between 1877 and 1890 that the Greek civilization was not unique but was preceded by much older cultures. By 1900 it was known that one such culture, the Mycenaean, had spread through the islands to the Greek mainland from its centre in Crete; Sir Arthur Evans had begun to excavate the legendary palace of King Minos, and J. L. Myres had shown a connection between the Bronze Age culture of Cyprus and those of the Aegean and Syria. Connections were also demonstrated between Egypt, Crete and the Aegean. These investigations and others in Mesopotamia made a lively appeal to the

---

[1] See Hallowell, A. Irving, 'The Child, the Savage, and Human Experience.' Proc. of the 6th Institute on the Exceptional Child, Oct. 1939., pp. 18-19.

imagination—it may be recalled that Freud had a lifelong interest in antiquities, and Jung has said that at one time he himself had wished to be an archaeologist.[1]

With the study of archaeology we come to the edge of the sciences and into the humanistic disciplines, though in German-speaking countries the distinction seems to have been less clear-cut, both being brought together, more often than separated, under the heading of *Wissenschaft*, or organized knowledge. And to a large extent it is the German-speaking world with which we are concerned. This is partly due to Jung's own origins in a German-speaking country; some other trends of thought can be found—the ethical and political philosophy of the English Utilitarian school, for instance—which do not seem to have left a mark upon his work. Nevertheless, in spite of these trends, and in spite of the French psychiatric movement and such great individual figures as Darwin and T. H. Huxley, one cannot fail to be struck by the predominance of German workers in so many fields—a circumstance which Huxley jokingly attributed to their habit of marrying one another's sisters and daughters, and Merz to the excellence of their University organization, drawing the best brains to itself during a time of intellectual ferment in an area that politically was divided and disorganized.[2] Whatever the reason for this remarkable activity, it is clear that the German literary men, historians, theologians and philosophers were no less productive than the German scientists.

Probably the most powerful and far-reaching influence was the Romantic movement of the late eighteenth and early nineteenth centuries. During the previous hundred and fifty years, as a reaction against the chaotic religious wars of the sixteenth and seventeenth centuries, there had grown up, mainly in France, but spread in varying degrees throughout the rest of Europe, a rather formalized, rationalistic cultural life belonging almost exclusively to the nobility. Now, especially among the middle classes, this culture was felt to have become too artificial, too remote from the emotions, too lacking in concern for individual liberty. 'Back to Nature' expressed many

[1] Interview with John Freeman, B.B.C. Television Programme, 'Face to Face', Oct. 22, 1959.

[2] *Op. cit.*, Vol. I, pp. 160–2: 'a great network, a vast organization for the higher intellectual work of the nation and of mankind' harbouring 'the largest and most efficient intellectual army.' Through 'nearly fifty larger or smaller towns, in the course of six centuries, learning and higher education have been spread over the German-speaking countries of Europe.'

aspirations of this school, originating to some extent in the writings of Jean-Jacques Rousseau. In Germany, Hölderlin as a forerunner, Novalis, Tieck, the Schlegels, Kleist and Uhland among others turned for inspiration away from the world of man-made objects to natural surroundings, and took for their artistic ideal emotional expression, in place of the eighteenth-century requirement of polished form. The simpler classes of society were represented as preserving basic human values with greater purity, and history was studied eagerly in the belief that periods could be found in which such values were more fully realized. In the political movements which characterized their era the Romantics were enthusiastically though rather vaguely revolutionary—condemning the old but having no detailed plans for reconstruction of the new. For a while the French Revolution of 1789 filled them with hope, but since this was followed by the Napoleonic Wars in which Germany together with the rest of Europe fought for independence, the Romantic and the nationalist movements become closely intertwined.

The Romantic interest in history, united with nationalist sentiment, brought about a revival of early Germanic literature—tales of the Migrations, gathered in the thirteenth century into the *Nibelungenlied*, and the medieval epics, *Parsifal*, the story of a naive youth who finds the Holy Grail, and *Tristan and Isolde*, with its theme of adulterous courtly love. Later in the nineteenth century these stories were brought forcefully before the world in the operas of Richard Wagner, who shared the Romantic vision of assisting the birth of a new Germany by glorifying its past. Interest in the past led also to the study of folklore, of which the best-known example is the collection of *Märchen* by the brothers Grimm in 1812, to the study of language, of which again a well-known example is Grimm's Law of Etymological Change, and the beginning of Oriental studies under Friedrich Schlegel. By the middle of the nineteenth century we find the more systematic historians, Ranke and Mommsen, and a powerful influence in Jung's student days at Basel was the historian Jacob Burckhardt, whose approach to history was essentially psychological in seeking to understand the history of a period by penetrating to the core of its beliefs.[1] Contemporary with the Romantics, but greater in realizing the need for holding to some of the values of classicism equally, were Goethe and Schiller, who perhaps did more than any to awaken a sense of the

---

[1] Progoff, *op. cit.*, p. 35.

unity of German culture; among their dramas, Goethe's *Faust*, commonly regarded as the greatest, is the outstanding example of a theme which seems to have had special meaning for the German people—that of the hero who sins but perseveres, is gradually cleansed of his shortcomings, and achieves his purpose.

The attitudes to Nature and the past do not entirely cover the Romantic movement, however, for in all of this the Romantics were seeking communion with that which lay beyond, with mysterious ultimate forces conceived in some way to be reached *through* the communion with Nature and the past, or to be mirrored in the emotional outpouring of the soul. Perhaps, indeed, the strength of the Romantic movement in Germany should be found in its affinity with more deeply rooted characteristics, in particular with that transcendental longing which has often been taken as typical of the Germanic peoples through many hundred years. At the same time, within the sphere of theology itself there were important applications of the new historical spirit. First, the Higher Criticism, or textual and historical examination of the Scripture records, drew attention to many contradictions, emendations, and discrepancies of dates, and even at times raised doubts, in the minds of the scholars concerned, about their total authenticity. This naturally led to reinterpretations of Christian dogma. For the philosopher Hegel, to take a rather extreme example, the doctrines of the death, resurrection and exaltation of Christ were statements in parable form that finite man is inevitably the prey of negation and decay but rises to a lofty and positive participation in the pantheistic world process. 'In this sense, but no other, the Word took flesh and dwelt among us.'[1] Such a tendency was reinforced by the studies of the history of religion; belief in a unique revelation through Christ seemed to many thinkers less credible than belief in a universal and gradual unfolding of religious understanding from the primitive rites of the savage to the enlightened concepts of the world religions. Another trend in the theology of the time was a search for the essential features of religion, which the theologian Schleiermacher, influenced by the Romantic emphasis on individual experience, defined as 'the sense of the all,' or 'a feeling of absolute dependency'. From this concern with individual experience a renewed interest developed in the mystical writers

[1] MacKintosh, H. R., *Types of Modern Theology*, p. 108. London: Nisbet & Co., 1937.

of the thirteenth century—Mechthild of Magdeburg, Meister Eckhart, Suso, Tauler—and the seventeenth-century Jacob Boehme, with their worship of the God Who dwelt within the human soul. It was this Liberal or humanistic theology, laying its stress on man's search for God, in history and within his own soul, that ruled throughout the nineteenth century.

Philosophy itself was far from idle. The end of the eighteenth century and the first few decades of the nineteenth saw the development of the great Idealistic systems of Kant, Fichte, Schelling, Hegel —a development which has been compared to the flowering of Greek philosophy from Socrates to Aristotle. The philosophy of Kant took as its starting point the question, How can we know the real? His answer was, of course, that with one exception knowledge of the real, the *Ding-an-Sich*, is an impossiblity, since experience is mediated by the activity of consciousness, which imposes its own order by means of categories inherent in itself—time, space, causality, etc. The exception he allowed was experience of the moral law. We find that we accept responsibility for our own actions, and experience the compelling power of the Categorical Imperative or moral perception even when it is not followed. Since this experience of freedom runs counter to the law of causality ordering all phenomenal experience, it has to be regarded as giving entrance to a noumenal world beyond the world of natural phenomena; it is to this world that the moral self belongs, though, in falling outside the phenomenal world, it cannot be further known.

Kant's successors did not remain content with the distinction between the phenomenal and the noumenal worlds, the fixed nature of the categories and the unknowability of the noumenal or moral self, but went back to the self as presented in consciousness, found that this self or subject implies also an object, i.e. the self does not exist except in relation to something else, and sought in the nature of the subject-object relationship a clue to the nature of ultimate reality.

Fichte, developing one aspect of Kantian thought, saw the interplay of subject and object, self and the world, in terms of moral experience. For the individual the world is there not simply by chance, but because he realizes it as a field for his endeavours—it is always a task to be performed, to be built up into a sphere of action; all selves are in some measure manifestations of the Absolute Self which creates the total world as a set of actions to be carried out. This formulation, while acceptable as an account of the individual's experience in ordering his life, and valuable in drawing attention to an element of affirmation or willing which accompanies all thought and awareness, does not do justice to the existence of physical objects independently, as it seems, of moral experience, i.e. knowledge, as G. H. Mead puts it, does not seem to be of the nature of a duty.[1]

Schelling then sought to interpret the subject-object relationship in terms of artistic intuition. Just as the artist gives himself up to nature and in so doing finds the very ideas which he is trying to bring to consciousness, so, too, we create our day-to-day experience. Considering the world-process, he suggested that Mind or subject and Nature or object have arisen from the same source, a state of indifference or identity, and form two sides of the world process, conscious and unconscious. The objective factor leads from matter to organism, the subjective factor, transcending morality and science, leads to the work of art; the total manifestation of the universe, or Absolute, is at one and the same time the most perfect organism and the most perfect work of art.

To Hegel, the third of the great systematists after Kant, it seemed that neither Fichte nor Schelling had traced in a sufficiently definite manner the path from the limited human reason to the Absolute or God. With his dialectical method he believed that he could do this, i.e. any content of thought, or thesis, is first defined by its opposite—that which it is not, and then more fully by what is common to the two, or synthesis—whereupon the synthesis becomes a thesis, requiring definition in its turn, and so the process is repeated. The inclusiveness eventually reached belongs not only to the realm of thought, but is the expression of ultimate reality—all dualities, all contrasts of subject and object, mind and matter, are transcended in the Absolute.

Among these philosophers Schelling, though the least notable academically, is of interest also for his close connections with Romanticism and his concern with the relationship between philosophy and art. Not only did he think of himself as putting into more explicit form what was implicit in the literary writings of his period—through his conception of the Absolute he saw art as in some way too the goal of philosophy, In order to bridge the gap new symbols are needed as mediating agencies, and since a new symbol is the creation not of a

---

[1] Mead, G. H., *Movements of Thought in the 19th Century*, p. 124. Chicago: Univ. of Chicago Press, 1936.

single poet but of an age, it becomes necessary, if we are to understand the symbol-creating process, to study the mythology of different cultures, especially the highly developed cultures of antiquity.

Somewhat later, Lotze, who, as a medical man in the mid-nine-
teenth century, was in more direct contact with the natural sciences,
made a fresh attempt to take account of their concepts while sub-
ordinating them to the ethical and metaphysical traditions of his
predecessors. Taking the law of universal causality itself, he found in
the fact that a change occurring in A can be connected with B, an
indication for discarding the theory of separate objects with independent existence, and held that what seems at first like an action taking
place between separate substances should be seen as an immanent
operation within a single entity, the World-Ground or Infinite. The
elements of the world as we know it are, therefore, merely modifications of the Infinite; these modifications are of two types, elementary,
and souls, which are distinguished from the rest by their capacity for
feeling, and for knowing themselves to be the active centres of a flow
of life. The Infinite itself, in the last resort, can be thought of only
as analogous to our own spiritual being, freed from finite limitations.

With Schopenhauer there occurred to some extent a break in
philosophical pattern. Although, as with Kant and Fichte, priority is
given to the Will, this Will of Schopenhauer is very different from the
moral force of the older philosophers, being simply an endless aimless
striving working itself out unconsciously in man and nature. Whereas
an outlook of optimism was implicit in the work of his predecessors
—man, through the exercise of his powers, can become a worthy
participant in an eternal supersensible order—Schopenhauer, under
the influence of Indian philosophy, to which he had been introduced
by Friedrich Schlegel, held that the best attainable by man is a state
of rest, which can be reached only by absolute renunciation of the
will to live. Von Hartmann, writing after Schopenhauer, accepted the
idea of the unconscious universal will, but endowed it with a mysterious purpose, and considered human reason to be its highest manifestation. However, the purpose of Hartmann's Unconscious Will is
not really different from the goal envisaged by Schopenhauer—
redemption from all effort and desire. Indeed, the Unconscious has
brought the Conscious into existence in support of its own purpose,
since the more consciousness deepens and widens, the more it will

perceive the evil of the world and, ultimately, decide to bring the process to an end.

Schopenhauer and Von Hartmann, together with Nietzsche, were being widely read as the century was drawing to its close. From the systematic point of view Nietzsche would hardly be considered a philosopher—he himself thought of philosophy not as the attempt to give a unified account of the universe, but as offering a criticism of thought and life. His own criticism took the form of an attack, expressed in aphorism, on all restricting, limiting modes of living, as they seemed to him, in particular the Christianity of European culture. Before the advent of Christianizing morality, he urged, the word 'good', had been applied to the qualities of the aristocrat; the remedy for the corruption of our civilization is to sweep away its restrictions, to deny any form of human equality, in favour of the few, those Super-Men who have courage to live dangerously in pursuit of self-determination, bowing to no higher power.

This, very broadly, is the philosophy which Jung would have in mind in regarding psychiatry as the meeting point of medicine and philosophy—Schopenhauer, Von Hartmann and Nietzsche in the foreground, in the background the great Idealistic systems. To meet the conception of the Unconscious, however ill-defined, both in psychiatry and in philosophy, was clearly stimulating. Are there any other trends in these differing systems which would be likely to coalesce, to form a residual impression? One such idea might well be that of polarity working toward unity, as seen in Schelling's conception of Mind and Nature and the Hegelian dialectic; another, the tendency to take some principle other than discursive reasoning—the Will, or intuitive feeling—as the means through which an apprehension of ultimate reality is gained; a third, perhaps, the habit of using terms ever more inclusively, contrasting sharply with the habit of minute analysis and insistence on referents, the What-precisely-do-you-mean? of the twentieth-century logical empiricists with whom many readers nowadays, at any rate in English-speaking countries, will be more familiar.

Returning to some of the factors in Jung's early cultural environment besides philosophy—the newly developed German and French psychiatry, applying the methods of observation, and even, occasionally, experiment, to its novel subject-matter; the scientific discoveries of other fields, especially biology; the widespread acceptance of evolutionary theory and controversies concerning the mechanism of evolution, centring round the Inheritance of Acquired Characters and Recapitulation Theory; the application of evolutionary ideas to man, including the study of his social organization and religion, and the controversy between the proponents of psychic unity and cultural diffusion in explaining similarities; the imagination-stirring finds of archaeology, and the great literary, historical and theological traditions of Germany, with a strong tincture of Romanticism—we can indeed speak with Jacobi of 'that many-layered native soil from which Jung's system drew its first nourishment and in which it is spiritually rooted.'[1] The situation is vividly conveyed by her account of the dream of a new student of Jung's work, in which he was reading a vast volume, on the right-hand side of which was printed Jung's own text, while the left-hand pages

'were covered in a small and crowded print with quotations from Meister Eckart, Paracelsus, Boehme, Leibniz, Kant, Goethe, Carus, Schopenhauer, Nietzsche and others. And suddenly he realized: all these thinkers' world of ideas belongs to Jung, is intimately related with his, and actually constitutes but a segment of the important intellectual and spiritual currents that have converged in his mind.'[2]

One intellectual influence of which we have not spoken is Jung's Swiss, as distinct from German-speaking, background. Jung feels, we are told, that the mediatory position of Switzerland has been significant for him—that by participating in the Swiss neutrality he has been able to take a similar mediatory position in the world of thought, close enough to European life to understand it, uninvolved enough to keep a vantage point above the turmoil.[3] To a visiting observer, the simplicity and quietness of the people, the medieval town buildings and the nineteenth-century style of many of the houses might suggest, on the one hand, an almost fairy world, and on the other, a stable country which has largely missed the impact of the two World Wars. Here it would be possible for a scholar to spend his life in thought and solitude, verging indeed on isolation, as it would not be possible to do in London.

[1] *The Psychology of C. G. Jung*, p. x.
[2] *Jacobi, J., Two Essays on Freud and Jung*, p. 19. Zürich, 1958.
[3] *Progoff, op. cit.*, p. 22.

caused her to make many reading errors. The messages were delivered after she had fallen into a trance ('S.W. grew very pale, slowly sank to the ground or into a chair, closed her eyes, became cataleptic, drew several deep breaths, and began to speak.') Gradually, out of a multitude of spirits, two gained the ascendancy and controlled the girl's body in turn—her grandfather, a clergyman, who indulged in many pious maxims, and a facetious individual who announced himself as 'Ulrich von Gerbenstein'. There also existed a somnambulic self by the name of Ivenes—apparently a distinguished figure in the spirit world, who seldom spoke during the trances but could be reconstructed from S.W.'s accounts shortly after her 'return to the body', i.e. for the most part S.W. had access to the subjective experiences connected with the name of Ivenes, though she could not recall the conversations of the grandfather and Ulrich von Gerbenstein.

By degrees a mystical system, taught by other spirits, was revealed, according to which the forces operating in the universe were arranged in ten concentric circles, with 'natural' forces in the seven innermost circles, and unknown forces, intermediate between matter and energy, in the three remaining circles. In addition to this, Ivenes evolved a system of reincarnations; in the early nineteenth century she was a well-known German seeress, the Prophetess of Prevost; at the close of the eighteenth century she was a clergyman's wife in central Germany; in the sixteenth century a French noblewoman, Mme de Valours; in the fifteenth century a Saxon countess, and so on. Into this system all S.W.'s friends and connections were fitted, e.g. as Mme de Valours Ivenes was the mother of Jung—himself, presumably, enjoying a previous existence. Besides the somnambulic attacks and momentary lapses, S.W. experienced semi-somnambulic states at the beginning and end of the 'great attacks' and sometimes independently. In these the most obvious feature was 'preoccupation' —the patient lent only half an ear to the conversation around her, answered at random and became absorbed in hallucinations; she also gave good results with table-turning and automatic writing. Closer observation revealed a change in the whole character. S.W. in these states seemed far more mature and dignified than a girl of fifteen; the semi-somnambulic ego was, indeed, almost identical with Ivenes of the somnambulic state. After the elaboration of the mystical and reincarnational systems, however, S.W. appeared to have played herself out; the visions lost in vividness and plasticity, and less and less new material was produced. The seances ended altogether six months later, when S.W., herself aware of and distressed by the decline of her supernatural powers, was discovered in deliberate cheating, though eighteen months after their termination she was stated to be giving every satisfaction in a large business, as an industrious, responsible and sympathetic person.

The report having been made, Jung offers explanations:

The table-turning of the semi-somnambulic state is accounted for in terms of unconscious sensitivity to movement. Without being aware of doing so, the experimenter or transmitter makes small movements to which the subject then responds, the motor function of his own arm being dissociated from ego-consciousness. All these movements are powerfully influenced by predominating thoughts, hence the thought-reading that apparently occurs. The situation is similar in automatic writing, but there the mental processes concerned with the content of the messages, as well as those controlling the hand, are dissociated from the main stream of consciousness. Dissociation is attributed to auto-suggestion. Especially with automatic writing, the subsequent recognition of what has been done, and the feeling of strangeness that results, may pave the way for the creation of an 'unconscious personality', in order that the subject may give an answer to the question, Who is responsible? Any name is introduced, generally one charged with emotion, and the division of the personality is accomplished. Very often leading questions assist in the division. Jung cites conversations between Janet or Myers and their subjects: (Janet asks): Do you hear me? . . . (Lucie answers, in automatic writing) *No*. But one has to hear in order to answer . . . Who is it? *Somebody besides Lucie* . . . Shall we give the other person a name? *No*. Yes, it will be more convenient. *All right, Adrienne*.[1] Once the subject has accepted the thought that an independent spirit is making itself known, it is no great step to concluding that it may be possible for the spirit to be seen. The origin of hallucinations is then discussed: contributing factors are, strong expectation on the subject's part, the fact that the thinking of somnambulists is apt to be carried on in plastic images which are then objectified, and in this case, the darkness of the room, which gave an opportunity for the retina's own light, usually very weak, to be seen with great intensity.

[1] *Psychiatric Studies*, p. 53; *Collected Papers*, p. 55.

P.J.—2*

Jung's main interpretation concerns, of course, the split-off figures and the somnambulic ego in S.W. Recalling that the subject's behaviour was sometimes anxious and retiring, sometimes unduly gay, Jung concludes that the grandfather and Ulrich von Gerbenstein each typify one aspect of her character. S.W. herself found the contradictions painful; the attempt to harmonize them created the dream of the ideal Ivenes, during which the other trends fell into the background and, as repressed ideas, began an independent existence; like other hysterical dissociations, however, they were relatively superficial: 'none of them goes so deep as to attack the firmly knit basis of the ego-complex.'[1] Comparing other cases in the literature, he notes that in all of them the Stage II personality subsequently replaced the Stage I, or waking, personality, as seems to have happened with S.W. 'It is therefore conceivable that the phenomena of double consciousness are simply new character-formations, or attempts of the future personality to break through.'[2]

Besides his own formulation, in which Progoff has traced the influence of Hartmann's theory of Unconscious Will, there are elements derived from Janet and the other French psychiatrists. Looking for more distant causes, he uses Janet's concept of exhaustion owing to psychopathic defect, suggesting that the early reading lapses developed into somnambulic attacks during the stressful period of puberty, as could easily occur in a subject of psychopathic heredity; at the same time he shows himself familiar with the German psychiatric literature, commenting on the lack of interest in this type of case among the German psychiatrists, and producing his own to fill the gap; the title of the study, as well as references within it, reveals his familiarity with the investigations of the Myers school. His reading of Freud's *Interpretation of Dreams* is also evident, in the suggestion that repressed ideas form the starting point of the autonomous personalities, and again in the interpretation of Ivenes' mother fantasies as 'nothing but a dream of sexual wish fulfilment'. It is the woman's premonition of sexual feeling, he declares, 'the dream of fertility, that has created these monstrous ideas in the patient.'[3] However, the attack is not pressed home in Freudian terms. For instance, although any explanation of details (the mystical

---

[1] *Psychiatric Studies*, p. 76; *Collected Papers*, p. 80.
[2] *Psychiatric Studies*, p. 79; *Collected Papers*, p. 84.
[3] *Psychiatric Studies*, p. 70; *Collected Papers*, p. 74.

system, or S.W.'s customary trance position) is sought in the patient's personal experience,[1] Jung does not follow up the early reading lapses through the technique of free association, as Freud would probably have done; there is a passage referring to S.W.'s unaccountable hatred of a lady acquaintance of his own[2] which would seem to indicate an emotional involvement of the type which Freud described as transference; and in his explanation of Ivenes' sexual dreams he lays the emphasis not so much on wish-fulfilment as on unconscious premonition, thereby drawing it nearer to his own hypothesis.

This quality of being on the edge of the Freudian epoch rather than within it may become more evident if we digress to consider, very briefly, how much of the Freudian work was then available.

Freud, coming from a Jewish and predominantly trading background, had entered the medical faculty of Vienna University in 1873, but being primarily interested in scientific research did not consider medical practice until 1882, after being warned by the physiologist Brücke, in whose laboratory he had spent several years, that in view of his restricted material circumstances it was not feasible to take up a theoretical career.[3] He then turned his attention to neurology, and since at that time the neurologist was the usual consultant for neurotic patients, he went in 1885 to Paris to study under Charcot. There he became acquainted with hypnosis as a method of treatment, and back in Vienna worked closely with a colleague, Josef Breuer, who found in treating a severe case of hysteria that if his patient remembered an emotional episode and talked it out in the hypnotic state she would awake with her symptoms much improved. This case and others were published jointly in 1895 as *Studies in Hysteria*.

During the years 1895–1900 several major steps were taken. Breuer, shocked by his patient's declaration that she had fallen violently in love with him, quickly withdrew, nor, according to Jones's account, were his own feelings entirely uninvolved. Freud,

---

[1] *Ibid.*, p. 40; p. 41: 'I can remember clearly that in the winter of 1899/1900 we spoke several times in S.W.'s presence of attractive and repulsive forces in connection with Kant's *Natural History and Theory of the Heavens*, also of the law of the conservation of energy, of the different forms of energy, and of whether the force of gravity is also a form of motion. From the content of these talks S.W. had evidently derived the foundations of her mystic system.'

[2] *Ibid.*, p. 38; p. 39: This lady, in the reincarnational system, was 'the incarnation of a celebrated Parisian poisoner. . . . '

[3] *Autobiographical Study*, p. 16. London: Hogarth Press, 1935.

more intrepid in the face of similar experiences, concluded that they did not represent a genuine attraction to himself but were to be regarded as substitute reactions, a transference to the physician of emotional attachments in the patient's former life. Hypnosis was given up, partly because it made the transference, as he called it, more difficult to manage, and partly because some method was needed for patients who could not readily be hypnotized. This was found in free association—the patient was simply instructed to relax, physically and mentally, and let his ideas come up spontaneously. The free association method led to fresh discoveries. In every case there were points at which the patient was stuck—associations ceased to flow. With persistence the blocks were overcome; always the associations which followed were painful to the patient, and as patient and doctor persevered it became clear that forbidden actions and emotions were involved. Thus the concepts of conflict and repression were developed—actions, emotions or memories coming into conflict with accepted standards were thrust out of consciousness, but continued their existence outside consciousness and sought expression through the symptom. To begin with it seemed that such repression might date from any period in life and involve any type of motive or unpleasant memory, but gradually, when Freud's patients, apparently cured, returned some time later with slightly different symptoms, he pushed his analysis farther and farther back into the early years. For a while he was confused by frequent reports of sexual assaults, most of which turned out to be imaginary, in so far as the circumstances could be verified. These, however, were interpreted as wish-fulfilments, indications of a sexually-toned attachment of the child, hitherto regarded as sexually innocent, to the parent of opposite sex—in short, an incest wish, or Oedipus complex, as Freud called it. The goal of therapy, therefore, was to bring the conflict out into the open, not merely through an intellectual recall of material, but through reviving the emotional attitudes of early childhood, positive and negative, in the transference to the analyst. The neurosis, it was hoped, would then be seen for the childish residue it was and dissolved in favour of a more mature adjustment. Another outcome of the free association method, reinforcing the whole structure of Freud's thought, was his study of dreams. Sometimes in the midst of associations the patient would remember a dream which made an excellent starting-point for further associations. Following such clues, including those obtained in self-analysis, Freud distinguished in the *Interpretation of Dreams* between the manifest and latent content: the manifest content conceals the latent content with the aid of such mechanisms as condensation of more than one image into one, displacement of affect from a major to a minor character, and above all, through the use of symbols acceptable to the dreamer's consciousness in order to conceal more primitive and unacceptable ideas which make up the latent content and are always concerned with fulfilment of a wish, usually a sexual wish. In the same work he elaborated the distinction between primary process, in which there is a quite uninhibited flow of energy, with no sense of time and of external reality, and secondary process, inhibiting energy and allowing it to flow only when satisfaction can be gained in accordance with the dictates of reality.

By 1900, therefore, many of the essential features of the Freudian position had been worked out, and while the *Interpretation of Dreams*, the only work by Freud which Jung had so far read, is not concerned with transference phenomena, the remaining ideas can certainly be found there. Returning to 'So-called Occult Phenomena', we can see in the fact of his having read this book at all so soon after publication an indication of unusual breadth of reading, and considering the highly unfavourable reviews of that year it is notable that he was able to use it as he did. At the same time, its unique and closely argued point of view does not really seem to have made a radical impression on him, as indeed he himself admitted later.[1]

With the *Studies in Word Association* he went further. Shortly after the publication of 'So-called Occult Phenomena' he began at the Burghöltzli some work with which, like Kraepelin and Aschaffenburg, he hoped in the first instance to throw light on diagnostic problems. The technique of the Word Association Experiment is of course quite simple: a list of words, usually a hundred, is read out to the subject, who is asked to respond to each with the first word that occurs to him, his reaction times are recorded, and at the end of the first reading the list is repeated and the subject required to reproduce his former associations.

When the completed records were examined the diagnostic aspect receded into the background—though some suggestions were made —in view of other peculiarities which they regularly showed. For

---

[1] *Supra*, p. 6.

instance, the reaction time to some of the stimulus words would be unduly prolonged, or the subject might even be unable to respond at all. The stimulus word might be misinterpreted or the instructions to respond with a single word neglected and some other word form, sentence or ejaculation, substituted. Some of the responses seemed to be unrelated to the stimulus word on any system of classification which could be employed objectively, such as contrast, or class membership, and to have a purely personal significance; or a series of associations which had run smoothly along one particular line, say, similarity, would be interrupted by an association of more superficial nature, such as rhyme or clang. Finally, in the second trial, the subject might be unable to reproduce his first association. All these peculiarities were indications, as Jung puts it, that certain stimulus words denoted actions, situations or things about which the test person could not think quickly and surely. It soon became clear that the difficulty in thinking was of emotional, not intellectual, origin. For instance, one subject responded to the word propriety with 'improper' after a reaction time of 3·6 seconds as against his mean reaction time of 1·2; he had no hesitation in tracing the difficulty to memories of 'improper' scenes in childhood. A young man who suffered from ear trouble misinterpreted 'deaf' as 'deft' and responded with 'neat' accordingly. A third subject, who responded to 'wild' with the apparently irrelevant word 'dentist' explained that he had recently visited his dentist, whose name happened to be Wild. And so on. In all these cases it was clear that the stimulus word had impinged on a set of experiences which had affective significance for the subject, usually of a painful type. To such a set of ideas or experiences Jung gave the name complex. He suggested that the underlying process was a clash between the associations stemming from the normal ego-complex and the associations connected with the affective complex, which was operating wholly or partially outside the control of the ego-complex and so could be called autonomous or unconscious. To this clash was due the inhibition, delay, or unusual response. In short, Jung from his own experience in research had moved more emphatically toward the concepts of psychic conflict and repression. These were the studies which caused Bleuler, as head of the Burghöltzli, to make the first contact with Freud in the autumn of 1904. By 1905 and 1906 Jung apparently had no difficulty in accepting the sexual nature of many of the associations; extending his discussion to hysteria, he described Freud as having '*found* that the hysterical symptom is essentially a symbol for presentations (sexual in the ultimate analysis) which are not present in the conscious but are repressed from the conscious by strong inhibitions'.[1]

As Jung himself points out, material elicited by single responses to standardized words is limited, compared with the material obtained in psychoanalysis through chains of association from personal dream-images. Most of the ideas coming to light are accessible to the subject's consciousness, if not at the time of reaction, soon afterwards or with a small amount of introspection. The clinical value of the test, therefore, lies in its overall survey, rather than exhaustive analysis of the patient's problems. Over and above its practical usefulness, however, the work is of theoretical significance as the first experimental confirmation of psychoanalytical findings, demonstrating, under conditions which are repeatable and open to all, the existence of inhibition or repression as postulated by Freud in his work on dreams and neuroses, the sexual nature of many complexes, and the value of the association method in detecting them. In Jung's own words, 'Association experiments have helped us to get over these first and chief difficulties'—namely, that 'Safe foundations are wanting from whence to start'.[2]

Besides this major contribution there is in the Word Association Studies much additional material. A lengthy paper by Jung and Riklin, 'The Associations of Normal Subjects', discusses variations in association according to age, sex and degree of education, and several association types are distinguished—the objective, with few complex signs, which responds either to the internal meaning (inner association) or the verbal form (outer association) of the stimulus word, the egocentric, producing many self-references and/or complex indicators, and a 'predicate type', which tends to respond with judgments of value. (This type, Jung thinks, is apt to make up in expressiveness for what is lacking in genuine emotion, and often possesses the further peculiarity of very rich and vivid imagery.) As Eder points out in his translator's preface, these distinctions are the first indications in Jung's work of an interest in typology. Another paper, by a pupil, Dr. Emma Fürst, follows up some hints in the paper on normal subjects and shows that close relatives have a tendency to belong to the same association type—the resemblance

[1] *Studies in Word Association*, p. 297. (Italics mine.)   [2] *Ibid.*, p. 299.

between mother and children being particularly close, closer than that between father and children. The diagnostic interest is expressed in a paper by Jung on the associations of an epileptic, and by a colleague on the associations of imbeciles and idiots, and finally two papers are included on the physical concomitants of the Word Association Test. All this work was carried out at the Burghöltzli, references to 'our honoured chief' appear from time to time, and Professor Bleuler himself contributes an introduction and a paper on 'Consciousness and Association' giving the theoretical basis of the studies. From this it is clear that Jung and his colleagues, like Freud, and nineteenth-century psychologists in general, are 'enlightened associationists'—they do not rely on the old laws of similarity and contiguity as sufficient explanatory principles, but realize the importance of emotional drives in welding the associations together; at the same time, individual associations remain for them the basic units from which mental life is built—there is not yet the interest in other principles of organization which came into prominence a few years later with the experiments of the Gestalt school and had been foreshadowed by the school of Gestaltsqualität in the 1890's. Most of the papers, similarly, can be fitted without difficulty into the framework of the dominant nineteenth-century psychology. Besides the diagnostic interest derived from Kraepelin and Aschaffenburg, another link with previous work is to be found in the extensive use, as above, of Wundt's classification into 'inner' and 'outer' associations. A later investigator has suggested that more might have been achieved diagnostically if Jung had been less concerned with analysis of grammatical relationships according to the custom of the time[1]— in effect, we may add, grafting the Freudian discoveries on to this foundation. However, while this may be relevant in considering Jung's own mode of thought, it does not alter the importance of his experimental work on psychoanalytical problems; we can also see him as an extremely detailed, even cautious, researcher, who defines his terms, e.g. 'educated' and 'uneducated' carefully[2] and gives a warning against over-generalization from his findings. ('I would observe,' he says at the end of the paper on associations in a case of epilepsy, 'that my analysis is for the moment of value only for this case, and that I do not venture to draw any universal deduction.

[1] Rapaport, D., *Diagnostic Psychological Testing*, Vol. II, p. 492. Chicago: Year Book Publishers, 1946.   [2] *Op. cit.*, pp. 64, 90, 114, 121.

There are many different kinds of epilepsy which perhaps exhibit different psychological characteristics.'[1])

In the midst of the work reported in the Word Association Studies, Jung was applying the psychoanalytical method in a novel way to the study of dementia praecox. Choosing a long-standing case, he first asked the patient directly what she meant by her repetitive expressions ('I am Socrates', 'I am the finest Professorship'), but succeeded only in evoking further neologisms. He then asked her to give *all* the thoughts occurring to her when certain stimulus words were presented, taking the words from those which she used frequently. From these trains of association he was able to demonstrate the emotional significance of the patient's delusional ideas. For instance, to 'Socrates', the associations ran: *'scholars—books—wisdom—modesty*—no words in order to express this wisdom—it is the highest *groundpostament'*—another neologism—'his teachings—had to die on account of bad people—falsely accused—sublimest sublimity—self-satisfied—that is all Socrates—the fine learned world—no thread cut—I was the best tailoress—never had a piece of cloth on the floor —fine artist world—fine professorship—is *doubloon*—twenty-five francs—that is the highest', etc.[2] As Jung remarks, the underlying set of ideas can easily be understood: 'I am an excellent sempstress and therefore claim financial rewards, instead of which I am ill-treated and imprisoned.' This single example reveals the two most prominent aspects of the patient's delusions—the wish-fulfilling and the persecutory. The third aspect is the sexual. Jung states now that wherever there exists such a richly developed symbolism the sexual complex is bound to be present. The most striking illustration is the train of associations to 'Amphi'. (Occasionally the patient would say, 'Doctor, this is again too much amphi', or complain of being disturbed at night by 'amphi'. '. . . they are really amphibians, snakes and that kind . . . a green little snake came as far as my mouth—it had the finest, loveliest, sense, just as if it had human reason, and wished to tell me something—just as if it wished to kiss me.' (Here the patient blushed and laughed timidly.)[3] The sexual significance of 'amphi' is sufficiently obvious, Jung adds, noting it also as an illustration of the Freudian principle of displacement from below to above. One other feature of the case is mentioned—the patient's 'telephone',

[1] *Op. cit.*, p. 226. [2] *Psychology of Dementia Praecox*, p. 103,
[3] *Ibid.*, p. 127,

During the interviews this 'telephone', much to the patient's chagrin, would call out such remarks as, 'The doctor should not be bothered,' or, when she was impeded in her associations, 'She is embarrassed and therefore she can say nothing.' It had, that is, the character of an ironical censor, convinced of the futility of the morbid symptoms— an indication, Jung believes, that the healthy as well as the unhealthy components of the personality can be repressed.

In short, as Meier says, 'for the first time in the history of psychiatry delusional material is treated as more than just unintelligible stuff and is looked upon as something worthy of interpretation.'[1] The problem of etiology is also reviewed. Comparing hysteria and dementia praecox, Jung finds a number of resemblances—states of 'emotional indifference', broken by excessive outbursts, disturbances of volition, e.g. both the hysteric and the dementia praecox patient complain of being automatons, difficulty in fixing attention, and a tendency to gyrate around the same set of expressions and ideas. Symptoms of this kind suggest the operation of an overwhelming complex, causing all other thoughts to lose their feeling tone. In dementia praecox, however, the symptoms are much more severe— the loss of rapport with the hysteric is remediable, but the dementia praecox patient remains inaccessible, and certain disturbances in thinking processes are found only in dementia praecox. The question therefore must be asked, Why does hysteria develop in one case and dementia praecox in another? Like so many workers in this field, Jung is uncertain ('At the question of etiology, that is, at the nucleus of the problem, one must halt.')[2] He suggests that given a predisposition in the subject, strong emotion may liberate a toxine which injures the brain more or less irreparably, so that the highest psychic functions become paralysed, but he thinks it not entirely impossible that the illness is very largely somatic in its origin—any complex which happens to be uppermost merely being seized and 'fixed' into pathological symptoms. At this stage of his work Jung is interested primarily in the investigation of the illness; no mention of psychotherapy for dementia praecox is made in the monograph of 1906. However, the therapeutic interest is apparently not far behind. In a slightly later paper ('Content of the Psychoses', 1908) he states that

[1] Meier, C. A., 'C. G. Jung's Contributions to Theory and Therapy of Schizophrenia.' *Congress Report of IInd International Congress for Psychiatry*, Vol. IV. Zürich, 1957.
[2] *Psychology of Dementia Praecox*, p. 30.

'analytic practice has given us experience of cases where patients on the borderline of dementia praecox have been brought back to normal life'.[1] Ernest Jones speaks of his ambition to cure the psychiatrist Otto Gross, who unfortunately developed schizophrenia and was admitted to the Burghöltzli,[2] and Meier, referring to the early correspondence between Freud and Jung, reports that Jung 'tried very hard to convince Freud of the possibility of helping those poor patients analytically . . . more than fifty years ago'.[3]

As in 'So-called Occult Phenomena' and the *Studies in Word Association*, we find in *Psychology of Dementia Praecox* a careful link-up with the work of earlier investigators, especially in Jung's summing up of 'thought deficiencies'. For instance, the identifications of these patients reveal an inability to discriminate between two ideas—they go beyond ordinary poetic licence in that the patients expect them to be accepted, and cannot discriminate between their own personalities and the role they have assumed; and confusion between important and unimportant material is seen in vague analogies. The earlier investigators were agreed in postulating as the basic disturbance some such condition as 'lowering of central control', i.e. inability of the ego to exercise its synthesizing function; and Jung mentions some experiments by Stransky, (1903); in which relaxation of attention in normal subjects led to the production of sentences very similar to those of dementia praecox patients. As A. A. Brill has said, this portion of the book 'contains everything worth knowing about dementia praecox that had been written up to that time'.[4] Jung himself remains keenly interested in the experimental approach, adding toward the end that 'It would be far beyond the power of a single person to carry out by himself in the course of a few years all the experimental work which alone could support my hypothetical views'.[5] In his attitude to symbolism he follows closely the writers on 'thought deficiency', citing on two occasions the statement of a French writer, Pelletier, that the symbol is to be regarded as a very inferior mode of thinking which reveals a deficiency in the power of discrimination, since it is 'a false perception of a relation of identity or of a very marked analogy between two objects which in reality present only a very vague analogy'.[6] We are indebted to the

[1] *Collected Papers*, p. 313.
[2] *Sigmund Freud*, Vol. II, 33.　　　　　[3] *Op. cit.*, p. 16.
[4] Brill, A. A., *Lectures on Psychoanalytic Psychiatry*, p. 21. London: Lehman, 1948.　　　　[5] *Op. cit.*, p. 141.　　　　[6] *Op. cit.*, p. 12; p. 58.

author, Jung adds, for the valuable observation on symbolism and symbolic relations so very frequent in dementia praecox. As in the other studies, he continues to search for connections with the patient's past experience, e.g. saying of the use of horses, cats, dogs, etc., as sexual symbols that it is from these animals that one is likely to see coarse sexual procedures, a thing which particularly impresses children.

Since in the next group of papers the influence of Freud becomes more prominent, it may be convenient to consider, so far as we are able, the relationship between Jung and Bleuler and the kind of influence which Bleuler is likely to have exerted on Jung's work. In this, as in other ways, the Jungian group has been reserved, making no open comment whatsoever. Freud, however, referred as early as 1914 to disagreements culminating in Bleuler's resignation from the Psycho-Analytical Society and the severance of Jung's connection with the Burghöltzli shortly after the society was founded in 1910,[1] and Ernest Jones, in an obituary of Karl Abraham, spoke of 'the uncomfortable atmosphere resulting from the tension between Bleuler and Jung' even in 1907 as one factor in Abraham's resignation from the hospital staff.[2] In his biography of Freud, Jones repeats that 'Bleuler and Jung never got on well together'[3] and includes a remark by Freud that Bleuler was 'a curious fellow'.[4] At the outset of Jung's career at the Burghöltzli Bleuler's personal influence seems to have been strong.[5] But certainly it would not be surprising if the older, more established man were less enthusiastic about the psycho-analytical alliance than his young assistant, and since by all accounts Jung's personality is a very forceful one, some degree of tension could very well arise—all the more so in view of the customarily dominant position of the European Professor, favouring little divergence of opinion within university departments. There are one or two very slight indications in Jung's papers, e.g. whereas in 1906 he stated, 'My views are no contrivances of a roving fancy, but thoughts which matured in almost daily intercourse with my venerable chief, Pro-

---

[1] *Collected Papers*, Vol. I, p. 331. ('History of the Psycho-Analytical Movement.')
[2] *Int. J. Psycho-Anal.*, Vol. VII, 1926; p. 157.
[3] *Op. cit.*, Vol. II, p. 80.   [4] *Ibid.*, p. 185.
[5] For instance, at this period he gave up the use of wine (of which he had previously been fond, and to which he subsequently reverted), even in the company of very close friends—Bleuler himself being a fanatical teetotaller. Oeri, *op. cit.*, p. 528.

fessor Bleuler',[1] in 1908 he speaks of 'a case of mental disorder known as Dementia Praecox, which Bleuler calls Schizophrenia. . . . The facts will not be altered if these disorders are called by some other name than dementia praecox.'[2]

On the intellectual side a fairly clear impression can be gained from Bleuler's own writings of the kind of pressure he would be apt to bring to bear. Not only does there seem to be a good accord in general between the detailed, dispassionate, rather descriptive style of the *Studies in Word Association* and the monograph on the *Psychology of Dementia Praecox* and that of his own treatise, *Dementia Praecox or the Group of Schizophrenias* which appeared a few years later. Bleuler also states explicitly in his contributions to the *Studies in Word Association* that obscure concepts have 'the great disadvantage that they stand in the way of impartial observation and must be first of all pushed aside by those who wish to arrive at any kind of useful view'[3] and that 'In Germany the concept of the unconscious has become so twisted by Edward von Hartmann, among others, that it has become quite useless for scientific psychology'.[4] Later, in his *Dementia Praecox*, he says that in his opinion Jung has been too gentle in dealing with certain of his predecessors, for

'Theories, which combine correct and false facts, are even more dangerous to science than complete errors; and hypotheses which are only "justified in a certain sense", always create confusion because the necessary reservations cannot always be stated. Clear-cut concepts can only be formed if we ruthlessly reject everything that does not belong to them, regardless of whether we are dealing with simple problems or with entire theories.'[5]

From this we can conclude that Bleuler stood very firmly in the scientific foreground, as it might be called, of nineteenth-century German thought.

At this point too it may be useful to review Jung's attitude to Freudian psychology immediately before he developed a more personal relationship with Freud. Once again his intention appears to be to use Freud's work to illuminate the whole rather than to con-

---

[1] *Psychology of Dementia Praecox*, p. iii.
[2] *Collected Papers*, p. 312.
[3] *Op. cit.*, p. 268. [4] *Op. cit.*, p. 266.
[5] *Dementia Praecox or the Group of Schizophrenias*, p. 465 n. New York: International Universities Press, 1950.

centrate exclusively upon it, nor does he seem to press the Freudian explanations quite so far as Freud himself. For instance, whereas Freud describes 'the resistance watching on the boundary between the unconscious and foreconscious',[1] Jung speaks of attention being withdrawn from the complexes, in consequence of which 'they manifest themselves in rather vague and symbolic expressions and become mixed up. A real censorship of dream thoughts in the sense of Freud we need not admit. The inhibition emanating from the sleep suggestion perfectly suffices to explain everything.'[2] That is, even though Jung is making use of the new psychology he is less dynamic—there does not seem to be quite the same degree of striving for expression of frustrated urges that is found in Freud; nor is sexuality emphasized quite so strongly as the cause of mental illness. 'Any strong complex may call forth hysterical symptoms in those predisposed; at least so it seems.'[3] It is interesting that no use is made of Freud's major work in the years we are considering—the *Three Contributions to the Theory of Sex*, which appeared in 1905. According to this theory, sexual energy, differentiated from other forms of energy by a special chemism, is derived not only from the sexual organs but from all parts of the body, especially certain sensitive zones, the oral and the anal; and the sexual instinct passes through stages in which the child gains pleasure of an essentially sexual kind first from the oral, then from the anal, and thirdly from the genital zone itself—a stage which includes both auto-erotic activity and the sexually-toned attachment to the parent of opposite sex, or Oedipus complex, which had previously been postulated. Eventually, after a latency period during which it is repressed through the strength of social prohibitions, the instinct re-emerges at puberty; fusion of the partial impulses occurs under the dominance of genital sexuality, which normally is directed toward members of the opposite sex; and some proportion of the infantile impulses finds direct gratification in the form of forepleasure associated with the adult genital act, as in kissing, while some undergoes repression and displacement. Perversions and neuroses result from fixation or regression to one of the earlier phases—hence the activities of the child, ranging over all these phases, are described as 'polymorphously perverse'. Freud on his side, although speaking highly of

---

[1] *Interpretation of Dreams*, p. 430. London: George Allen & Unwin, 1920.
[2] *Psychology of Dementia Praecox*, p. 59.   [3] *Ibid.*, p. 60.

Jung's work in bringing psychoanalysis into the field of the psychoses, expressed some disappointment a few years later that attention had been concentrated on interpretation of symptoms and that explanation in terms of toxic states had been introduced without any attempt to consider whether all neurotic and psychotic manifestations could be regarded as deviations of the libido from its normal developmental course. 'This point of view was overlooked by the Swiss investigators.'[1] In general, however, Jung's approach is not unreasonable. At the outset he explains, in his preface to the *Psychology of Dementia Praecox*, he entertained all the objections which were later advanced against Freud in the literature. But he said to himself that Freud could only be refuted by one who, making use of the psychoanalytical method, really investigated like Freud. 'He who does not or cannot do this should not judge Freud's views, otherwise he acts like those famous men of science who disdained to look through Galileo's telescope.' Fairness to Freud does not, however, imply surrender to a dogma—independent judgment can be maintained beside it. 'If I, for instance, recognize the complex mechanisms of dreams and hysteria, it by no means signifies that I ascribe to the infantile sexual trauma the exclusive importance seemingly attributed to it by Freud.' As for Freud's therapy, 'it is at best a possible one, and perhaps does not always offer what one expects from it theoretically'. Nevertheless, he concludes, these points are incidental and completely vanish when set beside 'the psychological principles, the discovery of which is Freud's greatest merit and to which the critics pay much too little attention'[2].

In April 1906, a couple of months before the *Psychology of Dementia Praecox* was actually published, the first direct contact between Freud and Jung took place when Freud wrote to Jung thanking him for his warm defence of psychoanalysis after attacks which Aschaffenberg had made, and during the next seven years no fewer than 330 letters passed between them.[3] In spite of Jung's defence, his letters of 1906, like the preface cited, have a note of caution and reserve. Freud wrote in October that he was aware of Jung's hesitation about the place assigned to sexuality, 'but I do not cease to expect that you may in the course of time come closer

[1] *Collected Papers*, Vol. I, p. 312. ('History of the Psycho-Analytical Movement.')
[2] *Op. cit.*, pp. iii–iv.
[3] Jacobi, *Two Essays on Freud and Jung*, p. 21.

to me than you now think possible'.[1] Jung for his part referred in December to the fact that 'My education, my environment, and my scientific premises are . . . very different from yours.'[2]

In February 1907, however, the two men met for the first time. The fullest description which we have of the meeting, at any rate at present, is that by Ernest Jones, based on Jung's own report to him in those early days. 'He had much to tell Freud and to ask him, and with intense animation he poured forth in a spate for three whole hours. Then the patient, absorbed listener interrupted him with the suggestion that they conduct their discussion more systematically. To Jung's great astonishment, Freud proceeded to group the contents of the harangue under several precise headings that enabled them to spend the further hours in a more profitable give and take.'[3] Some months afterwards Jung wrote to Freud that 'To know your science means to have eaten from the tree of paradise,'[4] and according to A. A. Brill, who visited the Burghöltzli at that time, he gave the impression of being fully convinced: 'You could not express any doubt about Freud's views without arousing his ire.'[5] What Jung's support meant to Freud has been described most sympathetically by Jacobi: 'In a hostile environment which put up a desperate resistance to the assertions of psychoanalysis, the youthful, enthusiastic man appeared to Freud as the longed-for and welcome "crown prince" indeed.'[6] In 1909, on the invitation of Stanley Hall, they lectured jointly at Clark University in the United States, Freud giving a résumé of theoretical developments in psychoanalysis and Jung a summary of the Word Association Experiments, together with a paper, 'Experiences Concerning the Psychic Life of the Child', which is one of several written between 1909 and 1911, apparently applying and defending Freudian views. This paper is made up of short reports on the attempts of a child, Anna, aged six—his own daughter, though the fact is well concealed—to solve the problem, Where do babies come from? Anna's attempts are compared with those of Hans in the longer study, 'Analysis of the Phobia of a Five-year-old Boy', which Freud had published earlier in the year.[7] For both children the problem, though existing before, is brought to a head by the birth of a

[1] *Ibid.*, p. 21.   [2] *Ibid.*, p. 21.
[3] *Sigmund Freud*, Vol. II, p. 36.   [4] *Op. cit.*,. 20.
[5] Cited by Edward Glover, *Freud or Jung*, p. 45.
[6] *Two Essays on Freud and Jung*, p. 20.
[7] *Collected Papers*, Vol. III, pp. 149–289.

sibling; both express jealousy of the new arrival, even speaking or
revealing fantasies about a permanent removal; both are sceptical of
the popular stork theory, and after partial enlightenment both
speculate as to how the baby got out of and into the mother. The
first question is answered in the same way (the 'anal' theory of birth),
and Anna's suggestion for the second, i.e. lying face downwards,
kicking and calling, 'Look, is that what Papa does?' is noted as
similar to Hans's fantasies of 'the black horse that kicked with its
legs'.

Another paper in this series, 'Significance of the Father in the
Destiny of the Individual', has the aim of reinforcing the view that
'the psycho-sexual relationship of the child toward his parents,
particularly toward the father, possesses an overwhelming importance in the content of any later neurosis'.[1] One of his patients is
attracted solely to men of her father's age and type. Another,
although sufficiently independent to reject the husband whom her
father chose, is haunted by a feeling of guilt, even though the man
chosen was an idiot of repulsive appearance and the father himself
was a drunkard. A child patient, interviewed for enuresis, is extremely
dependent on his mother and jealous of his father; he dreams of a
black snake which wants to bite his face or a tall man with a sabre or
gun who lies in his bed and wants to kill him. It is not difficult, Jung
adds, to see whence comes the black snake and who the wicked man
is, especially since the wicked man whom the boy describes has a
close physical resemblance to the father. In short, 'we are forced to
say that *in essence our life's fate is identical with the fate of our
sexuality.*'[2]

A dream interpreted mainly along Freudian lines forms the foundation of the next paper, 'Psychology of Rumour'. Marie X, a
thirteen-year-old schoolgirl, had related to her classmates a dream
which gave rise to sexual rumours in which their teacher figured.
Formerly Marie had liked this teacher well; more recently she had
lost his good opinion by misbehaviour and had received a poor
report. After indulging in murderous fantasies during the day she
dreamt of confused happenings which included the use of boys'
swimming baths, swimming out in a lake with the teacher, getting on
his back, and going for a journey 'like a honeymoon', of which Jung's
explanation is that the repressed part of herself which desired sexual

[1] *Collected Papers*, p. 156.   [2] *Ibid.*, p. 172.

union with the teacher fulfilled its desire 'as a compensation for the hate which had filled the day'.[1] A fourth study, 'On the Significance of Number Dreams', follows Freud's interpretations in the *Psychopathology of Everyday Life* (1904): all the numbers in the dreams of the patient who is analysed are traced to problems in his sexual life, e.g. to the number 315 the associations were, 'his doctor has three children, just lately there is one in addition. He himself would have five children were all living.'[2]

These, aside from the 'Content of the Psychoses' already mentioned, are the papers from 1909–11. Now although, as we have said, they seem at first sight to be a confirmation of Freud's work, a closer reading brings to mind the question, How deep, after all, did that influence really go?

To begin with, there is some difference in Jung's treatment of the sexual. Freud himself, of course, makes a distinction between the sexual and the genital, as in the libido theory, though it has often been pointed out that he has many passages in which the term sexual is employed in a way at least suggestive of the customary meaning. (For instance, he says of the child patient Little Hans, who had previously been allowed to sleep with his mother, that he can be assumed since then to have been 'in a state of intensified sexual excitement').[3] Jung in his accounts of psycho-sexuality is apt instead to link it with more general issues, without much exploration of the physical territory: psychoanalytical experience teaches us, he says in the paper on the 'Significance of the Father', that as a rule 'the first signs of the later conflict between the *parental constellation and individual independence, of the struggle between repression and libido* (Freud), occur before the fifth year'.[4] Jung's account of the part played by the parents in paving the way for a neurosis is also somewhat different. In one place, admittedly, he speaks, like Freud, of mothers who excite their children with unhealthy tenderness,[5] but the more usual impression is of 'a sensitive child whose intuition is only too quick in reflecting in his own soul all the excesses of his parents'. This can come about since 'The child imitates the gesture, and just as the gesture of the parent is the expression of an emotional state, so in turn the gesture gradually produces in the child a similar feeling, as it feels itself, so to speak, into the gesture'.[6] As Mullahy

[1] *Ibid.*, p. 190.　　[2] *Ibid.*, p. 194.　　[3] *Collected Papers*, Vol. III, p. 260.
[4] *Collected Papers* p. 160. (Italics mine.)　　[5] *Ibid.*, p. 170.　　[6] *Ibid.*, p. 127.

points out, attention is focused on the emotional interplay between child and adult rather than on the development or suppression of the instincts.[1] Again, there seems at this time to be uncertainty about the relative importance of the mother and the father in the child's development. On the one hand, Jung summarizes Fürst's paper on Familial Resemblances in the Word Association Studies, according to which the reaction types of children are in general nearer the type of the mother, and judging from his use of case material he accepts it. On the other hand, he writes in the same paper ('Significance of the Father') that 'the father is usually the decisive and dangerous object of the child's fantasy, and if ever it happens to be the mother, I have been able to discover behind her a grandfather to whom she belonged in her heart'.[2] In general terms he says: 'The most recent thorough investigations demonstrate the predominating influence of the father often lasting for centuries. The mother seems of less importance in the family. If this is true for heredity on the physical side'—an entirely pre-Mendelian view—'how much more should we expect from the psychological influences emanating from the father?'[3] And he even speaks of the father-child relationship as the foundation of religion.[4] Jung seems, therefore, to be caught between his own earlier orientation toward the mother and the more patriarchal emphasis of Freud. Another blend or juxtaposition can be found in 'The Psychology of Rumour'. Although Jung speaks of 'the censor' as pushing Marie's sexual complex away as long as possible, his main concern is not with conflict and repression but, as in 'So-called Occult Phenomena', with unconscious germination of ideas. Marie, he writes, was 'physically almost completely developed sexually, and in this respect ahead of her class; she is therefore a leader who has given the watchword for the unconscious, and thus brought to expression the sexual complexes of her companions which were lying there ready prepared.'[5]

Besides these points of theory there are other differences of emphasis which make it unlikely that Jung's papers would have been written by Freud or vice versa. These are particularly noticeable in their work on the psychic life of children. For Little Hans far more information is forthcoming on sexual development; no mention is

---

[1] *Oedipus Myth and Complex*, p. 131. New York: Hermitage Press, 1948.
[2] *Ibid.*, p. 175.　　　　　　　　　　[3] *Ibid.*, p. 157.
[4] *Ibid.*, p. 172.　　　　　　　　　　[5] *Ibid.*, p. 189.

made of auto-erotic activity or of interest in contemporaries of opposite sex on the part of Anna, but these aspects of Little Hans's life are fully documented. Altogether, Hans gives the impression of being a much more active, striving organism. He does not, like Anna, become 'elegiac and dreamy' with a tendency toward poetic fancies,[1] but consciously joins with his father in conducting the enquiry into the 'nonsense', as they have nicknamed his phobia of horses. '"D'you know what?"' he cries, '"Let's write something down for the Professor", i.e., Freud.[2] Or, as Philip Rieff puts it, 'Freud's great case study of infantile sexuality, "Little Hans", seems as much a study in infantile intellectuality. . . . Having grasped the principle that the Professor collected sex stories, Hans took to analysis as an intriguing game complete with rules.'[3] The parents, too, seem more active in approach. Hans's father repeatedly takes the initiative, and follows it up with long interpretative dialogues. Anna, on the other hand, is left to raise matters for herself, nor is anything in the nature of a true enquiry conducted. ('In this matter I believe much discretion is advisable; still if children come upon an idea, they should be deceived no more than adults.'[4]) Another difference is the greater attention paid by Freud to anatomical details. For instance, there is nothing in the case of Anna to set beside Hans's interest in the difference between the genital organs of his small sister and himself. ('She *has* got a tiny little widdler.'[5]) A similar difference in frankness, or in literalism, may be seen in the handling of an almost identical moment—the child's entry into the confinement room. Anna 'first threw a rapid glance at her somewhat pale mother and then displayed something like a mixture of embarrassment and suspicion as if thinking, "Now what else is going to happen?"'[6] Little Hans had an opportunity of observing 'the basins and other vessels, filled with blood and water, that were still standing about the room. Pointing to the blood-stained bedpan, he observed in a surprised voice: "But blood doesn't come out of *my* widdler".'[7] The same kind of difference is found in the enlightenment provided for the children. Anna is told that her little brother 'grew

[1] *Collected Papers*, p. 137; *Development of Personality*, p. 12.
[2] *Collected Papers*, Vol. III, p. 239.
[3] Rieff, Philip, *Freud—the Mind of the Moralist*, p. 92. London: Gollancz, 1959.
[4] *Collected Papers*, p. 154.
[5] *Collected Papers*, Vol. III, p. 157.
[6] *Collected Papers*, p. 135; *Development of Personality*, p. 11.
[7] *Collected Papers*, Vol. III, p. 154.

inside his mother as the flower grows out of the earth'[1] and later that 'the mother is like the soil and the father like the gardener; that the father provides the seed which grows in the mother and thus produces a baby.'[2] Hans learns that 'children grow inside their Mummy and are then brought into the world by being pressed out of her like a "lumf",' —i.e. faeces—'and that this involves a great deal of pain.'[3] There is even something which might be deemed a slight sentimentalism, without parallel in Freud, in Jung's account of Anna's interest in her father, i.e. 'Language has no words for the peculiar kind of tender curiosity that shone in the child's eyes.'[4] Elsewhere, also, traces can be found of a more poetical approach than Freud permits himself, e.g. in the hope that 'the experience of the coming years will sink deeper shafts into this still dark land which I have been able but momentarily to light up, and will discover to us more of the secret workshop of that fate-deciding demon . . .' i.e. the parental constellation.[5] Even so, Jung's attitude in the main is one of objectivity. 'What we have not yet been able to show,' he says again, as in the Word Association Experiments, 'is the universal validity of the observations; it is only by the accumulation of such observations that we shall gain complete insight into the laws of psychical development.'[6]

Reviewing now this period of ten years, what would we be most inclined to say about the work of Jung? First, he stands out as a scientific investigator and a keen experimentalist. The therapeutic interest, though apparently more important to him than the papers taken by themselves would indicate, is not at this stage a main preoccupation. In all his work he shows himself open to new ideas, indeed, enthusiastic toward them, though his own papers, with their careful exposition of existing knowledge, have perhaps a descriptive rather than hypothesizing bent. If a prediction were attempted it might be that Jung would find a place for himself as the experimentalist of the Freudian movement, perhaps anticipating some of the later laboratory work on psychoanalytical mechanisms. Jung's connection with the academic world, however, was clearly weakened somewhat in his withdrawal from the Burghöltzli in 1909, and Freud for his part saw little point in exhaustive investigations designed to substantiate what to him was obvious. Concerning a second function

[1] *Collected Papers*, p. 142; *Development of Personality*, p. 17.
[2] *Ibid.*, p. 152; p. 28.   [3] *Op. cit.*, p. 230.
[4] *Op. cit.*, p. 152; p. 26.   [5] *Collected Papers*, p. 175.
[6] *Ibid.*, p. 154.

which Jung might have developed, that of Freudian expositor, the material, slight as it is, has already begun to suggest that he might not have a sufficiently strong commitment to these doctrines and none other.

Personal relationships during and after 1909 seem to have been complicated. Freud, from his own account as well as Ernest Jones's, was particularly sensitive to anti-Semitism. In connection with one of his dreams he mentions having heard that 'a co-religionist had been forced to resign a position at a state asylum which he had secured with great effort' and refers to 'anxiety about the future of my children, who cannot be given a country of their own.'[1] Some years later he raises, 'with all reserve, the question . . . whether the personality of the present writer as a Jew who has never sought to disguise the fact that he is a Jew may not have had a share in provoking the antipathy of his environment to psycho-analysis.'[2] He admits that it was extremely important to him to render psychoanalysis respectable to the medical and academic world by securing a non-Jewish lieutenant, and Jung, with his position as chief assistant to Professor Bleuler, was well fitted for that role[3]; he was, accordingly, made first President of the International Psychoanalytical Society in 1910. To the Viennese supporters, who themselves were Jews, the favour shown to Jung was not quite acceptable, and during these years Freud made considerable efforts to bring them to his way of thinking. '"Be tolerant',." he wrote to Abraham, even in 1908, '"and don't forget that really it is easier for you to follow my thoughts than for Jung . . . racial relationship brings you closer to my intellectual constitution, whereas he, being a Christian and the son of a pastor, can only find his way to me against great inner resistances".'[4] After all, he added, later in the year, '"our Aryan comrades are quite indispensable to us; otherwise psychoanalysis would fall a victim to anti-semitism".'[5] Jung for his part does not seem to have felt warmly toward the Viennese, describing them to Jones as 'a medley of artists,

---

[1] *Interpretation of Dreams*, pp. 347–8.
[2] *Collected Papers*, Vol. V, pp. 173–4. ('Resistances to Psychoanalysis', 1925.)
[3] This function was to be combined with administrative duties. Jung 'was to be the liaison officer between the various societies, advising and helping wherever necessary, and supervising the various administrative work of congresses, editorial work, and so on. Freud would thus in this way be relieved from the active central position for which he had no taste' (*Sigmund Freud*, Vol. II, p. 160). In short, one may be tempted to add, a 'dog's body' for the movement.
[4] *Ibid.*, p. 53.   [5] *Ibid.*, p. 56.

decadents and mediocrities'.[1] Freud, again in writing to Abraham, surmised that he himself was spared 'the repressed anti-semitism of the Swiss' which was directed all the more strongly against others. It seems possible, however, from material not yet published, that an element of hidden strain in addition to overt enthusiasm may have existed in Jung's mind concerning this relationship as well.[2] At any rate, he has spoken openly about a period of uncertainty and doubt, following his return from the American trip, which had its roots in Freud's 'regrettable dogmatism'.[3] Shortly before going to America he had written to Freud, 'If there is a psycho-analysis there must also be a psycho-synthesis', and turning back to his old studies of Von Hartmann, Nietzsche and others, he urged that ' "We shall never fully explain neurosis and psychosis without mythology and the history of culture".'[4] For these reasons it seems that there is really a close continuity between this period and the one which follows.

[1] *Ibid.*, p. 38.   [2] See Makhdum, *op. cit.*, p. 27; pp. 31–2.
[3] *Development of Personality*, p. 67; Progoff, *op. cit.*, p. 26.
[4] Jacobi, J., *Two Essays on Freud and Jung*, pp. 24–5.

Chapter III

THE INTERMEDIATE PERIOD

Introduction

The years 1912–15 were ones of great activity. During this period Jung set forth his main criticisms of Freud, together with the beginnings of his own views on psychotherapy; his use of the symbolic method, leading to his later theories of the structure and functioning of mind; and the first form of his theory of psychological types. At the same time events which could not quite have been predicted, but which seemed not improbable, did in fact occur: after suggesting a number of modifications to the Freudian position in his *Theory oj Psychoanalysis*, 1912, Jung maintained somewhat uncertain relations with the psychoanalytical movement for a further two-year period, and finally, in the spring of 1914, resigned the Presidency of the International Psychoanalytical Society, so that all connection ceased. In the previous year, 1913, he had given up his University Instructorship in Psychiatry at Zürich,[1] and it was not until 1933, when he was approaching sixty years of age, that he took up an academic post again—this time at the Eidgenossische Technische Hochschule in Zürich and for one year, 1944, as Professor at the University of Basel. The writings of 1912–15—*Theory of Psychoanalysis*, *Psychology of the Unconscious* (published in German as *Wandlungen und Symbole der Libido* and recently revised as *Symbols of Transformation*), and several papers, 'On Psycho-Analysis', 'Some Crucial Points in Psychoanalysis', 'The Psychology of Dreams', 'On the Importance of the

---

[1] There is again a hint of disparagement in his 'Criticism of Bleuler's "Theory of Schizophrenic Negativism".' According to Bleuler there existed a primary schizophrenic splitting, so that the balance between opposite tendencies in the psyche is no longer maintained. But in every case of negativism that has been analysed, Jung argues in his paper, the disturbing factor has been found to be resistance set up by a complex. 'I feel myself bound to emphasize the complex theory, and am not disposed to surrender this conception, which is as illuminating as it was difficult to evolve.' (*Collected Papers*, p. 205.)

46

Unconscious in Psychopathology', and 'A Contribution to the Study of Psychological Types'[1]—can be grouped together on two counts. For one thing there is a similarity in aim. At any rate in his writings Jung still thinks of himself as a scientist rather than a practising physician,[2] and although he discusses the religious question in *Psychology of the Unconscious*, its solution has not yet become a main concern with him. In style, too, his work is somewhat simpler than it afterwards becomes; the papers on psychoanalysis are written in the same straightforward manner as the earlier papers, and while the terms used in *Psychology of the Unconscious* are rather concretistic (e.g. images *stream up* from the unconscious and enable the analyst to *work down to buried strata* of the soul) and the analogies are often hard to keep in mind, the book does not seem to possess that rather baffling quality which makes it possible for many academic readers to go through sentences, paragraphs, and even whole chapters, of the subsequent work without gaining any clear idea of content. Jung's critique of the Freudian viewpoint will be taken first, since this was the beginning of the search for other concepts.

Critique of Freud

Jung introduces his critique by saying that psychoanalysis seems to him to stand in need of a weighing-up from the inside. Theories are instruments, he quotes from William James, '"We don't lie back upon them, we move forward".' This does not mean, however, that 'a modest and moderate criticism' should be taken as a falling away or a schism: 'On the contrary, through it I hope to help on the flowering and fructification of the psychoanalytic movement.'[3]

He starts with the libido theory. Although he follows Freud in widening the scope of sexuality to include more than adult genital functioning, he does not accept the idea of a bundle of impulses which are later co-ordinated, but prefers the concept of one fund of psychic energy, manifesting itself in the two instincts, preservation of the species and self-preservation. Nor does he agree that any form of sexuality is to be found side by side with the function of nutrition in the infant in arms. Such an assumption seems to him to project into

---

[1] See *Collected Papers*, pp. 206–311.   [2] *Collected Papers*, p. 248.
[3] *The Theory of Psychoanalysis*, p. 2. New York: Journal of Nervous & Mental Disease Publishing Company, 1915.

the psyche of the child facts taken from the psychology of adults; even though oral activities can serve sexual purposes later in life, that does not tell us anything about the beginnings of sexual life. Everywhere in nature the vital processes consist for a considerable time of the functions of growth and nutrition only, and there is no need to make an exception in the case of the human infant. The Freudian interpretation rests on an assumption which he himself sees no reason to make, namely, that all pleasure is sexually toned. Beyond a few comments in *Psychology of the Unconscious* to the effect that children value their excretory products highly and that dementia praecox patients can regressively do likewise,[1] Jung does not concern himself with an anal stage of development, but he does acknowledge a connection between 'childish bad habits', such as nail-biting and thumb-sucking and masturbation. These he regards as expressions of 'displaced rhythmic activity'—a more generalized activity which is developed on the model of the sucking movement and leads in its explorations to the discovery of the genital function. Even here it is misleading, in Jung's view, to speak of the child as perverse; there is an analogy, and only an analogy, between the precursors of sexuality and the products of disintegration.

Jung's own developmental divisions are: the pre-sexual, lasting until between the third and fifth years, and characterized first by suckling and later by displaced rhythmic activity; the pre-pubertal, during which the genital zone is discovered; and the age of puberty onwards. No latency period is given—Jung apparently assumes a slow but uninterrupted development. The Oedipus Complex is handled similarly: it is in the first place only a formula or shorthand expression for the childish desire toward the parents and for the conflict evoked by this craving. The desire for food and protection is taken as sufficient to account for the little son's wish to have his mother to himself; it is conceded that 'a relatively germinating eroticism' is also connected with it, but Jung speaks as though the infantile 'root-complex' were only a general form, set in action subsequently—not until the puberty years does the libido take possession of the form and produce feelings and fantasies which unmistakably show the existence of the erotic component, and even then, Jung thinks, such a development occurs only in those individuals who have not succeeded in freeing themselves from father and mother. In accordance

---

[1] *Op. cit.*, pp. 116–18.

with this approach a different interpretation is given of the incest prohibition. Freud, of course, regards this prohibition as evidence for the existence of a powerful and universal urge. Jung, on the other hand, believes 'it is in the natural order of things that what surrounds us daily and has surrounded us loses its compelling charm and thus forces the libido to search for new objects'.[1] The same difference is found in their interpretation of childhood amnesia. For Jung the inability of the child or adult to remember his experiences before the age of five or six can be explained in terms of biological immaturity; the Freudian view, that repression of early sexual activities and desires carries with it the remainder of the child's experience, appears to him 'a conclusion *a posteriori* from the psychology of neurosis',[2] like the previously mentioned view of the child as polymorphously perverse. It is not surprising to find that Jung grants less importance to repression of infantile experience as a factor in the genesis of mental disorder, arguing that since infantile fantasies of the type discovered by Freud are latent in normals, and since they have been inoperative for a very long time in cases of neurosis which break out suddenly, it is necessary to look elsewhere for the essential cause of the illness. It cannot, therefore, be said of Jung, as Freud says of himself at this time, that the doctrine of repression is the foundation stone on which all else is based.[3] Such elements in the patient's past life, Jung continues, do not supply the dynamic, but only the form, of the symptoms. He considers it 'a very suspicious circumstance that these patients frequently show a pronounced tendency to account for their illnesses by some long-past event, ingeniously withdrawing the attention of the physician from the present moment toward some false track in the past,'[4] just as if 'the Germany of the nineteenth century had attributed its political dismemberment and incapacity to its suppression by the Romans, instead of having sought the actual sources of her difficulties in the present.'[5] If the present situation of the patient is examined, some task or obstacle is usually found to which he is not equal. Instead of applying his energies or libido to the real world around him, he has introverted it—turned back or regressed to the memories and fantasies of an earlier period. This turning back, or in long-standing cases refusal to move

[1] *Theory of Psychoanalysis*, p. 70.   [2] *Ibid.*, p. 78.
[3] *Collected Papers*, Vol. I, p. 297. ('History of the Psycho-Analytical Movement', 1914.)
[4] *Op. cit.*, p. 48.   [5] *Ibid.*, p. 81.

on at all, is thought of as occurring because the patient's weakness or inertia is such that he is unable to reach out to a more satisfying world. It is 'that unsuspecting thoughtless state of early childhood ... to which the inner longing always draws us back again and again, and from which the active life must free itself anew'.[1] In the Freudian conception of neurotic regression or fixation there is an element of more active pleasure-seeking; as Jung points out, 'it appears as if the incestuous desires of the Oedipus Complex were the real cause of the regression'.[2]

In one of its aspects analysis is not altered by this theoretical change: the regressive fantasies must still be brought into the light, since the energy which the patient requires for his full adaptation is attached to them. But treatment cannot be allowed to stop at that point. Unless fresh channels are found for the liberated libido, it will always sink back, and therefore patient and physician must work together to find the right path in the present. Jung is prepared for the objection that, far from being ill because he cannot carry out his life task the patient is unable to carry out his life task because he is ill, and replies that sensitive and somewhat inharmonious characters, such as neurotics always are, will meet with special difficulties and perhaps more unusual tasks than normal individuals, who as a rule have only to follow well-established lines. They try to follow the half-conscious way of normal people and do not realize their own critical and very different nature.[3] Some cases, it is true, are neurotic because they will not accept the demands of society; nevertheless, there are many who do not need to be reminded of social obligations, but instead have the task of working out new social ideals.[4]

Several aids can be adopted in the finding of the right path. Important among these is interpretation of dreams, which have the advantage of being psychic products that are independent of the patient's consciousness, and therefore reveal aspects of mental life which do not usually come into prominence. Like Freud, Jung uses the associations supplied by the patient as a basis for the interpretation of dreams, but he begins to rely, to a greater extent than Freud ever came to, on the symbolic method, seeking for parallels between

---

[1] *Psych. of the Unconsc.*, p. 199. London: Kegan Paul, 1944.
[2] *Collected Papers*, p. 230. ('On Pyschoanalysis.')
[3] *Collected Papers*, p. 233.   [4] *Ibid.*, p. 271.

myths and the dreams of his patients. Even in using the free association method he differs from Freud in the type of interpretation which he is prepared to give. Without denying the Freudian theory that dreams are traceable to wishes which have their roots in the past, he does not think it is exhaustive. For instance, although music is no doubt derived from the sexual sphere, it would be unjustifiable simply to look at it in that light. 'A similar nomenclature would then lead us to classify the Cathedral of Cologne as mineralogy because it is built of stones.'[1] Or again, let us suppose that we took the history of the English Parliament back to its first origin. In that way we should certainly achieve a perfect understanding of the factors determining its present form. But we should know nothing about its 'prospective function', i.e. about the work which it has to accomplish now and in the future. The same thing can be said about the dream—it faces two ways, toward the past and toward the future. At the beginning of analysis dreams are helpful chiefly in discovering the fantasies to which the patient's energy is tied, but in the later stages, when the patient is beginning to concern himself with problems of the present again, there is the possibility of discovering in the unconscious material 'those future combinations which are subliminal just because they have not reached the distinctiveness or the intensity which consciousness requires.'[2] Here, too, Jung uses his theory that unconscious functioning is compensatory to that of consciousness, which can be traced back to his earliest study, 'So-called Occult Phenomena', and is found also in the Freudian papers. Sometimes compensation may take the form of symptomatic actions in the Freudian sense, revealing trends rejected by the conscious personality, but the compensatory function which Jung stresses is that of pointing the way to possibilities. Or, as one writer puts it, whereas Freud sees in the fantasy and dream the gratification of a wish that is not actually fulfilled, 'the compensatory theory sees in the fantasy an effort to supply that which is absent in the waking life, and is therefore a "protective" mechanism with a teleological aspect[3]'. A great deal of mental illness arises, Jung believes, from failure to recognize these contributions and accept them. In cases where they are needed, neglected moral values

---

[1] *Psych. of the Unconsc.*, p. 136. [2] *Theory of Psycho-Analysis*, p. 110.
[3] Spinks, A. G. S., 'Archetypes and Apocalypse', pp. 479–80. Unpublished Ph.D. thesis: University of London, 1946.

find expression in this way. As an example he discusses the case of a patient who dreamt that he was going up a flight of stairs with his mother and sister; upon reaching the top he was told that his sister was soon to have a child. Obviously, on the Freudian interpretation, this is nothing but an incest dream—climbing the stairs being a symbol of the sexual act and the sister's child being the natural result. But, Jung argues, if the stairs are to be interpreted symbolically, why not also the mother and sister? This patient was delaying the choice of a profession unduly and also possessed homosexual leanings. The associations to the mother were expressions of regret for having neglected her. 'Mother' was then interpreted by Jung as standing for something which was neglected in an inexcusable manner. ' "My work," said the patient, with considerable embarrassment.' Associations to the sister were that upon taking leave of her years ago he ' "understood for the first time what love for a woman can mean" '—i.e. 'sister' represented 'love for a woman'. To the stairs the association was made, ' "climbing upwards, getting to the top." ' The child brought ideas of regeneration, becoming a new man. According to Jung, therefore, 'One has only to hear this material in order to understand at once that the patient's dream is not so much the fulfilment of infantile desires, as it is the expression of biological duties which he has hitherto neglected'.[1] These duties are not to be equated with restrictions externally imposed. In contrast to Freud, who holds that 'The child . . . knows no *enough* and insatiably demands the repetition of whatever has pleased it or tasted good to it'[2] and is made to conform to social requirements, e.g. the renunciation of the Oedipus wish, only through fear of punishment and loss of affection, Jung holds that there exists an innate urge to the domestication and taming of the libido which cannot be neglected without danger to mental health. 'Man . . . carries his social imperatives within himself, *a priori*, as an inborn necessity.'[3]

To Freud the Jungian view of dreams is possible only if the distinction between the repressed and the non-repressed is disregarded. Before the days of psychoanalysis, he wrote during this period, it was the custom to think that every latent idea had remained latent because it was weak, and that it grew conscious as soon as it became strong. Psychoanalysis soon gained the conviction that some latent

---

[1] *Collected Papers*, p. 220.   [2] *Interpretation of Dreams*, p. 227.
[3] *Collected Papers*, p. 263.

ideas do not penetrate consciousness, no matter how strong they become. 'Therefore we may call the latent ideas of the first type *preconscious*, while we reserve the term *unconscious* (proper) for . . . ideas with a certain dynamic character, ideas keeping apart from consciousness in spite of their intensity and activity.'[1] Only if the contribution of the unconscious proper is disregarded can the dream represent anything with which waking life has been concerned—a reflection, warning, intention, etc. The two theories involve very different views of symbolism. To Freud the symbol is a sign or symptom causally connected with a more forbidden thought that cannot force its way directly into consciousness; these thoughts are of a concrete nature and closely related to the primary instincts, usually the sexual instinct. To Jung the symbol is the best means that can be found at the time for expressing by analogy something that as yet is grasped imperfectly; even symbols which are apparently sexual may really be expressing a more general idea, e.g. a phallus in erection is sometimes to be interpreted as signifying the concept of virility. Or, as Spinks puts it again, for Freud such symbols as pole, steeple, sword, snake, can all be reduced to the phallus, while for Jung any one of these terms, including the phallus itself, may do duty for any one of the others—they are treated, that is, as inter-representations of ideas.[2] Especially during the later stages of analysis, Jung adds, after sexual problems are uncovered, the sexual fantasies of the patient may express aspirations of a different kind. 'Just as primitive man was able, with the aid of religious and philosophical symbol, to free himself from his original state, so, too, the neurotic can shake off his illness in a similar way.' To be healed the patient 'has to reassume that psychological attitude which, in an earlier civilization, was characterized by the living belief in a religious or philosophical dogma. . . . Thus the human being attains the same sense of unity and totality, the same confidence, the same capacity for self-sacrifice in his conscious existence that belongs unconsciously and instinctively to wild animals.'[3]

A further aid to finding the way and the framework within which the other aids are used is the patient-physician relationship. While admitting that transference of infantile attitudes and fantasies

---

[1] *Collected Papers*, Vol. IV, p. 25. ('The Unconscious in Psycho-Analysis', 1912.)
[2] *Op. cit.*, p. 400.   [3] *Collected Papers*, p. 224.

occurs, so that the physician is responded to as though he were the father or some other significant figure in the past life of the patient, and even admitting that such fantasies contain a sexual element, Jung places more emphasis on other aspects. Since he does not attach so much importance to the sexual element in the original parent-child relationship, it is easier for him to hold that through analysis of the infantile portion of the transference fantasies 'the patient is brought back to the remembrance of his childhood's relationship, and this—stripped of its infantile qualities—gives him a beautiful, clear picture of direct human intercourse as opposed to the purely sexual valuation.'[1] Although he does not develop the idea, it would seem from this passage that Jung thinks of the libido as going out toward others very early, whereas Freud is convinced that 'a child loves himself first and only later learns to love others and to sacrifice something of his own ego to them.'[2] Furthermore, according to Freud, even when the child does learn to love others, 'we have to conclude that all the feelings of sympathy, friendship, trust, and so forth . . . are genetically connected with sexuality and have developed out of purely sexual desires by an enfeebling of their sexual aim'.[3] Jung, however, holds that in human relationships as well as dreams sexuality itself can be used symbolically. The patient, not knowing the right way to 'lay hold of the doctor's personality', gropes toward it by means of this analogy. The personality of the physician is, indeed, one of the chief factors in a cure. Besides pointing out the need for the physician himself to undergo analysis on the ground that without it he will inevitably be blindfolded in all those places where he meets his own complexes, Jung believes that 'Patients read the doctor's character intuitively and they should find in him a human being, with faults indeed, but also a man *who has striven at every point to fulfil his own human duties in the fullest sense*'.[4] I think, he adds, that this is the first healing factor. If the doctor himself were neurotic 'the patient would copy the defect and build it up into the fabric of his own presentations'.[5] In so far as the sexual component does enter into the relationship it must be viewed against a wider background. It would not be clung to so obstinately, Jung declares, if the sexual did not have tremendous significance among the duties of life,

[1] *Collected Papers*, p. 273.
[2] *Introductory Lectures on Pyschoanalysis*, p. 172.
[3] *Collected Papers*, Vol. II, p. 319. ('The Dynamics of the Transference', 1912.)
[4] *Collected Papers*, p. 244.   [5] *Ibid.*, p. 272.

especially for the younger person. Although in the later stages of life a tendency to look back to the sexual may represent retreat from the task of developing a more individualized outlook, in the earlier stages the search for a valuable personality is only too often a cloak for the evasion of biological duty. However, he insists, at no stage is psychoanalysis a pedagogical procedure.

> 'What direction the patient's future life should take is not ours to judge. We must not imagine we know better than his own nature—or we prove ourselves educators of the worst kind. Psychoanalysis is but a means of removing stones from the path, and in no way a method . . . of putting anything into the patient which was not there before. So we renounce any attempt to give a direction, and occupy ourselves only with setting in proper relief all that analysis brings into the light of day, in order that the patient may see clearly, and be in a position to draw the appropriate conclusions.'[1]

These, then, are the chief divergences from Freud: Jung prefers to think of a general fund of psychic energy with varying manifestations rather than a series of component impulses organized into the adult sexual drive; he has less regard for the Oedipus complex, incest prohibition and repression as factors in the genesis of mental illness and more regard for the present situation and the patient's need to find his future line of development; he holds that the function of the unconscious is prospective and compensatory and that its natural means of expression, the symbol, provides analogies for concepts, often of a general kind, that are not yet fully grasped; he believes in the innateness of social and self-restraining impulses and the importance of a religious outlook broadly interpreted; and he considers the patient-physician relationship to be less repetitive and less influenced by sexual desire. There are also various smaller differences —for instance, Jung's opinion, as already noted, that it is inertia rather than fixation to infantile pleasures which impedes development. Another such difference is his attitude to confession, i.e. that the holding back of a secret cuts the patient off from intercourse with the rest of mankind. So far as the present writer is aware, nothing comparable to this inclusion of the community can be discovered in the work of Freud. Again, while Freud quickly accepted one of Jung's reasons for analysis of the physician—that without it he would be blind when meeting his own complexes in psychoanalytical

[1] *Ibid.*, p. 264.

practice and so 'would introduce into the analysis a new form of selection and distortion'[1]—no mention is made of the second reason —that the patient would build the physician's defect into his own personality.

The radical differences between Freud and Jung can of course be found in the later work as well, though as might be expected they form a smaller portion of the totality, and the minor differences can best be appreciated with the full range of their writings upon which to draw. There is, however, one feature of their presentation which is already rather marked. Although Jung can be seen to acknowledge the necessity of dealing with, for instance, infantile incestuous phantasies in terms that are not always symbolical, he does not, even so, appear to be happy with this aspect of the work. His attitude rather is that 'The psycho-analyst must put aside . . . aesthetic judgment, just as every physician must, who really tries to help his patients. He may not fear any dirty work.'[2] He admits that the fantasies can have a certain scientific interest, but thinks that this is best concealed, in order not to tempt the patient to have greater pleasure than necessary in them. In other words, the fantasies are to be examined, with the proviso that the patient should not be encouraged to tarry over them unduly. Now Freud himself speaks in one passage of being tired with rummaging in all this human filth and longing to get away, 'to see my children and then the beauties of Italy'.[3] But this is very unusual. In all the cases he records, the infantile and other sexual material is handled with unlimited dexterity and care; moreover, in the passage cited it is a complete rest that Freud is seeking, not an examination of the case in any other aspect. This difference in the handling of material is of course in harmony with the difference in their theoretical positions; we may recall its beginnings in the earlier period, before Jung's theoretical statements had really been worked out.[4]

Another feature at this time is the attitude which Jung begins to take toward the responsibilities of psychiatric practice. The scientist, he says, can have a different attitude, but in therapeutic practice 'I regard the conscience-searching question of the doctor's remaining true to his scientific convictions as rather unimportant in comparison

[1] *Collected Papers*, Vol. II, p. 328. ('Reconstructions in Treatment', 1912.)
[2] *Theory of Psychoanalysis*, p. 99.
[3] *Interpretation of Dreams*, p. 373.   [4] *Supra*, p. 40.

with the incomparably weightier question as to how he can best help his patient.'[1] A further difference is that the scientific interest of the investigator leads him to find rules and categories, whereas the physician would be well advised to

'put away his scholar's gown, bid farewell to his study, and wander with human heart through the world. There, in the horrors of prisons, lunatic asylums and hospitals, in drab suburban pubs, in brothels and gambling hells, in the salons of the elegant, the Stock Exchanges, Socialist meetings, churches, revivalist gatherings and ecstatic sects, through love and hate, through the experience of passion in every form in his own body, he will reap richer stores of knowledge than text-books a foot thick could give him, and he will know how to doctor the sick with real knowledge of the human soul.'[2]

These statements suggest that Jung's view of the relation between science and therapy is not identical with that of Freud, who had written two years previously that 'every advance in our knowledge means an increase in the power of our therapy . . . the more we understand the more we shall achieve'.[3] Or at any rate, while Jung would probably not wish to challenge the point of view which Freud expresses, he may be more inclined to envisage the possibility of a conflict between therapy and science in the immediate situation, and in his handling of the individual case may be tending toward the use of empathic understanding and richness of association rather than the application of formal diagnostic, or even developmental, patterns abstracted from previous case material.

Psychology of the Unconscious

Psychology of the Unconscious is largely an essay in the use of the symbolic method. In an introductory chapter on 'Two Kinds of Thinking', which gives its theoretical basis, Jung distinguishes a directed type of thinking, or layer of thought, as he describes it, which has the purpose of adaptation to the environment, including communication with others, takes place in words or substitute motor signs, is conscious throughout, and requires a definite effort; and a non-directed, which for adaptive purposes is wholly unproductive

[1] *Collected Papers*, p. 251.
[2] 'New Paths in Psychology,' 1912. Appendix, *Two Essays*, new ed., p. 244.
[3] *Collected Papers*, Vol. II, p. 286. ('The Future of Psycho-Analytic Therapy,' 1910.)

and in which image crowds upon image associatively, without effort and in accordance with the unconscious wishes of the subject. 'An extraordinarily important task, which even to-day is hardly possible, is to give a systematic description of phantastic thinking'[1] but at least, since the mode of thinking is the same, the myths of ancient and primitive man and the dreams of modern man can be used to clarify each other's meaning.

From this standpoint Jung investigates an individual fantasy system produced over a ten-year period by a young American woman, Miss Frank Miller, who some time afterwards developed schizophrenia. Jung himself never saw this girl, who had been associated for a period with the psychologist Flournoy at Geneva. His role was, therefore, entirely that of scientific investigator, nor had he heard of her illness at the time of making his interpretations. The opening poem begins:

> *When the Eternal first made Sound*
> *A myriad ears sprang out to hear,*
> *And throughout all the Universe*
> *There rolled an echo deep and clear*
> *All glory to the God of Sound!*

—the other verses ending, 'All glory to the God of Light' and 'All glory to the God of Love'.[2] First the personal circumstances and associations are examined. The poem was composed during a sea voyage when, after a period of isolated dreaming, the writer had become friendly with some of the officers; she states that the midnight singing of one of these officers had especially impressed her— to which Jung comments that after a condition of introversion, or inward turning of the libido, such as preceded it, an erotic impression has a deep effect which may easily be undervalued. Not infrequently at the time of first love, he continues, there is a regressive attempt at resuscitation of the father image, which seems to have happened in this case, since the idea of the masculine creative Deity is a derivation; confirmation is found in other associations, i.e. that as a girl of nine to sixteen she had been much impressed by a Presbyterian minister, 'without in the least being able to understand what he meant when he spoke to us of Chaos, Cosmos and the Gift of Love.' Here is a turning away from the natural father to the 'father of the church' and

[1] *Psych. of the Unconsc.*, p. 19. London: Kegan Paul, 1944.   [2] *Ibid.*, p. 28.

the Father God represented by him, 'because the original sin of incest weighs heavily for all time upon the human race.'[1]

Unfortunately, Jung goes on to say, the issue is never fairly and squarely faced: there is no conscious treatment of the erotic problem on the subject's part. It is this sort of undervaluation which Freud has formulated as repression; its disadvantage is that what is repressed may create fresh compensations and displacements elsewhere. He contrasts Miss Miller's poem with the religious solution of earlier Christian times, when the conflict, with its pain, care and anxiety, was kept in sight and consciously given over to a personality conceived to lie outside oneself. In fact, Jung considers, such a personality is no more than a projection ('In the Deity man honours his own libido'), and since a delusion cannot be kept up indefinitely it has had to be reinforced by appeal to the human community and the injunction of brotherly love; at the same time the belief in the Deity has had value in preventing psychological intimacy from 'creating certain shortened ways . . . to the sexual relation.'[2] Miss Miller's poem, however, is not much more than a sentimental transformation of the erotic. A second poem, 'The Moth to the Sun', is taken as an illustration of the way in which such an unfaced complex continues to be worked over in the unconscious:

> . . . having gained
> One raptured glance, I'll die content.[3]

The first poem reveals an unconscious longing to solve the conflict through positive religion, as in earlier centuries. When this does not succeed a death wish is substituted, since anyone who refuses to experience life must stifle his desire to live. The identity of the theme is seen from the personal associations, among which are the words, 'the passionate longing of the moth for the star, of man for God. . . .'[4] This passionate longing for God is to be equated with the longing for the singing morning stars in the earlier poem, i.e. for the ship's officer who sings on deck in the night watch.

From this material with its images of warmth and light Jung moves to a more general consideration of libido symbols. These are classified as symbols based on analogy, e.g. sun and fire; those which designate the libido by its object, e.g. the sun again; those derived from the place of origin or analogies, e.g. the phallus or the snake;

[1] *Ibid.*, p. 33.   [2] *Ibid.*, p. 41.   [3] *Ibid.*, p. 47.   [4] *Ibid.*, p. 50.

and finally, those arising from the activity comparison, e.g. lion or boar, which, together with fire, are used especially for the destructive aspect of libido. When the element of personification is added the gods come into being. A very usual god, met in many guises, is the sun hero 'who again mounts to the height of the sun and again descends to the coldness of the winter, who is the light of hope from race to race, the image of the libido'.[1] But the phallus is important here as well, giving the model for Tom Thumb and other hero dwarfs, and for the phallic god Dionysius, who 'stands in an intimate relation with the psychology of the early Asiatic God who died and rose again from the dead and whose manifold manifestations have been brought together in the figure of Christ into a firm personality enduring for centuries.'[2] The basis of the Trinity, also, is to be found in the male genital organs, and 'The traditional representation of the Crucified flanked by John and Mary is closely associated with this circle of ideas, precisely as is the Crucified with the thieves.'[3] In addition, however, the Christian scheme includes God and the Devil, personifications of the creative and the destructive aspects of the libido. Without the destructive quality something essential would be lost, he continues, in passages which are among the most obscure in the book, and 'Through the loss of the Devil, God himself suffered a considerable loss, somewhat like an amputation upon the body of the Divinity.'[4]

A reconstruction of these symbolizing activities in the life of mankind is attempted. Jung puts forward the hypothesis that in prehistoric times much of the energy which to modern man is available in a generalized form was of a sexual nature. Having been desexualized in the history of the race, some portions of libido remain permanently directed into other channels. The impulse bringing this about is conceived to be an actual resistance against sexuality, which aims at the prevention of the sexual act by seeking analogies for it. An example is found at the present time in the custom of an Australian aboriginal tribe of thrusting spears into a bush-covered hole, made to resemble a woman's genitals; there seems to be a compulsion to perform such activities—no outer obstacle exists to normal satisfaction, but 'will opposes will; libido opposes libido'.[5] In prehistoric times fire-making may have originated as just such a substi-

---

[1] *Ibid.*, p. 69.   [2] *Ibid.*, p. 74.   [3] *Ibid.*, p. 126.
[4] *Ibid.*, p. 66.   [5] *Ibid.*, p. 94.

tute; Jung cites, among other examples, a Hindoo cult in which the two pieces of wood are personified as man and woman.[1] He suggests also that immense opportunities of applying the libido have arisen through the regression of part of it, in the face of the incest prohibition, to the stage of rhythmic activity, after which the search for an external object is continued. For instance, the application of infantile boring activities to the outer world may have given another mode of fire discovery, and the secrecy with which fire is prepared in some religious rites would seem to indicate an attempt to find an alternative expression for the genital form of those activities. For the real mother object an ideal substitute is the earth, with its combined associations of nutrition and fertilization—hence the development of agriculture. Primitive speech, implying directed thought, may have developed from a strengthening of the already existing love call when the repressed libido turned again to the external world in search of substitute objects; Jung lists a number of Indo-Germanic words with the meanings of 'to desire, to play, to radiate' as well as 'to sound'. In short, he believes, for primitive thought the so-called objective world was, and had to be, a subjective image: the fire-tool, for instance, did not receive its sexual significance as a later addition—the sexual libido was the driving force behind its discovery.

Jung now returns to the series of fantasies which was his starting point. Between the first poem in 1898 and the fantasies about to be discussed four years have gone by, concerning which Miss Miller gives no information, but this lack, he suggests, may have advantages, i.e. our interest is not diverted by sympathy for the personal fate of the author, and thus 'something is obviated which often prevents the analyst in his daily task from looking away from the tedious toil of detail to that wider relation which reveals each neurotic conflict to be involved with human fate as a whole'.[2]

After a state of passivity, indicating, Jung thinks, a tendency to move away from real solutions, Miss Miller describes a Sphinx-like figure which, in the absence of personal associations, he himself interprets as a representative of the mother: such half-human, half-animal figures have had this significance very often in mythology—above, the human and attractive half, below the horrible animal half, converted into a fear animal through the incest prohibition. Then follows an Aztec by the name of Chi-wan-to-pel; from Miss Miller's

[1] *Ibid.*, pp. 90–2.　　　　[2] *Ibid.*, p. 106–7.

association, 'Popocatepetl', he suggests that this figure was influenced by the anal interests of childhood—the implication of the association is, 'I make, produce, invent him out of myself'. A second association —Ahasuerus or Ahasverus—leads to a different trend of thought, the Wandering Jew; Jung refers to a parallel Islamic figure of Chidr, or 'al Chadir', and an earlier legend of the cave of the seven sleepers, who escaped persecution by sleeping in a cave for three hundred and nine years and awoke in a new era. The model for this is the course of the sun, which 'sets periodically but does not die. It hides in the womb of the sea or in a subterranean cave, and in the morning is "born again", complete'.[1] The wish-fulfilment is obvious—a return to the womb of the mother. Traces of this are found in other legends, e.g. 'the dying and resurrected gods are the lovers of their own mothers or have generated themselves through their own mothers. Christ as the "God becoming flesh" has generated himself through Mary; Mithra has done the same.'[2] The wandering of these heroes is also symbolic. It makes the sun comparison easily intelligible, but expresses really 'the myth of our own suffering unconscious, which has an unquenchable longing for all the deepest sources of our own being; for the body of the mother, and through it for communion with infinite life in the countless forms of existence'.[3]

After the creation of the hero Miss Miller has a vision of a throng of people and a 'City of Dreams'. The first image Jung interprets as a symbol of mystery—the bearer of the mystery being placed in opposition to the multitude of the ignorant—and in its streaming and moving aspect it signifies the great excitement in the unconscious, but more attention is paid to the city, as a mother symbol, i.e. 'a woman who fosters the inhabitants'. Evidence of this is found, for example, in the description of the heavenly Jerusalem in the Book of Revelation: ' "And he shewed me a pure river of water of life. . . . In the midst of the street of it, and on either side of the river, was there the tree of life, which bare twelve manner of fruits, and yielded her fruit every month, and the leaves of the tree were for the healing of nations." '[4] 'Water' and 'tree', Jung continues, are themselves maternal symbols, e.g. in the Vedas the waters are called Matritamah, which means, 'the most maternal'. The maternal significance of the tree can be seen in myths where the hero is enclosed in a tree—the dead Osiris in a column, Adonis in the

---

[1] *Ibid.*, p. 119.   [2] *Ibid.*, p. 120.   [3] *Ibid.*, p. 127.   [4] *Ibid.*, p. 135.

myrtle—though there is also evidence for a masculine and phallic significance, e.g. in the medieval family trees, where the trunk grows upwards from the first ancestor in the place of the phallus. The bisexuality of the symbol is illustrated by the Latin word 'arbor' with a masculine termination and feminine gender. But in conjunction with the symbolism of the city, both the water and the tree 'refer to that amount of libido which unconsciously is fastened to the mother imago'.[1]

However, Jung holds, we can see clearly in these myths that the 'incestuous' desire does not aim at cohabitation but at the thought of becoming a child again, of coming into the mother once more in order to be born again. 'There shall be no more sins, no repression, no disharmony with one's self, no guilt, no fear of death and no pain of separation more!'[2] Since incest stands in the path of this goal, some means of circumventing the prohibition must be found, such as transforming the mother into another being, and fantasy gradually produces possibilities in which the libido becomes 'spiritualized in an imperceptible manner', again through analogy. In the Christian scheme 'man becomes a child again and is born into a circle of brothers and sisters; but his mother is the "communion of the saints", the church, and his circle of brothers and sisters is humanity, with whom he is united anew in the common inheritance of the primitive symbol'.[3] Valuable though it is, this process is not free from drawbacks—infantilism on the one hand, and on the other, doubt. Though much is said of pious people who wander through the world unshaken in their trust in God, 'I have never seen this Childher yet. It is probably a wish figure.'[4] At the present time another way is needed—the way of conscious recognition. For instance, instead of doing good to others for the love of Christ, we should do it from the knowledge that humanity could not exist if the one could not sacrifice himself for the other. 'I think *belief should be replaced by understanding*; then we would keep the beauty of the symbol, but still remain free from the depressing results of submission to belief. This would be the psychoanalytic cure for belief and disbelief' and the higher course of action, for man without compulsion or delusion to '*wish that which he must do*'.[5]

Besides those myths in which the primitive thought of incestuous

---

[1] *Ibid.*, p. 138. [2] *Ibid.*, p. 138. [3] *Ibid.*, p. 140.
[4] *Ibid.*, p. 144. [5] *Ibid.*, pp. 144–5.

reproduction occurs, Jung mentions cults in which man is sufficiently advanced to believe that eternal life is reached not through incest but through the sacrifice of the incest wish. This is expressed in the Mithraic sacrifice, where Mithra conquers his animal nature, 'the bull'. A similar interpretation is given to the Crucifixion: 'The first-born sacrifices its life to the mother when he suffers, hanging on the branch, a disgraceful and painful death.'[1] After a more extended consideration of the cross symbolism—the resemblance of the cross to the form of the human body, its possible relation to the two pieces of wood in religious fire production, and its use, e.g. in Plato's 'Timaios', as a symbol of union—Jung continues with the Miller fantasies. The drama enters a new phase, which he calls 'The Battle for Deliverance from the Mother'.[2] This begins with the vision of a forest and bushes; retaining the symbolism of 'tree' as equivalent to 'mother', he interprets it as meaning that the act takes place in or near the mother. Chiwantopel appears on horseback and an Indian prepares to let fly an arrow at him, but since he presents his breast in an attitude of defiance the Indian slinks away. Jung finds an intimate connection between the hero and the horse. They are an artistic formation of the idea of humanity with its repressed libido; the horse possesses the significance of the animal unconscious, which appears domesticated and subjected to the will of man. Mythological parallels are 'Agni upon the ram, Wotan upon Sleipneir, . . . Christ upon the ass, Dionysus upon the ass, Mithra upon the horse. . . .'[3] Various superhuman powers are attributed to the horse in myth—he can prophesy evil, hear the words of a corpse, and see phantoms, achievements which are typical manifestations of the unconscious. It is understandable that the horse, as the image of the wicked animal component of man, including sexuality, should have connections with the devil, e.g. the devil has a horse's hoof. Other phallic indications can be found, such as the myth that Balder's horse gave rise to a spring through his kick, and thus became 'the dispenser of fruitful moisture'. On the other hand, the horse is also connected with the symbolism of the tree—a neo-Persian word for coffin means 'wooden horse', and the Trojan horse is obviously a mother symbol. The horse, in short, is a libido symbol of the same type as the tree, of partly phallic and partly maternal significance.

[1] *Ibid.*, p. 162.   [2] *Ibid.*, pp. 169–87.   [3] *Ibid.*, p. 170.

Chiwantopel's gesture in baring his breast is scrutinized. Miss Miller is reminded of the scene between Cassius and Brutus in *Julius Caesar*, to which Jung adds that Cassius has something very infantile about him. As Brutus says, '"O Cassius, You are yoked with a lamb."' The association implies that Chiwantopel is like that. Death is to come to this infantile hero in the form of an arrow wound, i.e. in contrast to the inactive nature of the previous symbols those of this vision have a threatening aspect. The theme of being wounded by an arrow is found in mythology—sometimes, too, the theme of being wounded by one's own arrow, which signifies that will turns against will, libido against libido. This implies a state of introversion—the libido sinks into the unconscious and finds there a substitute for the upper world which it has abandoned—the world of childhood and the mother, or, strictly, the mother-imago, or idea that the child has of the mother. Regularly, when some great work is pending, before which a human being is doubtful of his strength, his libido returns to this source. In this dangerous phase the decision takes place between annihilation and new life. If, through any decrease in the forward-striving movement—ageing, external difficulties, or very often enslavement by woman in the mother-role—the libido remains arrested in this childhood kingdom, the man is, for the world above, a phantom. If the libido succeeds in tearing itself loose and pushing up into the world above, the journey proves to have been one of self-renewal, *reculer pour mieux sauter*, and new fertility springs from apparent death.

Of the Miller fantasy Jung comments that the arrow is not shot, the hero does not die. But it is high time for him to take his departure, since all bonds and limitations need to be renounced. Jung reinforces his interpretation by reference to the dreamer's personal circumstances. From various hints it appears that she is still living in the family circle at an age when independence is urgently required—he who does not heed life's call because of childish indolence and fear is threatened by neurosis. Admittedly, the arrow wound has a sexual significance as well, but, Jung considers, nothing is gained by the sexual reduction—'it is a commonplace that the unconscious shelters coitus wishes, the discovery of which signifies nothing further'[1]—and, indeed, he takes the coitus wish itself as a symbol of the conquest of an independent life.

[1] *Ibid.*, p. 187.

After the disappearance of the assailant, Chiwantopel begins a monologue in which he declares that after leaving his father's palace he has sought for a hundred moons '"her who will understand"'; reviewing the women he has known he concludes, '"There is not one among them who has known my soul."' This again suggests the mother, who in the infantile language is 'she who understands'; the fact that the dreamer herself is a woman makes no difference, for 'The daughter takes a male attitude towards the mother.' At the same time it also means the life companion, and therefore a repressed striving toward the natural destiny. Miss Miller states that the hero's departure from his father's palace reminds her of the young Buddha, who similarly renounced luxury. Jung notes this as a confirmation of his previous suggestion that in her own case, too, the battle for independence is at stake. Before continuing with this line of thought he examines the myth of Hiawatha, which Miss Miller cites as a source of influence. Here the same cycle of ideas is found as in the hero-myths discussed already. First there is a strange birth—in this case from a maiden, Wenonah, and the West Wind; Wenonah dies after the birth and the grandmother Nikomis takes her place. The theme of the two mothers suggests self-rejuvenation, the fulfilment of the wish that it might be possible for the mother to bear one again; the same theme is found in the story of Buddha, who has a stepmother, and the myth of Romulus and Remus with the fostering animal, while in the Christian mythology it is replaced by the motif of twofold birth through baptism. Eventually, after preliminary encounters with animals, Hiawatha battles with the father, Mudje-keewis, in order to avenge the dead mother, Wenonah. Behind this lies the thought that he slays the father in order to take possession of the mother, for the father 'in the psychologic sense, merely represents the personification of the incest prohibition; that is to say, resistance, which defends the mother'. The hero, Jung continues, is a hero because he sees in every difficulty of life resistance to the forbidden treasure, and fights that resistance single-mindedly. 'When one has slain the father, one can obtain possession of his wife, and when one has conquered the mother, one can free one's self.'[1] On his return journey Hiawatha stops at a clever arrow-maker's, who possesses a lovely daughter, Minnehaha, Laughing Water. The name alludes to the mother so clearly that the hero's

---

[1] *Ibid.*, pp. 200–1.

secret yearning is powerfully touched. However, he does nothing directly to win Minnehaha, but fasts in isolation for three days. Other adventures follow, all of which are concerned with the backward pull toward the mother and the effort to turn this regression into a life-creating experience. One of these is with Mishe-Nama, a fish monster. Challenged to battle, the monster devours Hiawatha and his boat. Inside it Hiawatha strikes its heart with his fist and drags his canoe carefully through its jaws—the typical myth of the sun hero. Another adventure is with the magician, Megissogwon, representing the fearful aspect of the mother. A terrible struggle takes place—Megissogwon is invulnerable, and at evening Hiawatha retires wounded to rest beneath a pine tree whose trunk is coated over with a special kind of fungus, Dead Man's Moccasin Leather— a dangerous step for him, because in so doing he resigns himself to the devouring mother 'whose garment is the garment of death'. At this stage of despair a helpful bird, Mama the Woodpecker, representing the benevolent aspect of the mother, advises him where the magician should be shot—beneath the hair, the 'phallic' point at the top of the head, which still appears as the birth place in the sexual theories of children. Into this place Hiawatha shoots three arrows, a well-known sexual symbol, and thus kills Megissogwon. By this great deed, vanquishing the death-bringing mother, he frees himself for marriage with Minnehaha. In the years that follow Hiawatha discovers writing and brings other blessings to his people—and then begins the decline. His best friend, Chibiabos, the embodiment of the joy of life, is ambushed by evil spirits and drowned, he loses another friend, Kwasind, the embodiment of physical strength, famine comes, and the death of Minnehaha, and finally he prepares for a last journey.

> *I am going, O Nokomis,*
> *On a long and distant journey,*
> *To the portals of the Sunset . . .*
> *Thus departed Hiawatha,*
> *Hiawatha the Beloved,*
> *In the glory of the sunset . . .*
> *To the land of the Hereafter.*[1]

The sun image was the first carrier of human destiny, and fully entitled to become such: 'in the morning of life man painfully tears

[1] *Ibid.*, p. 215.

himself loose from the mother, from the domestic hearth, to rise through battle to his heights.' Bearing within himself

'a deadly longing for the depths within, for drowning in his own source, for becoming absorbed into the mother, his life is a constant struggle with death, a violent and transitory delivery from the always lurking night. This death is no external enemy, but a deep personal longing for quiet and for the profound peace of non-existence, for a dreamless sleep in the ebb and flow of the sea of life.'

If man is to live,

'he must fight and sacrifice his longing for the past, in order to rise to his own heights. And having reached the noonday heights, he must also *sacrifice the love for his own achievement, for he may not loiter*. The sun also sacrifices its greatest strength in order to hasten onwards to the fruits of autumn, which are the seeds of immortality.'[1]

Returning to the Miller fantasies after further mythological study, Jung reviews a later portion of Chiwantopel's monologue: ten thousand moons will wax and wane before that pure soul is born who will understand. Temptation will assail her but she will not yield. '"I have come ten thousand moons before her epoch, and she will come ten thousand moons too late. But she will understand."' Together with his horse, which succumbs first, Chiwantopel is stung to death by a green serpent, repeating as he dies, '"I have kept my body inviolate. Ah! She understands. Ja-ni-wa-ma, Ja-ni-wa-ma, thou who comprendeth me."'[2]

The motif of coming too late, Jung comments, is characteristic of the infantile love: father and mother cannot be overtaken, and separation by ten thousand moons is a wish-fulfilment, effectively annulling the incest relationship. The statement, 'I have kept my body inviolate'—which only a woman would be likely to make— refers to refusal of the coitus fantasy, and the bold assertions that temptation is resisted and that only once in ten thousand moons is such a soul born, point to an enormous infantile megalomania, concealing the fact that all enterprises have remained but dreams. Punishment inevitably follows:

'In place of the positive phallus, the negative appears, and leads the hero's horse (his libido animalis), not to satisfaction, but into eternal peace—also the fate of the hero. This end means that the mother,

---

[1] *Ibid.*, p. 215.   [2] *Ibid.*, p. 238.

represented as the jaws of death, devours the libido of the daughter. Therefore, instead of life and procreative growth, only phantastic self-oblivion results.'[1]

And yet, Jung suggests, there is a deeper stratum of meaning, in explaining which he goes back to the comparison of Chiwantopel and Cassius. Chiwantopel is the dreamer's infantile personality, which is unable to understand that one must leave father and mother. Therefore, when Chiwantopel dies, it means the fulfilment of a wish, that this infantile hero who cannot leave the mother's care may die, since if the bond is severed a step into independence will be made. Examining the symbols again, he concludes that while the sacrifice of the horse symbolizes renunciation of the sexual wishes, the sacrifice of the hero 'has the deeper and ethically more valuable meaning of the sacrifice of the infantile personality'.[2] The significance of the horse and the serpent is contrasted also. As a rule the horse is not an animal of fear but signifies the living positive part of the libido, and the serpent represents fear, the fear of death. This antithesis symbolizes an opposition of the libido within itself—a striving forward and a striving backward. It appears to Jung as though the libido is not only an endless life and will for construction, meeting death and every end through some outside catastrophe, but as though it also wills its own destruction. 'In the first half of life its will is for growth, in the second half of life it hints, softly at first, and then audibly, at its will for death.'[3] In the young it is repressed sexuality that is symbolized by the serpent, because the arrival of sexuality puts an end to, i.e. is the death of, childhood. With Miss Miller, therefore, it is the insufficiently expressed sexuality which as serpent takes the role of sacrificer and delivers the hero over to death and rebirth.

Finally, from the last words of Miss Miller's hero, we learn that his longed-for beloved, she alone who understands him, is called Ja-ni-wa-ma. Here again are the syllables familiar from the early childhood of the hero Hiawatha—wawa, wama, mama. Taking etymological examples, Jung links *verstehen*, *comprendre* and *erfassen*. 'The thing common to these expressions is the surrounding, the enfolding. And there is no doubt that there is nothing which so completely enfolds us as the mother. When the neurotic complains

[1] *Ibid.*, p. 239.   [2] *Ibid.*, p. 265.   [3] *Ibid.*, p. 266.

that the world has no understanding, he says indirectly that he misses the mother.'[1]

Coming now to a review of this material in *Psychology of the Unconscious*, a fundamental question is, of course, the soundness or otherwise of the theoretical basis. Is it true that there are the two types of thinking, directed and non-directed, and that childhood, primitive and psychotic thinking can be equated? And how far is Jung right in the kind of interpretations that he gives to the symbols of dreams and other fantasies, i.e. how far do the dream images represent general ideas which the dreamer can grasp only vaguely, and how far should they be interpreted as standing for more concrete, forbidden ideas as the Freudians have urged? These problems, like those of the libido theory, etiology of neurosis and therapeutic aim, belong also to the later work, but whether or not any restatement may be needed then, an impression does emerge that the same thread is running through both the clinical and the mythological material—the need of mankind in general and the individual whose fantasies are being examined in particular, to live an independent life, the mingled desire and reluctance to achieve this, and use of the themes of sacrifice and rebirth in order to express it. It is surely a notable achievement to have hit off the young woman's mentality so well, as Flournoy later assured him,[2] with no personal contact, at a time when the psychological study of symbolism was only just beginning.

On the other hand, there is a diffuseness in the mythological material, a piling of parallel upon parallel with, in fact, varying degrees of similarity between them, which, rather than enhancing the general impression, at times detracts from it. It seems on occasion as though the usual distinctions are lost sight of, so that, for instance, the truly mythical hero, representing moral orientation, the fairy-tale hero, representing simple wish-fulfilment, and the culture hero, like Hiawatha, who stands intermediate between them, are all handled on one level. There also seems to be a blurring of historical fact. It is perhaps especially noticeable that the Crucifixion is dealt with as a sacrifice of the animal nature, comparable to Mithra's sacrifice of the bull, and the Cross is seen as a symbol of union, as representing the human figure, and so forth, but during this exploration of associative accretions the Crucifixion itself as an actual or probable event

[1] *Ibid.*, p. 267.   [2] *Symbols of Transformation*, p. xxviii.

has largely disappeared. A similar failure to consider outer reality is found in some of Jung's historical accounts. Having pointed out that the ancient world, despite its mathematical knowledge, never developed a technology, he says that 'There is necessarily only one answer to this': men at that time, with the exception of a few extra-ordinary minds, lacked the capacity to think objectively about the processes of nature. But surely the commonly accepted interpretation would have been worthy of consideration, i.e. that failure to make advances in technology was due to the abundance of slave labour and the contempt in which practical activities were held by the trained minds of the period. In this respect—consideration of alternative hypotheses—Jung seems less critical than in the days of the Word Association Studies. He himself was evidently intoxicated by his findings. 'I feel,' he wrote to Freud during the preparation of the book, 'as if I had journeyed alone to a foreign land, to see marvellous things there that no one has seen before.'[1] Many years afterwards he referred to *Psychology of the Unconscious* as 'the explosion of all those psychic contents which could find no room, no breathing space, in the constricting atmosphere of Freudian psychology and its narrow outlook'.[2] For many people, however, a number of less comprehensive examples might have been helpful at this stage.[3] And in fact, despite his bursting out of Freudian psychology, Jung often makes a blend or juxtaposition of his own and Freudian views which is at least as confusing as in the previous papers. In one respect—the importance given to the mother—he reverts to the position of the Word Association Studies, but from his assumption of a wish-fulfilling motive behind the fantastic type of thinking, the sexual derivation of many of the symbols—e.g. the association of the Trinity and the male genitals—the theory of desexualization of libido in the course of history and the derivation of religious activity

---

[1] Cited by Jacobi, *Two Essays on Freud and Jung*, p. 26.
[2] *Symbols of Transformation*, p. xxiii.
[3] One such example is given in the *Theory of Psycho-Analysis*, pp. 124–6, where a child patient, aged eleven, had objected that all fairy tales do not have a meaning, and had named in illustration Sleeping Beauty and Snow White. It was pointed out to her that ' "The Sleeping Beauty had to wait for one hundred years in an enchanted sleep until she could be freed. . . . So one must often wait a long while to obtain what one longs for." ' In his commentary Jung adds that the story of Snow White in her glass coffin 'arose from the same unconscious sources as the Sleeping Beauty, that is, a complex consisting of the expectation of coming events, which are altogether comparable with the deliverance of the earth from the prison of winter and its fertilization through the sunbeams of spring.'

from 'those impulses which in childhood are withdrawn from incestuous application through the intervention of the incest taboo', it is not easy to decide how far Jung is still incorporating Freudian doctrines. An example of this ambiguity can be found in the concluding portion of the book. On the one hand, the death of the hero and the horse means that 'the mother, represented as the jaws of death, devours the libido of the daughter', i.e. Jung interprets the fantasy according to his own view that such material gives a picture of the actual state of the psyche. On the other hand, there is a deeper stratum of meaning, a wish that this infantile hero who cannot leave the mother's care may die.

Now in the new edition, where *Psychology of the Unconscious* has been revised as *Symbols of Transformation*, these traces of Freudian influence have disappeared. Nothing is said of a wish-element in fantastic thought, most of the sexual derivations have dropped out, the Deity is less closely connected with infantile themes but becomes 'an image of all the necessities and inevitableness of life', and the lack of co-ordination at the end is remedied. (The dream solution, Jung says here, represents an attempt on the part of the unconscious to help the dangerous situation of the conscious mind. 'But if it requires so drastic an annihilation of the hero . . . we may justifiably conclude that the human personality of the author is threatened in the highest degree.'[1]) Other criticisms are met to some extent, i.e. Jung allows that his comparative method often joins figures which from other points of view can hardly be put together at all, and in his account of historical development he acknowledges the lack of any external pressure toward technology in the ancient world. Nevertheless these small points in *Psychology of the Unconscious* may be helpful to us in discovering where and how it is that Jung and many sections of the learned world have parted company. Perhaps, too, we may refer to another rather confusing point in *Symbols of Transformation*—one which can be found from time to time in other volumes of the new edition. Continuing with the example of the ancients, Jung adds again, immediately after admitting the lack of external compulsion: 'We must also remember that the interest of the man of antiquity was turned in quite another direction: he reverenced the divine cosmos, a quality which is entirely lacking in our technological age.'[2] It is as though

[1] *Symbols of Transformation*, p. 397.   [2] *Symbols of Transformation*, p. 16.

there were some difficulty in admitting so much of external reality into his formulation of the problem. A matter of more significance for Jung's work in general is his handling of the Recapitulation theory. Whereas in *Psychology of the Unconscious* he is prepared to say that 'the state of infantile thinking in the child's psychic life, as well as in dreams, is nothing but a re-echo of the prehistoric and the ancient',[1] in *Symbols of Transformation* he says,

'one must certainly put a large question mark after the assertion that myths spring from the "infantile" psychic life of the race. They are on the contrary the most mature product of that young humanity. Just as those first fishy ancestors of man, with their gill slits, were not embryos, but fully developed creatures, so the myth-making and myth-inhabiting man was a grown reality and not a four-year-old child.'[2]

Even so, something of the old view remains; speaking of the 'royal foundlings myth' of Moses, and Romulus and Remus, he adds, only three pages further on: 'What, with us, is a subterranean fantasy was once open to the light of day. What, with us, crops up only in dreams and fantasies was once either a conscious custom or a general belief.'[3] It almost seems as though there had been an attempt to modernize his thought, with, however, the same tendency toward confusion in the formulation of ideas as could be seen during his years within the psychoanalytical movement.

At least two differences can be noted between *Psychology of the Unconscious* and the earlier papers. In the first place the symbol has assumed a different function. From being a very inferior mode of thought, revealing a deficiency in the power of discrimination, it becomes the chief vehicle of the civilizing process. ('We must agree thoroughly with Steinthal when he says that an absolutely overweening importance must be granted to the little phrase "gleich wie" (even as) in the history of the development of thought.')[4] In the second place, Jung is taking a rather different attitude to causality. At this period he still maintains its importance, saying that there are no accidents, no just as wells—the supposition that there can be 'arises from the fact that the law of causation in the psychical sphere is not taken seriously enough'.[5] There is, however, some tendency to seek for explanations not in the details of the individual life, as

---

[1] *Op. cit.*, p. 14. [2] *Symbols of Transformation*, p. 24.
[3] *Ibid.*, p. 27. [4] *Psych. of the Unconsc.*, p. 86. [5] *Ibid.*, p. 31.

formerly, but in the history of the race. This trend may be seen by comparing the discussion of S.W.'s mystical system in 'So-called Occult Phenomena' with a note added at this time. Although Jung mentions in the original paper that parallels can be found with Gnostic systems down the centuries, the emphasis is clearly placed on the sources of the system in S.W.'s individual experience.[1] Now, the accomplishment is 'revealed as a consequence of energetic introversion, which again roots up deep historical strata of the soul and in which I perceive a regression to the memories of humanity condensed in the unconscious'.[2] The same difference in emphasis seems to be at work in a passage we have cited, where Jung suggests that lack of personal information for the years intervening between Miss Miller's poems and fantasies may have an advantage, in that attention is not distracted from the universal theme.

An additional question which arises in reading *Psychology of the Unconscious* is Jung's attitude to a Death Instinct. As we have seen, he is inclined to believe that 'the libido wills its own destruction', and at times, too, he speaks of the destructive as well as the creative aspect of libido. Does he, then, anticipate or come close to the later Freudian conception, according to which there are two separate instincts, Eros, preserving the organic substance and binding it into ever larger units, and Thanitos, seeking to dissolve these units and restore their antecedent inorganic state, but directed also toward the outer world as an instinct of aggression? The differences are perhaps more important than the similarities. Not only does Jung continue to operate with the concept of one fund of psychic energy— in the passages referring to the destructiveness of the libido he seems to have an outward rather than a self destructiveness in mind. The self-destructive aspect is at no time linked with this outer destruction but seems more akin to an instinct for peace: 'a deep personal longing for quiet and for the profound peace of non-existence, for a dreamless sleep in the ebb and flow of the sea of life.'[3]

Finally, in view of the large number of citations in *Psychology of the Unconscious*, it may be asked, How far or in what sense is it an independent work, and how far is it derived? It is evident from the work of Bastian, Bachofen and others that some of these ideas were in the air, e.g. there is a remarkable similarity between Jung's

<hr>

[1] *Supra*, p. 25. [2] *Psych. of the Unconsc.*, p. 285.
[3] *Ibid.*, p. 215.

statements about symbolism and those of Bachofen,[1] and again, Nietzsche had suggested that ' "In sleep and in dreams we pass through the entire curriculum of primitive mankind . . . as even to-day we think in dreams mankind thought in waking life through many thousand years." '[2] However, the application of these theories to psychiatry was only just beginning. Within the psychoanalytical school Abraham and Rank were also taking up the study of mythology. But Freud himself states plainly, even after the 1914 break, that 'C. G. Jung was the first to draw explicit attention to the striking similarity between the disordered fantasies of sufferers from dementia praecox and the myths of primitive peoples'.[3]

Within the Jungian school work which has considerable affinity with *Psychology of the Unconscious* can be found, on the clinical side, in Baynes's *Mythology of the Soul*, and on the anthropological, in Erich Neumann's books, *The Origins and History of Consciousness* and *The Great Mother*. *Mythology of the Soul*, which is made up of two case studies of borderline schizophrenic patients whom Baynes himself had treated, is probably easier for the majority of readers to follow than *Psychology of the Unconscious*, since, although the same basic concepts are used, a much more detailed description is given of the individual fantasies, which in these cases have been expressed in drawings, and attention is paid to differences as well as similarities between the clinical and the mythological material. Neumann seeks to bring order into the mythmaking of mankind and the psychic development of the individual by distinguishing in more detail the stages through which he conceives both to have passed— first a state of 'uroboric incest' in which the individual is content to be absorbed in unconsciousness, completely contained as in the mother; a second stage in which ego-consciousness struggles to develop, becomes ambivalent about its former state, and produces two images, of the Good Mother, and the Bad Mother, against whom it is not yet able to defend itself successfully but by whom, mythologically, it is castrated and destroyed, e.g. in the myths of

---

[1] ' "The symbol awakens intimations, speech can only explain. . . . Only the symbol can combine the most disparate elements into a unitary impression. . . . Words make the infinite finite, symbols carry the mind beyond the finite world of becoming, into the realm of infinite being." ' Bachofen, J. J., *Mutterrecht und Urreligion*, Kröner, 1954, p. 52, cited by Jacobi, J., *Complex/Archetype/Symbol*, p. 78.

[2] Cited by Spinks, *op. cit.*, p. 600.

[3] *Collected Papers*, Vol. V, p. 129. ('Psycho-Analysis,' 1922.)

Attis and Osiris; thirdly, myths of the separation of the World Parents, the equivalent of which in individual development is the splitting off of consciousness and unconsciousness; fourthly, with the reinforcement of the Father Divinity (consciousness) a new phase of fighting the dragon, interpreted as an image of the Terrible Mother, expressing all the devouring, castrating tendencies of the unconscious, and threatening not only sexuality but the higher masculinity of consciousness; and finally the stage of winning the treasure hard to attain—often in mythology the liberation of a maiden, signifying the separation of the positive feminine element so that woman becomes a human creature opening the way to individual relationship. To those who have been brought up in association with the British school of anthropology, in which the line of development has been from the study of physical anthropology to the study of social institutions, such attempts to recreate the 'consciousness' of earlier times are bound to seem strange, if not a little improbable. Professor E. O. James puts this point of view in his *Beginnings of Religion*. Primitive man, he says, 'is neither a philosopher, a scientist, nor a neurotic. He is just a plain unsophisticated practical person living in a precarious environment and continually confronted with perplexing situations which he endeavours to meet as well as he is able by natural and supernatural means.'[1] The American anthropologist Kroeber is similarly reserved. Without being in a position to adjudicate between these viewpoints we may perhaps suggest that the 'symbolic' school might reasonably do one of two things. Either, they might attempt a closer study of the interaction between the psychological tendencies they posit and other factors which go to make up cultural life, or they might state more clearly than they do that they are aware of the need for studying these complexities but prefer for the time being to follow the single strand so far as it will lead them.

The Beginning of Jung's Typology

To set beside *Psychology of the Unconscious* as a forerunner of the later Jungian concepts is a short paper on Psychological Types[2]

---

[1] *Beginnings of Religion*, p. 137. London: Hutchinson's University Library.
[2] 'A Contribution to the Study of Psychological Types.' *Collected Papers*, pp. 287–98.

which some years afterwards was massively expanded. Its starting point is a distinction which Jung makes between hysteria and dementia praecox. In addition to the difference, as Jung believes, that the imaginings of the hysteric can be accounted for by his previous history, while the inventions of the dementia praecox patient resemble mythological creations more than personal memories, the hysteric shows exaggerated emotionality and the dementia praecox patient extreme apathy. Jung therefore describes the direction of the libido in hysteria as extraverted—the fundamental interest is given to the external world—and in dementia praecox as introverted—'the objective world suffers a sort of depreciation or want of consideration for the sake of the individual himself'. Admittedly, each possesses the capacity for the alternative reaction— hysterics have periods of being unable to live outside their rooms, and dementia praecox patients have fits of morbid compensation. Nevertheless, extraversion, associated with feeling, and introversion, associated with thinking, respectively dominate the picture of these two disorders. In the previous lives of the patients a similar, though less extreme, preponderance of the one mechanism or the other can be found, and Jung concludes that it is reasonable to look for something of the sort in normal people also.

As supporting evidence he lists the dichotomies of several well-known writers. For instance, William James divides philosophers into the tender-minded, interested in the inner life and spiritual values, and the tough-minded, who emphasize objective reality and material things, or, as Jung interprets it, the introvert and extravert. A second parallel is taken from the work of Wilhelm Ostwald, who divides scholars and men of genius into classics and romantics. The romantics are noted for rapid reactions, abundant production and love of teaching. 'Herein our type of extraversion is easily recognized.'[1] The classics live apart, make few disciples and produce after great labour and difficulty works of finished perfection. 'All these characteristics correspond to introversion.'[2] A third example is Worringer's theory of aesthetics. Worringer suggests two forms of aesthetic activity, sympathy (Einfühlung) and abstraction. By sympathy the artist or spectator is carried 'into the presence of the object in order to assimilate it and penetrate it with emotional values,'[3] by abstraction the object is deprived of all living qualities

[1] *Ibid.*, p. 292.   [2] *Ibid.*, p. 293.   [3] *Ibid.*, p. 293.

and grasped solely by intellectual thought, so that sympathy corresponds to extraversion and abstraction to introversion. Jung also connects extraversion and introversion with Schiller's naive and sentimental poets. The naive poet, or extravert, '"pursues only nature and feeling in their simplicity, and all his effort is limited to the imitation and reproduction of reality"'.[1] The sentimental poet, or introvert, reflects the impressions he himself receives from objects. Another illustration is Nietzsche's contrast between Apollonian and Dionysian states of mind. The one is calm, self-contained, withdrawn into the self, or introverted, the other is a state of psychic intoxication, unloosening a torrent of libido which expends itself upon 'the multiplicity of the objective world' in the manner of the extravert. Next a linguistic hypothesis is utilized: according to the philologist Finck, language structure is of two main types—in one, the subject is generally conceived as active, 'I see him', 'I strike him down'; in the other, it is the object which is active, 'He appears to me', 'He succumbs to me'. In the first type, energy is going out of the subject, and therefore extraverted; in the second, energy is coming out of the object toward the subject, and therefore introverted. From the field of psychiatry Jung introduces a distinction made by Otto Gross between two forms of 'mental debility'—diffuse shallow consciousness, found in manic-depressive insanity, another extraverted condition, and concentrated, deep consciousness, characteristic of the paranoiac shut up within himself. Lastly, an interpretation is given of the Freudian and Adlerian theories. Freud's standpoint is essentially reductive, causal and sensualist, regarding psychological life as only a reaction to the environment, and is therefore extraverted. Adler's standpoint is finalistic—the history of the patient and the concrete influence of the environment are of less importance than the subject's 'guiding fictions'—he does not have to depend upon the object, but aims at protecting his own individuality against threatening influence from outside, and so is introverted.

Most of these ideas are met subsequently, and discussion will therefore be postponed, but one comment may be made at present. Whereas in this paper it is the *differences* between hysteria and dementia praecox which have been stressed, in *Psychology of Dementia Praecox* it is the *similarities*. Possibly, then, Jung has been

---

[1] *Ibid.*, p. 295.

rather inclined to fit the material into a form suggested by his interests—in the one case, the creation of a clear-cut typology, in the other, demonstration of the applicability of Freudian methods and discoveries.

Looking back on this period, we may wonder whether the split which occurred between the Zürich and the Viennese practitioners was unavoidable, or whether Jung's contributions could have been accepted as the 'modest and moderate criticism' from within which he apparently considered them to be. In so far as questions of theory are involved, the answer naturally depends upon the interpretation given to the psychoanalytical movement. If psychoanalysis itself is to be defined in terms of the theories which Jung either rejected or emphasized less strongly, he could not, of course, have continued to function as a member, let alone the President, of the International Psycho-Analytical Society. If, on the other hand, the psychoanalytical movement is to be regarded as a body of investigators and therapists 'with the goal that both'—psychiatrist and patient—'may learn to understand the troublesome aspects of the patient's life and bring them and their hidden causes to the patient's awareness',[1] he might have remained. Freud, of course, at all times insisted on the former construction. Not only the assumption that there are unconscious mental processes, but 'the recognition of the theory of resistance and repression', he said, years later, 'the appreciation of the importance of sexuality and of the Oedipus complex—these constitute the principal subject-matter of psychoanalysis and the foundations of its theory. No one who cannot accept them all should count himself a psychoanalyst.'[2] Acceptance in this context involves more than 'acceptance under some circumstances', or 'acceptance from some points of view'. It implies acceptance of the principles laid down, not only as universally valid, but as the most important aspects of mental life. 'Psychoanalysis does not permit itself to be ranged with other conceptions,' said Anna Freud, contributing at a later period to a book of child psychology, 'it refuses to be put on an equal basis with them. The universal validity which psychoanalysis postulates for its theories makes impossible its limitation to any special sphere. ... Instead of taking its place beside the others, it usurps the function

[1] Fromm-Reichmann, Frieda, 'Remarks on the Philosophy of Mental Disorder.' *Psychiatry*, Vol. IX, 1946; pp. 293–308 (p. 304).
[2] 'Psycho-Analysis.' *Int. J. Psycho-Anal.*, Vol. XXIII, 1942; pp. 97–107 (p. 102).

of writing the entire text book . . . on the basis of its own discoveries.'[1] It was this priority that Jung, with his wide and longstanding interest in the humanistic studies, was not prepared to give. On the other hand, in fairness to the psychoanalytical standpoint, it may be suggested that if Freud and his followers were engaged in tracing the effects of developmental factors in mental illness—if they felt, as of course they did, that they had contributed a new dimension of causality, in addition to heredity and precipitating stresses, which had always been acknowledged—while Jung was showing himself relatively indifferent to such developmental aspects, the extent to which they could work together constructively would inevitably be diminished, even with the utmost personal goodwill. And, as we have seen, goodwill was not always present. For interpretation of the personal difficulties during these years we are again dependent on the Freudians, though their contributions do not sound entirely convincing. The view that Jung has wished to sidestep the less pleasant aspects of the human psyche is to an appreciable extent refuted by published case material—especially, perhaps, that by H. G. Baynes. Even admitting that Jungian psychology is likely to attract a fringe of sentimentalists who do wish to avoid the discoveries of Freud, it is hardly feasible to judge Jung and his closer associates in those terms. As Baynes says in his paper, 'Freud or Jung', the assumption that a modern mind is still 'horrified and disgusted at laying bare the "bones of the ape", is immensely exaggerated'.[2] Freud's statement in 1914 that he had had no inkling that he had 'lighted upon a person . . . whose energies were ruthlessly devoted to the furtherance of his own interests'[3] comes a little strangely from one whose own self-interest was so manifest. His suspicions of anti-Semitism would seem to need some modification, since Jung has not been entirely without Jewish supporters. But whatever the underlying causes, it is clear that the situation has been felt very keenly by both sides. In addition to Freud's own statements, we find a reference by Ernest Jones to the Swiss Society of Psycho-Analysis as holding its own 'in rather difficult circumstances'.[4] Jung,

---

[1] Murchison, C. (ed.), *Handbook of Child Psychology*, p. 561. Mass.: Clark Univ. Press, 1931.

[2] *Analytical Psychology and the English Mind*, p. 100.

[3] *Collected Papers*, Vol. I ('History of the Psycho-Analytical Movement'), p. 329.

[4] Business Report of the Central Executive, 1934. *Int. J. Psycho-Anal.*, Vol. XV, p. 515.

for his part, speaks as late as 1950 of having been 'acutely conscious
. . . of the loss of friendly relations with Freud and of the lost
comradeship of our work together'. 'The practical and moral support
which my wife gave me at that difficult period', he continues, 'is
something I shall always hold in grateful remembrance'.[1]

[1] *Symbols of Transformation.* (Introduction to the 4th Swiss Edition, p. xxvi.)

Chapter IV

JUNG'S LATER CONCEPTS OF MIND: EXPOSITION

Introduction

From *Two Essays in Analytical Psychology*, 1916, onwards, several features appear or develop in Jung's work which give some grounds for making a distinction between this and earlier periods. For one thing, there are differences in aim. Jung does not entirely abandon scientific claims: in one place he speaks of confining himself to the limits of science,[1] and in another of pursuing science, 'not apologetics or philosophy'.[2] However, in contrast to what he tells us in the previous period,[3] the therapeutic aim has now become his main one: 'Analytical psychology is eminently practical. It does not investigate for the sake of investigation, but for the very immediate purpose of giving help.'[4] Any account of the structure and functioning of mind is a by-product, not its main purpose: 'I may allow myself only one criterion for the results of my labours: Does it work? As for my scientific hobby—my desire to know *why* it works—this I must reserve for my spare time.'[5] The contrast between Jung and Freud in this respect[6] can be seen more plainly: Freud declares within this period that after forty-one years of medical activity his self-knowledge told him he had never really been a doctor in the sense of desiring to succour suffering humanity, and goes on to express concern lest the therapeutic aspect of psychoanalysis should destroy the science.[7]

Jung also has a third aim, or perhaps he might be said to generalize

---

[1] *Contribs.*, p. 268.
[2] Letter cited by Victor White in *God and the Unconscious*, p. 235. London: Harvill Press, 1952.
[3] *Supra*, p. 47.   [4] *Contribs.*, p. 349.
[5] *Practice of Psychotherapy*, p. 43.   [6] *Supra*, pp. 56–7.
[7] *Collected Papers*, Vol. V, pp. 208–9. ('Discussion on Lay Analysis,' 1927.)

the aim of individual therapy, in endeavouring to contribute his psychiatric findings to the solution of spiritual problems. He refers often to the deep disturbance which the World Wars have brought about. Nearly two thousand years of Christianity have been followed, not by the millenium, but by these wars. 'I believe I am not exaggerating when I say that modern man has suffered an almost fatal shock, psychologically speaking, and as a result has fallen into profound uncertainty.'[1] And he suggests that, while many gaps remain, analytical psychology 'goes beyond itself to fill the hiatus that has hitherto put Western civilization at a psychic disadvantage as compared with the civilizations of the East'.[2] Especially from about 1930 this aim is uppermost, with the discovery of alchemistic parallels, the study of Chinese and other Eastern texts, the lectures on *Psychology and Religion*, and various essays on contemporary problems. Jung's main writings on the structure and functioning of mind—*Two Essays on Analytical Psychology*, *Psychological Types*, and some of the papers in *Contributions to Analytical Psychology*—appear during or before the 1920's, together with many, though not all, of his papers on individual psychotherapy. However, there is so much in these writings which has bearing on religion, and so much in the religious writings which involves the concepts of mental structure and functioning, that a further chronological division has not now been made.

In so far as Jung does concern himself with science in this period he tends to subordinate it to other ways of experiencing the Universe. Scientific knowledge, he writes, 'is satisfying only to the modern forefront of the personality, but not to the collective psyche, which reaches back into grey antiquity'.[3] He also expresses doubts about the use of some of the methods and assumptions of science in psychology. In particular, the experimental method, in which he had formerly been interested, 'will never succeed in doing justice to the nature of the human soul, nor . . . trace even an approximately faithful picture of the complicated psychic phenomena.'[4] Whereas formerly he held that the law of cause and effect could not be taken too seriously, now he feels uncertain of the possibility of tracing its operation in psychic life. Once a level is reached of greater com-

---

[1] *Mod. Man*, pp. 230-1.
[2] *Practice of Psychotherapy*, p. 75; *Mod. Man*, p. 62.
[3] *Integ. of Person.*, p. 108.　　　　[4] *Psych. Types*, p. 519.

plexity than reflex actions or psychophysiological instincts, 'the psychologist must content himself with more or less widely ranging descriptions of happenings and with the vivid portrayal of the warp and weft of the mind in all its amazing intricacy'.[1] More recently the principle of synchronicity has been introduced, i.e. 'the temporal coincidence of two or more events linked together by meaning, but without any causal connection'.[2] These statements, in spite of the difference in attitude to the law of cause and effect, can perhaps be taken as developments of the earlier work, in which there seemed at times to be a descriptive rather than hypothesizing orientation.[3] In addition, Jung regards the concepts of analytical psychology as 'in essence, not intellectual formulations but names for certain areas of experience', so that 'they remain dead and irrepresentable to anyone who had not experienced them'.[4] He introduces the distinction which has often been made between *knowledge* and *understanding*, toward which, again, he seemed to be moving in the intermediate period.[5] It is possible, he says, to build up a universally valid anthropology or psychology, with an abstract picture of man as an average unit from which all individual features have been removed. But for understanding it is precisely the individual features which are of paramount importance. 'If I want to understand an individual human being, I must lay aside all scientific knowledge of the average man and discard all theories in order to adopt a completely new and unprejudiced attitude . . . the positive advantages of *knowledge* work specifically to the disadvantage of *understanding*.'[6]

Not only science, but the activity of the reason in general, is felt to be inadequate to the human situation. 'Did reason and good intention save us from the World War,' Jung asks, 'or have they ever saved us from any other catastrophic nonsense?'[7] More positively, he states that 'in the greatest and really decisive questions the reason proves inadequate. . . . When the rational way has become a cul-de-sac—which is its inevitable constant tendency—then, from the side where one least expects it, the solution comes.'[8]

The difficulty of effecting a rapprochement between Jung and the

[1] *Mod. Man*, p. 176.
[2] Bach, H. J., 'C. G. Jung's "Synchronicity".' Guild of Pastoral Psychology, October, 1953, p. 5.
[3] *Supra*, p. 43.   [4] *Archetypes and the Collective Unconscious*, p. 271.
[5] *Supra*, p. 57.   [6] *The Undiscovered Self*, pp. 10–11.
[7] *Mod. Man*, p. 222.   [8] *Psych. Types*, p. 322.

more academic type of reader is increased by the rather baffling style referred to previously. Here it should be said that many passages can be found, especially in the new translation, without which psychology would be the poorer, even when the actual content is put forward by other writers too. It is perhaps the task of the literary rather than the psychological critic to analyse this quality of style, but the impression is that Jung is at his best in communicating ideas which are not unduly abstract, but sufficiently simple to provide an anchorage for his attitude to life. This applies particularly to his writings on psycho-therapy. (For instance, where a later psychoanalytical writer may speak of many of his patients as coming to him on account of 'difficulties in living', Jung will say that about a third are suffering, not from any clinically definable neurosis, but from the senselessness and emptiness of their lives.) It seems, however, that when he tries to meet the need for a conceptual framework this suffusing of idea and attitude is less successful. Thus, a not inconsiderable portion of his work is made up of statements such as, 'Spirit is life', 'the un-conscious is life', 'Life and spirit are a pair of opposites', from which the chief meaning to be taken is, possibly, an attitude of wonder and reverence toward all living things. It is true that the conveying and evoking of such attitudes is one of the important functions of speech, as well as the imparting of ideas and information, but, as Crawshay Williams says, unless the printed word 'is written (and read) openly as a contribution to fantasy thinking (e.g. fiction, poetry, art and some of its criticism) it tends to be taken for granted as a contribu-tion to our knowledge of the external world'.[1] Jung's lack of ex-plicitness on this point is likely to be confusing to readers with a mainly academic training. Often, indeed, his main concepts are expressed in terms that make them very difficult to define or analyse. The unconscious is 'a realm of nature that cannot be improved upon or perverted. It is part of nature's secret, which we can listen to but cannot handle.'[2] It contains 'the hidden treasure upon which man-kind ever and anon has drawn'.[3] Like the sea itself it 'yields an end-less and self-replenishing abundance of living creatures, a wealth beyond our fathoming'.[4] If it were permissible to personify it, 'we might call it a collective human being combining the characteristics

[1] Crawshay-Williams, R. *The Comforts of Unreason*, p. 150. London: Kegan Paul, 1947.   [2] *Integ. of Person.*, p. 101.
[3] *Two Essays*, new ed. p. 66; old ed. p. 68.
[4] *Practice of Psychotherapy*, p. 177.

of both sexes, transcending youth and age, birth and death, and, from having at his command a human experience of one or two million years, almost immortal'.[1] Many other matters are touched on in this way. Describing the changes taking place in an immigrant population he writes, 'The virgin soil demands that at least the unconscious of the conqueror sinks to the level of the authochthonic inhabitants.'[2] Or again, the modern Germans are described as possessed by 'an old god of storm and frenzy, the long quiescent Wotan',[3] and 'Thundering and intoxicating, early Germanic history comes surging up from a remote past, to fill the yawning breach in the Church.'[4] Casting our minds back over the previous stages of Jung's work, we will remember some slight tendency toward poetical expressiveness during the early years, e.g. in the hope that 'the experience of the coming years will sink deeper shafts into this still dark land . . .',[5] and similar passages have been cited from *Psychology of the Unconscious*. For the most part, however, the contrast is quite marked, and in itself makes not altogether incomprehensible the attitude of those psychologists who, as Baynes put it, allude to the earlier work of Jung in a tone appropriate to an author who has died.

Equally striking are the contradictions in Jung's work. For instance, to set against the more usual equating of childhood, primitive and psychotic thought, seen already in *Psychology of the Unconscious*, there is a statement that 'Nothing goes to show that primitive man thinks, feels or perceives in a way that differs fundamentally from ours. His psychic functioning is essentially the same— only his primary assumptions are different.'[6] Or again, it is said in *Psychological Types*: 'Between the religion of a people and its actual mode of life there always exists a compensatory function; if this were not so, religion would have no practical significance at all.'[7] But in a later book, *Psychology and Religion*, the expressive function is brought into prominence, i.e. 'any religion which is rooted in the history of a people is as much an expression of their psychology as the form of political government, for instance'.[8] It would seem that Jung really considers religion to have both these functions, but omits to specify the conditions under which the one or the other

[1] *Mod. Man*, p. 215.   [2] *Contribs.*, p. 140.   [3] *Contemp. Events*, p. 2.
[4] *Contemp. Events*, p. 68.   [5] *Supra.*, p. 43.   [6] *Mod. Man*, p. 148.
[7] *Psych. Types*, p. 174.   [8] *Psych. and Religion*, old ed. p. 97.

comes into operation. His statements on morality also are not uniform. On the one hand he says 'the force of life is beyond the moral judgment'[1] and dissociates himself from those who think 'the beautiful tree of humanity can only thrive by dint of being pruned, bound, and trained on a trellis, whereas Father-Sun and Mother-Earth have combined to make it grow joyfully in accordance with its own laws, which are full of the deepest meaning'.[2] On the other hand, for resolution of man's conflict 'the highest moral effort, the greatest self-denial and sacrifice, the most intense religious earnestness and saintliness, are needed'.[3] Taken together, these statements mean, perhaps, that some kinds of moral code are, and others are not, consistent with the realization of human potentialities, and that on man lies the responsibility of finding and adhering to the ones that are consistent with such realization. But the statements are not brought together by Jung himself, and the making of interpolations to this extent carries one further beyond the text than a reader often cares to go, while acceptance of them in an unco-ordinated form is, for some minds at any rate, unsatisfying. A similar contradiction seems to exist in Jung's social philosophy. On the one hand, 'the great, liberating deeds of world history have come from leading personalities and never from the inert mass that is secondary at all times and needs the demagogue if it is to move at all'.[4] On the other hand, 'Great innovations never come from above; they come invariably from below . . . it is just people of the lower social levels who follow the unconscious forces of the Psyche; it is the much-derided, silent folk of the land—those who are less infected with academic prejudices than great celebrities are wont to be.'[5] This difficulty could be resolved in part by saying that it is 'the silent folk of the land' who prepare the ground, and the leading personalities who finally bring new ideas to fruition. But once against the statement is not made.

Other features of Jung's writing in this period are a tendency to ready generalization quite unlike his handling of the early data, and comparatively little analysis of concepts. For example, of the second half of life he says, 'How often it happens that a man of forty or fifty years winds up his business and that his wife then dons the trousers and opens a little shop where he sometimes performs the duties of handyman.'[6] But how often does this happen, really? Not many

---

[1] *Psych. Types*, p. 334.　　[2] *Collected Papers*, p. 369.　　[3] *Psych. Types*, p. 153.
[4] *Integ. of Person.*, p. 281.　　[5] *Mod. Man*, p. 243.　　[6] *Mod. Man*, p. 124.

people will be able to recollect more than one or two cases in their own experience, if indeed a single case. Again, throughout the later work the 'primitive' is dealt with on a general footing, although knowledge of the differences between one tribe and another has increased enormously in the last two generations; and his statement of the Recapitulation theory, i.e. that 'the history of the development of the species repeats itself in the embryonic development of the individual'[1] does not take account of the controversy concerning recapitulation of the adult or the embryo form so prominent in the biology of the late nineteenth and early twentieth centuries.

A further source of confusion is the tendency to make a transition from one concept to another which is related to it only loosely. In the following passage, for example, we do not really know how far Jung is speaking of society and how far of the State, or whether he believes the two to be identical. Society, he writes,

'is nothing more than a term, a concept for the symbiosis of a group of human beings. A concept is not a carrier of life. The sole and natural carrier of life is the individual, and that is so throughout nature. "Society" or "State" is an agglomeration of life-carriers and at the same time, as an organized form of these, an important condition of life. It is therefore not quite true to say that the individual can exist only as a particle in society. At all events man can live very much longer without the State than without air.'[2]

This transition is fairly easy to follow associatively. Less easy is the statement that 'Even the most far-reaching abstraction of the personal in favour of the general value never renders a complete elimination of personal admixture possible. Yet, in so far as this exists, thought and feeling contain also those destructive tendencies which proceed from the self-assertion of the person in face of the inclemency of social conditions.'[3] To account for this linking of the personal and the destructive, it may be suggested that a double transition has been effected, from the personal to the egocentric, and from the egocentric to the destructive—and indeed, unless some such transition had taken place, one would expect Jung to assume that self assertion in face of the inclemency of social conditions could be, at any rate sometimes, constructive. A still greater jump

[1] *Contribs.*, p. 317.
[2] *Practice of Psychotherapy* p. 106. *Contemp. Events*, p. 31.
[3] *Psych. Types*, p. 52.

seems to have been made from the statement that 'The symbols of the self arise in the depth of the body' to the conclusion that 'The body's carbon is simply carbon. Hence "at bottom" the psyche is simply "world".'[1]

Perhaps the most baffling are passages with a 'sic et non' quality about them. For instance, the wise old man[2] is described as 'the father of the soul, and yet the soul, in some miraculous manner, is also his virgin mother'.[3] And 'the anima and life' are 'meaningless in so far as they offer no interpretation. Yet they have a nature that can be interpreted, for in all chaos there is a cosmos, in all disorder a secret law, in all caprice a fixed law, for everything that works is grounded on its opposite.'[4] For this reason especially the reading of the later Jung is rather like translation from a foreign language which has been learnt imperfectly—only a few pages will be gone through at one time, and even with these some doubt about the meaning may remain.

This is not the first time that such considerations have been raised. In addition to the doubts already cited[5] we find that W. R. D. Fairbairn, distinguishing several different senses in which the term complex has been used—as instinct, sentiment, part-personality, etc.—comes to the conclusion that Jung renders it 'almost meaningless to any investigator who attaches value to coherent conceptualization'.[6] In so far as Jung is aware of the difficulty, however, he does not seem to be disturbed by it. Concerning the emotive quality of his writing he says, for instance, that in order to describe the condition of the German people it would be possible to speak of the *furor teutonicus* instead of Wotan, but we should only be saying the same thing and not as well.[7] We merely render emotion into prose when we describe 'the awful and revered beings that inhabit the shadows of the primeval forest as "psychological complexes"'.[8] The 'sic et non' quality, furthermore, reflects for him the nature of the universe, i.e. the paradox is 'one of our most valued spiritual possessions, while uniformity of meaning is a sign of weakness'.[9] Or again, he contrasts 'the niggardly European "either-or"' with the 'magnificently

---

[1] *Archetypes and the Collective Unconscious*, p. 173.   [2] *Infra* p. 96.
[3] *Archetypes and the Collective Unconscious*, p. 35.   [4] *Ibid.*, p. 32.
[5] *Supra*, pp. x–xi.
[6] 'Observations in Defence of the Object-Relations Theory of the Personality.' *Brit. J. Med. Psychol.*, XXVIII, p. 146.
[7] *Contemp. Events*, p. 8.   [8] *Contribs.*, p. 262   [9] *Psych. and Alchemy*, p. 15.

affirmative "both-and"' of the Eastern world.[1] His followers, also, are prepared to accept the situation. 'A mind that is rushing on for new hypotheses', Progoff writes, 'cannot always stop to look behind and make sure that its definitions are covered.'[2] Often, indeed, their own style is much the same, as when H. G. Baynes asks, 'What is this dark fear of our archaic past . . . ?'[3] or conceives of the German nation as going back 'with deep instinctive purpose to recover a primitive soul . . .'[4] More realistically, perhaps, Murray Jackson has acknowledged that Jung's writing 'is often obscure, apparently contradictory and difficult to relate to immediate problems of clinical practice'. But, he believes, despite the drawbacks, the concepts are there to be found.[5] In this and the chapters following it will be our task to state and discuss these concepts so far as we are able.

Three divisions of the mind, or psyche, are given—the conscious, the personal unconscious, and the collective unconscious.

The conscious mind, or simply consciousness, is understood as 'the state of association with the ego'.[6] Jung suggests that consciousness may be thought of as a powerful cohesive force, drawing the various parts— images of the sense functions and of past processes— in the direction of a virtual centre. This centre, the ego, is chiefly concerned, as in the Freudian system, with adaptation to external reality. In one of his latest books, *Aion*, he refers to its psychophysical nature: 'It seems to arise in the first place from the collision between the somatic factor and the environment, and, once established as a subject, it goes on developing from further collisions with the outer world and the inner.'[7]

The personal unconscious is formed of all those experiences in the individual's life from which attention is diverted—anything, that is, which loses a certain energic intensity. Some of the unconscious contents have the special quality of being repressed, i.e. consciousness puts up an active resistance to their entry, but simple forgetting is more usual, occurring whenever any mental content is connected only loosely with other conscious contents.

Concerning the collective unconscious two main types of state-

---

[1] *Psych. and Religion*, new ed. p. 511.   [2] *Op. cit.*, p. 20.
[3] Preface to *Psych. Types*, p. 6.
[4] *Analytical Psychology and the English Mind*, p. 5.
[5] "Jung's 'archetypes' and Psychiatry" J. Ment. Sci. Vol. 106. No. 445 1960; pp. 1518–26.   [6] *Contribs.*, p. 81.   [7] *Aion*, p. 5.

ment can be found. On the one hand, Jung writes that the collective unconscious is the hypothesis of 'a universal similitude or identity of the basic structure of the human psyche'[1] or 'a potential system of psychic functioning' mediating between consciousness and the physiological functioning of the body.[2] On the other hand, he describes it as 'the sediment of all the experience of the universe of all time . . . an image of the universe that has been in process of formation for untold ages'[3] including 'not only the instincts from the animal stage but also all those differences of culture which have left behind transmissible memory traces'.[4] There are also traces of a third meaning. For instance, the Christian era was conditioned by developments that were taking place in almost everybody, i.e. 'by a process in the collective unconscious',[5] and again, Nietzsche's Zarathrustra brought to light 'the contents of the collective unconscious of our time'.[6] Here the collective unconscious seems to stand for a climate of thought rather than for anything transmitted biologically, or at any rate there is a lack of differentiation between the social and the biological. This third meaning, however, does not have the importance in Jung's work of the other two.

The relationship between the personal and the collective unconscious varies somewhat in Jung's writings. Sometimes it seems that the personal unconscious must have been disposed of before the collective unconscious can be experienced,[7] and sometimes, judging from the use of personal imagery in experiencing architectural themes, as though they are combined. The second is probably the predominant meaning, especially in the more recent publications, i.e. each image, or 'content' has a personal, and a collective or universal, aspect, and each individual experiences the collective aspect in a way that is conditioned by his needs. The relationship of the unconscious—usually the collective unconscious—to consciousness is twofold: it moulds all experience into certain forms, even in the exact sciences, where it is 'at the root of indispensable auxiliary concepts, as of the ether, energy and the atom'[8] and it is also, and more predominantly, compensatory, as in the previous work. 'The psyche is a self-regulating system that maintains itself in equilibrium as the body does. Every process that goes too far

---

[1] *Integ. of Person.*, p. 50.   [2] *Mod. Man*, p. 216.
[3] *Collected Papers*, p. 432. ('Psychology of the Unconscious Processes,' 1917.)
[4] *Contribs.*, p. 58.   [5] *Ibid.*, p. 266.   [6] *Psych. Types*, p. 237.
[7] *Integ. of Person.*, p. 111.   [8] *Contribs.*, p. 280.

immediately and inevitably calls forth a compensatory activity. Without such adjustments a normal metabolism would not exist, nor would the normal psyche.'[1]

Both these functions are exercised through the archetypes, described by Jung as modes of apprehension which are correlates of the instincts. He thinks it is impossible to say which of the two is prior, apprehension or impulse to action—it is as though they form together one vital activity which we cannot adequately imagine as single and therefore dissect into separate processes. For the most part it is the archetypes, not the instincts, with which Jung is concerned, and here, also, two types of statement can be found. On the one hand, archetypes are 'factors determining the uniformity and regularity of our apprehension',[2] arranging the material of consciousness into definite patterns. On the other hand, they 'represent the precipitate of psychic functioning of the whole ancestral line, i.e. the heaped up, or pooled, experiences of organic existence in general, a million times repeated and condensed into types'.[3] Owing to the large number of passages in which Jung speaks of the *contents* of the collective unconscious as *breaking through*, or being *reactivated*, the second view, implying Inheritance of Acquired Characters, is more prominent, though since it is also denied in several places we cannot hold Jung to it. The uncertainty of his position can be seen, for instance, in the new edition of *Psychology and Religion*, where he writes at first: 'Since many unconscious contents seem to be remnants of historical states of mind, we need only go back a few hundred years in order to reach the conscious level that forms the parallel to our dreams.'[4] and later: 'I have never maintained that the archetype *an sich* is an idea, but have expressly pointed out that I regard it as a form without definite content.'[5]

Normally, the conscious and the unconscious are co-ordinated, but under the conditions of modern life, requiring too much specialization, there is a danger that the regulating function of the unconscious will not be acknowledged by the conscious mind, and that its contents will break forth explosively in bizarre thoughts and actions. But even apart from such explosions, the thinking processes of the collective unconscious are not identical with those of consciousness. For instance, the archetypes are not isolated from each other, but are

[1] *Mod. Man*, p. 20.   [2] *Contribs.*, p. 280.   [3] *Psych. Types*, p. 507.
[4] *Psych. and Religion*, new ed. p. 53.   [5] *Ibid.*, p. 307.

in a state of fusion—differentiation, implying limitation and exclusion, is a property of the conscious mind. As one aspect of their lack of differentiation the archetypes contain within themselves both 'positive' and 'negative' features—'not only all the fine and good things that humanity has ever thought and felt, but the worst infamies and devilries of which men have been capable'.[1] Jung sometimes states that the collective unconscious has at its disposal 'the wisdom of the experience of untold ages',[2] and that it is 'continually active, creating combinations of its materials . . . considerably superior to the conscious combinations both in refinement and extent'[3] and sometimes that 'The general aspect of unconscious manifestations is in the main chaotic and irrational.'[4] But on the whole he is inclined to think that whether its contents turn out to be a curse or blessing depends upon 'the quality of the consciousness which has to cope with them'.[5] The moment will infallibly come when the individual must hold fast so as not to be thrown catastrophically off balance, and this holding fast can be achieved only by a conscious will. 'That is the great and irreplaceable significance of the ego.'[6]

Another feature of the unconscious is its capacity to personate. Here, certainly, Jung is far from clear. On the one hand, he writes that the impersonal, like differentiation, is a category of consciousness, and that it is not we who personify the powers of the unconscious—'they have a personal nature from the very beginning'.[7] On the other hand, he also writes that it is only our *conscious* mind which is personal. What we mean in speaking of unconscious disturbance is more like an error in psychic diet upsetting the equilibrium of digestion, but this 'unpoetical comparison' is far too mild in view of the far-reaching effects of the condition,[8] and 'Patients often suffer so much from intrusions of the unconscious that it helps them considerably to know their opponent "personally".'[9] It is possible that if the matter were inquired into closely, Jung would wish to confine himself to the latter statements; nevertheless, when the later work is compared with the early study of S.W., the impression grows that he is taking up a rather different attitude to the unity of personality. Whereas formerly the dissociations were held to be relatively super-

---

[1] *Two Essays*, new ed. p. 69; old ed. p. 72.   [2] *Collected Papers*, p. 442.
[3] *Ibid.*, *loc. cit.*   [4] *Integ. of Person.*, p. 17.   [5] *Contemp. Events*, p. 83.
[6] *Archetypes and the Collective Unconscious*, p. 319.
[7] *Secret of the Golden Flower*, p. 119.
[8] *Two Essays*, new ed. p. 233; old ed. p. 261.   [9] *Integ. of Person.*, p. 22.

ficial ('none of them goes so deep as to attack the firmly knit basis of the ego-complex')[1] now, 'in spite of our carefully wrought theory affirming the "unity of the self", according to which autonomous complexes cannot exist, Nature does not appear in the least concerned about such intelligent notions'.[2] Or again, 'the psyche is not an indivisible unity, but a more or less divided totality. Although the separate parts are connected with each other, they are none the less relatively independent of each other.'[3] This impression is also brought to the fore by accounts of the archetypal figures. Not all archetypes appear in personal form—there are, for instance, archetypes of transformation, which are not personalities but typical situations, places, ways, animals, plants, etc. which symbolize a change. But some of them do appear as personalities, and of these certain ones have important parts to play in mental life.

First, however, Jung discusses the persona, which he describes as a compromise between the individual and society as to the kind of semblance to adopt, or as we might say, those aspects of the ego which are concerned with adaptation to social roles. The persona in its way is a necessity:

> 'Society expects, and indeed must expect, every individual to play the part assigned to him as perfectly as possible, so that a man who is a parson must not only carry out his official functions objectively, but must at all times and in all circumstances play the role of parson in a flawless manner . . . each must stand at his post, here a cobbler, there a poet. No man is expected to be both.'[4]

Since no human being can fit these expectations to perfection or fulfil all his capacities within their bounds, the construction of an artificial personality is unavoidable. But as the name persona indicates, this remains a mask. Expressing an attitude in which one psychological function is dominant to the exclusion of the others, it is a hindrance to the development of full individuality and its "dissolution" is required.

With the dissolution, or analysis, of the persona the collective unconscious may be experienced. 'An infallible sign of collective images seems to be the appearance of the "cosmic" element, i.e. the images in the dream or fantasy are connected with cosmic qualities such as temporal and spatial infinity, enormous speed and extension

[1] *Supra*, p. 24.   [2] *Psych. Types*, p. 306.   [3] *Contribs.*, p. 256.
[4] *Two Essays*, new ed. pp. 190–1; old ed. p. 208.

of movement, "astrological" associations, telluric, lunar, and solar analogies, changes in the proportions of the body, etc.' The dreamer may think he is the earth, or the sun, or a star, 'or else is inordinately large, or dwarfishly small; or has died, has come to a strange place, is a stranger to himself, is confused, mad, etc.'[1] The analogy with mental disorder is very close—in fact, the condition differs from the initial stages of mental illness 'only by the fact that it leads in the end to greater health'.[2]

The first figure of the unconscious is the shadow—the personification, often in the form of the devil, or a dark-skinned or mongoloid human being, of all those tendencies that the individual rejects on moral or aesthetic grounds, and keeps in suppression because they are contrary to his conscious principles. It also contains qualities that the individual has not developed in his conscious life—in some cases capacity for thinking, in others capacity for relationships, and so forth. The shadow has indeed two aspects—it includes much of the personal unconscious, but has a collective archetypal aspect too, as the personification of the principle of evil within the human psyche. In order to develop an objective attitude to his own personality, or in order to *be* a fully developed personality, the individual must accept the existence of those trends within himself which are least approved and those which have not yet been lived.

The next stage is meeting with the soul-image, called the anima in men and the animus in women—or really, animi; in accordance with the compensatory function of the unconscious, Jung believes, the animus is plural, since woman is consciously monogamous, while the anima is a single figure in the consciously polygamous male. These figures represent partly the contra-sexual portion of the psyche, i.e. the latent feminine qualities in the man and masculine qualities in the woman;[3] partly the precipitate of all human experience pertaining to the opposite sex;[4] and partly the function of relationship between conscious and unconscious.[5] The anima as the attitude to inner processes is contrasted with the persona, or outer attitude, and apparently does not differ greatly from the anima as representing latent feminine qualities: 'The persona, the ideal picture

---

[1] *Two Essays*, new ed. p. 158; old ed. p. 168–9.
[2] *Ibid.*, new ed. p. 160; old ed. p. 170. (During the second half of the period these introductory experiences are less strongly emphasized.)
[3] *Two Essays*, new ed. p. 88 n.
[4] *Ibid.*, p. 188.   [5] *Ibid.*, p. 222.

of a man as he should be, is inwardly compensated by feminine weakness, and as the individual outwardly plays the strong man, so he becomes inwardly a woman, i.e. the anima'.[1] His unconscious femininity is often projected on to some actual woman, who then acts in accordance with it. 'I once made the acquaintance of a very venerable personage—in fact, one might easily call him a saint. I stalked round him for three whole days, but never a mortal failing did I find in him. . . . Then, on the fourth day, his wife came to consult me.'[2] In women the phenomena corresponding to the moods of the anima-ridden man are 'opinions', based upon unconscious and unanalysed assumptions.

> 'If the woman happens to be pretty, these animus opinions have for the man something rather touching and childlike about them, which makes him adopt a benevolent, fatherly, professorial manner. But if the woman does not stir his sentimental side, and competence is expected of her rather than appealing helplessness and stupidity, then her animus opinions irritate the man to death, chiefly because they are based on nothing but opinion for opinion's sake.'[3]

Since these qualities are inferior and unconscious, the anima and the shadow are frequently 'contaminated with each other'.[4]

After an understanding has been gained of the anima and animus, so that the man acknowledges and develops, but does not live exclusively in, his feminine side and the woman does likewise with her masculine side, the archetypes of the old wise man (in men) and magna mater (in women) may be encountered, signifying 'for the man the second and real liberation from the father, and for the woman, liberation from the mother, and with it comes the first genuine sense of his or her true individuality'.[5] Or, we might suggest, the two figures represent the patient's liberation from old conflicts, his desire for recovery, and his expectation of achieving it.

The final stage in the developmental process, to which Jung gives the name of individuation, is the emergence of the archetypal image of the self. Jung himself states that this concept is not a very clear one, but considers the vagueness to be unavoidable, for while we can think of ourselves easily enough as possessing part-souls, e.g. personas, 'it transcends our powers of imagination to form a clear

[1] *Ibid.*, new ed. p. 193; old ed. p. 210.
[2] *Ibid.*, new ed. p. 192; old ed. p. 209.
[3] *Ibid.*, new ed. p. 206; old ed. pp. 228–9.   [4] *Psych. and Alchemy*, p. 169.
[5] *Two Essays*, new ed. p. 233; old ed. p. 262.

picture of what we are as a self, for in this operation the part would have to comprehend the whole'.[1] At times it seems uncertain whether the self is unveiled or created. For instance, Jung says in one place that 'The aim of individuation is nothing less than to divest the self of the false wrappings of the persona on the one hand, and the suggestive power of primordial images on the other.'[2] But in another place he states: 'the self has somewhat the character of a result, of a goal attained, something that has come to pass very gradually and is experienced with much travail'.[3] However, the essential meaning seems to be contained in the passage following:

> 'If we picture the conscious mind, with the ego as its centre, as being opposed to the unconscious, and if we now add to our mental picture the process of assimilating the unconscious, we can think of this assimilation as a kind of approximation of conscious and unconscious, where the centre of the total personality no longer coincides with the ego, but with a point mid-way between the conscious and the unconscious. This would be the point of new equilibrium, a new centring of the total personality.'[4]

Or, as Jung says elsewhere, 'In face of the dangerous tendency to disintegration there arises . . . a counter action, characterized by symbols which point unmistakably to a process of centralization.'[5] These symbols frequently take the form of mandalas, or circles which enclose a flower, cross or wheel, with a tendency to repeat the number four—representing the four psychic functions[6]—in their petals, bars, or spokes.

A second account of individuation conceives the psyche in terms of opposites—conscious-unconscious, masculinity-femininity, nature-spirit. The interplay of conscious and unconscious has been discussed to some extent. Of masculinity-femininity Jung writes that the conscious psychology of man is founded on logos, or objective and factual interest, and that of woman on eros, or psychic relationship. ('The man's world is the nation, the state, business concerns, etc. . . . his world consists of a multitude of co-ordinated factors, whereas her world, outside her husband, terminates in a sort of cosmic mist.')[7] Their primeval opposition 'represents symbolically all conceivable

[1] *Ibid.*, new ed. p. 175.   [2] *Ibid.*, new ed. p. 172; old ed. p. 185.
[3] *Ibid.*, new ed. p. 237–8; old ed. p. 268.
[4] *Ibid.*, new ed. p. 219; old ed. p. 245.
[5] *Contemp. Events*, p. 26.   [6] *Infra*, p. 99.
[7] *Two Essays*, new ed. p. 208; old ed. p. 226.

oppositions that may occur, as warm-cold, light-dark, south-north, dry-wet, good-bad, etc. In the masculine psyche it also represents the opposition conscious-unconscious.'[1] In nature and spirit we have the primitive instincts and an inherent principle which regulates them: 'the multiplicity and inner division of part contradicting part is opposed by a contractive unity, the power of which is just as great as that of the instincts';[2] the self is created through detachment of libido from both sides, by means of the symbol.

It is in connection with the opposites that Jung has most to say of mental energy, though once more he is not always consistent. For instance, in defining mental energy he insists at times that 'whether or no a specific psychic force exists has nothing to do with the concept of libido',[3] but when, as often, he speaks of it as being transformed through the symbol,[4] 'flowing away' or 'sinking down', it seems reasonable to assume that in practice his usage has not altered. Similarly, although he says at least once that 'the unconscious contains and is indeed the source of libido',[5] his predominant view appears to be that energy arises from the tension between opposing mental factors, among which are conscious and unconscious. Principles governing its distribution are: equivalence, according to which the disappearance of a quantity of energy in one direction is followed by the appearance of a corresponding amount in another form; and entropy, according to which contradictions balance each other in the development of a lasting and relatively unchanging attitude.[6] These seem closely related to the principle of compensation, already met in Jung's theory of unconscious functioning. In addition to the principles of equivalence and entropy there are two pairs of movements—extraversion-introversion and progression-regression. Extraversion, as before, is the turning of energy outward to the external world, and introversion the turning of energy toward the subject himself and his own inner processes. Progression is the continuous satisfaction of environmental demands; if an obstacle is encountered, regression sets in, bringing forth both 'slime' and 'seeds of new possibilities of life'.[7] Extraversion-introversion and progression-regression are not identical—Jung states that the movement forward or backward can proceed in two different

---

[1] *Integ. of Person.*, p. 156.   [2] *Contribs.*, p. 57.   [3] *Psych. Types*, pp. 571–2.
[4] *Contribs.*, p. 54.   [5] *Collected Papers*, p. 461.   [6] *Contribs.*, p. 27.
[7] *Ibid.*, p. 38.

forms, extraverted or introverted—but there is some tendency for regression and introversion to be defined in similar terms, as when Jung says that 'introversion into the unconscious' achieves 'that original state of unconsciousness, where a discriminating consciousness has not yet distinguished subject from object'.[1]

Extraversion and introversion bring us to Jung's expanded form of psychological types, the third account of mental structure and functioning. In his major work on types the previous connection with mental disorders is not stressed, but in a subsidiary paper Jung reproduces it in modified form—extraversion still being connected with hysteria, introversion with psychasthenia, or in present-day terms, obsessional and anxiety neuroses, rather than dementia praecox. In the extravert, interest and attention follow primarily those of the immediate environment, including its views on art and morals, while the introvert's attitude is one of abstraction—a reservation of the ego as if an attempted ascendancy on the part of the object had to be continually frustrated. A parallel is drawn between these two ways of adaptation and two ways of adaptation in Nature—the one by increased fertility, together with relatively slight defensive powers, the other by powerful equipment for individual self-defence but relatively slight fertility, i.e. following William Blake's terminology, the 'prolific' and the 'devouring'. Ideally, a rhythmical alternation of both these forms of activity would take place, but owing to peculiarities of individual disposition and the complicatons of life under civilized conditions, one mechanism of adaptation is favoured rather than the other, and in this way the types are produced. At the same time there exists in each type a tendency toward compensation for its one-sidedness; consequently it is often very difficult to determine type-membership, although a guide may be found in the fact that the compensating tendency, being unconscious, is likely to be infantile and unco-ordinated in its ways of expression.

To these attitudes are now added four functions—thinking, or the function of intellectual cognition, forming logical conclusions; feeling, or subjective evaluation leading to acceptance or rejection; sensation, or all perception by means of the sense organs; and intuition, or perception by way of the unconscious. The first two functions are rational, in that they form judgments, according to logic and feeling respectively; the others are irrational, not in the

[1] *Psych. Types*, p. 147.

sense of being unreasonable, but in the sense of aiming at pure perception. At the outset the functions are undifferentiated, but owing to constitution or to early circumstances, as with the attitudes, one function comes to dominate. Although he states that each function is possessed by everyone, and that the *products* of all may be conscious, Jung speaks of the *consciousness of a function* only when the life of the individual is mainly ruled by it, so that with thinking, for example, the logical conclusion in any given case holds good, without the backing of any further evidence. Since it is absolutely necessary for adaptation that the individual shall have clear-cut, unambiguous aims, it is impossible for him to develop a second function as strongly as the first, but it is usual for an auxiliary function to be developed, e.g. besides being introverted and mainly thinking in type, a man may make use of intuition. Thus a variety of personality types are built up—thinking-intuitive, feeling-sensation, and so forth, but Jung considers that a rational function can only be joined to an irrational, and vice versa, on the ground that the evaluation of the two 'rational' functions, thinking and feeling, and the perception of the 'irrational', sensation and intuition, are diametrically opposed.

Jung does not describe the more complicated types, but has a good deal to say of the extraverted and introverted attitudes combined with one or the other of the four functions. Extraverted thinking is governed by objective data, being liable to heap up fact upon fact, without proceeding to any illuminating generalization. The extraverted feeling type relies on conformity with traditional and generally accepted standards to secure the feeling-rapport with the environment which is his chief concern. The extraverted sensation type aims at concrete enjoyment; objects matter in so far as they release sensation, so that 'the orientation of such an individual corresponds with purely concrete reality'.[1] The extraverted intuitive is concerned with facts in so far as they open up fresh possibilities in the external world. On the other side, introverted thinking 'formulates questions and creates theories . . . but in the presence of facts it exhibits a reserved demeanour'.[2] Facts are collected as evidence or examples for a theory, not for their own sake. Intensity is the aim, not extensity, and in the case of the human object there is a definite lack of relatedness. 'This negative relation to the object—indifference, and even aversion

---

[1] *Psych. Types*, p. 457.   [2] *Ibid.*, p. 481.

—characterizes every introvert.'[1] Introverted feeling 'strives after an inner intensity, to which at the most objects contribute only an accessory stimulus',[2] and is continually presented with the problem of finding an external form which is not only subjectively satisfying but also conveys feeling to others. Introverted sensation, similarly, is coloured by what the subject brings to the percept, so that it always seems as though objects were not so much forcing their way into the subject in their own right, as that the subject were seeing quite different things from the rest of mankind. Introverted intuition perceives all the background processes of consciousness. Just as the extraverted intuitive is continually scenting out new possibilities in the outer world, 'so the introverted intuitive moves from image to image'. This is fruitless from the standpoint of immediate utility, but 'since these images represent possible ways of viewing life, which in given circumstances have the power to provide a new energic potential',[3] the function of introverted intuition is really indispensable. All the types develop difficulties if they are allowed to go to extremes. For instance, the thinking of the extraverted thinker may become mere imitation, while the impoverishment of introverted thinking in relation to objective facts may find compensation in an abundance of unconscious facts, so that 'Finally, images are produced which no longer express anything externally real, being "merely" symbols of the simply unknowable.'[4]

As supporting material, which in the book itself precedes his own, Jung includes expansions of several previous lines of evidence— Nietzsche's division of Apollonian and Dionysian, Otto Gross's types with deep and shallow consciousness', Worringer's distinction of the feeling-into and abstracting types, William James's tough and tender-minded, and Ostwald's division of classic and romantic. Another classification, the 'impassioned' and the 'less impassioned' is added from a late nineteenth-century physician, Furneaux Jordan: the 'impassioned' is identified with the introvert, who 'has to rise above an archaic, impulsive, passionate nature to the safer heights of abstraction', and the 'less impassioned' with the extravert, whose 'less deeply rooted emotional life is more readily adapted to differentiation and domestication'.[5] In a chapter on 'The Type Problem in History' Jung gives interpretations of several theological and philo-

---

[1] *Ibid.*, p. 485.   [2] *Ibid.*, p. 490.   [3] *Ibid.*, p. 507.
[4] *Ibid.*, p. 483.   [5] *Ibid.*, p. 187.

sophical controversies. For instance, in the Arian controversy, the formula of Homoiousia, or 'essential similarity' of Christ with God, 'definitely lays the accent upon the sensuous and humanly perceptible'[1] and is therefore extraverted, while the purely conceptual and abstract standpoint of Homoousia, or complete identity of Christ and God, is introverted. In the controversy concerning the Eucharist, transubstantiation, as the extreme concretization of a symbol, is extraverted, while the more abstract, commemorative view is introverted.

There remain two more difficult chapters, one based on Schiller's 'Letters on the Aesthetic Education of Man', the other on Spitteler's 'Epimetheus and Prometheus'.[2]

In the work of Schiller two basic instincts are distinguished, the sensuous and the formative. The sensuous instinct is concerned with ' "the placing of man within the confines of time, and making him material" ';[3] it turns to all material being and all things directly present to the senses and accordingly demands change. The formative instinct is concerned with abstraction, with all formal qualities of things, and seeks changelessness, eternity. In Jung's own terminology the one is extraverted, the other introverted, for 'the extravert finds himself in the fluctuating and changeable, the introvert in the constant'.[4] A means of reconciling them is needed—the symbol, whose message always is, 'In some such form as this will a new manifestation of life, a deliverance from the bondage and weariness of life, be found'.[5] Through the symbol-creating function energy is drawn from both sides and 'an individual nucleus' created.

Spitteler's work is taken as dealing with rather different aspects of extraversion and introversion—the social or collective and the solitary or individual. Epimetheus realizes that his aim is the world and what the world values. Prometheus 'surrenders himself unconditionally to his own soul', repressing every impulse toward adaption to the outer world. However, in spite of this repression, the soul of Prometheus seeks the world of men, and plans a work to alleviate its sufferings. This is symbolized by a jewel which his youngest daughter, Pandora, brings him. But in the kingdom of Epimetheus the symbol is strange, immoral, unlawful, and threatens it with 'inundation' and disintergration. It is obvious, Jung says, that although this is nowhere

[1] *Ibid.*, p. 30.   [2] Chapter II, pp. 87–169; Chapter V, pp. 207–336.
[3] *Ibid.*, p. 124.   [4] *Ibid.*, p. 116.   [5] *Ibid.*, p. 320.

stated the image is a naked human figure, representing man as he might be through Nature and not through some preconceived and artificial form; in the world of social values this is bound to be disturbing. Finally, Prometheus rescues a child, Messias, who becomes heir to the kingdom, brings about what the first symbol could not do and reconciles Prometheus and Epimetheus. This corresponds very closely, Jung adds, with what is often found in analytical psychology —an energizing symbol is rejected on account of its crudity, a counter-reaction occurs, and in the end a simplification and re-integration comes about, connecting the matured personality with the energy sources of childhood.

From these chapters it can be seen again where Jung's special interest lies, i.e. in the study of rather obscure integrative processes taking place within the adult personality. He traces these processes also in the work of the medieval alchemists. While there were many alchemists who thought of nothing more than learning to make gold, others used their chemical substances in order to project a psychic transformation.*

> 'The situation is enveloped in a kind of fog, and this fully accords with the nature of the unconscious content: it is dark and black—"*nigrum, nigrius nigro*," as the alchemists rightly say—and in addition it is charged with dangerous polar tensions, with the *inimicitia elementorum*. One finds oneself in an impenetrable chaos, which is indeed one of the synonyms for the mysterious *prima materia*. . . . Hunted for centuries and never found, the *prima materia* or *lapis philosophorum* is, as a few alchemists rightly suspected, to be discovered in man himself.'[1]

In addition to the more symbolic descriptions, Jung states in general terms that 'Every life is, at bottom, the realization of a whole, that is, of a self, so that the realization can also be called individuation.'[2] A difficulty for the reader is, not only a lack of experience of the central-izing process in analysis—though that may be conceded as a factor— but lack of co-ordination in the written material, i.e. there is a frag-

---

* Up to a point, Jung had been anticipated by Herbert Silberer and two mid-nineteenth-century writers, E. A. Hitchcock and N. Landur, whom he mentions in his book, *Problems of Mysticism and Its Symbolism* (New York, 1917, pp. 151–6). Hitchcock and Landur, however, were more concerned to interpret the alchemistic symbolism in the conventional terms of moral life (e.g. mercury or sulphur was equated with conscience) and Silberer himself had more to say of the psychoanalytical aspects of their imagery (*ibid.*, p. 137).

[1] *Practice of Psychotherapy*, p. 187.

[2] *Integ. of Person.*, p. 200.

mentation in Jung's writings, so that statements which might logically be placed together are found instead in separate chapters or even separate works. Perhaps it might be said that the human mind is endowed with a capacity for organization; that this capacity has to exercise itself upon a number of opposing trends, such as need for social adaptation and need for individual autonomy, conscious and unconscious components of the personality, and masculine and feminine components; and that for many patients it is helpful to personify the forces which are involved in the struggle.

The individuation process will be returned to in discussing therapy and values. Here we may note that Jung states emphatically, individuation is not for the young. 'Before individuation can be taken for a goal, the educational aim of adaptation to the necessary minimum of collective standards must first be attained. A plant which is to be brought to the fullest possible unfolding of its particular character must first of all be able to grow in the soil wherein it is planted.'[1] In so far as he concerns himself with personality development in the early years, he uses very largely the concept of *participation mystique*, i.e. his own developmental stages of the intermediate period seem to disappear, and he assumes, with Durkheim and Levy Bruhl, that in primitive psychology there exists 'a state of identity in a common unconsciousness', or failure to differentiate oneself from the surroundings, and that the small child, recapitulating the history of the race, exists in a similar state of *participation mystique* with the parents. Even at the age of six the child is still 'nothing but the product of his parents, endowed, it is true, with the nucleus of an ego-consciousness, but in no way capable of asserting his individuality to any marked degree'.[2] In spite of the passivity which this and other passages suggests,[3] the child is said elsewhere to 'possess a treasury of constantly accessible libido', a 'joy, which, undismayed by things without, streams all-embracing from within'.[4] At the same time, the child is only gradually emerging out of the collective unconscious. Even his relation to the mother is affected by it: 'she is known by the more or less unconscious child not as a definite, individual feminine personality, but as the mother, an archetype loaded with significant

---

[1] *Psych. Types*, p. 562.   [2] *Contribs.*, p. 318.
[3] *Ibid.*, p. 125: 'The soil of the earth on which the child plays, the fire at which he warms himself, the rain and storms that freeze him, although always realities, were at first, because of his twilight consciousness, seen and understood only as characteristics of the parents.'   [4] *Psych. Types*, p. 308.

possibilities'.[1] 'My own view differs from that of other medico-psychological theories,' he says explicitly, 'in that I attribute to the personal mother only a limited aetiological significance'.[2] Looking back now at the material in the present chapter, it will be realized that we have not altogether been able to avoid certain difficulties in Jung's work—the peculiarities of his style of writing, the two main interpretations of the collective unconscious and the Archetypes, the rather scattered accounts of individuation, and the brief handling of earlier developmental stages. Postponing for the most part a search for the explanation of such difficulties, we will next look more closely at some of the theoretical problems which are involved in them. One other feature of Jung's later expositions may, however, be mentioned—not only a dropping out of Freudian influence, but a lack of interest in, almost, it would seem, an unawareness of, psychoanalytical developments. For instance, in 1923 Jung describes psychoanalysis as 'a psychology which deals exclusively with the ramifications of the sexual instinct in the psyche'.[3] But as early as 1914 Freud had distinguished between sexual and ego instincts.[4] Jung also says nothing of Freud's division of mind into Ego, Id and Super-Ego, and continues to think of the Freudian Unconscious as consisting purely of repressed material. But in 1923 Freud wrote: 'We recognize that the Ucs. does not coincide with what is repressed; it is still true that all that is repressed is Ucs., but not that the whole Ucs. is repressed. . . . Pathological research has centred our interest too exclusively on the repressed.'[5] Again, in 1924 Jung writes, 'In the Freudian doctrine the collective unconscious has no place.'[6] But Freud had written in 1923 that 'in the id, which is capable of being inherited, are stored up vestiges of the existences led by countless former egos . . .'[7] In short, as Marjorie Brierley comments,

'The uninformed reader would be likely to gather that Freud's contributions to psychological theory ended with the formulation of the libido theory and the infantile-wish origin of dreams; also that the psychoanalytic unconscious is still to be equated with the repressed, i.e. with Jung's personal unconscious. There is no reference anywhere to the new classification of instincts, to modern concepts of mental structure and function, or, indeed, to meta-psychology at all.'[8]

[1] *Contribs.*, p. 123.   [2] *Archetypes and the Collective Unconscious*, p. 83.
[3] *Contribs.*, p. 314.   [4] *Collected Papers*, Vol. IV, 'On Narcissism,' p. 35.
[5] *Ego and the Id*, p. 17.   [6] *Contribs.*, p. 368.   [7] *Op. cit.*, p. 52.
[8] Review of Jolande Jacobi: 'Psychology of C. G. Jung.' *Int. J. Psycho-Anal.*, Vol. XXIV, 1943; pp. 81–4.

On the other hand, Freud himself does not seek a meeting-point. In his own work there are no comparisons between the Id and the Collective Unconscious, nor does he make any reference to Jung's hypothesis of an innate urge toward domestication of libido in suggesting, as he does in 1929, 'Sometimes one imagines one perceives that it is not only the oppression of culture, but something in the nature of the function itself, that denies us full satisfaction and urges us in other directions.'[1] And indeed, as so often when Freud and Jung appear to draw together, differences remain in the midst of similarities. In Freud's description of the Id as 'a chaos, a cauldron of seething excitement' knowing 'no values, no good and evil, no morality'[2] we are reminded again of the more active, striving nature of his formulations. For Jung, as Crichton Miller says, 'The emergence of unconscious material in consciousness is much more a process for the conscious to develop, than one in which the conscious has ever to defend its own peace.'[3] The second point, concerning the urge to seek satisfaction in other directions, is one where the difference in emphasis is very great—the rare conjecture in the work of Freud, followed by the proviso that 'This may be an error; it is hard to decide,' to set against a major tenet in the work of Jung. There even seems to be a slight difference in the concept itself—Freud's attention being focused more fully on *the denial of full satisfaction*, and Jung's on the spontaneous turning to other modes of expression. The personal attitude of the two men to one another during these later years seems to have been on Freud's side one of dismissal, and on Jung's one of ambivalence: Freud writes of the secession of Jung and Adler that 'After a lapse of ten years, it can be asserted that both of these attempts against psycho-analysis have blown over without doing any harm,'[4] and Jung writes on the one hand, that 'To Freud belongs the undying merit of having laid the foundations of a psychology of the neuroses'[5] and on the other, that 'The partly one-sided, partly erroneous conceptions of Freud really tell us nothing.'[6]

Especially in the first half of the period some references are made to Adler. As before, the Adlerian psychology, with its stress on the power urge, is seen as an introverted psychology, in contrast to Freud's, in which the subject depends upon the object. Jung also

[1] *Civilization and its Discontents*, pp. 76–7.   [2] *New Introd. Lectures*, pp. 98–9.
[3] *Psycho-Analysis and its Derivatives*, p. 190.   [4] *Autobiographical Study*, p. 97.
[5] *Two Essays*, new ed. p. 9.   [6] *Contribs.*, p. 150.

draws attention to the goal-seeking concept in the work of Adler, pointing out that Adler, unlike himself, is concerned chiefly with social adaptation. (Other differences are, of course, that Adler follows Freud in giving a great deal of attention to the early years, and that compensation, which figures so prominently in his work as well as Jung's, is for him less a matter of homeostasis, a redressing of the balance, than an urge to 'make it up to oneself' in the face of overwhelming insecurity.) This material, however, was available to Jung within the intermediate period—it remains the case that developments falling within the later period, either in psychoanalysis or modern psychology and psychotherapy in general, do not receive very close consideration.

Chapter V

JUNG'S LATER CONCEPTS OF
MIND: DISCUSSION

We come now to the question of the *value* of Jung's later concepts on the theoretical side, i.e. how far do the collective unconscious and the archetypes, the opposites and mental energy, psychological types and the account of personality development assist the psychologist to order existing data and make further observations?

Taking first the collective unconscious: since Jung expressly denies that form of the theory which implies the biological transmission of life experience from one generation to the next, we need not concern ourselves with it, other than to note that the existence of so many passages which do in fact assume such a process of transmission is a drawback in his writings, in view of the trend of modern biology and psychology against it. The second sense in which the term is used—as a potential system of psychic functioning—seems, viewed academically, to have drawbacks of its own. Let us suppose that the innately determined drives of hunger, sex, etc., together with certain modes of perceptual organization, are described as attributes of the collective unconscious. Is there not a danger that those employing the term will be inclined to assume that problems have been solved, when in reality they have been shelved? That is, owing to the inclusiveness of the term, and the sense of apparent understanding which it gives, there may be less likelihood than before of inquiring, what is the range of individual differences in this mental function, under what conditions does it express itself most fully, and so forth. This may be illustrated by comparing two passages on infant development, the one from a standard work on Jungian, the other from a standard textbook of academic, psychology. 'At the beginning of life,' says Jacobi, the human being 'must struggle out of infancy, which still is wholly imprisoned in the collective unconscious, to the differentiation and demarcation of his ego.'[1] 'The ego is not present at birth in the human child,' says Sherif:

> 'The activity of a baby in the first weeks of his life is determined chiefly by the biogenic needs with which he is born. From the standpoint of a socialized adult his behaviour may seem utterly chaotic and haphazard. But as Gesell put it so colorfully: "From the standpoint of 4-week-oldness his behaviour is patterned, meaningful, significant." And the determiners of this "standpoint of 4-week-oldness" are the physiological states of his organism.'[2]

However indefinite the phrase, 'physiological states of the organism,' may be itself, it would seem to hold out more possibilities for inquiry, and to be less of a blanket term, than the collective unconscious. Theories, as Jung himself has quoted from William James, are instruments, '"We don't lie back upon them, we move forward".'[3] The danger of *lying back upon* the collective unconscious may trouble many readers. And indeed, at any rate until very recent times, there does not seem to have been a great deal of theoretical development within the Jungian school. Clarifications of meaning there sometimes are,[4] case studies, and further gathering of myths. But even Michael Fordham, who believes that the analytical school should pay more attention to the psychology of childhood, has operated very largely within the existing framework of archetypes, collective unconscious, and *participation mystique*.

Supporters of Jung's work will feel that the collective unconscious is being used, not as a blanket term but as a convenient shorthand term, to cover especially those regularly recurring patterns of apprehension which Jung distinguishes as archetypes, together with the mode of thinking of which they are the most outstanding examples. Even so, it can be argued that the blanket quality is not entirely absent from the archetypes themselves. This may be illustrated by Jung's comparison of the theory of conservation of energy with primitive ideas of spirit, in both of which he sees the operation of an archetype. As Theodor Merz has said, naturally quite independently, although obscure notions of the attractive and repulsive forces of nature have floated before the minds of philosophers since the time

---

[1] *The Psychology of C. G. Jung*, p. 142.
[2] *Outline of Social Psychology*, p. 253; p. 51.
[3] *Supra*, p. 47.   [4] *Infra*, p. 120.

of Empedocles, 'It is the scientific method, the exact statement, which was wanting, and which raises the vague guesses of the philosophical or the dreams of the poetic mind to the rank of definite canons of thought, capable of precise expression, of mathematical analysis, and of exact verification.'[1] That is, the difference between the primitive and the scientific conceptions is at least as important for the understanding of human thought as any similarity. Again, is there not an echo of the early nineteenth-century anthropology in Jung's method of comparing myths and symbols in isolation from the cultures of which they are components, i.e. without consideration of the interrelationships and modifying factors within the cultures themselves. John Layard, himself a Jungian, has pointed out in his *Stone Men of Malekula* some of the problems which arose when a Christian missionary attempted to draw parallels between the doctrines of the Church and the beliefs of the native population. The priest compared the native *bakeran* with the Christian Heaven. However, Layard comments, the native conception 'is not one of any place at all, but simply one of great and glorious height'. Again, the figure of the native Ta-ghar, who begat men by the moon and ordained the earth, the sea, the stars, the light, all for the greatest good of man, cannot really be identified with the Christian God, since no formal ritual or act of worship is connected with him, 'Nor have I met with any signs of gratitude nor of any other kind of emotion towards him other than one of simple acceptance of the fact that he exists.'[2] That is the very thing—omission of differences relevant for precision of understanding—of which some critics are likely to accuse Jung and his school.

Not only the archetypes, but also Jung's discussion of the mode of thinking of the child, the primitive, the psychotic and the normal dreaming adult, i.e. the thinking of the collective unconscious in general, may be subjected to this kind of criticism. Is it true, for instance, that the child and the primitive are alike in their thinking, and that the difference between their thought and the waking thought of the civilized adult is so great? Some anthropologists believe that it is not. The supposition that it is, says Irving Hallowell, rests on two things—an overvaluation of verbal expression as a measure of thought and an exaggerated view of the logicality of the civilized

[1] Merz, J. T., *op. cit.*, Vol. I, p. 313.
[2] *Stone Men of Malekula*, pp. 215–16. London: Chatto & Windus, 1942.

adult mentality.[1] Paul Radin, similarly, attacks Levy Bruhl's concept of *participation mystique* which Jung has borrowed. Primitive man, according to Radin, in no sense merges himself with the object as Levy Bruhl maintains. 'He distinguishes subject and object quite definitely. In fact the man of action spends a good part of his time in attempting to coerce the object.'[2] Norman Cameron, considering the thought of the child and the psychotic, doubts whether the similarities in that direction are so great as has sometimes been supposed. Presenting the same logical problems to normal children and to schizophrenics, he found nothing comparable to the characteristic schizophrenic peculiarities—over-inclusion, interpenetration of themes, etc.—in normal children. His conclusion therefore is: 'It is hardly more correct to assert that as the schizophrenic loses his adult organization he becomes a child in his thinking, than it is to say of normal children that as they grow up they recover from schizophrenia.'[3] Heinz Werner, on the other hand, in his *Comparative Psychology of Mental Development*, brings together a great deal of material suggesting *formal* similarities, even though, as he points out, the different life situations of the child, the primitive and the psychotic will modify the patterns of behaviour which they actually show. Syncretism and diffuseness are the common qualities which he finds in their mental operations. In the perceptual field the syncretic quality is displayed in a relatively limited differentiation of perception and feeling—things do not stand 'out there', discrete and fixed in meaning, but are determined, more than in the case of civilized adults, by the whole affective situation; for instance, a rattle to a small child is not an independent object but 'something to be shaken', or 'something to be bitten'. It is easy for objects perceived in this dynamic way to appear animistic—a schizophrenic will say, for instance, 'The door is devouring me.' The greater diffuseness of perception implies that objects are less well-organized into essential and non-essential characters—a trivial variation may be interpreted as a revision of the whole, a revolutionary change. The concepts of these groups are apt to be syncretic also, being based simply on the affective experience

---

[1] See: 'The Child, the Savage, and Human Experience.' *Proc. of the Sixth Institute on the Exceptional Child. Child Research Clinic of the Woods Schools.* Oct. 1939.
[2] *Primitive Man as Philospher*, p. 246.   New York, Appleton & Co., 1927.
[3] Kasanin, J. (ed.) *Language and Thought in Schizophrenia.* 'Experimental Analysis of Schizophrenic Thinking,' pp. 50–64 (p. 60).

of togetherness in a concrete situation rather than on logical abstraction, e.g. in one Australian aboriginal tribe 'water' and 'thirst' are given the same name because both are experienced as elements in a common situation, or a child may use the same word for water and for glass, because the two objects form a realistic concrete unity. There is a diffuseness in such groupings too, since first one element of a collective unity is stressed and then another. Diffuseness and syncretism affect attitudes to personality. A lack of discrimination between essential and constant elements, and peripheral and transitory ones, gives rise to a belief in the transmutability of personality—to the child, the primitive and the psychotic one human being can possess a multiplicity of souls, nor is there so clear a distinction between one person and another, or between the individual and the social groups of which he is a member.

Many writers, indeed, have felt the need for making a distinction between logical thinking processes and thinking which is more closely bound up with the affective characteristics of the subject and/or with the immediate concrete situation—Bleuler, for example, distinguishes autistic and reistic thinking, Freud primary and secondary thought. Owing to the far-reaching influence of nineteenth-century evolutionary theory the problems of thinking and its development have often been tied up, as in Jung's own work, with the assumption that the child recapitulates and the psychotic regresses to the thinking of the primitive. In view of the differences as well as similarities, in view also of the indications of logical thinking in the child and the primitive *as well as* non-logical thinking in the civilized adult, it might be more satisfactory simply to acknowledge the existence of non-logical, more concrete and affectively influenced thinking processes which can be found, in varying degree, in any human being, though the child, primitive and psychotic may be more prone to depend on them—all the more so since a tradition of logical, reality-directed thinking presses less heavily upon them. In this sense a 'collective unconscious' might be admitted.

In addition to the question of the existence of some such type of thought, there is the question of its significance in human life. Is it something to be brushed aside or overcome, or does it have a constructive part to play? Jung, of course, takes the latter view—for wholeness of personality the unconscious must be assimilated in some way by the conscious mind—it is not good to be divorced from it. Werner, without developing the idea, conceives of the primitive functions not only as the base from which the more developed functions have arisen, but as being 'continually present' and 'of vital importance in supporting the highest forms of mentality'.[1] Among psychoanalytical writers J. C. Flugel is prepared to consider the possibility that 'as Jung and his followers appear to hold, a temporary regression to a deep level . . . can sometimes act recuperatively, or perhaps even creatively, in such a way as to enable us to deal more efficiently with grave problems and difficulties, both those presented by the external world and by our own inner conflicts,' though he thinks that 'our present knowledge scarcely enables us to say whether these are, as it were, secondary and incidental benefits that we have contrived to extract from the deeper levels . . . which in themselves are merely an encumbrance, or whether these levels have a primary function of their own without which the human psyche might not have achieved its unique capacity'.[2] In cognitive terms a rather more specific suggestion has recently come from within the Jungian school, viz., a distinction by Plaut between the focusing and defocusing of consciousness. The phenomena of consciousness, Plaut thinks, are bound up with rhythmic alterations. Focusing, or a high degree of paying attention, makes for acute awareness in one direction only, while little or no heed is being paid to what is going on elsewhere. It provides the necessary intensity of experience for the defocused consciousness to reflect on and integrate with a wider area. 'This raises interesting questions: Are such phasic alterations in keeping with the natural organization of our central nervous systems? Does the increasing emphasis which we put on rationality constitute an interference with this rhythm by attempting to focus consciousness all the time?'[3] In a broad sense, of implication for the total personality, which is what Jung has most in mind, a statement by an American psychoanalytical writer, Andras Angyal, may clarify his meaning. In our ordinary experience, Angyal remarks, the objects of our environment do not conform to some conventional definition but have a rich personal content. For instance, the picture of someone who is dear to one is not only a piece of paper with some colours on it. It is as if something of the person portrayed were incorporated in

[1] *Op. cit.*, p. 4.
[2] *Man, Morals and Society*, pp. 237–8. London: Duckworth, 1945.
[3] Plaut, A., 'Aspects of Consciousness,' *Brit. J. Med. Psychol.*, Vol. XXXII Pt. 4, 1959; p. 242.

it, and in harming it one would almost feel as though the person too were harmed. This formulation, he continues, 'may seem akin to "magic" or "primitive" thinking, but actually we function in this way in all matters which are close to life and refrain from doing so only in highly abstract scientific speculations. This "primitive" way of thinking seems to be rather a sign of close contact with life and of personal refinement than of primitivity.'[1] In Jung's work, however, it seems that the kind of thinking which he is describing has exerted some influence on his own conceptions. The anima, for example, standing for the contra-sexual portion of the psyche, the precipitate of all experience with the opposite sex, and the individual's attitude to his own psychic processes, is certainly a diffuse and labile concept, and the same is true of the collective unconscious itself, representing at times a potential system of psychic functioning, at times the accumulated traditions of society, whether handed on biologically or otherwise, and possibly other things as well.

But from the psychoanalytical school there comes a different question, which we found in essence in the intermediate period, namely, How far can Jung in his descriptions of the collective unconscious be said to be dealing with truly unconscious processes, at a still deeper level than the Freudian, as he and his followers believe, and how far, by lessening his emphasis upon repression, has he been concerned with pre-conscious thinking only?

To begin with, it may be admitted that if some of Jung's statements on the unconscious are compared with descriptions of 'the sub-conscious' or 'the subliminal' given by the earlier writers, William James and F. W. H. Myers, a close resemblance will be found. William James's description of the subconscious as the source of all non-rational operations has been noted, together with his statement that 'just *how* anything operates in this region is still unexplained'.[2] Myers, too, writes that the subliminal is 'in closer relation that the supraliminal . . . to the primitive source and extra-terrene initiation of life',[3] and that sometimes, therefore, 'we seem to see our subliminal perceptions and faculties acting truly in unity, truly as a Self'. But 'it seems that this degree of clarity, of integration, cannot be long

---

[1] Angyal, A., *Foundations for a Science of Personality*, pp. 156–7. New York: Commonwealth Fund, 1941.

[2] *Supra*, p. 6.

[3] *Human Personality and its Survival of Bodily Death*, p. 76. London: Longmans, Green & Co., 1918.

preserved. Much oftener we find the subliminal perceptions and faculties acting in less co-ordinated, less coherent ways.'[1] Nor do we know how to get our suggestions to *take hold of* the subliminal self. To Jung, similarly, the unconscious has at its disposal 'the wisdom of the experience of untold ages' on the one hand, and is apt to be 'chaotic and irrational' in its manifestations on the other.

However, this comparison, though historically it may be of some interest, cannot by itself take us far. The argument of the Freudian school is that the kind of symbol formation which Jung attributes to the activity of the unconscious is in fact only possible for the conscious or pre-conscious mind. Perhaps the fullest account of the difference is that by Ernest Jones, in his paper, 'The Theory of Symbolism'.[2] After defining a symbol in general terms as 'a representative or substitute of some other idea, from which in the context it derives a secondary significance not inherent in itself',[3] Jones distinguishes 'true symbolism' from all other forms of indirect representation. In the case of 'true symbolism' the concept symbolized may, in itself, be known to the individual, but in addition to the fact that the process of symbolization is carried out unconsciously, so that the individual is quite unaware of the meaning of the symbol, or even of having employed a symbol at all, 'the affect investing the concept is in a state of repression, and so is unconscious'.[4] While the number of symbols encountered is very high, the number of ideas symbolized in this sense is very limited indeed. 'All symbols represent ideas of the self and the immediate blood relations, or of the phenomena of birth, love and death. In other words, they represent the most primitive ideas and interests imaginable.'[5] Because of the powerful affective and conative processes connected with these ideas but inhibited from direct entry into consciousness, energy flows from them and never to them. Therefore, a church tower in a dream often (though not always) symbolizes the phallus, but a phallus in a dream is never a symbol of a church tower. These ideas and interests are also very concrete. Whereas to Jung the image of a serpent in a dream will symbolize the abstract idea of sexuality more often than the concrete idea of the phallus, to the psychoanalytical school it only symbolizes the latter, though of course it is commonly *associated*

---

[1] *Ibid.*, p. 58.
[2] *Papers on Psychoanalysis*, pp. 129–86. London: Ballière, Tindall & Cox, 1920.
[3] *Ibid.*, p. 131.   [4] *Ibid.*, p. 139.   [5] *Ibid.*, p. 145.

with the former; 'the practical difference this makes is that, according to the latter school, any meaning of the dream context which is expressed in terms of the general idea is secondary to, derived from, and dependent on a deeper meaning in the unconscious which can only be expressed in terms of the concrete'.[1] We are concerned, Jones says later, with three groups of psychical material, the unconscious complexes, the inhibiting influences that keep these in a state of repression, and the sublimated tendencies. Symbols, like the third group, or sublimated tendencies, are the product of intrapsychical conflict between the first two groups. The *material* of the symbol is taken from the third group, though the second group, made up of the inhibiting influences, is to some extent represented in its formation. But 'the dynamic force that creates the symbol, the meaning carried by the symbol, and the reason for the very existence of the symbol, are all derived from the first group, from the unconscious complexes'.[2] Some patients become exceedingly adept at the method of protecting themselves from realization of their unconscious by stressing the secondary meanings, so that even openly erotic dreams are desexualized into poetic allegories.

> 'If, now, the psychoanalyst allows himself to be deceived by these defensive interpretations, and refrains from overcoming the patient's resistances, he will assuredly never reach a knowledge of his unconscious, still less will he be in a position to appraise the relative importance of unconscious trends and those of the surface. By this I do not in any sense mean that the latter are to be neglected, or in their turn to be underestimated, but simply that one should not put the cart before the horse and talk of something secondary and less important being *symbolized* by something primary and more important.'[3]

Now in some measure, since Jung himself holds that each dream faces two ways, toward the past and toward the future, and Jones acknowledges secondary meanings, we are dealing with differences of emphasis. In practical dream interpretation something will depend on the type of explanation that is sought. The customary view, to which evolutionary theory gave additional support, has been that a phenomenon is explained if it can be traced to antecedents in the past. More recently there has been some leaning toward a different type of explanation, i.e. relating a phenomenon to its context in the existing situation. For example, D. W. Winnicott describes a dream in which

---

[1] *Ibid.*, p. 170. [2] *Ibid.*, p. 183. [3] *Ibid.*, pp. 167–8.

he believed himself to have no right side to his body and was in consequence extremely anxious; his explanation is that one of his patients had aroused this anxiety by her demand that he and she have no body. Whatever other interpretations might be made, he adds, the result of having dreamt it and remembered it was that he could take up the analysis again without the irritability which had begun to damage it.[1] Even so, it is difficult not to feel that Jung is sometimes rather too ready to step over a root complex to the associative accretions. Reverting to his example in the intermediate period, of a young man who dreamt that he was climbing the stairs with his mother and sister and added that upon taking leave of the sister years before he had 'understood for the first time what love for a woman can be'—one may well feel that the associations themselves point to an incestuous complex. Similarly in the later period, Jung gives the example of a patient 'fifty-five years old and unmarried' who dreamt that the lower part of her body was thrust into the earth or among boulders; that Jung himself passed by in the form of a sorcerer with a magic wand; she called to him for help; he touched the rock with his wand; it broke apart and she emerged. His interpretation is that only the upper half of her personality was alive, all that seemed to her 'good' and 'genteel', while the lower half was unconscious, mere earth or stone.[2] The lack of any reference to phallic symbolism is rather striking if the interpretation is recalled which Jung gave to 'amphi' and the creeping snake in the early monograph, *Psychology of Dementia Praecox*. In a slightly revised version of this material[3] a direct reference is in fact made to sexual symbolism; Jung merely states, however, that this, 'which for many naive minds is of such capital importance, was no discovery for her. She was far enough advanced to know that explanations of this kind, however true they might be in other respects, had no significance in her case.' Adding that 'we would do well to abandon from the start any attempt to apply ready-made solutions and warmed-up generalities of which the patient knows just as much as the doctor',[4] Jung considers the egg-like boulders, as in the previous account: 'The egg is a germ of life with a lofty symbolical significance. It is not just a cosmogonic symbol—it is also a "philosophical" one. As the former it is the

---

[1] 'Hate in the Counter-Transference.' *Int. J. Psycho-Anal.*, Vol. XXX, Part II, 1949; pp. 69–74   [2] *Integ. of Person.*, p. 34.
[3] *Archetypes and the Collective Unconscious*, pp. 292–3.
[4] *Ibid.*, pp. 292–3.

Orphic egg, the world's beginning; as the latter, the philosophical egg of the medieval natural philosophers, the vessel from which, at the end of the *opus alchymicum*, the homunculus emerges, that is, the Anthropos, the spiritual, inner and complete man, who in Chinese alchemy is called the *chen-yen* (literally, "perfect man").[1] This difference brings us almost to consideration of therapeutic outlook, for clearly the Freudians are seeking their therapeutic solution primarily in a direct working out of the complex which they conceive to be the root one, while Jung and his supporters, even though they may not deny the existence of the sexual complex altogether, are seeking guidance to a far greater extent from associations which the Freudians would regard as secondary.

In favour of the Jungian point of view it can be said that the Freudians are apt to confuse the issue in speaking of 'true symbolism' when the representations to which they are referring differ from those which have generally been described as symbolic, and can better be described as signs or symptoms. It is the Jungian sense of the term— the symbol as a means of expressing ideas not yet fully grasped— which is more usual. That, however, is a terminological matter only, and does not touch the underlying question, whether or not the unconscious, as distinct from the preconscious, can symbolize in the way Jung thinks it can—using 'unconscious' to denote mental activities which have either been repressed or never been in consciousness at all, and 'preconscious' to denote activities and presentations which have been conscious and can become so again without the barrier of repression. Dalbiez believes not: 'Since any reality can be symbolized in an infinite number of ways, the concept of symbolism would appear so indeterminate that it could have no practical use unless choice intervened. But how could this choice possibly not be conscious? Symbolism, in the meaning which it bears elsewhere than in psychoanalysis, seems essentially to imply a conscious comparison.'[2] Comparison there must be, certainly, but need the comparison be conscious? Might it be the case that a movement of thought toward general concepts could take place through unconscious comparison with concrete objects, at a stage intermediate between the most concrete thinking of all, and thought which either operated with

---

[1] *Ibid.*, p. 293.
[2] *Psychoanalytical Method and the Doctrine of Freud*, Vol. II, p. 102. Longmans, Green & Co., 1941.

general concepts directly, or consciously employed concrete symbolism? Such a movement of thought might be as inaccessible in its early phases, as much in need of discovery by special methods, as the repressed unconscious. Aside from this, the primitive symbolizing of, for example, a phallus by a snake, is, after all, a rational operation of the mind, even if a rudimentary one. If it seems desirable to retain the distinction between Freudian and all other symbolism, it might be useful nonetheless to think of a continuity of rational process, from the phallus-snake level to a conscious or near-conscious perception that the desire for integration of personality can be expressed appropriately by a circle.

A review of the thinking processes which seem to be implied in the collective unconscious and the archetypes has carried us rather far from other objections which have commonly been raised. The most usual form which our previous 'blanket' criticism has taken is that Jung has neglected the cultural influences affecting symbolism. W. H. R. Rivers puts this objection clearly: he once asked one of Jung's leading disciples for an example of some universal belief which could be taken as an illustration of Jung's primordial thought image. The example chosen was the representation of good by right and evil by left. However, Rivers comments, there is no evidence whatever for that association among most peoples of the earth, and a large number of languages are quite devoid of words for right and left—orientation being effected instead by cruder methods such as the direction of prevailing winds. Much of Jung's material has been drawn, he thinks, from Indo-European cultures, where a common tradition has existed. 'The possibility cannot be excluded that this common tradition reaches the individual in infancy, childhood and youth through the intermediation of parents, nurses, schoolfellows, the overhearing of chance conversations, and many other sources.'[1] That is, in the controversy concerning cultural diffusion or psychic unity, Jung has accepted the latter point of view too uncritically. In the clinical field, W. C. M. Scott, writing of mandala symbolism, acknowledges the existence of such symbols but does not find it necessary to use the collective unconscious and the archetypes in explanation. Such drawings appear to him to be attempts to isolate and enclose good and/or bad objects which the patient has previously internalized, i.e. they are related to understandable objects in the

---

[1] *Conflict and Dream*, p. 178. London: Kegan Paul, 1923.

patient's life—natural objects, other people, or the patient's own body. He states also:

> 'In contrast to what I find while reading what Jung and his pupils write, these symbols never remain for very long in the same form in patients being psychoanalysed by me. They tend to develop into the bodies of animals or persons or into outlines of bodies. They also develop into boundaries of body openings or body cavities. They also expand until they become equivalent to the imagined boundaries of the cosmos— then they contain the universe and all the people within.'[1]

To some extent these objections are allowed for by Jung himself or by his school. Jung points out differences between medieval and modern mandala symbols: whereas the former contained the figure of Christ, the latter contain 'a star, a sun, a flower, a cross with equal arms, a precious stone, a bowl filled with water or wine, a serpent coiled up, or a human being, but never a god'.[2] Baynes compares the use of myths in analytical psychology to the use of specific dye stains in histology. While differences will be found between the mythological and clinical material, 'The developed myth-pattern brings into relief just those elements of the dream-structure which correspond to it.'[3] Concerning the fluidity of the developmental process, another Jungian writer, Frances Wickes, admits that 'As soon as one attempts to give a precise definition of these images, one is confronted with the fact that they are vague, shifting, imprecise. An image rarely arises in sharply defined form, nor does a particular image appear only at a certain period of life. They are always changing, appearing, disappearing, returning in some new form as the conscious problems change.' All that can be claimed, she adds, is that 'as one studies the material of the unconscious one gains a certain familiarity with typical traits of the psyche, even though these traits appear in varying guises'.[4] Nevertheless, there are many passages in Jung which give sufficient grounds for raising such objections—as when he writes that 'myths and symbols which can arise authochthonously in every corner of the earth . . . are none the less *identical*, just because they are fashioned out of the same world-wide human unconscious'.[5] An

---

[1] 'The Psycho-Analytic View of Mandala Symbols.' *Brit. J. Med. Psychol.*, Vol. XXII, Pts. 1 & 2, 1949; pp. 23–5.
[2] *Psych. and Religion*, new ed. p. 80; old ed. p. 97.
[3] *Analytical Psychology and the English Mind*, p. 149. London: Methuen, 1950.
[4] *The Inner World of Man*, p. 18. New York: Henry Holt, 1938.
[5] *Psych. Types*, p. 152. (Italics mine.)

example which particularly suggests diminished critical sense is his handling of a dream series in the *Integration of the Personality*. The material consisted of more than a thousand dreams and visual impressions of a highly educated man who dreamt, for instance, that he was surrounded by nymphs. 'But the dreamer's education in history, philology, archaeology and ethnology is not the question here. The bearing of his dreams upon the subject matter of these fields was almost wholly unknown to him.'[1] Even so, it would seem that the influence of such training should be taken into account. Jung, however, continues with the statement that regression has gone 'even further back to an antiquity that is out of question . . . contact with distant times—that is, with deep layers of the psyche—has taken place'.[2]

Any objections which can be raised against the archetypes in general will naturally apply to the archetypal figures. In addition it may be asked whether the figures do not have further limitations on the side of theory. One danger is that they will be taken literally rather than as a conceptual device. How far Jung himself sometimes goes in this direction has been pointed out by a recent critic in philosophy,[3] who cites the following passage from the *Answer to Job:* '"the archetypes of the collective unconscious . . . are spontaneous phenomena which are not subject to our will, and we are *therefore* justified in ascribing to them a certain autonomy . . . they possess spontaneity and purposiveness, or a kind of consciousness and free will".' In this, Hepburn comments, we can see an illicit transition from the denial of conscious control over the archetypes to the philosophically misleading personification of them as conscious beings existing over-against the subject concerned. 'Metaphor has taken over the work of argument.' Another possibility is that the archetypal formulations may lead on the one hand to a disregard for the carry-over from one sphere of an individual's activities to another, and on the other hand to a confusion of aspects of mental life which should be separated. The first of these difficulties may arise in connection with Jung's concept of the self. Granted that the self represents a new centring of the total personality, extended, reinforced though the personality may be, is the difference such as to warrant

---

[1] *Integ. of Person.*, Ch. IV, pp. 96–204 (p. 97).   [2] *Ibid.*, p. 124.
[3] Hepburn, R. W.: 'Poetry and Religious Belief' in *Metaphysical Beliefs*, ed. A. MacIntyre, pp. 85–166 (pp. 106–7). London: S.C.M. Press, 1957.

the introduction of a separate entity? Perhaps there really is need of the new term—though Jung himself admits in one place that the change is only relative and that continuity with the previous state is largely preserved.[1] It is the second difficulty—confusion of aspects which are really separate, as in the case of the anima—which seems the more serious handicap to thinking. Jung's supporters might wish to make the point that the appropriateness of any set of concepts depends in part upon the field in which it is being used: in the field of psychiatry and psychotherapy, or any other dealing with whole persons, it is necessary to employ broad concepts such as would be quite unsuited to the purpose of laboratory analysis. Furthermore, it might be said that later psychoanalytical writers, notably Klein, and following Klein, Fairbairn, Scott and Winnicott, have approached the Jungian type of conceptualization with their theories of 'internal objects'—defined by Fairbairn as endopsychic structures other than the ego-structure with which the ego-structure has a relationship comparable to a relationship with a person in external reality.[2] To these arguments two answers can be given. First, from the point of view of objectively directed thinking there is a considerable difference between such terms as shadow, animus, wise old man, etc., with their emotive overtones, and the more matter-of-fact language of these later writers. Not that there is no place for terms of the kind that Jung has used. There is indeed some evidence that his accounts may fit the need of certain patients for expression very well, and that mythology and folklore, as he puts it, may be 'a treasure house . . . from which the doctor can draw helpful parallels and enlightening comparisons for the purpose of calming and clarifying a consciousness that is all at sea.'[3] 'Joanna Field' in her book *Experiment in Leisure* speaks of the significance that she herself found in the symbolism of the alchemists:

> 'I was particularly interested in the phrase—"Fire of the Sages", and in the fact that all the processes of the Great Work were carried on in a special closed receptacle to which great importance was attached. For images of this kind had often come into my mind when trying to describe processes of concentration, long before I had heard anything at all about alchemy. I had felt my thought to be a glowing crucible and the process

[1] *Psych. and Religion*, new ed. p. 166.
[2] 'Observations in Defence of the Object-Relations Theory of the Personality.' *Brit. J. Med. Psychol.*, XXVIII, 1955; p. 145.
[3] *Psych. and Alchemy*, p. 33.

of becoming concentrated in order to find forms of expression had seemed like a gradual raising of inner fires. Images of fiery vessels held me with a curious power. . . . Another alchemical image which interested me particularly was a process called sometimes corruption or dissolution or blackness. It reminded me now of the depression and emptiness that so often came upon me before I could begin to raise the inner fires of concentration.'[1]

However, a distinction which Marjorie Brierley makes between the language of the consulting room and that of science may clarify the problem. Reviewing the work of the Kleinian writers, who are themselves apt, she thinks, to lose sight of the distinction, she points out that,

'The work of psycho-analysts is carried on almost entirely in terms of perceptual experience. We recognize the necessity of this when we say that theory and theoretical formulations have little or no place in interpretations to patients. On the whole, we are less vividly alive to the corresponding conclusion that perceptual terms have little place in theory. Theory is primarily concerned with generalization from the particulars of the consulting-room. These particulars are, indeed, our data and also to a great extent our ultimate criteria, but theory itself is a body of concepts and should be expressed in the language of abstraction. Terms such as "ego" and "object" have no appropriate place in the consulting-room. What happens there happens in terms of "I", "you", "he", "she", "it", and "they", and is dealt with in these specific and personal terms, the terms in which we lead our ordinary lives. But personal terms have no authentic place in general theory.'[2]

The error is not merely a linguistic one, but may result in a seriously confused view of the real events, since in psychological as in physical medicine the same perceptual account may accompany conditions that need careful differentiation and quite different treatment. A second point is that the object-relations school, together with other psychoanalytical groups, gives very close attention to the earliest phases of childhood development, and has been largely responsible for pushing reconstruction back to infancy. The division of the Freudian oral period into an early sucking and a later biting stage, first made by Karl Abraham, is continued—the depressive position in psycho-pathology being attributed to unresolved conflict in the later oral phase ('to suck or to bite—to love, or to destroy by hate'), while the schizoid position is associated with the early oral phase

---

[1] *Experiment in Leisure*, pp. 157 *et seq.* London: Chatto & Windus.
[2] *Trends in Psycho-Analysis*, p. 66. London: Hogarth Press, 1951.

('to suck or not to suck—to love or not to love'). It might be argued that this kind of reconstruction is outside the predominantly descriptive and therapeutic tasks that Jung has set himself. As Progoff puts it, Jung 'is content to leave to others the implications of variations in nursing, toilet training, and other developmental tasks of childhood. His interest centers on the adult who, in one way or another, has mastered life's demands for nourishment, elimination, locomotion, speech, occupation, marriage and social relations. What follows next?'[1] Unfortunately, we are entitled to question the conceptual utility of the hypothesis that Jung does introduce, if he has not first explored the very early years. For instance, a similarity has been pointed out by Michael Fordham between the child's fantasy of attacking the mother, destroying her and tearing out her insides, which the Kleinian school has stressed, and the mythological theme of the hero killing the dragon.[2] Is it useful, however, to invoke the collective unconscious to explain the latter, or is it sufficient to regard it as a secondary elaboration—no doubt carrying highly significant overtones of meaning—of the primary infantile experience? In the long run, too, the reconstructions of early infantile experience may be of therapeutic value, since if we know exactly where a lack has occurred, it may be easier to remedy it, and in general to decide more coherently, What next? In practice, members of the Jungian school do not ignore the past history of their patients, even if they do not carry their investigations so far as the Kleinians, and there is some reason to think that they themselves are feeling the need for a more adequate account. Erich Neumann, after saying that psychoanalysis regards man essentially as a being who must be understood in terms of his personal history, while analytical psychology has shifted the emphasis from the temporal and personal to the transpersonal and timeless, then continues: 'For us who, a generation later, can take our stand on the sum total of Jung's discoveries and experiences, the task must surely be to combine the aspects of the personal and the transpersonal, the temporal and genetic and the timeless, which have grown too far apart, in an altered picture of man and his development.'[3] One contribution to this task is a paper by Plaut, in which a distinction is

---

[1] *Op. cit.*, p. xvi.   [2] *Life of Childhood*, p. 7.
[3] Neumann, E., 'The Significance of the Genetic Aspect for Analytical Psychology.' *J. of Analytical Psychol.*, Vol. IV, No. 2, July 1959; pp. 125–37 (p. 126).

made between zonal ego elements and a central ego nucleus. Interpreting infantile experience Plaut suggests that during feeding the sum-total of an infant's awareness lies in his mouth; in this state he is unable to distinguish between mouth and nipple, let alone between himself and the mother, and neither space nor time is apprehended— a state of wholeness which may be the forerunner of later, more differentiated experiences of the self. But during the periods when the infant is neither feeding nor sleeping he develops responses which indicate that he can also be aware of what is happening around and in him. To this capacity, independent of zonal excitation, Plaut ascribes the formation of a central ego nucleus, able to anticipate situations and experience fear and hope. An important function of the nucleus is the creation of an ego-boundary, integrating the component parts of the ego in such a way that the ego can distinguish between itself and others, and between the inner and the outer world. However, this nucleus is extremely vulnerable to adverse influences. If the relations between the zonal ego elements and the ego nucleus are disturbed, if, for instance, the experience of wholeness remains exclusively linked with a zonal ego element, a pseudo or emergency ego is likely to develop, which can control archetypal situations, checking destructive potential, but without enabling any fruitful relationship between ego and archetype to become established. This account, while retaining the concept of the archetype without, perhaps, linking it very fully with the rest, points toward an increasing rapprochement between analytical psychology and psychoanalysis itself.[1]

Before continuing with our other topics—the opposites, mental energy and psychological types—let us review what has so far been said about the collective unconscious and the archetypes. The collective unconscious has been criticized on account of a blanket quality which at times obscures differences in favour of similarities; much of what Jung has to say about its mode of thought has been tied rather closely to the assumption, influenced by nineteenth-century evolutionary doctrine, of identity with or very great similarity between childhood, primitive, psychotic and dream thinking, and very little consideration has been given to the part played by cultural and developmental factors in the production of its dominant themes

---

[1] 'Hungry Patients: Reflections on Ego Structure.' *J. of Analytical Psychol.*, Vol. IV, No. 2, July 1959; pp. 161-8

or archetypes. Nevertheless, it has become clear that some form of non-logical thinking, such as Jung describes, takes place, and the possibility cannot be ruled out that it has constructive functions. While we have felt that Jung has been too ready to bypass the implications of the Freudian view of symbolism, it has seemed also that other aspects of symbol formation may be unknown to the patient and therefore in need of investigation by special methods; and in his archetypal figures, for all their neglect of developmental factors, Jung has apparently anticipated the internal objects theories of psychoanalysis of the present day. Are there, then, any other meanings which have been attached to the collective unconscious, or any other concepts which it covers?

One possibility is that Jung with the collective unconscious has been endeavouring to break away from the narrowness and intensity of the psychoanalytical situation, in which, as Trigant Burrow puts it, 'there is the close, private, specialized relationship of one individual to another . . . a personal situation of mutual secrecy'.[1] Jung himself writes of stepping 'out of your narrow, stuffy, personal corner into the wide realm of the collective psyche, into the healthy and natural matrix of the human mind, into the very soul of humanity'.[2] H. G. Baynes, similarly, finds that 'As soon as we have admitted the hypothesis of a fundamental impersonal psyche upon which our personal psyche rests, the facts of our inner life assume a perspective which is not only convincing to the reason but deeply satisfying to feeling.'[3] For analyst as well as patient there are advantages: 'To those of us whose *métier* it is to try to understand the activities of the unconscious in the lives of our patients, it is refreshing to open our sails to a wide impersonal breeze.'[4] Others have tried to avoid or counteract onesidedness by means of group therapy; but here, as well as in more definite ways, it may have happened that the evolutionary thinking of the nineteenth century led Jung away from a social solution toward a biological substitute. An additional factor which may have caused the Jungian school to lean toward the 'collective' or 'impersonal' material is the difficulty, which they seem to have felt keenly, of making personal material public. Baynes, again, expresses this quite clearly. The reader will appreciate, he says, that it is objectionable, if

[1] *The Social Basis of Consciousness*, p. 234. New York: Harcourt, Brace & Co. 1927.
[2] *Practice of Psychotherapy*, p. 35.   [3] *Mythology of the Soul*, p. 35.
[4] *Analytical Psychology and the English Mind*, p. 17.

not ethically impossible, to disclose intimate material—even, he thinks, when the patient himself has given his consent. The difficulty would be insurmountable, were it not that the causes of morbid processes, in mind as well as body, are general and can be presented impersonally. 'Even though its forms of expression are distinctly individual, the impersonal material, which is the true object of our study, can and should be treated from a general standpoint.'[1]

A second possibility, involving the concept of 'depth' in mental life, will be put forward tentatively. One of the difficulties in describing and explaining mental processes is, of course, the necessity of using terms which were developed originally for more practical and immediately utilitarian purposes. Exactly what, for instance, should be understood by the phrase 'deeper levels' when applied to mental life? On the one hand there is the psychoanalytical interpretation of 'more inaccessible', and, usually, prior in development, requiring to be brought into consciousness through the specialized technique of free association. On the other hand there is the philosophical interpretation of 'having more meaning or significance'—either cosmic significance or significance for human life.

Now suppose it is agreed that the facts of infantile sexuality are undeniable, and that the exploration of its ramifications, pre-genital as well as genital, the opposing forces and the mechanisms they utilize, will throw much light on normal personality development, besides making the difference between mental health and mental illness in at any rate a proportion of neurotic cases. Even so, there may be a feeling on the part of some readers that Freudian discoveries do not contribute greatly to the understanding of the deeper levels of mental life in the second, philosophic, sense. As those who have experienced such a feeling might say, reading Freud is in one respect rather like reading the novels of Jane Austen, little though either might care for the comparison. That is, the works of both possess a similar clarity, a similar working out of point after point, once the basic assumptions are accepted—and since the assumptions in both cases function admirably within the world that opens up before us, there may seem, as we read, no ground for doubting them. However, just as it is, after all, possible to doubt, let us say, the assumption that three hundred pounds a year in the eighteenth century was not a marriageable income, when one stops to think, so it is possible to

[1] *Mythology of the Soul*, p. 6.

doubt whether the depths of the personality, in the second sense, are really plumbed, once we know how it is that a young lady has not been able to take pleasure in her birthday presents, or why an unmarried man living with his mother has given way to exaggerated fits of weeping at the prospect of her being afflicted with a mortal illness—and it is this type of information which Freud often gives in 'making conscious the most hidden recesses of the mind'.[1] The Jungians evidently feel a difficulty here, their argument being that values and aspirations connected with them can become, and in the mature personality do become, orienting points to an extent that counterbalances the primitive experiences. As Jung says himself, 'What stands behind sexuality or the instinct to power is the *attitude to sexuality and power*.'[2] Values, that is, are 'deeper' in the sense of going beyond the instinctual drives and determining the individual's mode of handling them. Holding such a view, a writer who had had contact with the psychoanalytical school, and whose ideas were formed in the 'biological century', might become rather concretistic in his interpretation of depth, saying, in effect, that we must 'dig deeper' for the source of values and creative inspiration than it is necessary to dig for childhood material on the Oedipus complex, etc., and hence that we must work back to buried layers of thought deposited by the experience of the ancestors. This suggestion is not inconsistent with the trend of Jung's work, and one reference—to 'the old pagan in ourselves; that piece of eternal unspoiled nature and natural beauty which lies unconscious but living within us . . . who is . . . the bearer of that beauty which we elsewhere unavailingly seek'[3]—comes very near it.

A third possibility is that we have not quite done justice to Jung's view of the collective unconscious as 'the psychic event that mediates between consciousness and the physiological functioning of the body'.[4] That is, in his use of the principles of compensation, or homeostasis, and maturation, e.g. in the individuation process, Jung is implying that there is a continuity of living process from the physiological to the psychological, and that among the processes which lie outside the range of conscious awareness but nonetheless have significance for conscious life and personality development, are some which can be compared to the regeneration of bone or skin

[1] *Collected Papers*, Vol. III, p. 94. [2] *Psych. Types*, p. 271.
[3] *Psych. Types*, p. 110. [4] *Integ. of Person.*, p. 224; *supra*, p. 91.

tissue. Or, as H. G. Baynes has put it, 'In a developing personality the growing point is the centre of intense formative activity. Therefore we can speak of continual embryology in the realm of the psyche.'[1] The same interpretation has recently been given by Dr. Murray Jackson. The physical organism, he writes, has its maturational and defensive repair processes, its compensatory reactions, its inflammation and immunological responses. Why should it be so difficult to envisage the psyche as having similar functions of repair and growth? Most of Jung's concepts are large-scale or macroscopic ones. 'They may be of little help in the unravelling of the detailed dynamisms of behaviour and they tell us next to nothing of the intricacies of the defensive manoeuvres of the ego which are clearly illuminated by psycho-analytic theory.' On the other hand, they do offer a view of neurosis which 'seems to me to bring psychological disorders more into line with organic disorders, however different they may be in other respects'.[2]

In Jung's handling of the opposites the molar quality of his concepts seems again to reach blanketing proportions. The pairs to which he chiefly refers—conscious-unconscious, masculinity-femininity, nature-spirit—are so complex that they can hardly be taken as ultimate units of mental life, nor does he give guidance as to the relation of the separate pairs to one another or their mode of operation, e.g. under what circumstances one member of a pair 'passes over into' its opposite, which at times seems to happen almost automatically, and under what circumstances a synthesis is reached. His view of mental energy as generated from the tension between them perhaps lays too much emphasis on conflict as a source of energy, although conflict of an impersonal nature, and would seem to be only one of the possible mechanisms at work, unless the opposites are widened in such a way as to include under 'the object' all stimuli impinging on the subject, or experiencing organism, all reactions then being subsumed under the heading of tension between them. This Jung seems at times inclined to do, thereby producing another blanketing conception. In itself, the concept of a general fund of psychic energy is more workable, though once more, most clinicians, whatever modifications they

[1] *Mythology of the Soul*, p. 144.
[2] 'Jung's "archetypes" and Psychiatry.' *J. Ment. Sci*, Vol. 106, No. 445, 1960; p. 1522.

may themselves introduce, do not feel that they can afford to neglect in favour of a purely general account the impulses centring round the oral and anal zones which will inevitably have significance in the early stages of personality development. There is perhaps more of a tendency also to think in psycho-physical rather than purely or mainly psychic terms. For instance, Gardner Murphy writes:

'All points in the body are at all times the site of chemical reaction, of energy changes that pass, gradient-wise, in many directions. The nervous system . . . is itself the site of many tensions . . . the brain, even under deep ether anesthesia and pocketed off from the viscera and muscles, shows its own continuous discharges. . . . Thus every cell in the body is an initiator of motivation.'[1]

As we saw, mental energy is closely connected with Jung's other major concept, psychological types, since its predominating direction, inward or outward, is taken as their basis. In reviewing this concept several questions come to mind concerning mode of presentation, methods used, consistency of the main formulations and steps which have been or can be taken to advance the study further.

Some criticism, as always, may be made of the mode of presentation. For instance, in his main work on psychological types Jung introduces new material even as late as the concluding chapter, 'Definitions'—in particular, a distinction between 'active' and 'passive' forms of introversion and extraversion: 'Introversion is *active*, when the subject *wills* a certain seclusion in face of the object; it is *passive* when the subject is unable to restore again to the object the libido which is streaming back from it.'[2] Similarly, 'One should speak of an *active* extraversion when deliberately willed, and of a *passive* extraversion when the object compels it, i.e. attracts the interest of the subject of its own accord, even against the latter's intention.'[3] It would seem that the active and the passive types of introversion and extraversion might represent radically different conditions, and that their ramifications might have been explored more fully and the reader acquainted with them earlier.

One of the methods used is of course the literary and historical—a method which shows that a given concept or something like it has been used by various writers, so that a case exists for further study, without by itself being able to establish it. Jung also gives a résumé of his clinical impressions, though not, however, case material. From

[1] *Personality*, p. 88.   [2] *Psych. Types*, p. 567.   [3] *Psych. Types*, p. 543.

what we know so far, it would be surprising if no inconsistencies or vagueness were found in the conclusions that he sets before us. For instance, when he speaks of 'the subject', and 'the object', we presently notice more than one meaning allotted to those terms. At one time 'the subject' is used as equivalent to the 'I', e.g. 'cognition must have a subject, for there exists no knowledge, and therefore, for us, no world where "I know" has not been said'.[1] At another it is said to include *more* than the 'I', and in the definitions it is even the unconscious.[2] The object, too, is sometimes a specific object but more often the entire outer world. Again, the generalizations, determination by object or by subject, seem to cover states of mind which are really very different. For determination by the object Jung gives the following examples: 'St. Augustine says, "I would not believe in the Evangels if the authority of the Church did not compel it." A daughter says, "I could not think something that would be displeasing to my father". . . . Someone has said, "One need not be ashamed of a thing if nobody knows about it".'[3] As contrasting examples of determination by the subject it is added: 'A man of this type might say, "I know I could give my father the greatest pleasure if I did thus and so, but nevertheless I have a different idea about it"; . . . Another typical example is . . . "Everybody believes I could do something, but nothing is more certain to me than the fact that I can do nothing".[4] But how much has the person who says, "I could not think something that would be displeasing to my father" really got in common with the person who says, "One need not be ashamed of a thing if nobody knows about it"? Of the first case it might be said, insufficient emancipation from earliest ties, of the second, insufficient internalization of social norms, i.e. in the one case there appears to be an immaturity of super-ego formation, and in the other a relative lack of super-ego formation. In the case of the man who knows that he could give his father pleasure but has other ideas, and the man who is convinced he can do nothing, in spite of other people's good opinions, the information which we have been given is insufficient to lead to a clear-cut suggestion, but it easily might be that differences in ego-strength, degree of socialization, etc. would have more relevance for the understanding of their behaviour than the generalization, determination by the subject, from which,

[1] *Ibid.*, p. 473.   [2] *Ibid.*, p. 591.
[3] *Contribs.*, pp. 301–2.   [4] *Ibid., loc. cit.*

by comparison, content seems to have been largely removed. Such reclassifications according to psychoanalytically derived theory, to which many psychological workers would be driven, brings to mind the argument that, clinically, a typology is most useful if based upon a detailed study of development. A somewhat similar conceptualiza- tion, of peripheral significance for the theory of types, but relevant, perhaps, in illustration of Jung's mode of thought, is his grouping of the two beliefs, Christ's 'essential similarity' to God and Tran- substantiation, as extraverted, since they 'lay the accent on the sensuous and purely perceptible' and are 'the extreme concretization of a symbol' respectively, while the opposing beliefs, Christ's 'com- plete identity' with God and Communion as a commemorative feast, are classified as introverted, because more abstract, views. In Church history, however, these pairs have been differently united—those who hold that Christ is identical with God may or may not hold also the doctrine of Transubstantiation, but those who hold that Christ is 'essentially similar' to God have never accepted Transubstantia- tion. It seems, therefore, that this material too could be reclassified— this time according to the more syncretic or more logical nature of the concepts involved.[1]

It can also be argued that aside from the ambiguities in Jung's use of the terms subject and object, the formulation itself, inward or outward turning of libido, gives an oversimplified picture. As Gardner Murphy says, 'He who has the gift of response is able to use it either inwardly or outwardly.' Or, 'to put the matter more broadly, there is no necessary compensatory role by which a surplus of affect for any one component in one's world automatically robs another component. There may well be a general tendency for each to increase in value with the rest. . . . We may find that the individual discovers a means of maintaining a balance between the *self* and *other*, or a characteristic way of losing it; but it does not follow that introversion implies the want of extraversion, or vice versa.'[2] Con- tinuing this idea, we might imagine that the difference between those described as introverts and those described as extraverts would often lie at least as much in the particular aspects of the external world by which their interest is aroused, and the manner in which it is ex-

---

[1] A further description—that of Freudian psychology as extraverted and Adlerian as introverted—seems again unduly molar—if not positively misleading, in view of the stress laid by Adler on social adaptation.

[2] *Personality*, p. 597.

pressed, as in any straight out inward or outward turning of libido. If so, a formulation such as the Gestalt-influenced 'patterns of integration' would be more appropriate than the nineteenth-century 'determination by subject or by object'. The replacement of one formulation by another which may take certain facts more fully into account is, however, a normal process in the development of theory; what is perhaps less to be expected is the degree of confusion which seems to lurk in Jung's initial concept.

Another portion of Jung's work which theoretically seems vulnerable is his description of the functions—thinking, feeling, sensation and intuition—and their mode of operation. For example, the chief meaning assigned to the feeling function is, as we have seen, that of valuation; this function is rational, since 'values in general are bestowed according to the laws of reason'.[1] Now the latter statement is far from being self-evident; if, however, we accept it, would it not be possible to speak of the application of thinking to a certain kind of subject matter, instead of holding that 'thinking belongs to a category quite incommensurable with feeling'?[2] A subsidiary meaning which Jung has introduced into the feeling function, i.e. very slight affects, may also be examined. Every feeling, Jung says, on attaining a certain strength releases physical innervations and becomes an affect. 'On practical grounds, however, it is advisable to discriminate affect from feeling, since feeling can be a disposable function, whereas affect is usually not so. . . . Pronounced affects, i.e. affects accompanied by violent physical innervation, I do not assign to the province of feeling but to the realm of the sensation function.'[3] But the assigning of slight affects to the feeling function and more pronounced affects to sensation seems an arbitrary division, making a distinction at some point unspecified where there is really a continuum. The relations between intuition and sensation give rise to much the same problem. Jung's predominating view is that in the intuitive individual 'Thinking, feeling and sensation are relatively repressed; of these, sensation is the one principally affected, because, as the conscious function of sense, it offers the greatest obstacle to intuition.'[4] And yet, if sensation covers all perception by means of the sense organs, and intuition is perception by way of the unconscious, and if at the same time

---

[1] *Psych. Types*, p. 545.
[3] *Ibid.*, p. 522–3.
[2] *Psych. Types*, p. 545.
[4] *Ibid.*, p. 462.

there is a less hard and fast division between conscious and unconscious in Jung's psychology than in the psychology of Freud, it might be expected that the two functions would shade into one another. Jung himself, indeed, makes—again in the Definitions—a further distinction between *concrete* and *abstract* forms of intuition, 'according to the degree of participation on the part of sensation'.[1] A more radical objection, perhaps, is made by Philp, who argues that the four functions are too static. The traditional psychological classification has been that of cognition, feeling and conation. If cognition and feeling are included as functions, why, then, should conation be omitted?[2] It may be wondered, too, whether Jung has adequately surveyed all the modes of operation of the functions, and their interaction with the attitudes. Is it true, for instance, that the differentiation of one function necessarily leads to inferiority of the rest, and that a second or third function can only be differentiated in some measure at the expense of the superior function? May it not happen sometimes that an apparently submerged function is called into play through intensification of the predominating function itself, and not at its expense, e.g. the emotional accessibility or reactivity of the introverted thinking type—presumably assigned to feeling or sensation—may lie in an appeal to intellectual life. Or changes may occur in mental set, according to the sphere of life in which the individual is operating, e.g. emotional accessibility or reactivity in the introverted thinker may even be 'consciously disposable' in the sense that the individual will order his conduct in accordance with it, but concentrated on a comparatively small number of people in domestic life. These difficulties, together indeed with Jung's willingness to classify so many different states of mind under the heading of determination by subject or by object, can be taken as practical illustrations of the argument that Jung is apt to be sketchy in his treatment of conation, and this lack of interest in the forces lying behind behaviour is probably connected with, or part of the same attitude to phenomena as, his lack of interest in the earlier phases of personality development. At the same time, it is possible that the critical approach does not quite do justice to the significance of the functions as orienting points in psychotherapy, enabling the analyst to direct the patient's attention to certain capacities which an integrated personality should have at its com-

---

[1] *Psych. Types*, p. 568.　　　[2] *Op. cit.*, p. 73.

mand—the power of logical thought, readily accessible sympathies co-ordinated by values, ability to perceive and respond to sense impressions without the grosser types of distortion or neglect, and ability also to deal with more complex situations through the synthesizing of unconscious cues.

Since in psychology as a whole it is the attitudes, introversion-extraversion, which have engaged attention, we will turn to these. Here, in spite of the blanket quality of the terms subject and object and occasional discrepancies, a fairly consistent picture has emerged of the introvert as characterized by 'a defective relation to the object'—indifference to, aversion from, or fear of being over-whelmed by direct experience; he therefore dislikes change and is concerned more with individuals than groups ('His whole mentality is one of depth and intensity') and is apt to suffer from feelings of inferiority and distrust arising from a sense of being out of touch with his environment; on the other hand, although his productivity is limited and he is often rigid and inaccessible to the ideas of others, this partial independence also gives him the possibility of being creative. Similarly we have seen the extravert as one who is interested in the outside world, especially in the events and visible objects of the immediate environment, is friendly and accessible, always concerned with the life of the community and possessing the self-assurance that comes from the knowledge of having it behind him, but insufficiently independent to become creative. In some such form Jung's extravert and introvert, like Adler's inferiority complex and the Oedipus complex of the Freudian school, have become familiar far beyond the world of professional psychology, and in describing trends and personalities in a practical way almost everyone would feel handicapped without these terms. The problem then is, to introduce more exactitude into the analysis—to determine, for instance, how far extraversion and introversion represent unitary traits, or single modes of integration, and how far they are convenient shorthand terms for one or more clusters of traits commonly though not invariably associated. Concerning the methods to be employed in studies of the types there has been a good deal of controversy—the Germans, as Vernon pointed out years ago, having preferred the method of clinical observation, hoping in that way to preserve the organized form quality of the personality, the Americans and British seeking to establish statistical trends with the help of comparatively simple tests. The disadvantage of the first method is of course that each investigator develops his own broad typology, similar to but not identical with those of his predecessors, and does not go beyond the global level, while the second method, in spite of its apparent numerical precision, still relies on the insight—often inferior to that of the clinician—with which the test items are selected.[1] One of the more interesting investigations is that in H. A. Murray's well-known book, *Explorations in Personality*. Combining paper and pencil tests, the psychiatric interview, projective techniques and laboratory situations, he and his collaborators worked out a classification of 'needs', one application of which was the breaking down of introversion into several syndromes, described as the passive introvert, the sensitive, avoidant introvert, the reserved inviolate introvert, the abstractive imaginative introvert, and the contracted perseverative introvert, with varying correlations between them.[2] A classical questionnaire study is that of the Guilfords, who, administering a thirty-item introversion-extraversion questionnaire to 1,000 students, extracted three main factors, D (depression), S (seclusiveness), and T (thinking), making up the introverted picture, with the opposite composite, sociability, cheerfulness, and lack of meditative thinking as the extravert.[3] In recent years H. J. Eysenck has regarded introversion/extraversion as sufficiently stable and unitary to be treated as *dimensions* of personality. Presenting a considerable amount of experimental and test data, he believes that Jung's hypothesis concerning the relationship of extraversion and hysteria, introversion and psychasthenia, or, as he describes it, dysthymia, can be established, and connects both with the rate of development of inhibition, i.e. persons who develop inhibition rapidly are predisposed to extraverted patterns of behaviour and hysterico-psychopathic disorders in the event of neurotic breakdown; persons who develop inhibition slowly are predisposed to introversion and dysthymia. For a full appreciation of the work of Eysenck and his school a high degree of statistical competence is needed; the less statistically minded can, however, follow certain

[1] Vernon, P. E., 'The American v. the German Methods of Approach to the Study of Temperament and Personality.' *Brit. J. Psychol.*, Vol. XXIV, Pt. 2, 1933–4; pp. 156–77.

[2] Murray, H. A., *Explorations in Personality*, pp. 232–42. New York: Oxford University Press, 1938.

[3] Eysenck, H. J., *Structure of Human Personality*, pp. 103–10. London: Methuen, 1953.

doubts which have been raised as to whether the evidence, especially that regarding inhibition, is as convincing as Eysenck would have his readers believe.[1] But whatever the outcome there may be, for discussion of Jung's work it is the main outline of the situation which is most important. That is, Jung with his theory of psychological types has produced a concept which has become not only a household word but also a standard topic of investigation for professional psychologists. None of the detailed work of verification or disproof, however, has been carried out by Jung himself or by his followers.

This brings us to the final question of the chapter, namely, to what extent can Jung's subsidiary claim, of scientific status, be accepted? Let us first consider what is meant by science. At least two writers in the clinical field itself have recently given definitions. 'The essence of science', says Dr. Marjorie Brierley, 'is its realistic mode of approach to the object of study. Any subject can therefore be studied scientifically and any technique can claim to be regarded as scientific which devises adequate checks and standards of probability suited to its individual field.'[2] *'The picture of reality provided by science,'* says W. R. D. Fairbairn, *'is an intellectual construct representing the fruits of an attempt to describe the various phenomena of the universe, in as coherent and systematic manner as the limitations of human intelligence permit, by means of the formulation of general laws established by inductive inference under conditions of maximum detachment and objectivity on the part of the scientific observer.'*[3]

So far as intellectual constructs are concerned, we could not, even in the exposition, avoid referring to the lack of clarity and the contradictions in Jung's writings, and these impressions have been increased in the discussion. Certainly Jung does not seem to have succeeded in putting into practice the view which, at least on one occasion, he expresses, that in psychology the 'precision which exact measurements lend to the observed fact can be replaced only by the precision of the concept'.[4] Turning back to such a passage as that in which he extols the value of 'the magnificently affirmative "both-and"', we may feel with Fairbairn that the chief difficulties arise

---

[1] See Storms, L. H. and Sigal, J. J., 'Eysenck's Personality Theory with Special Reference to *The Dynamics of Anxiety and Hysteria.' Brit. J. Med. Psychol.,* Vol. XXXI, 1958; pp. 228–46.

[2] *Trends in Psycho-Analysis,* p. 155.

[3] 'Observations in Defence of the Object-Relations Theory of the Personality.' *Brit. J. Med. Psychol.,* Vol. XXVIII, Pts. 2 and 3, 1955; pp. 144-56 (p. 154).

[4] *Psych. Types,* p. 519.

not from rushing on to new hypotheses, as we are sometimes asked to believe, but from the abandoning of the laws of rational discourse out of which science itself has evolved.[1] Perhaps it should be suggested that in spite of passages in which Jung appears to recognize the importance of hypothesis, he is to be regarded not as a theoretical, but as a primarily descriptive, scientist. Some of his doubts about going beyond description have been noted,[2] and other passages of similar import can be found. For instance, in his *Practice of Psychotherapy* he declares that his main concern is to establish facts. 'How these facts are named and what further interpretation is then placed upon them is of secondary importance. Natural science is not a science of words and ideas, but of facts.'[3] We ourselves have thought that the descriptive rather than hypothesizing bent could be taken as a feature common to Jung's earlier and later work.[4] Whether the distinction can be strictly maintained is, however, doubtful. It may be that the descriptive element in science was more strongly stressed at the beginning of the century than it is at present, i.e. in our own generation there may be more awareness that the relation between fact and hypothesis is two-way—not only does the gathering of facts confirm, refute or modify hypotheses, but the kind of hypothesis which the investigator brings to his subject, e.g. its clarity or vagueness, will affect his gathering of the facts. Unless he is satisfied to remain with an overall impression, a sense of totality almost as much emotional as cognitive, it is necessary to ask specific questions—he cannot leave Nature to 'answer out of her fullness' as Jung has suggested.[5] For this reason Jung's attitude to experiment in his later work seems too extreme; even in such complicated fields as social and personality psychology the use of experiment, or often, strictly speaking, controlled observation, can bring more precision.[6] But still more vital is the question of achieving 'maximum detachment', of devising 'adequate checks and standards of objectivity'. It is there that the special difficulty lies. It would surely not be suggested for a moment that Jung had based his reports on data which did not come to him in the course of therapeutic work, but over and above the communication problems which analytical psychology shares with psychoanalysis and related schools, e.g. the

[1] *Supra*, pp. 89–90.   [2] *Supra*, p. 84.
[3] *Practice of Psychotherapy*, p. 317.   [4] *Supra*, p. 84.
[5] *The Interpretation of Nature and the Psyche*, p. 50. New York: Bollingen Foundation, 1955.   [6] *Infra*, p. 176.

difficulty of allowing for personal bias in the eliciting of information, or of putting a full set of observations before other qualified investigators, it seems to be just the realism of approach referred to by Brierley and Fairbairn which is often lacking. A clinical example is that of the ethnologically educated patient with the dream of nymphs—omitted from the revised translation of Jung's works, but relevant as an illustration of the working of his thought. The principle of synchronicity seems to show the same lack: no attempt is made to discover how far the meaning attached to the series of acausally connected events springs from associations supplied by the perceiver.[1] In addition there is the emotive style of the reporting with which the reader has so often to contend.

For these reasons the more academically minded psychologist is likely to think of Jung in his later work as a pre-scientific rather than scientific investigator, realizing, however, that he may have more than this to offer. Indeed, had it not been for the claims put forward at times by Jung himself and by his followers, it might have seemed preferable to pass more rapidly to other aspects; Theodor Merz's remark, of Goethe, comes to mind: 'Such natures are wronged whenever one tries to construct from their scattered expressions, by hook or by crook, a rounded philosophical system; we can ever attempt only an indefinite indication of the essence of their views.'[2] The direction in which the 'more' of Jung's contributions can be sought may become clearer if the *limitations* of science are considered. In the first place, science deals with abstractions, not with immediate experience, in which, as we have seen, Jung is specially interested. In the second place—a point which Jung does not always seem to grasp[3]—it is detached from values and emotions

---

[1] For instance, Jung reports that one Friday while engaged on a study of fish symbolism, he found that he had fish for lunch, that he made a note of an inscription which referred to fish, that a former patient brought him some impressive pictures of fish which she had painted, that in the evening he was shown a piece of embroidery with fish-like monsters on it, and that on the following morning another patient came to him with a dream of fish. He adds that only one of the persons involved knew anything about his current interest. (*The Interpretation of Nature and the Psyche*, p. 14.) Confronted with this series of happenings, the critic may wonder whether the selective influence of perception and recall should be taken into account, and whether it would have been taken in account by Jung also in his earlier work.

[2] *Op. cit.*, Vol. IV, p. 573.

[3] See, e.g. *Two Essays*, new ed. p. 146: 'My conscience as an investigator is concerned not with quantity but with quality. Nature is aristocratic, and one person of value outweighs ten lesser ones.'

Chapter VI

THE JUNGIAN THERAPY AND
RELATED INSIGHTS

Many of Jung's ideas which can be stated as independent insights, and do not necessarily stand or fall with the theories already summarized, are found also in his critique of Freud during the Intermediate Period, i.e. his reinterpretation of the Oedipus material and affirmation of the prospective significance of dreams and neurotic symptoms, and the purposiveness of mental life, the innateness of a drive toward socialization and morality, the need for a *Weltanschauung*, the importance of finding the individual way of the patient, and the significance of the patient-physician relationship, involving the total personality of both, together with other points such as the belief that psychic inertia rather than fixation to infantile pleasures is the cause of the neurotic's clinging to childhood, and that sexuality can be used as a means of expressing non-sexual needs. On the other hand, a considerable amount of fresh material is given for methods and practical procedures, and although essential ideas may be found in outline at the earlier stage, the impression is that Jung does not stand exactly where he was at the time of writing the *Theory of Pyschoanalysis* but has continued to work over his thoughts in a way that expresses his point of view more fully. Here the obscurity of his writing no longer forms a stumbling block, since most of the questions he discusses are handled as simply as before.

The division of the therapeutic process which Jung most commonly employs is that of the analytic and reductive stage, where causes are explored, and the prospective and synthetic stage, where trends for the future are considered, but in one of his essays[1] the two stages are

---

[1] 'Problems of Modern Psychotherapy.' *Mod. Man*, pp. 32–62; *Practice oj Psychotherapy*, pp. 53–75.

141

sub-divided into four—confession, explanation or elucidation, education and transformation.

Therapy begins, he says in this essay, with the act of confession, including not only the patient's conscious recollections but the recovery of unconscious material. As formerly,[1] stress is laid on the value of confession in restoring the patient to full membership of the community. In small doses, and shared with an inner group, concealments may be beneficial, in preventing the individual from 'dissolving in the featureless flow of unconscious community life'.[2] But a secret kept purely to oneself acts like a psychic poison. Recovery of unconscious contents that have been repressed, i.e. concealed even from oneself, is not sufficient by itself, for the patient still continues in his state of isolation. It is only with the help of confession that he is able to throw himself into the arms of humanity, represented by the physician, and be 'freed at last from the burden of moral exile'.[3]

But through this very act of confession the patient is apt to be tied to the physician and to fall into a condition of childish dependence—unless indeed he is so fascinated by the hinterland of his own mind that he goes away 'bound to the unconscious' instead. Generally speaking, the second stage, explanation or elucidation, begins. It must be explained to the patient that this tie corresponds to the relation between father and child, or rather, that the patient projects on to the person of the physicians fantasies connected with the parents. In this essay, as often elsewhere, Jung writes as though both Freud and Adler were his guides in the explanatory stage. It is the great merit of Freud, he says, to have explained the incestuous elements in the patient's early fantasies, which are then transferred —though, as before, he thinks that Freud makes the mistake of speaking too much as though such fantasies were repressed from consciousness, instead of being, most probably, essentially unconscious from the outset. In another essay, however, it seems that Jung is unable to make up his mind about this component: the patient, he declares—and this is more in accordance with the general drift of his writings—is seeking not incest but 'the universal feeling of childhood innocence, the sense of security, of reciprocated

---

[1] *Supra*, p. 55.
[2] *Practice of Psychotherapy*, p. 56; *Mod. Man*, p. 36.
[3] *Ibid.*, p. 59; p. 41.

love, of trust, of faith',[1] and his regressive tendency only means that his development was one-sided and left important items of character and personality behind—'That is why he has to go back'.[2] Many cases, too, usually introverts, can be explained equally well or better by Adler's power principle.

But insight, however necessary, is not enough by itself: 'the crooked paths of a neurosis lead to as many obstinate habits, and . . . for all our insight these do not disappear until replaced by other habits.'[3] If the patient is sensitive, and able to draw independent conclusions, explanation may suffice; in a very large number of cases, however, 'The patient must be *drawn out* of himself into other paths, which is the true meaning of "education", and this can only be achieved by an educative will.'[4] Adler is particularly helpful in educating patients to social adaptation, but, Jung thinks, patients can be divided into two main groups, 'individualists with under-developed collective adaptation', and 'collective people with under-developed individuality'. It is patients in the latter group to whom Jung feels that he himself has most to offer. Following Indian teaching especially,[5] he considers that the basic facts of the psyche undergo a marked change in the course of life, 'so much so that we could almost speak of a psychology of life's morning and a psychology of its afternoon'.[6] The life of a young person is characterized by general expansion and striving toward concrete ends; his neurosis seems mainly to be an expression of shrinking back from such necessities. The life of an older person is characterized by a contraction of forces and curtailment of further growth; neurosis comes mainly from his clinging to an attitude appropriate to youth. Fully two thirds of his patients have been in the second half of life, and, as we have seen, it is these patients who are most likely to undergo a further process of development—though among some of Jung's followers at the present time there is less tendency to tie the development to any given age.[7]

The individuation process has been met already, and clearly a

[1] 'Some Aspects of Modern Psychotherapy.' *Practice of Psychotherapy*, p. 32.
[2] *Ibid.*, p. 33.
[3] 'Problems of Modern Psychotherapy.' *Practice of Psychotherapy*, p. 68.
[4] *Practice of Psychotherapy*, p. 68.
[5] See Zimmer, H., *Philosophies of India*, p. 44. New York: Bollingen Foundation, 1959.
[6] *Practice of Psychotherapy*, p. 39.
[7] See Martin, P. W., *Experiment in Depth*, p. 165: 'there is no uniformity about it. "Ripeness is all"; and a man or woman may be ripe in the early twenties, the late fifties, or perhaps never.'

relationship exists between it and the fourth stage, transformation, given in the paper on psychotherapy which we have been taking as a guide. For instance, in another paper dealing specifically with psychotherapy, Jung states that one of the criteria for giving up the analytical-reductive method and treating symbols anagogically is the appearance of mythological or archetypal contents.[1] However, just as in discussing individuation he spoke of every life as being at bottom the realization of a whole which, too, can be called individuation,[2] so now it seems that transformation is not confined to individuation in the sense of the full archetypal or symbolical experience, but includes as well a form of integration effected primarily by means of the patient-physician relationship. Perhaps—again interpolating, as in dealing with the individuation problem previously—we might suggest that in addition to the majority of people, who find sufficient integration by following the ways of their society more or less unthinkingly, others develop a more individualized personality of themselves, e.g. through devotion to an external cause or object, as Jung suggests in one place;[3] and that among those who do seek aid many are helped to a new synthesis by means of this relationship, without passing through experience of a more directly archetypal nature.

At any rate, Jung's conception of the patient-physician relationship is of considerable importance in his work. Especially in the later stages of therapy, when the infantile material is exhausted, the doctor's own personality takes on more significance. In this relationship, described as 'a personal one within the impersonal framework of professional treatment',[4] 'the man in the patient confronts the man in the doctor upon equal terms'.[5] No longer does the patient stand alone, 'but someone whom he trusts reaches out a hand, lending him moral strength to combat the tyranny of uncontrolled emotion. In this way the integrative powers of his conscious mind are reinforced until he is able once more to bring the rebellious affect under control.'[6] More than that:

---

[1] 'Principles of Practical Psychotherapy.' *Practice of Psychotherapy*, p. 20.
[2] *Supra*, p. 103.
[3] *Secret of the Golden Flower*, p. 89.
[4] *Practice of Psychotherapy*, p. 71; *Mod. Man*, p. 56.
[5] *Contribs.*, p. 292; *Practice of Psychotherapy*, p. 137 ('. . . the patient confronts the doctor upon equal terms.').
[6] *Practice of Psychotherapy*, p. 132; *Contribs.*, p. 286.

'By no device can the treatment be anything but the product of mutual influence, in which the whole being of the doctor as well as that of his patient plays its part. . . . For two personalities to meet is like mixing two different chemical substances: if there is any combination at all, both are transformed. In any effective psychological treatment the doctor is bound to influence the patient; but this influence can only take place if the patient has a reciprocal influence on the doctor. You can exert no influence if you are not susceptible to influence.'[1]

The procedure can be described as dialectical, a dialogue or discussion between two persons. Dialectic, Jung explains, was originally the art of conversation among the ancient philosophers, but very early it became the term for the process of creating new syntheses. 'A person is a psychic system which, when it affects another person, enters into reciprocal reaction with another psychic system.'[2] This becomes possible

'only if I give the other person a chance to play his hand to the full, unhampered by my assumptions. In this way his system is geared to mine and acts upon it. . . . In all circumstances the prime rule of dialectical procedure is that the individuality of the sufferer has the same value, the same right to exist, as that of the doctor, and consequently that every development in the patient is to be regarded as valid, unless of course it corrects itself of its own accord.'[3]

In other words, 'the therapist is no longer the agent of treatment but a fellow participant in a process of individual development.'[4] This means, in concrete terms, that not only questioning, but also answering, is demanded of the doctor—he 'must emerge from his anonymity and give an account of himself, just as he expects his patients to do.'[5] He must even 'give serious consideration to the possibility that in intelligence, sensibility, range and depth the patient's personality is superior to his own.'[6]

Jung is not unaware of the dangers of this kind of participation for the doctor. The unconscious changes which the patient brings about are well-known to many psychotherapists; their nature, he thinks, can best be conveyed by the old idea of the demon of sickness, according to which the sufferer can transmit his disease to a healthy person whose powers then subdue the demon, but not without impairment of well-being. He refers briefly to 'cases where, in dealing

---

[1] *Practice of Psychotherapy*, p. 71; *Mod. Man*, p. 57.
[2] *Practice of Psychotherapy*, p. 3.   [3] *Ibid.*, p. 5.
[4] *Ibid.*, p. 98.   [5] *Ibid.*, p. 18.   [6] *Ibid.*, p. 10.

with borderline schizophrenics, short psychotic attacks were actually "taken over", and during these moments it happened that the patients were feeling more than ordinarily well'.[1] The situation, he adds, is 'difficult and distressing for both parties; often the doctor is in much the same position as the alchemist who no longer knew whether he was melting the mysterious amalgam in the crucible or whether he was the salamander glowing in the fire'.[2] And yet 'A genuine participation, going right beyond professional routine, is absolutely imperative. . . . The doctor must go to the limit of his subjective possibilities, otherwise the patient will be unable to follow suit. Arbitrary limits are no use, only real ones.'[3] The remedy for the dangers, as before,[4] is that the doctor himself shall undergo analysis, in the wider sense also of facing whatever task he wishes the patient to face. For instance, he must become socially adapted, 'or, in the reverse case, appropriately non-adapted'.[5] In order to exercise his function constructively he must *be* the man through whom he wishes to influence others, and here an important aspect is the possession of 'avowable, credible, and defensible convictions which have proved their viability either by having resolved any neurotic dissociations of his own or by preventing them from arising'.[6] Perhaps it could be said that what Jung envisages in the patient-physician relationship is an introjection of or identification with the doctor figure, especially on the side of values. The patient 'suns himself, as it were, in the analyst's commonsense, poise, and normality'.[7]

As in the intermediate period the symbolic method is used extensively, modified now by the introduction of 'objective' and 'subjective' modes of interpretation. Interpretation is on the objective plane when the symbols are treated as representations of real objects, and on the subjective plane when every fragment of the dream is connected with the patient himself. For instance, a patient dreamt that a big crab seized her foot. Interpreted objectively, the crab is a friend who fastens on her in an unhealthy manner. Interpreted subjectively, the crab is her own untamed libido which makes the relationship possible. The objective mode is 'analytical and reductive', dissecting the dream contents into complexes and finding their

[1] *Ibid.*, p. 172 n.   [2] *Ibid.*, p. 198.   [3] *Ibid.*, p. 199.
[4] *Supra*, p. 54.   [5] *Practice of Psychotherapy*, p. 72; *Mod. Man*, p. 58.
[6] *Practice of Psychotherapy*, p. 78; *Contemp. Events*, p. 39.
[7] *Contribs.*, p. 354.

relation to real conditions. The subjective mode is 'synthetic and constructive', detaching the underlying complexes from their actual causes, regarding them as tendencies or parts of the subject, and reintegrating them with the main stream of psychic life. While Jung tends to think of the first type of interpretation as belonging to the earlier stages of analysis, there is, as Father Hostie points out,[1] no 'really satisfactory standard of judgment' which can be applied to their use, and in practice his followers seem to vary somewhat, with a tendency, however, to prefer the latter. The patient's own associations to the symbols are still required, as well as amplification by mythological material, but a modification is introduced, which Jung describes as association *around* the dream image instead of association in a straight line from it; the free association technique will reveal complexes, he argues, but will seldom give the meaning of the individual dream. For this to be revealed it is necessary to keep as close to the dream images as possible. If, for instance, the patient has dreamt of a deal table, Jung asks him to describe the object and give its history in a way that would be intelligible to anyone who had never seen an object of that kind. 'We succeed in this way in establishing a good part of the context of that particular dream image. When we have done this for all the images in the dream we are ready for the venture of interpretation.'[2] Jung also uses a method of 'active imagination', in which the patient is encouraged to take an attitude which can be described as both active and passive, letting the images of his dream or fantasy develop of their own accord, with the conscious ego standing somewhat aside and reporting on them. Of this method one analysand has commented that while a daydream may stay the same for years, a fantasy under Jungian analysis changes rapidly, and that whereas the satisfaction given by a daydream has a spurious quality—the feeling underlying it being one of emptiness and unreality—in active imagination 'there is a positive feeling of coming to grips with reality',[3] or, as another follower of Jung has said, of achieving 'something more in the nature of a synthesis of the conscious and the unconscious standpoints'.[4] This accords with the aim that Jung sets forth, of bringing about 'a psychic state in which my patient begins

---

[1] Hostie, R., *Religion and the Psychology of Jung*, p. 39. London: Sheed and Ward, 1957.
[2] *Practice of Psychotherapy*, p. 151; *Mod. Man*, p. 16.
[3] Makhdum, *op. cit.*, pp. 73–4.   [4] Martin, P. W., *op. cit.*, p. 57.

to experiment with his own nature—a state of fluidity, change, and growth where nothing is eternally fixed and hopelessly petrified'.[1]

Unlike Freud, who believes that 'far more frequently dreams are not attached to one another but are interpolated into a successive series of fragments of waking thought',[2] Jung makes more use of dream series than of single dreams. In this way, he thinks, 'the continuity of the unconscious pictorial flood' is best revealed[3] and 'It is as if there lay before us not a single text but a large number which throw light from all sides upon the unfamiliar terms, so that the reading of all the texts is sufficient in itself to clear up the difficulties of meaning of each single one.'[4] Painting is recommended as an adjunct to the other methods, since it encourages activity on the patient's part—he does not merely talk about his fantasy but is actually doing something about it—enforces a study of all parts of the vision, and provides an objective record of the state toward which the personality is tending. The patient is aware that this creative activity is socially unimportant, but feels it as a way of working at himself for his own benefit and freeing himself from dependence on the doctor; indirectly, however, this will be an advantage in his social life as well, since 'an inwardly stable and self-confident person will prove more adequate to his social task than one who is on a bad footing with his unconscious'[5]. A practical point is the timing of the patient's visits; Jung states that whereas the psychoanalyst thinks he must see his patient for an hour a day for months on end, he himself manages with three or four sessions in the week, generally, indeed, with only two, and once the patient has got going he is reduced to one, working at himself in the intervals under Jung's control. He also breaks off the treatment every ten weeks or so, in order to throw the patient back on his normal milieu and avoid too much dependence on medical authority.

'In such a procedure time can take effect as a healing factor, without the patient's having to pay for the doctor's time. With proper direction most people become capable of making their contribution—however modest at first—to the common work. In my experience the absolute period of cure is not shortened by too many sittings. It lasts a fair time in all cases requiring thorough treatment. Consequently, in the case of the patient

---

[1] *Practice of Psychotherapy*, p. 46; *Mod. Man*, p. 75.
[2] *Collected Papers*, Vol. V, p. 139. ('Remarks on Dream Interpretation.')
[3] *Practice of Psychotherapy*, p. 12.   [4] *Integ. of Person.*, p. 101.
[5] *Practice of Psychotherapy*, p. 50; *Mod. Man*, p. 82.

with small means, if the sittings are spaced out and the intervals filled in with the patient's own work, the treatment becomes financially more endurable.'[1]

In addition to what has been noted about the age group of the patients, a little more can be gathered of the type of cases which Jung has most commonly encountered, i.e. it seems that he has been dealing in the main with 'neuroses or psychotic borderline states in complicated and intelligent people'.[2] About a third are suffering, not from any clinically definable neurosis but from the senselessness and emptiness of their lives. Denominationally the larger number have been Protestants, a smaller number Jews, and not more than five or six believing Catholics. Just as formerly the patient needed to 'reassume that psychological attitude which, in an earlier civilization, was characterized by the living belief in a religious or philosophical dogma',[3] so now Jung states in a passage which is often cited,

'Among all my patients in the second half of life—that is to say, over thirty-five—there has not been one whose problem in the last resort was not that of finding a religious outlook on life. It is safe to say that every one of them fell ill because he had lost that which the living religions of every age have given to their followers, and none of them has been really healed who did not regain his religious outlook.'[4]

Most of the patients who come to him have already had some form of psychotherapeutic treatment, usually with partial or negative results. From the references to cases of schizophrenia or dementia praecox it would seem either that a fair number have fallen into this psychiatric category or that Jung has been strongly impressed by those that he has met. In fact, he says that nothing has struck him more forcibly during many years' experience than the large number of mild schizophrenics who are 'partially camouflaged as compulsion neuroses, obsessions, phobias and hysterias' and 'are very careful never to go near an asylum'.[5] For the most part, however, Jung seems to pay rather less attention to diagnosis than is usual among psychiatrists; classifications are unsatisfactory, he considers, and a specific diagnosis seldom means anything real. 'In general, it

---

[1] *Practice of Psychotherapy*, p. 27. [2] *Ibid.*, p. 117.
[3] *Supra*, p. 53. [4] *Mod. Man*, p. 264.
[5] Cited by H. G. Baynes, *Mythology of the Soul*, pp. 43–4.

is enough to diagnose a "psychoneurosis" as distinct from some organic disturbance—the word means no more than that.'[1]

Besides the account of the patient-physician relationship and the information on methods and to some extent on patients, there are several attitudes running through Jung's work which have bearing on his therapy. Corresponding to the earlier statement that 'What direction the patient's future life should take is not ours to judge . . .'[2] is the later statement that the physician should not have too fixed a goal. 'What is it, at this moment and in this individual, that represents the natural urge of life? That is the question.'[3] The doctor 'can hardly know better than the nature and will to live of the patient'[4] and should 'do his utmost to avoid influencing the patient in the direction of his own philosophical, social and political bent'.[5] He must be able to 'let things happen', for 'It is rewarding to observe patiently what happens, quietly, in the psyche, and the most and the best happens when nothing is instilled from without and above by regimentation.'[6] Confronted with difficulties the doctor 'would do better to take the fact as an indication of his own growing inability to understand the situation'.[7] In order to rule out conscious suggestion he 'must consider any dream interpretation invalid that does not win the assent of the patient, and he must search until he finds a formulation that does'.[8] A new beginning is possible at any time: 'I have often seen cases where abnormal sexual fantasies disappeared suddenly and completely in the moment when the mind became aware of a new thought or psychic content'[9] and 'I have been deeply impressed with the fact that the new thing prepared by fate seldom or never corresponds to conscious expectation.'[10] 'Just the most unexpected, just the alarmingly chaotic . . . reveals the deepest meaning.'[11] '"And still to-day one findeth rarely that people come to great things without they first go somewhat astray."'[12]

To some extent Jung's accounts of the therapeutic situation can be analysed in terms of the factors which he thinks of as contributing to cure. Expression counts for something in itself, as we see in his statement that the patient may be greatly helped by painting. Ra-

---

[1] *Practice of Psychotherapy*, p. 86.   [2] *Supra*, p. 55.
[3] *Two Essays*, new ed. p. 285.   [4] *Practice of Psychotherapy*, p. 41.
[5] *Ibid.*, p. 26.   [6] *Integ. of Person.*, p. 129.
[7] *Mod. Man*, p. 10.   [8] *Mod. Man*, p. 12.   [9] *Contribs.*, p. 152.
[10] *Secret of the Golden Flower*, p. 90.   [11] *Integ. of Person.*, p. 80.
[12] Citation from Meister Eckhart, *Psych. Types*, p. 299.

tional insight plays a part—unconscious problems are uncovered and the patient becomes aware of unsuspected possibilities. There is also a social linking-up process, directly through the relationship with the physician as an individual, indirectly through the relationship with the physician as representative of humanity, and finally, there is the gaining of a workable attitude to life, and the putting of this attitude into operation. It would be handling Jung in too logical a way to attempt a ranking of these factors in the precise order of importance, nor is it likely that any psychotherapists would wish to do this for their work, but some rough-and-ready comparisons might be made between them. One feature of Jung's own discussions seems to be a wavering in his attitude to rational analysis. On the one hand, 'The doctor must probe as deeply as possible into the origins of the neurosis in order to lay the foundations of a subsequent synthesis'.[1] On the other hand, it is often a mistake for the patient to 'go searching about in his memory—perhaps for years—for some hypothetical event in his childhood, while things of immediate importance are grossly neglected'.[2] Perhaps the explanation may be found in his use of the term, understanding. Understanding, he says, 'acts like a life-saver. It integrates the unconscious, and gradually there comes into being a higher point of view where both conscious and unconscious are represented.'[3] Taking into consideration the commonly accepted meaning of the term and the trend of Jung's own writings, it seems likely that what he is really seeking is rational analysis blended with, or infused into, the other factors.

Freud's approach to therapy can readily be seen as more strictly rationalistic. This is apparent in the technique that he develops. Freud, that is, places more reliance than Jung on the patient's verbal material—there does not seem to be anything in his work comparable to the non-verbal, yet organized, expressiveness which Jung endeavours to foster in his patients through their painting. The attitudes to images and words which they actually state point in the same direction. For Jung the image is 'the preliminary stage of the *idea*, its maternal soil'.[4] 'Our intellect is born from mythology,' he says, 'and mythology is nothing but a translation of inner experience into the language of pictures.'[5] Speech itself is 'a storehouse of images

---

[1] *Practice of Psychotherapy*, p. 135.   [2] *Ibid.*, p. 143; *Mod. Man*, p. 7.
[3] *Ibid.*, p. 269.   [4] *Psych. Types*, p. 557.   [5] *Contribs.*, p. 267.

founded on experience'.[1] Freud speaks in reverse terms of the peculiarity which the dream has of 'transforming its content of ideas into plastic images'.[2] He is never found to say, like Jung, that 'with talk you get nowhere',[3] but becomes as eloquent about the word as Jung about the image:

> 'Words and magic were in the beginning one and the same thing, and even to-day words retain much of their magical power. By words one of us can give to another the greatest happiness or bring about utter despair; by words the teacher imparts his knowledge to the student; by words the orator sweeps his audience with him and determines its judgments and decisions. Words call forth emotions and are universally the means by which we influence our fellow creatures. Therefore let us not despise the use of words in psychotherapy.'[4]

More rationalistic also is Freud's insistence on the patient's acceptance of psychoanalytical interpretations, coupled with a relative lack of interest in the patient's value system. This can be illustrated by his use of suggestion. Both Freud and Jung acknowledge an element of suggestion in the therapeutic situation. Freud, however, holds that 'In psycho-analysis the suggestive influence which is inevitably exercised by the physician is diverted on to the task assigned to the patient of overcoming his resistances, that is, of carrying forward the curative process.'[5] We give the patient the conscious idea of what he may expect to find 'and the similarity of this with the repressed unconscious one leads him to come upon the latter himself'.[6] Some patients need more of such assistance and some need less, 'but there are none who get through without some of it'.[7] How far Freud may have been prepared to go along these lines can be seen from occasional dialogues between his patients and himself. In particular, Dora, the patient in his 'Analysis of a Case of Hysteria', had dreamt that a house was on fire, her father was standing by her bed and woke her up; she dressed quickly, then her mother wanted to stop and save her jewel case, but the father said, 'I refuse to let myself and my two children be burnt for the sake of your jewel case.' Associating to the jewel case, Dora recalled a dispute between her parents about a piece of jewellery which the mother did not like:

[1] *Mod. Man*, p. 102.
[2] *Interpretation of Dreams*, p. 435.
[3] *The Symbolic Life*, 1939, p. 23.
[4] *Introductory Lectures*, p. 13.
[5] *Collected Papers*, Vol. V, p. 126.
[6] *Ibid.*, Vol. II, p. 286.
[7] *Ibid.*, Vol. III, p. 247.

Freud: I daresay you thought to yourself you would accept it with pleasure.

Dora: I don't know. (*This, Freud comments in a footnote, was her regular formula for confessing to anything that had been repressed.*) I don't in the least know how Mother comes into the dream; she was not with us at L—— at the time.

Freud: I will explain that to you later. Does nothing else occur to you in connection with the jewel case?

Dora: Yes, Herr K. had made me a present of an expensive jewel case a little time before.

Freud: Then a return present would have been very appropriate. Perhaps you do not know that 'jewel case' is a favourite expression for the female genitals.

Dora: I knew you would say that.

Freud: That is to say, you knew that it *was* so. The meaning of the dream is now becoming even clearer.[1]

However, Freud assures us, in the same passage where he admits the inevitability of some suggestive influence, 'The analyst respects the patient's individuality and does not seek to remould him in accordance with his own—that is, according to the physician's—personal ideals'.[2] Freud, in short, is willing to exert a not inconsiderable amount of pressure on behalf of psychoanalytical interpretations, but leaves the patient's values as his own affair. Jung, by contrast, is reluctant to press his intellectual formulations of the patient's material—speaking as he does of the need for searching until one finds a formulation that the patient can accept—but he *is* prepared to exert some influence on behalf of certain values. One illustration is the dialogue between Jung and the young man who was delaying his choice of a profession.[3] It will be recalled that the young man's associations to 'Mother', were expressions of regret at having neglected her, and that 'Mother' was then interpreted by Jung as standing for something which had been neglected in an inexcusable manner. '"And what is that?" "My work," said the patient, with considerable embarrassment."' It might, indeed, be argued that, as with his attitude to rational analysis, there is a degree of ambiguity in Jung's position—on the one hand the doctor should avoid influencing the patient in the direction of his own philosophical, social and political bent, on the other hand, there is need of an educative will—though Jung himself would seek to harmonize the

[1] *Collected Papers*, Vol. III. 'Analysis of a Case of Hysteria,' 1905; pp. 13–146 (p. 84).
[2] *Collected Papers*, Vol. V, p. 127.   [3] *Supra*, p. 52.

apparent contradiction through his interpretation of education as a 'drawing out', that is, by seeing the values which he advocates as part of the patient's inmost self, coming to expression spontaneously in dreams and fantasies, and merely needing some measure of reinforcement and interpretation. Such a difference in outlook naturally affects the goal of therapy. Freud, unlike the older therapists employing hypnosis, who were treating patients largely at the symptomatic level, concentrates on reorganizing the trends which underlie the symptoms, in such a way that they neither recur nor are replaced by a fresh set springing from the same instinctual roots. The impression is gained, however, that the individual will be in most respects the same old XYZ, so to speak, that he always has been—the personality pattern remains essentially unchanged. Indeed, Freud deliberately restricts himself. Many people fall ill precisely from an attempt to sublimate their instincts beyond the degree permitted by their organization. In those who do have the capacity for sublimation, the process usually takes place of itself, as soon as the inhibitions have been overcome by the analysis. 'In my opinion, therefore, efforts to bring about sublimation of the impulses in the course of psychoanalytic treatment are no doubt always praiseworthy but most certainly not in all cases advisable.'[1] With much of this Jung no doubt would agree, i.e. that patients differ in their capacity for sublimation, or, in his own thinking, individual development, and that the developmental process is often independent, or largely so, of the doctor's intervention. Nevertheless, whether rightly or wrongly, he aims at yet another level, that of developing and bringing to maturity individual personalities.[2] A fairly direct contrast may be found in their handling of two patients whose life-situation in some respects was similar. The story of Freud's patient, who had developed obsessional symptoms relating to his mistress, was that

> 'After more than two decades, when they had both lost something of their youth, the woman naturally more than he, he felt the need of detaching himself from her; he wanted to be free, to lead his own life, and to have a house and family of his own . . . I may add that my patient was able with the help of analysis to make a love choice outside the magic circle within which he had been spell-bound.'[3]

[1] *Collected Papers*, Vol. II, p. 332. ('Recommendations on Treatment,' 1912.)
[2] *Practice of Psychotherapy*, p. 110; *Contemp. Events*, p. 35.
[3] *New Introductory Lectures*, pp. 64–5.

Jung's patient, or prospective patient, had brought a detailed manuscript analysing the symptoms of his illness with remarkable acumen ('He called it a compulsion neurosis—quite correctly, as I saw when I read the document.') and wished to know why, in spite of this insight, the illness was not cured. During the preliminary inquiries it transpired that the young man had a mistress, a poor schoolteacher who stinted herself in order to provide him with expensive holidays.

> 'Obviously I had to tell this young gentleman what I thought of him. If we could have reached agreement on this point, treatment would have been possible. But if we had begun our work by ignoring the impossible basis of his life, it would have been useless. . . . I believe firmly in the power and dignity of the intellect, but only if it does not violate the feeling values.'[1]

His want of conscience was the cause of his neurosis, Jung says in discussing this case elsewhere, 'and it is not hard to see why scientific understanding failed to help him.'[2]

It is not likely that all differences in the therapy of Jung and Freud can be reduced to the difference in their emphasis on rational analysis or values, though some connection may ultimately be found between this and other points. In the present context we may note that for Freud the psychoanalytical situation requires the existence of a 'superior' and 'inferior'; in the case of Little Hans, for instance, he considers that it was only because the authority of a father and a physician were united in the one person that the study could be made.[3] He speaks, similarly, of the *struggle* between patient and physician: 'The situation is the same as when to-day an enemy army needs weeks and months to make its way across a stretch of country which in times of peace was traversed by an express train in a few hours and which only a short time before had been passed over by the defending army in a few days.'[4] Unlike Jung, who conducts the analysis as 'a perfectly ordinary, sensible conversation',[5] Freud is of course strict in demanding the use of the psychoanalytical couch. He reports that some patients, when denied their request to take up another position, 'make in their own minds a division of the treatment into an official part, in which they behave in a very inhibited

---

[1] *Development of Personality*, pp. 99–100.   [2] *Mod. Man*, p. 223.
[3] *Collected Papers*, Vol. III, p. 149.   [4] *Ibid.*, p. 478.
[5] *Collected Papers*, p. 257.

manner, and an informal, "friendly" part, in which they really speak freely'. The physician, however, 'does not fall in for long with this division of time, he makes a note of what is said before or after the sitting, and in bringing it up at the next opportunity he tears down the partition which the patient has tried to erect'.[1] In keeping with this attitude is a high degree of scepticism about the statements of the patient. In some rare cases his 'No', turns out to be the expression of a legitimate dissent. Far more frequently it expresses a resistance; generally speaking, in a dispute between doctor and patient as to what has occurred, the doctor will be in the right. However, even the patient's 'Yes', cannot be taken uncritically:

> 'It can indeed signify that he recognizes the correctness of the construction that has been presented to him; but it can also be meaningless, or can even deserve to be described as "hypocritical", since it may be convenient for his resistance to make use of an assent in such circumstances in order to prolong the concealment of a truth that has not been discovered.'[2]

Freud's capacity for catching the patient out is practically unlimited. There is a most convenient method, he declares, by which light can sometimes be thrown on unconscious and repressed material: '"What," one asks, "would you consider was about the most unlikely thing in the world in that situation? What do you think was furthest from your mind at that time?" If the patient falls into the trap and names what he thinks most incredible, he almost invariably in so doing makes the correct admission.'[3] As for dreams of recovery, which Jung handles with respect as indications of the future,[4] quite as often they 'only have the value of dreams of convenience: they signify a wish to be well at last, in order to avoid another portion of the work of analysis which is felt to lie ahead'.[5]

Besides being a relationship of superior and inferior, the patient-physician relationship has other limitations. These exist not only as a matter of fact—Freud considers them desirable. Invariably, he says, the patient looks for substitutive gratification in the treatment itself, and may even strive to compensate himself for all other privations:

---

[1] *Collected Papers*, Vol. II, pp. 359–60.   [2] *Collected Papers*, Vol. V, p. 364.
[3] *Ibid.*, p. 181.   [4] See *Contribs.*, pp. 390–400 for an extended instance.
[5] *Collected Papers* Vol. V, p. 140.

'a certain amount must of course be permitted to him, more or less according to the nature of the case and the patient's individuality. But it is not good to let it become too much. . . . As far as his relations with the physician are concerned, the patient must have unfulfilled wishes in abundance. It is expedient to deny him precisely those satisfactions which he desires most intensely and expresses most importunately.'[1]

In other words, a strictly limited relationship provides the environment in which the best therapeutic results will be achieved. 'I cannot recommend my colleagues emphatically enough,' Freud says in a celebrated passage,

'to take as a model in psychoanalytic treatment the surgeon who puts aside all his own feelings, including that of human sympathy, and concentrates his mind on one single purpose, that of performing the operation as skilfully as possible. . . . The justification for this coldness in feeling in the analyst is that it is the condition which brings the greatest advantage to both persons involved, ensuring a needful protection for the physician's emotional life and the greatest measure of aid for the patient that is possible at the present time.'[2]

The physician, he adds, 'must bend his own unconscious like a receptive organ towards the emerging unconscious of the patient, be as the receiver of the telephone to the disc'.[3] He should be 'impenetrable to the patient, and, like a mirror, reflect nothing but what is shown him'.[4]

These recommendations, clearly, form the direct opposite of the Jungian approach, according to which 'the man in the patient confronts the man in the doctor upon equal terms' in the endeavour to secure 'a mutual agreement which is the fruit of joint reflection', the meeting of the two personalities, far from being like the reflection in a mirror, is 'like mixing two different chemical substances: if there is any combination at all, both are transformed', and the doctor, instead of ensuring for himself a needful protection, goes right beyond professional routine to the limits of his subjective possibilities. It is not surprising, therefore, that Jung and Freud sometimes show misunderstanding of each other's meaning. Jung, for instance, says that Freud 'would vouchsafe the instincts an unfettered excursion toward their objects'.[5] Freud protests that the making conscious of repressed sexual desires has, on the contrary, the aim of

---

[1] *Collected Papers*, Vol. II, p. 398.   [2] *Ibid.*, pp. 327–8.
[3] *Ibid.*, p. 328.   [4] *Ibid.*, p. 331.   [5] *Psych. Types*, p. 81.

achieving a mastery over them which the previous repression had been unable to achieve.[1] For his own part, referring to the dissention with the Swiss school, he declares that he and his followers

'rejected most emphatically the view that we should convert into our own property the patient who puts himself into our hands in search of help, should carve his destiny for him, force our own ideals upon him, and with the arrogance of a Creator form him in our own image and see that it was good'.[2]

Even though it may be felt that Jung, as often, is somewhat uncritical in failing to inquire into the culturally determined element in values, we can hardly allow that Freud has summed the situation up impartially. Nevertheless, in spite of exaggerations and inaccuracies, such statements are attempts to express the major differences in their orientation. It seems likely that some interchange of patients has taken place along those lines. Jung says that he has 'seen a good many patients injured by so-called psychoanalysis, and without exception it was from the lack of rapport that the evil took its origin',[3] while Freud cites the report of a former Jungian patient that

'Instead of freedom through analysis, every day brought fresh terrific demands on me, which had to be fulfilled if the neurosis were to be conquered—for instance, inward concentration by means of introversion, religious meditation, resuming life with my wife in loving devotion, etc.'[4]

So far comparatively little has been said about the characteristics which the renewed, transformed or individuated personality can be expected to possess, or those which can be looked for in the pre- or potentially individuated personality. On the second question Jung does not give much guidance, saying that the development is more what could be called fate, but some impressions relevant to the first can be gathered from his writings. In particular, of course, he speaks of an increasing wholeness, or harmonious synthesis of all trends and capacities. Almost equally he stresses autonomy, or ability to make decisions with full freedom and consciousness. The process requires 'unreserved self-surrender'[5] on the one hand, and yet, on

---

[1] *Collected Papers*, Vol. II p. 399. [2] *Ibid.*, Vol. II, p. 398.
[3] *Contribs.*, pp. 353–4. [4] *Collected Papers*, Vol. I, p. 355.
[5] *Contemp. Events*, p. 43.

the other hand, it is necessary to separate oneself from the unconscious not by repressing it but by presenting it to oneself as
something that is totally different.[1] That is, Jung seems to be aiming
at the development of a type of personality which achieves in relation
to its own experience a balance between participation and detachment not unlike that which the physician must take to the experience
of his patients. At the same time, not only is individuation in-
appropriate before a minimal adaptation to collective standards has
been made—it also entails no alienation from life and from the
world. ('Quite the contrary, for such a way is possible and profitable
only when the specific worldly tasks which these individuals set
themselves are carried out in reality.')[2] Nor is it to be confused with
individualism—whereas individualism sets a man in conflict with
the collective norm, individuation confirms his relation to it, 'precisely because it makes us aware of the unconscious, which unites
and is common to all mankind'.[3] Now at times Jung shows himself
not totally unaware of social circumstances. A neurosis, he says,
'is more a psycho-social phenomenon than an illness in the strict
sense. It forces us to extend the term "illness" beyond the idea of
an individual body whose functions are disturbed, and to look upon
the neurotic person as a sick system of social relationships.'[4] When
the patient comes to the therapist with a neurosis 'he does not bring
a part but the whole of his psyche and with it the fragment of world
on which that psyche depends. . . . Try as we may to concentrate on
the most personal of personal problems, our therapy nevertheless
stands or falls with the question: What sort of world does our
patient come from and to what sort of world has he to adapt himself?'[5] Implicit in these statements is a critique of society—the
thought that society might be based on values which accorded more
closely with the psychic needs of man. Such passages are comparatively rare—more representative are the statements that 'Individuation is an at-one-ment with oneself and the same time with humanity',
and that it 'leads to a natural appreciation of the collective norm'[6]
and is possible and profitable only when specific worldly tasks are
carried out. Both attitudes, however, seem more favourably disposed
toward human nature than the Freudian view of society as largely

---

[1] *Collected Papers*, p. 416. [2] *Two Essays*, new ed. p. 222; old ed. p. 248.
[3] *Practice of Psychotherapy*, p. 108. [4] *Ibid.*, p. 24.
[5] *Practice of Psychotherapy*, p. 94; *Contemp. Events*, p. 18.
[6] *Psych. Types*, p. 563.

Chapter VII

JUNG'S CRITIQUE OF FREUD AND
PSYCHOTHERAPY: DISCUSSION

In turning to Jung's critique of Freud—arising, he has said, directly out of therapeutic practice—and the development of his own psychotherapeutic methods, a question which comes readily to mind is that of similarities or differences between his own ideas and those of other contemporary and later writers, i.e. is he alone in holding the views he does hold, or can parallels be found elsewhere?

An early group which seems to have had much in common with Jung is that of the British psychiatrists—among them William McDougall, W. H. R. Rivers, J. A. Hadfield, H. Crichton Miller and William Brown, with Ian Suttie as a slightly later representative —who in the 1920's and early 1930's were developing a psychological approach to mental illness. All these writers, making use of the methods of dream analysis and free association, considered sexual difficulties to be one of the great sources of disorder; in greater or lesser degree they made use of the hypothesis of the Oedipus complex, and they recognized that conflict and repression play an important part in the aetiology of the neuroses. They were, in short, strongly influenced by Freudian practice and ideas.

However, even a statement of the Freudian influence has had to be phrased in such a way as to allow for differences. For instance, although regarding sexual difficulties as one of the great sources of disorder, the British school, or group, is inclined like Jung to adopt a formulation which will avoid the problem of the 'narrow-broad' connotation of sexuality found in Freudian writings. McDougall, especially, stresses the desirability of thinking in terms of one supply of psychic energy, flowing into channels of which two of the most important, though not in his scheme the only ones, are the instincts of

161

sex and of self-preservation. Their psychiatric experience in the First World War led them to maintain that neurosis can arise from conflict between self-preservation, as well as sexuality, and the requirements of society, and that no more subtle interpretation of the situation need be sought. Several other objections to the libido theory in its Freudian form bring them close to Jung. McDougall criticizes the developmental aspect of the theory, or the doctrine of erogenous zones, in very similar terms. Freud's connection of thumb-sucking, and other early pleasure-bringing activities, with the sexual impulse could only be justified, in his view, if the 'obviously false' premiss were accepted, that all pleasure is sexually toned. Although prepared to admit the existence of an Oedipus complex in some individuals, he is not convinced that its fully fledged sexual form is a normal stage of personality growth; and the Freudian explanation of all social impulses as 'aim-inhibited sexuality' seems to him unnecessary—all the more so in view of the fact that a tendency to succour, cherish and protect, functioning quite independently of sex, is found in all mammalian species. Another argument put forward previously by Jung is used by Rivers, namely, that if the Oedipus complex is (a) universal and (b) an important cause of mental illness, it is necessary to devote more attention to the problem, why some people suffer from psychoneuroses and others are able to escape. We have to distinguish a highly complex chain of causation, he continues, and the history of psychoanalysis shows a tendency to lay undue stress on early factors and a relative neglect of recent conflicts.[1]

Differences of this kind are reflected in their attitude to dreams. Several dreams are reported by McDougall which seem to him to have been motivated by repressed fear rather than repressed sexuality, among them a dream which occurred during his own analysis with Jung, i.e. that he was swimming on a lake with two other men behind him in a small boat. 'The fog grew denser. I turned around to look for the boat, but could not see it. I felt alarmed and shouted; I got no answer. I shouted more loudly, despairingly. . . .'[2] He is afraid, that is, lest he should 'get into deep water' in his analysis and be unable to extricate himself. His interpretation is an indication

---

[1] Rivers, W. H. R., *Conflict and Dream*, p. 144. London: Kegan Paul, 1923. Cf. Jung, *supra*, p. 49.
[2] *Outline of Abnormal Psychology*, p. 150. London: Methuen & Co., 1926.

too that like Rivers and again like Jung he is more inclined than the Freudian school to concentrate on the present situation of the patient. But in this school or group it is Rivers who has most to say on dreams. In the book already cited he disputes Freud's theory that a dream is necessarily the fulfilment of a wish, saying that it seems to him too simple. Not infrequently, he argues, a dream can be the expression of a conflict between a number of wishes, 'or more accurately between a number of conative trends, some of which might be called wishes, while others were rather of the nature of fears or apprehensions'.[1] For instance, a patient of his who was contemplating suicide dreamt that he was about to shoot a man who could easily be recognized as a surrogate, but heard the voice of his son saying, 'Don't do it, Daddy, you'll hurt me too.' In this dream the two wishes, or conative trends, desire for death and consideration for family welfare, found expression at the same time; it is therefore 'at least equally possible to regard the dream as a whole as an attempted solution of a very complicated kind which was going on in the mind of the dreamer'. Rivers comes close to Jung again in his suggestion that the dream 'though in fantastic form, may express conclusions better than those reached by the waking consciousness'.[2]

The prospective orientation to mental life is another feature. On this question McDougall with his hormic psychology is the major representative. There seem, he writes in the introductory pages of his *Energies of Men*, to be in Nature events of two different kinds, the physical and the psycho-physical. The physical can be accounted for with ever-increasing success in terms of the causal influence of preceding events, without any reference to possible events in the future. But when we observe the behaviour of living creatures, whether men or animals, e.g. a dog seeking prey or finding its way home, we cannot begin to understand it without attributing to them some activity essentially similar to our own conscious foresight of and desire for a goal. The two types of causation are difficult to reconcile—it may be that in future years the problem will be solved by a radical re-casting of conceptions. Pending such re-casting, it is most fruitful to assume, for instance, that the *goal* of seeing home and family may in some way guide the traveller's steps, or that foresight of a rise in prices may have some causal relation to the buying

---

[1] *Op. cit.*, p. 17.　　　　[2] *Op. cit.*, p. 49.

of stocks.[1] Other members of the group make use of this principle in psychotherapy. For instance, Hadfield gives the case of a patient who dreamt that he was back in Oxford to take the crew out. '"But the boatman says the boat is out of repair. . . . Then I go on to the landing stage and you"'—Hadfield—'"meet me and say, There is an abundance of coal and now is your opportunity."' The patient's association to coal was, the crude material of fire, life; and the dream as Hadfield interprets it is saying in its symbolic language that it is useless to look back to the age of prowess—it is out of date and must be given up, but as soon as he abandons it 'there comes the great opportunity, an abundance of crude material, of life and power within, which awaits development'.[2] Hadfield also uses compensation as an explanation of neurotic symptoms in a way that seems identical with that of Jung:

> 'the man with a psychology characterized by extravagant self-importance, who represses his humbler submissive instincts, is made to suffer a nervous breakdown in which the sense of impotence and failure is the characteristic feature; the man who has too great ideas of himself as a hero suffers from fear; the man who is too intellectual, placing all the weight of his psychology on reason, is haunted by the fear of madness, in which the irrational and emotional side of his nature finds expression. Such symptoms as these come to restore the balance, to make articulate the silenced functions of the soul.'[3]

It will already have been seen that these writers emphasize the expressiveness of the dream with the means at its disposal, rather than its effort to secure forbidden satisfaction. Both Rivers and McDougall discuss Freud's early concept of the censor in terms similar to Jung's, regarding it as too much of a dramatization to fit the facts. Parallels for unconscious processes are to be sought in the physiological sphere rather than the social, they consider, and the analogy which they suggest is that of levels of functioning. Just as the nervous system is arranged in a number of levels, forming a hierarchy in which each level controls those beneath it and is in turn controlled by those above, so a similar organization of mental life may be assumed. The most natural explanation of the dream is that its appearance in consciousness is due to the

---

[1] *The Energies of Men*, pp. 5–9. London: Methuen, 1932.
[2] *Psychology and Morals*, pp. 107–19. London: Methuen, 1923.
[3] *Ibid.*, p. 65.

removal in sleep of higher controlling levels; it may have the characteristics of infancy not because its *material* is derived from the *experience* of infancy, but because any experience finding expression in the dream is moulded according to the *forms* of feeling, thought and action which are normal in infancy. Rivers for his part prefers to use the term, transformation, to describe the processes through which thoughts are expressed in the language of the dream, and considers that the Freudian formulation in terms of repression 'tends to obscure the essential character of the dream as a product of a general principle of the development of mind'.[1] He is sceptical also about the importance which Freud attaches to repression of the Oedipus complex in accounting for childhood amnesia, though unlike Jung his argument is of a social rather than a biological nature, i.e. that the mental efficiency of the adult would be greatly impeded if modes of thinking, feeling and acting proper to infancy and childhood regularly intruded into his waking activities.

The same writers are far readier than the orthodox Freudians to admit questions of value and life philosophy into psychotherapy. One of the best known statements of their viewpoint is Hadfield's *Psychology and Morals*. While recognizing the familiar theoretical distinction between psychology, the descriptive science of mental processes, and ethics, the normative science of moral conduct, Hadfield denies that the practising physician can detach himself from moral standards. Especially in formulating the *goal* of therapy it is impossible to eliminate values. Even the psychoanalyst, who says, in effect, you 'ought not' to repress, has sprung at one leap out of the realm of pure science—a conclusion similar to that of Jung, who adds that an unacknowledged *Weltanschauung* is likely to affect the work of the therapist less satisfactorily than one which has been more thoroughly examined. The nature of the values advocated will be taken up again in the chapter following, but some reference to them may be made in noting the interpretations which are given of the therapist's task. Hadfield conceives the therapist to be concerned with assisting the patient to build himself up into a higher unity and completeness and to maintain his integrity—the urge to do this being part of his very nature, 'a compulsion from which we cannot escape'. McDougall declares, perhaps more militantly,

---

[1] *Instinct and the Unconscious*, p. 232. London: Cambridge University Press, 1924. See also McDougall, *Outline of Abnormal Psychology*, pp. 155–6.

'The most desirable procedure . . . is to help the patient to understand the genesis of the disorder, to lead him to a critical evaluation of all the factors involved and, where necessary, a revaluation of them, and to inspire him to the adoption of a new attitude dominated by some strong purpose; to set before him a worth-while goal towards which he may strive, sustained by motives which he wholly accepts and approves, and which are in harmony with the whole of his character.'[1]

Jung's division of therapy into the analytical and constructive phases seems to be implicit in McDougall's passage.

Again, in discussing the nature of the patient-physician relationship through which the goal is realized, the members of this school find themselves unable to accept the theory of the transference in its full Freudian sense. Being, like Jung, less inclined to view the original relationship with the parents as having a sexual significance, they do not consider the patient-physician relationship to be sexually toned in so far as it repeats that early relationship; they resemble Jung also in being less inclined to regard it *as* a repetition and more inclined to regard it as an essentially new relationship which is merely coloured by previous experience. In McDougall's opinion one cannot better sum up the role of this relationship than by citing Jung himself:

'"The therapeutic effect of the minute and scrupulous pursuit of all the infantile fantasy-roots depends not so much upon these relatively inessential demonstrations as upon the labour the physician gives himself to enter into the patient's psyche, thereby establishing a psychologically adapted relationship. For the patient is suffering precisely from the absence of such a relationship . . ."'[2]

Jung, in short, 'seems to me to have given psychoanalytic theory a turn in the right direction'.[3]

There does not, then, seem to be a great deal of difference between the outlook of the British school and Jung's own outlook in his *Theory of Psychoanalysis*, and from McDougall's references it is clear that he, at any rate, was in close touch with Jung. On the other hand, it was their own experience of wartime neuroses which led the members of this school to psychotherapy, and the concept of level, introduced in their discussion of repression, was derived from the work of the neurologist Hughlings Jackson. The criticisms made are,

[1] *Outline of Abnormal Psychology*, pp. 470–1.
[2] *Outline of Abnormal Psychology*, p. 468.   [3] *Ibid.*, p. 481.

indeed, of a kind which would be likely to occur to any worker at this period who endeavoured to steer a balance between complete discipleship in the psychoanalytic movement and complete rejection of it. Unlike Jung and his disciples, however, they are hesitant about accepting the theory of the collective unconscious. Even McDougall, the most favourably disposed, is careful to state that while he regards Jung's 'more speculative doctrines with great interest and sympathetic respect', he 'cannot at present accept them as even provisionally established'[1] and Rivers, as we have seen, is considerably more stringent.[2] Nor do they base their concepts of mind quite so predominantly on their work as depth psychologists. For instance, McDougall had laid the foundations of his hormic psychology before psychoanalysis had become at all widely known—as he frequently points out—nor did he ever greatly modify them. The concern of this school is rather to incorporate psychoanalytical findings into the general body of psychological theory, with a strong leaning toward comparative psychology, a tendency which can be seen in Mc-Dougall's reference to the urge to succour and protect, found in all mammalian species, and Rivers' desire to develop a theory of the dream which will be in harmony with general principles in the development of mind. Rivers goes further in endeavouring to understand some aspects of conscious and unconscious mental processes by analogy with the theory of epicritic and protopathic sensibility propounded by Sir Henry Head. According to this theory, the diffuse, all-or-none qualities of an older, more primitive type of cutaneous sensibility, the protopathic, are suppressed by a later, more localized and finely graded type of sensibility, the epicritic, in so far as they are incompatible with it, and otherwise are fused. In much the same way, Rivers suggests, the uncontrolled and undiscriminating, highly emotional characteristics of those processes which arise from the operation of the thalamus are held in check by the more discriminating and rational processes which result from the possession of a highly complex cerebral cortex, but are also fused with them. The details of the analogy cannot be sustained, since the theory of cutaneous sensibility on which it was based is no longer generally accepted. It can, however, be taken as an illustration of the difference in the biological orientation of Freud, Jung and the British group. Although both Freud and Jung can be seen to make

[1] *Ibid.*, p. 481.   [2] *Supra*, p. 119.

use of biological assumptions current in their day—the Lamarckian theory of heredity, for instance—Freud's interest from the early days of psychoanalysis onward lay entirely in its human applications. And while Jung is more aware than Freud of the world of nature to which human life itself belongs, it is probably not unfair to say that his attitude is of a rather general, philosophic type reminiscent of the Romantic writers,[1] and that only in the British group is there such a detailed interest in the linking up of man and other animals.

An exception to the statement that the British school is concerned more with the incorporation of psychoanalysis into general psychology than with systematizations of clinical experience is found in the work of the slightly later writer, Ian Suttie, whose work forms to a greater extent an ordered account of conclusions reached from psychotherapeutic practice and is more detailed than that of the others in its discussion of human relationships. Therefore, although belonging geographically and by his own associations with the British group, Suttie will be mentioned in conjunction with a second group whose views also resemble Jung's in some respects.

These practitioners, often known as the neoanalysts, came into prominence in the United States from the 1930's onwards. Strictly, perhaps, they should be divided into three groups—those with the most markedly cultural orientation, in particular Erich Fromm and Karen Horney; those working mainly with psychotic patients, among whom H. S. Sullivan and Frieda Fromm-Reichmann have been leading figures; and the psychosomatic group of Franz Alexander in Chicago. All, however, raise much the same objections to orthodox psychoanalysis as have been found already in Jung and the early British eclectics. Karen Horney, for instance, writing of the libido theory, declares: 'The assumption that every striving for pleasure is at bottom a striving for libidinal satisfaction is arbitrary.'[2] The existence of the Oedipus complex in its accepted form, i.e. the presence, as she puts it, of sexual desire strong enough to arouse so much jealousy and fear that they can be dissolved only by repression, seems to her exceptional rather than a universal phenomenon, and unlikely to occur without a strong environmental influence. For example, children may cling to one parent, the stronger or more protective, from sheer anxiety, which does not necessarily take on a

[1] See, for instance, *supra*, p. 139 n.
[2] *New Ways*, p. 68. London: Kegan Paul, 1947.

sexual colouring but may easily do so. Or there may be a gross sexual approach to the child, sexually tinged caresses, or 'an emotional hothouse atmosphere'.[1] This is reminiscent of Jung's statement in his later work that 'Unless diseased, children play these strange and unnatural roles only when they are unconsciously forced into them by their parents' attitude.'[2] Suttie, too, without denying the existence of a germ of erotic feeling, has pointed out various aspects of patriarchal cultures, such as early childbearing and age-disparity between wife and husband, which may foster the typical Oedipus complex. Since the woman is compensating in her relations with her children for the companionship and reality interests which she is denied elsewhere, it is easy for a premature sexualization of the infant's sensual feelings toward her to occur. 'Finally, under patriarchal conditions, the mother *allows the child* to perceive the father as the chief obstacle to its exclusive possession of herself—sexually or otherwise.'[3] Freud's own antecedents, Suttie comments, 'lie in perhaps the most patriarchal of all cultures'.[4]

Turning to the interpretation of the Oedipus myth itself, Suttie, followed later by Erich Fromm, points out that in the naming of his complex, Freud has not paid attention to the fact that the hero himself was not the original transgressor; instead it was the father who, having consulted the oracle about the danger of being supplanted in his kingdom, rid himself of the rival at birth. This would not affect the clinical findings—it could even be argued along Freudian lines that the prominence given in the Oedipus story to the aggression of the father was a displacement of the affect really felt by the infant. Suttie thinks, however, that in stressing the infant's jealousy of the father Freud has lost sight of the jealousy that men may feel of women on account of their close relations with the child. In the importance that Suttie and Fromm give to the child's relationship with its mother they again resemble Jung, especially in the *Psychology of the Unconscious*. Fromm in particular repeats almost exactly the Jungian view of incest: 'The essence of incest is not the sexual craving for members of the same family. This craving, in so far as it is to be found, is only one expression of the much more profound and fundamental desire to remain a child attached to those

---

[1] *Ibid.*, p. 82 *et seq.*   [2] *Contribs.*, p. 341.
[3] *Origins of Love and Hate*, p. 106. London: Kegan Paul, 1935.
[4] *Ibid.*, p. 104.

protecting figures of whom the mother is the earliest and most influential.'[1]

In keeping once more with the modified attitude to early family relationships is a lesser regard for repression of infantile experience and greater interest in present-day conflicts in neurosis. Horney suggests that the recall of infantile material can even be evasive in its character, since the patient 'hopes thereby to avoid facing trends which actually exist within him'[2]—a statement which comes close to Jung's, that it is 'a very suspicious circumstance that these patients frequently show a pronounced tendency to account for their illnesses by some long past event . . .'[3] For childhood amnesia they suggest the same explanation as Rivers—that the impact of new experience is such that the old experience no longer fits the framework of living, and drops out. In their discussion of repression they are concerned at least as much with repression of 'the good' as with 'the bad'. The necessity of maintaining a certain façade, Horney writes, 'leads not only to repressing "bad", anti-social, egocentric, "instinctual" drives, but also to repressing the most valuable, the most alive factors in a human being'[4]—a simpler expression, perhaps, of Jung's view that 'There are actually people who have the whole meaning of their life, their true significance, in the unconscious, while in the conscious mind is nothing but inveiglement and error.'[5] This point is emphasized, if anything, even more by Fromm. According to his view of dreams 'we are not only less reasonable and less decent . . . but we . . . are also more intelligent, wiser, and capable of better judgment when we are asleep than when we are awake.'[6] For instance, a well-known writer was offered a position in which he would have had to give up his integrity as a writer in exchange for money and fame. While considering the offer he dreamt that at the foot of a mountain were two very successful men of his acquaintance whose opportunism he despised; they told him to drive his car up the narrow road which led to the peak; he followed their advice, and near the top his car fell off and he was killed. The dream, that is, was saying in its symbolic language that acceptance of the position offered was equivalent to destruction as an integrated human being.[7]

[1] *Psychoanalysis and Religion*, p. 85. New Haven: Yale Univ. Press, 1950. Cf. Jung, *supra*, pp. 62–5.   [2] *Op. cit.*, p. 283.   [3] *Supra*, p. 49.
[4] *Op. cit.*, p. 229.   [5] *Two Essays*, new ed., p. 46; old ed. p. 46.
[6] *The Forgotten Language*, p. 38. London: Gollancz, 1952.
[7] *Man for Himself*, p. 165. Rinehart: 1947.

It becomes evident too that these writers are more concerned than the early Freudians with questions involving moral values. My own opinion, says Horney, 'is that an absence of value judgments belongs among those ideals we should try rather to overcome than to cultivate.'[1] Fromm writes similarly:

> 'My experience as a practising psychoanalyst has confirmed my conviction that problems of ethics cannot be omitted from the study of personality, either theoretically or therapeutically. . . . In many instances a neurotic symptom is the specific expression of moral conflict, and the success of the therapeutic effort depends on the understanding and solution of the person's moral problem.'[2]

In short, they maintain with Jung that 'The moral attitude to life is a real factor in life with which the psychologist must reckon if he is not to commit the gravest errors.'[3] This means that more stress is laid on the synthesizing aspects of psychotherapy; the dangers of too much analysis are sometimes stated in terms which bring to mind Jung's strictures against the philosophy of 'Nothing but.' The tendency to deny that mental faculties may exist in their own right fosters insecurity of judgment, Horney declares. For instance, it may lead the analysand not to take a stand against anything without making the reservation that his judgment is probably no more than an expression of unconscious preference or dislike. 'But it is merely dogmatic to assert, for instance, that a judgment cannot be simply the expression of what one holds to be right or wrong, that one cannot be devoted to a cause because one is convinced of its value, that friendliness cannot be a direct expression of good human relationships.'[4] The same criticism is made by Fromm: while psychoanalysis has tremendously increased our knowledge of man, its main function in the sphere of ethics has been that of 'debunking', of demonstrating that value judgments and ethical norms are often rationalized expressions of irrational fears and desires. Although this debunking is valuable, it becomes increasingly sterile when it fails to go beyond mere criticism.[5]

For the patient-physician relationship within which the re-synthesis is attempted certain implications follow from the different estimation of infantile experience, as with Jung and the early British eclectics.

---

[1] *Op. cit.*, p. 297. [2] *Man for Himself*, p. viii.
[3] *Mod. Man*, p. 224. [4] *Op. cit.*, pp. 187–8.
[5] *Man for Himself*, p. 6.

Frieda Fromm-Reichmann is representative in pointing out that since

> 'our thinking does not coincide with Freud's doctrine of the ubiquity of the Odeipus complex, the positive (sexual) attachment to the parent of the opposite sex, with concomitant rivalrous hatred for the parent of the same sex . . . we do not understand as a foregone conclusion that the difficulties of therapists in their relationships with patients and vice versa stem from, or are only a repetition of, their unresolved Oedipus constellations'.[1]

Granted that the patterns of our later interpersonal relationships are formed in early life, she continues, there is a danger of carrying this insight too far and neglecting the interchange between therapist and patient in a new experience. Similarly, Karen Horney, discussing sexual feelings towards the analyst, thinks that 'A great part of what appears as sexuality has in reality very little to do with it, but is an expression of the desire for reassurance'[2]—a passage which comes close to that of Jung, who states at a much earlier period that the patient, not knowing the right way to lay hold of the physician's personality, gropes toward it by means of this analogy.[3]

Of interest also to the student of Jung's work is the attention which is now being paid elsewhere to the personality of the psychiatrist and his own reactions to the therapeutic situation. In the early days of psychoanalysis, as Fromm-Reichmann explains, it was thought that any psychiatrist of integrity and emotional stability who was well-trained in the use of psychotherapeutic tools could treat any type of patient. More recently it has been realized that success or failure depends in addition upon the existence of an empathic quality between psychiatrist and patient.[4] Erich Fromm, among others, has suggested that Freud's neutral, distant attitude toward the patient was his greatest error in technique. 'One cannot help anyone emotionally or understand him psychologically if one remains distant and looks at him as an object.'[5]

But it is probably from those engaged, like Fromm-Reichmann, in the treatment of psychotic patients that the fullest statements have come of the need for deeper involvement on the part of the physician.

---

[1] *Principles of Intensive Psychotherapy*, p. 6. London: Allen & Unwin, 1953.
[2] *The Neurotic Personality of Our Time*, p. 157. London: Kegan Paul, 1937.
[3] *Supra*, p. 54.   [4] *Op. cit.*, p. 62.
[5] 'The Social Philosophy of "Will Therapy".' *Psychiatry*, Vol. 2, No. 2, 1939; pp. 229–37 (p. 232).

M. Grotjahn, for instance, reports the experience of an analyst who tried to show the patient that since her hallucinations were no different from those he could produce in his fantasies, he and she might find a world of hallucination together. 'When he attempted to "hallucinate" with her, the patient began to listen to him for the first time, and thus the beginning of some kind of communication was established.'[1] Such involvement is acknowledged to have dangers, in reactivating the psychiatrist's own conflicts; even so, it is considered to hold out the best hope of cure or amelioration by psychotherapeutic means. Here we may recall Jung's statements that the therapist is 'a fellow participant in a process of individual development' and that this participation must go 'right beyond professional routine . . . to the limits of his subjective possibilities', together with his report of 'cases where short psychotic attacks were actually taken over . . .'[2] Remembering also the direct evidence for believing that a fair proportion of Jung's patient's have fallen into the borderline psychotic rather than neurotic category, we can see him as, in effect, a pioneer in this field.[3]

At the same time Jung and these other therapists have in common a tendency to move away from the clear-cut diagnostic terminology current in most psychiatric work. In the first place, Fromm Reichmann argues, diagnosis can often be misleading, since the older classifications are bound to be revised in the light of recent progress. In the second place, as Erich Fromm explains, there has been an increasing tendency for patients to seek psychoanalytic aid not because they are suffering from any definite psychotic or neurotic symptoms, but because they experience 'difficulties in living'—a development which recalls Jung's own report that about a third of his patients were suffering, not from any clinically definable neurosis but from the senselessness and emptiness of their lives.[4] Owing to this change, emphasis has been shifted more and more from the therapy of neurotic symptoms to the therapy of the neurotic character, and it is in doing this that more account of values has been taken. For,

---

[1] 'Some Features Common to Psychotherapy of Psychotic Patients and Children.' *Psychiatry*, Vol. 1, No. 3, 1938; pp. 317–22 (p. 318).

[2] *Supra* p. 146.

[3] A technical point of similarity is avoidance of the classical free-association method, though slightly different reasons are put forward, i.e. Jung believes that the meaning of the dream or image is elucidated more fully by association around it, while these later writers stress the undesirable effects of free association in increasing the patient's lack of integration.   [4] *Supra*, p. 149.

as Fromm points out, while it is comparatively simple to decide what the therapeutic aim should be in a case of hysterical vomiting or obsessional thinking, it is not so simple to decide on a therapeutic aim in cases of 'character neurosis'.[1]

It would, however, be giving an unnecessarily limited impression of present-day psychoanalytical thinking to seek views of this kind only among the early British eclectics and the neo-analysts. Especially since the death of Freud in 1939 there has been a fairly widespread tendency toward that 'continuous self-criticism and tentative modification from within',[2] in the words of the English writer Marjorie Brierley, which Jung had sought to bring about in 1912. As Brierley declares, 'psychoanalysis should no longer be identified with Freud any more than the theory of evolution is now identified with Darwin, although this also happened for a time and had to be outgrown'.[3] Among the modifications of writers who have remained more closely affiliated to the psychoanalytical movement are, once more: a greater willingness to take account of the present situation, including, at times, the interpretation of dreams in accordance with its problems; fuller discussion of the effects of practice on the therapist himself; more concern with synthesis as well as with analysis; and the admission of needs other than the material, which seek satisfaction in the arts and in the creation of a philosophy of life. The first two points may be illustrated by Winnicott's dream already cited.[4] Under the latter headings, Marjorie Brierley speaks, like Hadfield and Horney as well as Jung himself, of the individual as 'a living being, whose psychological goal remains the attainment of optimum personal integrity'.[5] The term 'psycho-analysis', she says,

> 'is misleading when, as happens too often, it is understood to imply that psychoanalysts have no interest in synthesis. While they are trying to disentangle and trace the history of the various components of the total personality pattern, they are inevitably confronted with all the phenomena of synthesis and dissociation which have determined that pattern. Therapeutic success is proportionate to the degree and kind of reintegration initiated by the psycho-analytic process.'[6]

She objects to the reduction of human activity to 'nothing but' primary instinct gratification, insisting that the transformations of

[1] *Psychoanalysis and Religion*, p. 73. [2] *Op. cit.*, p. 117.
[3] *Ibid.*, p. 14.   [4] *Supra*, p. 117.   [5] *Op. cit.*, p. 245.
                  [6] *Ibid.*, p. 124.

the instinct which are brought about by mental organization are just as real as the primal impulses themselves: 'Probably many thwarted suckling wishes are gratified in the sublimated forms of listening to music, but the adult lover of music would seldom experience any pleasure if he were offered a wet nurse instead of a symphony.'[1]

These ideas—perhaps the easiest to gather together—by no means exhaust the affinities between Jung and other writers. Previously we mentioned his anticipations of the Kleinian school;[2] some interest on Flugel's part in his idea that regression may have adaptive significance in enabling the organism to recuperate;[3] and an acknowledgment by Angyal of the place to be given to the more primitive modes of thinking in our daily lives.[4] Other instances are Ferenczi's concern with the patient's responsiveness to hidden attitudes in the analyst and the child's responsiveness to such attitudes in the parents;[5] the re-birth theme used by Otto Rank, who sees man's development as a process leading from blind impulse through conscious will to self-conscious knowledge, which corresponds to a series of births, with their struggle and pain, separation from the universal, and creation of an individual cosmos;[6] and the stress on *play* in the work of Fromm and Suttie, who—in contrast to Freud with his emphasis on forcible socialization—take up as it were Jung's concept of the child as possessing a storehouse of constantly accessible libido[7] and point to the value of this surplus in enabling him to experiment and to create.[8]

But, it may very well be asked, what value can we hope to find in the making of citations from writers who in other respects will differ from one another and from Jung? What can reasonably be concluded from a survey of this kind? Two points may be suggested. In the first place, these anticipations of later writers have some importance independently of truth or falsehood as a possible source of Jung's appeal. If, forty, or even twenty, years ago exponents of these views who possessed standing in the psychiatric world were considerably less common, individuals who inclined toward them, whether as lay-

---

[1] *Ibid.*, p. 165. Cf. Jung, *supra*, p. 51: 'A similar nomenclature would then lead us to classify the Cathedral of Cologne as mineralogy, because it is built of stones.' [2] *Supra*, p. 124. [3] *Supra*, p. 113. [4] *Supra*, p. 114.
[5] See Ferenczi, S., 'Confusion of Tongues Between the Adult and the Child.' *Int. J. Psycho-Anal.*, Vol. XXX, Pt. 4, 1949; pp. 225–30.
[6] See Mullahy, P., *Oedipus Myth and Complex*, pp. 162–207. New York: Hermitage Press, 1942. [7] *Supra*, p. 104.
[8] Suttie, *op. cit.*, p. 19. Fromm, *Man for Himself*, pp. 186–7.

men or trainees, would be likely to be drawn to Jung. In the second place, although the circumstance that a number of other writers have had similar ideas is insufficient in itself to prove that these ideas are sound, the existence of a body of clinical opinion in their favour indicates a need for further study. The question then arises of finding ways in which clinical opinion can be rendered more precise and of subjecting it to some form of proof or disproof. For this, improved methods of recording and analysing data are required. Whether or not it will ever be feasible, as one investigator hopes,[1] to introduce tape-recorder and cine-camera into individual sessions, or to make other arrangements comparable to that of the observer in group psychotherapy, it is clearly not impossible to build up teams of depth psychologists largely agreed on diagnostic and therapeutic criteria, able to pool at any rate a certain amount of case material, recorded in ways sufficiently uniform to make comparison practicable, and with the resources necessary for long-term follow-up, including checks on such of the patient's statements as can be verified by independent means. A supplementary line of attack is experiment, both with animals and human beings. This approach has not always been favoured by clinicians, on the ground that the experimental situation is too simple to do justice to analytical complexities, and that in the case of animal experiments, analogies drawn from the mental processes of creatures whose symbol-forming capacities are so much more rudimentary than our own may be less helpful than misleading. Nevertheless, from the animal experiments of Masserman, Liddell and others have come not only indications of processes resembling conflict and repression in the psychology of man, but also observations which may be relevant in therapy. For instance, from one such experiment it was concluded that the animal's learning to control the situation—corresponding, the experimenters suggested, to 'working through' in humans—was more effective than rest or reassurance; an experiment with human subjects can be cited in which a simple interpretative technique proved more successful than a purely non-directive method in facilitating recall of complex indicators on the word-association test;[2] and learning experiments, both animal

---

[1] See Kubie, L. S., 'Problems and Techniques of Psychoanalytic Validation and Progress' in *Psychoanalysis as Science*, ed. E. Pumpian-Mindlin. Stanford Univ. Press, 1952, pp. 46–124.

[2] Keet, cited by E. Hilgard: 'Experimental Approaches to Psycho-Analysis,' in *Psychoanalysis as Science*, pp. 3–45.

and human, in which the best adaptations and acquisitions of skill were made when anxiety was at a minimum, would also seem to have bearing on the handling of the therapeutic situation.[1] However, as would be expected from the attitude to experiment which has been found already in Jung's later work, together with the more precise nature of psychoanalytical formulations, it is the influence of the latter school, often on non-analysts, to which we are indebted for a continuation of the search for links between clinical and general or comparative psychology in which Rivers and McDougall had been interested in the previous generation.[2]

With this we are brought again to Jung's distinction between knowledge and understanding. How far is it true that, as he several times declares, 'the positive advantages of *knowledge* work specifically to the disadvantage of *understanding*'[3] so that all scientific knowledge must be laid aside in the understanding of the individual? Material such as that above suggests that in the long run the therapist will be less effective if he lacks ordered knowledge of the events which are likely to be taking place within the therapeutic situation. The need for a knowledge of developmental processes, even from the therapeutic standpoint, has been touched on briefly in discussing Jung's concepts of mind.[4] In the present context we may take this up again, i.e. does the knowledge that, for instance, maternal deprivation is frequently found in the background of juvenile thieves, or a clinical hunch that some kinds of phobia are common in dependent personalities with dominating mother figures, interfere with the empathic process of understanding individual cases? Or does it not enable understanding to be mobilized more rapidly in the directions where it is required? Jung himself admits at least once that 'If one individual were totally different from every other individual, then psychology would be impossible as a science.'[5] Nevertheless, the statements we have cited seem to have more than poetical significance, suggesting that— probably as a consequence of his lack of interest in the earlier developmental phases—concentration on the individual case, which we see well expressed in his provisions for psychotherapy, can be

[1] See Russell-Davis, D., 'Clinical Problems and Experimental Researches.' *Brit. J. Med. Psychol.*, Vol. XXXI, Pt. 2, 1958; pp. 74–82.
[2] Very recently some interest has arisen within the Jungian school in a possible similarity between the archetypes and the innately determined perceptual patterns studied by Lorenz, Tinbergen and other students of animal behaviour in the last twenty years, but this has not yet been worked out clearly.
[3] *Supra*, p. 84.   [4] *Supra*, p. 124.   [5] *Practice of Psychotherapy*, p. 5.

taken as one 'pole' of his psychology, with the collective unconscious functioning as the other.

A marked difference between Jung and the later writers with whom we have compared him is indeed their interest in the development of personality in the early years. Aside from the orthodox Freudian, supplemented by Kleinian or neo-Kleinian, theory, the most thorough-going reconstruction is probably that of H. S. Sullivan, who distinguishes in the infant the needs for satisfaction, i.e. of physical requirements, and security, both of which are first experienced in the relation with the mother, who becomes split into a 'Good Mother', allaying these needs and giving the infant her approval, and a 'Bad Mother' who does neither.[1] Much of this is consistent with the Kleinian theory, but Sullivan, like Suttie in his discussion of the mother-child relation,[2] lays his emphasis not on impulse gratification but on the give and take between the infant and significant others in his personal environment. Sullivan makes a further contribution to the study, or interpretation, of these years in distinguishing three modes of experience, the prototaxic, which is present at birth, and is a mere sentience, an experiencing of happenings as they come along; the parataxic, which develops during infancy and is that mode of experience in which symbols are used, but in a private, incommunicable way; and the syntaxic, beginning in childhood with the development of the ability to utter articulated sounds, which can be subjected to consensual validation. This account seems helpful in counteracting any impression than experiences of too advanced a nature are being attributed to the very young infant. If Sullivan's theory were being considered in and for itself, it could, like theories in general, be inquired into at some points. For instance, in his emphasis on interpersonal relations Sullivan seems to go to the opposite extreme to that of Jung, taking so much account of such experience— indeed, defining personality itself as 'the relatively enduring pattern of recurrent interpersonal situations which characterize a human life'[3] —that the reader may almost lose sight of the fact that these relatively enduring patterns are tied to particular organisms. Considering his work more specifically in relation to that of Jung, it may be said that a point of view which Jung expresses in his handling of the patient-

[1] See Sullivan, H. S., *Interpersonal Theory of Psychiatry*, 1952, pp. 85–91; pp. 111–24.
[2] *Origins of Love and Hate*, pp. 29 et seq.   [3] *Op. cit.*, p. 110–11.

physician relationship[1] is elaborated by this more systematic writer into a theory of personality and its development.

Fromm and Horney, though less concerned than Sullivan with the early phases of development, have interpreted the Freudian stages in such a way that the various types of libido organization are taken as representing the kinds of relatedness to the world which can result from the child's early interactions. According to Fromm's interpretation, the child may develop a receptive ('oral-sucking') orientation, feeling that the only way to get what he wants is to receive it as a gift from outer sources. Or he may become an exploitative, or 'oral-biting', type, expecting to receive things not as a gift but by taking them away from others through force or cunning. Or thirdly, he may become a hoarding, or 'anal-retentive', type, expecting to receive little from the outer world and hoarding what he has. Freud's 'genital character', Fromm suggests, is a term which adequately symbolizes the individual who is fortunate enough to develop a *productive* orientation—the stage of sexual maturity being that in which man has the capacity for natural productiveness, and in a wider sense the ability to use his powers freely. Horney makes much the same suggestions. As a result of many adverse influences—lack of love, lack of respect for the child's own potentialities—disturbances may be produced in the child's relations to himself and others. First he reacts with a feeling of basic anxiety, of weakness and helplessness in a dangerous world. This anxiety makes it necessary for him to find ways of coping with life safely. He may embark on a quest for affection at all costs, no matter what the price may be in submissiveness and hanging on to others; he may seek power to compensate his inner weakness, or he may withdraw from emotional participation to avoid being hurt.

In the main, of course, it is for a study of certain cultural factors that one would turn to these two writers. Horney gives in vivid terms her picture of 'the middle-class neurotic of Western civilization'. This type is characterized by 'a great potential hostility, by much more readiness and capacity for hate than for love, by emotional isolation, by a tendency to be egocentric, ready to withdraw, acquisitive, entangled in problems concerning possession and prestige'.[2] Among the factors bringing this about the most important is the individual competitiveness on which the culture is based. This 'not only domin-

[1] *Supra*, pp. 144–6.   [2] *New Ways*, pp. 168–9.

ates our relations in occupational groups, but also pervades our social relations, our friendships, our sexual relations and the relations within the family group, thus carrying the germs of destructive rivalry, disparagement, suspicion, begrudging envy into every human relationship'.[1] Fromm presents a similar picture in his description of the marketing orientation of modern man, i.e. the attitude of the individual, both to others and himself, is determined by the abstract and relatively unknown demands of the market in our time. Just as some shoes will be sentenced to economic death, no matter how much *use value* they possess, if the supply is greater than the demand, so 'Clerks and salesmen, business executives and doctors, lawyers and artists all appear on this market.' Success depends on how well a person sells himself, how well he gets his personality across, and the degree of success achieved largely determines self-esteem. But success in a competitive market with ever-changing conditions beyond one's own control is too shaky a foundation, and the result is a deep sense of inferiority, insecurity and helplessness. 'If the vicissitudes of the market are the judges of one's value, the sense of dignity and pride is destroyed.' Both the individual's powers and what they create become estranged, 'something different from himself, something for others to judge and to use; thus his feeling of identity becomes as shaky as his self-esteem'.[2]

These contributions lead us to a further difference, or group of differences, not unlike some of those already noted between Jung and Freud. For instance, although the neo-analytical writers are inclined to believe that hate and aggression are not primary but arise from frustration of the needs for affection and security, they certainly have much more than Jung to say about them. Horney's middle-class neurotic of Western civilization and Fromm's individual with the marketing orientation do not differ greatly from each other; they do seem to differ from the Jungian patient, troubled by the search for some meaning in life other than 'blank resignation and mournful retrospect'.[3] Also, in some respects the attitude of these writers to the patient seems nearer that of Freud. Horney, at any rate, adheres to the rule that 'analysis should be carried on with a certain amount of frustration of the patient'—the analyst has an 'obligation to be reserved toward the patient's desires and demands'.[4] This, like Freud's

---

[1] *Ibid.*, p. 173.   [2] *Man for Himself*, pp. 67–73 *et seq.*
[3] *Two Essays*, new ed. p. 73.   [4] *New Ways*, p. 163.

own statements, can be contrasted with Jung's requirement that the doctor shall go 'to the limits of his subjective possibilities'.[1] Horney is also more suspicious of the patient: 'The patient wants to achieve his ends on his own terms. He may wish to be freed of suffering without his personality being touched. . . . Even his quest for happiness, in itself the most effective of all motivations, cannot be taken at its face value, because the happiness the patient has in mind secretly entails the fulfilment of all his contradictory neurotic wishes.'[2]

At the same time the motives of the therapist are investigated closely. Horney speaks of the analyst as struggling, like the patient, with the problem of competition. Fromm-Reichmann considers it a difficulty in therapeutic practice that he may be so preoccupied with the idea that his paitients have to get well for the sake of his reputation as to deafen himself against their real needs. Similarly, 'insecure psychiatrists may insist upon their patients doing and accomplishing things before they are ready for it'.[3] Or 'The psychiatrist may be afraid of appearing ridiculous in the eyes of his colleagues or of the secretaries of his clinic. . . . The quest for prestige in our culture is so great that it will interfere with some doctor's efforts to become desensitized to it.'[4] This, surely, is a more complicated picture than that which Jung presents, of someone whom the patient trusts, lending moral strength.[5]

Altogether, there seems in the writings of the neo-analysts something that might be described as more exactitude and specificity. For example, after giving injunctions that before proceeding to treatment the psychiatrist will need to know the patient's age, social and economic status and family background, present family constellation and so forth, Fromm-Reichmann goes on to say that the psychiatrist will also 'pay attention to the way in which information is given. Does the prospective patient, for instance, show despair or apathy? Does he speak diffidently? Does he display discomfort, fear or anxiety, unhappiness or grief, etc.? . . . Special attention should be paid to the way in which the patient behaves as he first enters the psychiatrist's office . . .'[6] In making this citation it is not, of course, implied that such questions are anything but relevant to the therapeutic situation, nor is it supposed that therapists of other schools,

---

[1] *Supra*, p. 146. [2] *New Ways*, p. 288. [3] *Op. cit.*, pp. 14–15.
[4] *Ibid.*, pp. 30–1. [5] *Supra*, p. 144. [6] *Op. cit.*, pp. 48–9.

including Jung himself, would not seek this type of information. Nevertheless, an impression does arise that the patient in these circles is less *taken for granted as an individual* than he is with Jung, but is subjected to a closer scrutiny. These accounts are, perhaps, indications also of a greater concern with rational analysis—if not causal analysis, then analysis of present motives and their ramifications, but in any case analysis, usually of both past and present, rather than simple undeveloped statements.

So far as can be gathered from the written material, the therapy of these workers is often more active and dynamic in its style. Every analyst, says Horney, 'will *actively interfere* when he notices that the patient persistently avoids certain topics'.[1] He should listen, Fromm-Reichmann advises, 'sufficiently alertly so that he can interrupt and direct the patient toward the production of more relevant material'.[2] The temptation is very great, Alexander and French consider, 'merely to treat the patient's problems as he brings them to us and thus, as it were, to let the patient drift into an analysis. Such a planless therapy obviously entails the danger that the therapist may later find himself in unanticipated difficulties'. It is therefore highly important

> 'to outline as soon as possible a comprehensive therapeutic plan, to attempt to visualize in advance (even if only tentatively) just what we shall attempt with our patient, what we hope to accomplish, and in particular what complications we expect and how we plan to deal with them—in other words, to outline a sort of grand strategy for our treatment instead of trusting to our therapeutic intuition on a day-to-day basis to deal with the patient's difficulties as they arise.'[3]

Consciously directed effort, they add, reaches its goal 'more easily and more rapidly than does random effort'.[4] Now Alexander, ten years later, has begun to lay somewhat less emphasis on planning, saying that 'it is scarcely possible, even for the experienced man, to decide in advance what course a treatment will take'.[5] Even so, he compares psychoanalytically oriented treatment and chess, as 'procedures of strategy in which two minds oppose each other', states the technical problem: Can the most prolonged part of the treatment, the tedious middle game, be shortened by improved strategy?—and

---

[1] *New Ways*, p. 285. (Italics mine.)   [2] *Op. cit.*, p. 10.
[3] *Psychoanalytic Therapy*, p. 110. New York: Ronald Press Co., 1946.
[4] *Ibid.*, p. 107.
[5] *Psychoanalysis and Psychotherapy*, p. 169. London: Allen & Unwin, 1957.

concludes that it can. All this is markedly in contrast to Jung's statements that 'It is rewarding to observe patiently what happens quietly in the psyche', that the physician should not have too fixed a goal, since he 'can scarcely know what is wanted better than do nature and the will-to-live of the sick person' and that 'the new thing prepared by fate seldom or never corresponds to conscious expectation'.[1]

On the other hand, there is some reason to think that this school is less favourably disposed than Jung toward any *unconscious* influence on the part of the physician. The statement from Alexander and French, that 'Consciously directed effort reaches its goal more easily and more rapidly than does random effort', conveys this attitude in some degree. More indicative of a definite wish to avoid unconscious influence is Fromm-Reichmann's warning that the psychiatrist should keep his personal evaluations 'sufficiently apart from his professional life to avoid their inadvertent emanation'[2] and that while responsive reactions on his part are not barred, he must be careful to see that they 'cannot be used by patients as a means of orientation inadvertently guiding their productions and behaviour'.[3] Much, however, is said of the consciously determined modifications which may be introduced into the transference relationship. Alexander and French describe it as a tool, and 'To make any tool serve our purpose most effectively, we must first understand its full potentialities'.[4] For instance, the feelings which the therapist arouses in the patient when he sits behind a desk are very different from those produced when he sits near him as in a drawing room conversation or even more informally beside him on the couch. Or if therapist and patient smoke a cigarette together, the atmosphere may change immediately from the formal one of a standard psychoanalytical session to one of friendly co-operation in which they are on equal terms. There is need for constant alertness and agility, the writers add, since 'It is in this handling and *manipulation* of the transference relationship that the power of the therapist lies'.[5] Again one would not wish to throw doubt upon the desirability of the analyst's introducing some variations in approach from one patient to another, or within the same analysis. Nevertheless, the attitudes referred to—desire to avoid unconscious influence and closer attention to

---

[1] *Supra*, p. 150.   [2] *Op. cit.*, p. 35–6.   [3] *Op. cit.*, p. 12.
    [4] *Op. cit.*, p. 41.   [5] *Op. cit.*, p. 51.

manipulation of the patient-physician relationship—seem to involve more rationality and more activity than Jung's injunction to '*be* the man through whom you wish to influence others'.[1] Another way of viewing the matter might be to say that although the physician is a participant observer, patient and physician are still kept slightly more apart—there is less *merging* between them than in the case of the Jungian patient and physician, where the meeting of two personalities is 'like mixing two different chemical substances . . .'[2] and the physician would appear to be using his whole self more freely. Support for these suggestions is gained also from a statement made some fifteen years ago by Michael Fordham ('I can see no advantage in deliberately provoking a transference nor in deliberately avoiding it'.)[3] and by his recent formulation of the 'analytical ideal', i.e. a personality who does not need rules of procedure or techniques, 'but can use dreams, fantasies, affects, reflexions, etc., with safety because they are integrated into himself and adapted to the patient's needs'.[4]

The more externalized approach of the later people is indicated once again by Fromm-Reichmann's discussion of the psychiatrist's liking and disliking of his patients: 'As he learns about the historical data which are responsible for the characterological development, and for the psychopathology of the patient, the temptation of moral evaluation with the implication of acceptance or non-acceptance will be replaced by genetic understanding and therapeutic curiosity.'[5] Beside this may be put Jung's attitude of 'unprejudiced objectivity', which is 'a human quality—a kind of deep respect for facts and events and for the person who suffers from them—a respect for the secret of such a human life. . . . It is a moral achievement on the part of the doctor, who ought not to let himself be repelled by illness and corruption.'[6] Even the American-born H. S. Sullivan, though less saturated with such differences than some, is more matter-of-fact than Jung in his attitude to the patient-physician relationship. The psychiatrist, he says, 'is an *expert*, having *expert* knowledge of interpersonal relations, personality problems and so on'.[7] He 'must be

[1] *Supra*, p. 146.   [2] *Supra*, p. 145.
[3] *The Life of Childhood*, p. 140. London: Kegan Paul, 1944.
[4] 'Counter-transference.' *Brit. J. Med. Psychol.*, Vol. XXXIII, Pt. 1, 1960; pp. 1–7 (p. 4).
[5] *Op. cit.*, p. 39.   [6] *Mod. Man*, p. 271; *Psych. and Religion*, new ed. p. 339.
[7] *The Psychiatric Interview*, p. 12. New York: Norton, 1954.

sure that the other person is getting something out of it, that his expectation . . . of attaining whatever has motivated him in undergoing the interview, gets encouragement.'[1] He should 'have a very serious realization that he is earning his living, and that he must work for it' and he 'can legitimately expect only the satisfaction of feeling that he did what he was paid for'.[2]

There seems also to be a difference in their conception of a cure, of a kind that might be expected from the accounts of personality development. While Jung on one occasion defines 'that man as normal who can somehow exist under any circumstances that yield him in one way or another the necessary minimum of the means of life',[3] Fromm-Reichmann considers that a person 'is mentally healthy to the extent to which he is able to be aware of, and to handle, his overt relationships with other people'.[4] Much the same difference can be found in the degree of immediate contact with the social environment which Alexander and French envisage in defining neurosis as 'a failure to deal successfully with a given situation, a failure to find socially acceptable gratification for subjective needs under given circumstances'[5] and that which is conveyed in Jung's description of neurosis as 'the illness of one who has not found what life means for him'.

At the same time, in their attitude to commonly accepted values the neo-analysts seem less closely in touch with society than Jung. For instance, Fromm-Reichmann cites an explanation given at her hospital that 'homosexuality was nothing of which to be ashamed or any reason for hospitalization, provided that it did not impair the patient's security of living among the average prejudiced inhabitants of this culture'.[6] It can be assumed that Fromm-Reichmann approves the giving of this explanation, since she describes it as an instance of the psychiatrist's 'stating her own and the hospital's unprejudiced attitude regarding homosexuality'.[7] Jung, however, although seeking an attitude of 'unprejudiced objectivity' in the therapist, is more inclined to represent homosexuality, in the terms of his associate H. G. Baynes, as a breach of the human pact.[8] In referring to a homosexual youth whom he was treating, he speaks of 'that highly unpoetical affair which impelled him to come to me', adding later

[1] *Ibid.*, p. 17. [2] *Ibid.*, p. 19.
[3] *Two Essays*, old ed. p. 54; new ed. p. 55. [4] *Op. cit.*, p. xiv.
[5] *Op. cit.*, p. 8. [6] *Op. cit.*, p. 29. [7] *loc. cit.*
[8] *Analytical Psychology and the English Mind*, p. 198.

that while a hopeful prognosis could be discovered in the dreams, the patient consciously was 'full of hesitation and resistance . . . ever ready to slip back into his previous infantilism'.[1] A different conception of objectivity may be involved. Fromm-Reichmann apparently regards adherence to the conventional morality as endangering, if not destroying, the analyst's objectivity. Jung seems to hold that acceptance of the customary view is quite compatible with objectivity, i.e. that *without passing judgment on* the patient, an analyst may legitimately regard homosexuality as a condition which falls short of full mental health.

For the most part, the members of this group seem to regard neurotic symptoms as resulting from the stifling of the individual's own, essentially superior, intuitions by a more corrupt society, as in the case of Fromm's patient who had been offered a lucrative but soul-destroying job. Jung, too, is aware of this possibility, saying that not a few are neurotic because 'they are born or destined to become the bearers of new social ideals'.[2] But to a large extent his patients seem to suffer, in the earlier phases of their life, from an inability to throw themselves into the tasks which, as he considers, society has a right to demand that they fulfil; and in the later phases, from an inability to recognize the need for relinquishing the place which they have won and devoting themselves quietly to self-culture. We may recall his view that among young persons the search for a valuable personality is often a cloak for the evasion of biological duty,[3] and that on the other hand, an old man who cannot bid farewell to life is as sickly as a young man who cannot enter it.[4] In short, as we have said, on questions of value Jung is lined up with society as he conceives it rather more fully than the neo-analysts.

Reverting briefly to the British school, we may remember the slightly militant and spartan note encountered in one of McDougall's statements on therapy. This can be seen more readily in his use of the self-regarding sentiment. Above all, he writes, appeal may properly be made to the patient's sentiment of self-respect, in showing him that his sickness is 'something which would lower him in the esteem of his friends, if they understood it'.[5] The same note is found in

[1] *Development of Personality*, pp. 157–62.   [2] *Supra*, p. 50.
[3] *Supra*, p. 55.   [4] *Mod. Man*, p. 128.
[5] *Outline of Abnormal Psychology*, p. 473.

his conception of a well-knit character as 'one that can face all problems, all critical alternatives, and can make a decision".[1] Suttie's suggestion of a 'taboo on tenderness' is similar. After recording his surprise that any plea for sympathy evoked impatience and embarrassment, whereas sexual and excretory interests in the patient left him undisturbed, Suttie concludes that 'there is a *taboo on tenderness* every bit as spontaneous and masterful as the taboo on sex itself'.[2] Much the same preference for manly independence may lie behind various comments on the transference situation. Rivers in his account of one of his own patients explains that it had been 'a regular part of my treatment to guard against the process known to the psychoanalysts as transference . . . and . . . to inculcate independence, "fighting ahead on his own" '.[3] Later he expresses his reservations openly about 'the usual psycho-analytic procedure in which the patient is made to lie down in the presence of the analyser and started by him upon the process of free association, for I believe that in the majority of persons a state of a hypnoidal kind is thus set up which greatly assists the occurrence of a process of morbid transference'.[4] McDougall's reference to 'the ritual' which some psychoanalysts are apt to make of the technique of free association is almost identical.[5] It would appear that while the psychoanalysts, together with the neo-analysts, are stringent in their warnings against any attempt to exert undue influence on the patient in the transference situation, Rivers and McDougall are reluctant to evoke such a condition of dependence to begin with. Jung's statements do not have the note of militancy, but his conception of 'the man in the patient confronting the man in the doctor upon equal terms' brings to mind the possibility that he has in common with the British eclectic group a belief in the patient-physician relationship as one which is close without necessarily being infantile or damaging to the patient's independence. It would seem, too, that the British school, like Jung,[6] has less interest in, or less facility in the manipulation of, the more complicated Freudian concepts than is found in orthodox psychoanalytical circles. For instance, Freud's theory of homosexuality— that the boy defends himself against his desire for the mother by turning to the father and hence to other male objects—produces in

---

[1] *Ibid.*, p. 538.   [2] *Op. cit.*, p. 78.
[3] *Conflict and Dream*, pp. 35.   [4] *Ibid.*, pp. 59.
[5] See *Outline of Abnormal Psychology*, p. 466.   [6] *Supra*, p. 40; p. 56.

McDougall the reaction: 'Surely one would need to be very strongly under the influence of Freud if one is to accept this involved and complicated derivation of homosexuality from the Oedipus complex! Surely the two factors which he, in common with all others, recognizes are sufficient, namely, the organic factor and seduction!'[1]

Finally, the world of the British group appears to share with that of Jung some measure of security and stability, in comparison with the world as shown us by the neo-analysts. We may compare, for instance, Fromm-Reichmann's picture of the analyst's anxieties with what Rivers tells us of his own, namely, doubts 'whether I was not being influenced in my decision to separate two patients by other than purely medical considerations',[2] whether or not 'to leave my chief in Edinburgh, who was in a situation of peculiar difficulty, in which I knew that I might be of considerable service', and 'whether I ought not to return to the College my income as Fellow', since 'I was at this time making an amply sufficient income for my needs through my pay as a Captain in the R.A.M.C.'[3] The question in all these situations is: What might reasonably be expected of a man occupying such and such position in the duly constituted order —a Medical Superintendent, a second-in-command, a Cambridge Fellow with another source of income? That is, attention seems to have been focused on fulfilment of commitments, rather than enhancement of personal security or competition against others.

It will be remembered that in discussing the British school or group at the beginning of this chapter it was not possible to decide at all points how far their ideas were independent and how far they had been influenced by Jung. With the neo-analysts there is no doubt that contact has been slight. Very few references to Jung are made, and those that do occur are apt to be unsympathetic, if not mis-representations of his point of view. To give an illustration: Clara Thompson, reviewing *Modern Man in Search of a Soul*, gives us to understand that Jung speaks there of Freudian 'filth'.[4] In fact, his statement is: 'Only a great idealist like Freud could devote a life-time to the unclean work' of draining 'a miasmal swamp.'[5] Similarly, Karen Horney, writing of the transference relationship, considers that psychologists who have examined this further—among whom

---

[1] *Op. cit.*, p. 411.   [2] *Op. cit.*, p. 48.   [3] *Ibid.*, pp. 85–6.
[4] *Int. J. Psycho-Anal.*, Vol. XV, Pt. 3, pp. 349–51.   [5] *Mod. Man*, p. 247.

she mentions Jung—have failed to give Freud sufficient credit for pioneering work.[1] On the other hand, one of Jung's supporters, Dr. E. A. Bennet, writes—and from the material above it would seem justly—that although this is not generally acknowledged by the later writers, 'Many features in the "flexible" approach have been current practice for many years amongst analysts whose work is based on the views of Jung.'[2] It seems, then, that the attitude of the neo-analysts to Jung can be summed up as not so very different from that of orthodox Freudian analysts following the break.

Perhaps, however, even more than the British group, the neo-analysts, or any representatives of the later psychoanalytical school, the writer most reminiscent of Jung, at any rate so far as practical recommendations are concerned, is the German psychiatrist Hans Prinzhorn, whose book, *Psychotherapy*, was written shortly before most of the papers in *Modern Man in Search of a Soul*.

Just as in Jung the patient throws himself into the arms of humanity, represented by the physician, 'freed at last from the burden of moral exile',[3] so to Prinzhorn psychotherapy 'is fundamentally an affair of two persons, wherein the suffering, isolated seeker after help, separated from the community, finds in the leader, the mediator thro' whom he can return to the world, to the human community'.[4] The patient, in giving himself to another person in confession, 'sets foot on the slender bridge of trust in humanity', and the confessor, not in his private capacity, but 'as a speaking tube for something which is not his, but in whose service he is and in whose name he acts . . . pours forth the free strong breath of life'. In order to do this the therapist must possess '*real superiority*', without any touch of egotism, which transforms itself completely into 'an effluence that penetrates' the patient.[5] And just as in Jung the doctor must *be* the man through whom he wishes to influence others, so to Prinzhorn the superiority of the therapist springs not from any method but from the maturity of his own personality, which enables him to be 'adequate to the highly complicated human and cultural situation'.[6] This can never be achieved intellectually—Prinzhorn stresses, like

[1] *New Ways*, p. 154.
[2] 'Psycho-Therapy,' *Recent Progress in Psychiatry*, Vol. II, 1950, ed. Fleming, G. W. T. H. Journal of Mental Science. pp. 615–34 (p. 616).
[3] *Supra*, p. 142.
[4] *Psychotherapy*, p. 267. London: Jonathan Cape, 1932 (German edition, 1928).   [5] *Ibid.*, pp. 261–6.   [6] *Ibid.*, p. 169.

Jung, that it depends on 'a life not of talk but of deeds'.[1] Once again, just as for Jung an important part of such maturity is the possession of 'avowable, credible, and defensible convictions . . .',[2] so Prinzhorn too believes that it is necessary for the therapist to form a picture of the world. As soon as he has done this for himself 'all his activities will probably receive . . . their one consistent meaning'.[3] It simply is not true, he writes, 'that one can discuss with a neurotic, even for a single hour, his quite ordinary troubles (headache, sleeplessness) without the personal view of the world being revealed and urged, in estimates and even in questions'. In discussing sexuality, especially, 'even the most general question contains, if not in the words themselves, yet in the tone and manner, an orientation of values which the patient of fine feeling apprehends quite spontaneously'.[4] Or, as Jung has said, 'What stands behinds sexuality or the instinct to power is the *attitude to sexuality and power*.'[5]

Every psychotherapy, from its very nature, leads into the realm of religion, as soon as the patient reaches that point—which really constitutes the psychotherapeutic situation—where he realizes the opportunity he has, of guiding himself, with outside help, better than before. At this moment 'the therapist is the representative of the supreme law; in the religious sense, the *mediator*. This is the reason why his person, his character, his view of the universe, his ethic, play such an immensely important part in the treatment.'[6] In so far as a therapist is neutral and insusceptible he is unfit for the work. But this does not imply domination. Psychoanalysis is essentially 'an excursion of two persons who, although one is the leader, and the other the person led, are gaining experiences in common',[7] and in this relationship it is of vital importance to have regard for 'the atmosphere of the other person, which, as foreign territory, even the helper may only enter as a guest'.[8]

Like Jung, Prinzhorn is especially interested in therapeutic work with older patients. Already at about the fortieth year, he thinks, 'it is a case not so much of clearing a way for oneself by better orientation in the basis of life, but rather of setting one's life-experience in order and finding dominant notes for a world picture already, in the main planned'.[9] In his philosophy of life he stresses two aspects—a

---

[1] *Ibid.*, p. 331. [2] *Supra*, p. 146. [3] *Op. cit.*, p. 265.
[4] *Ibid.*, p. 122. [5] *Supra*, p. 128. [6] *Op. cit.*, p. 65.
[7] *Ibid.*, p. 238. [8] *Ibid.*, p. 268. [9] *Ibid.*, p. 126.

tendency, on the one hand, '*to pass from the impersonal group being to the ever more sharply, more consciously, delimited individual being,*[1] which corresponds to the movement from *participation mystique* to 'conscious relationship'; and a sense, on the other hand, of 'vital harmony with the cosmic powers', the assured conviction, 'the faith, if you please—very seldom clear, but carrying with it a boundless responsibility, that *one* great meaning connects the whole of life, from the cosmos, through the nature of the earth, the vegetable and animal kingdoms, up to man',[2] which is similar to the sense of oneness with humanity that Jung regards as another aspect of the individuation process.

The chief differences seem to be as follows: First, Prinzhorn has more to say than Jung of the *loneliness* of the neurotic. What worries and oppresses the neurotic throughout all his multiplicity of symptoms 'is the dread of loneliness, of being useless, of not being wanted any more'.[3] He 'would never have gone to the psychotherapist if he had not been tortured by loneliness!'[4] Secondly, while declaring that the Jungian concepts of mind are too complicated to be workable,[5] Prinzhorn does not attempt to put forward others in their place.

In view of the similarities it would be interesting to know whether Jung and Prinzhorn had any influence on each other's work. Since Prinzhorn's book appeared in 1928 and Jung's essential ideas were available in 1912, it is clear that priority belongs to Jung. On the other hand, the expressions in Prinzhorn which resemble Jung's most closely are not used by Jung until the early 1930's. It seems likely, therefore, that their therapy was developed independently—similarities arising not from the direct influence of the one upon the other, but from some common source in their background of reading or of living.

[1] *Ibid.*, p. 93. [2] *Ibid.*, p. 121. [3] *Ibid.*, p. 127.
[4] *Ibid.*, p. 238. [5] *Ibid.*, p. 69.

Chapter VIII

SOME NOTES ON RELIGION IN
THE WORK OF JUNG

Already, both in the intermediate and the later periods, Jung has been seen to believe that spiritual needs are inherent in man's nature, and that a *Weltanschauung*, or conceptually organized attitude, is of great importance in the ordering of his life. Especially in view of the claims which have been made on his behalf, i.e. that he has succeeded in reconciling science and religion, we will consider more closely what his teachings on these problems are.

Turning back to *Psychology of the Unconscious*, we find that although religion was not then a central issue in his work, some of Jung's basic ideas are to be found there. That is, he gave an important civilizing role to Christianity, and to a lesser extent other mystery religions, in the concluding centuries of the Graeco-Roman era especially, but held that the time had now come to withdraw the projection of the Deity—in reality, an honouring of man's own libido—replace belief by understanding, and move toward moral autonomy.[1]

During the later period, particularly, as we have noted, after about 1930, Jung became increasingly aware of 'modern man's dilemma', i.e. that for many people of the present era the old religious forms have been outgrown, even to the extent of becoming almost meaningless, while the needs to which they ministered remain. In exploring this situation, encountered regularly in his therapeutic practice, he expanded his account of the historical development and functions of religion, and paid a great deal of attention to the psychological phenomena of religious experience. From 1948 onwards these contributions have been followed by massive comparisons of Chris-

[1] *Supra*, p. 59 *et seq.*

tian and other symbolism and reconstructions of dogma,[1] which, together with the accounts of religious experience, have evoked considerable comment, not so much from psychologists as from theologians, on whose sphere they can be said to impinge.

The account of historical development runs broadly as follows. For the primitive, religion has a compensatory function in strengthening the ego. At any moment, since he is almost wholly a 'collective being', his rudimentary sense of I-ness may be swept away by invasions of the unconscious. Jung cites the case of a primitive, enraged by the failure of a hunting expedition, who first strangled his small son and then mourned for him with the same lack of comprehension. Religion helps the primitive by objectifying such psychic contents; in viewing them as demons, spirits of the dead, etc., he separates them from his ego and is able to cope with them more easily. Among the civilized, religion no longer has to reckon with a weak ego function, but in the development of Christianity there has also been a compensatory element, since its ascetic trends were a protest against the licentiousness of the ancient world, and its belief in the immortality of each individual soul was a reaction against the degradation of the individual in slavery.

Besides possessing a compensatory function, religion has contributed to the onward flow of life for both primitive and civilized by giving expression in ritualistic and symbolic form to the fundamental human relationships, thus weakening the ties in actuality. Everywhere, at all times, life must continue—children must be liberated from their parents, take a wider place in the community, and become parents in their turn. Even the most primitive peoples take special measures, such as initiation rites in adolescence, at the periods of psychic transition. On a higher level the same tasks are undertaken by the great religions. Within Christianity, Jung considers, the Catholic system is by far the most complete:

'Here the father and mother world of childhood is dissolved by a rich system of analogical symbols; a patriarchal order adopts the adult into a new relation of childhood by means of spiritual generation and rebirth. ... The Pope as Pater Patrum and *Ecclesia Mater* are parents of a family which includes the whole of Christendom, except such parts of it as

[1] See especially 'A Psychological Approach to the Dogma of the Trinity,' *Psych. and Religion*, new ed. pp. 107–200; 'Transformation Symbolism in the Mass,' 1954, *Ibid.*, pp. 201–96; and 'Answer to Job,' 1952, *Ibid.*, pp. 355–470.

protest against this . . . a place is found both for the still active parental imagos and for that feeling of being a child which nothing can extinguish from the heart of man.'[1]

At the Reformation much of this was lost—to Protestants the Catholic symbolism had become outworn. The Germanic peoples, in particular, seemed to feel the need of a less controlled experience of God, 'as often happens to adventurous and restless people who are too youthful for any form of conservatism or domestication'.[2] It appears that with the passage of time the 'aura' of a symbol disappears, it becomes 'saturated with consciousness' and no longer has the same effect of reconciling conscious and unconscious; and that a force exists within the psyche which urges man away even from the more spiritualized form of primitive unity, toward individual differentiation, in spite of the suffering that it brings. At any rate, the denudation process has continued to the present day, 'the bridge from dogma to the inner experience of the individual has broken down', leaving the Protestant with nothing but the historical figure of Christ and a much-debated idea of God, to whom his relationship, owing to the progressive impoverishment of symbolism, has 'developed into an unbearably sophisticated I-You relationship'.[3]

The break-up of a dogmatic system which adjusted the inner and the outer worlds has serious consequences. The conscious mind becomes severed from its roots in the instincts; at the same time the energy which was formerly projected on to outer forms comes streaming back, 'the waters rise, and inundating catastrophes burst upon mankind'.[4] But in many cases there is no returning to the earlier times: 'it is just from the theologian that many of my patients come . . . they were shed like dry leaves from the great tree'— i.e. the Church—'and now find themselves "hanging on" to the treatment'.[5] Some have attempted to console themselves with the symbols of the East, but this is no solution; religion cannot be borrowed—it has to be experienced. It is 'from the depths of our own psychic life that new spiritual forms will arise'.[6]

Religion for Jung is to be defined as a peculiar attitude of the human mind in which there is

[1] *Contemp. Events*, p. 21.
[2] *Psych. and Religion*, old ed. p. 58; new ed. p. 47.
[3] *Archetypes and the Collective Unconscious*, p. 8.
[4] *Integ. of Person.*, p. 71.   [5] *Psych. and Alchemy*, p. 28.
[6] *Mod. Man*, p. 250.

'a careful consideration and observation of certain dynamic factors that are conceived as "powers": spirits, daemons, gods, laws, ideas, ideals, or whatever name man has given to such factors in his world as he has found powerful, dangerous, or helpful enough to be taken into consideration, or grand, beautiful, and meaningful enough to be devoutly worshipped and loved'.[1]

The essential religious experience is a numinous one, in Rudolf Otto's term. It involves being seized and controlled by such factors —a state of mind which has complete superiority to the conscious will of the subject and can 'enforce or bring about a standard of accomplishment that would be unattainable to conscious effort'.[2] There is also a quality of awesomeness about it. Such an experience possesses the power of bringing wholeness to the personality, through reconciliation of the opposites conscious and unconscious, good and evil, and is often symbolized by the God-imago —usually a dying and rejuvenated god, since this is a highly appropriate way of expressing a transformation of attitude or new manifestation of life. A further characteristic of the experience is its absolute nature. For the individual who has undergone it, it is entirely convincing; he who has not remains incapable of understanding what it is.

The experience of the God-imago seems identical with the coming into being of the self:

'It is as though, at the culmination of the illness, the destructive powers were converted into healing forces. This is brought about by the fact that the archetypes come to independent life and serve as spiritual guides for the personality, thus supplanting the inadequate ego with its futile willing and striving. As the religious-minded person would say: guidance has come from God. With most of my patients I have to avoid this formulation, for it reminds them too much of what they have to reject. I must express myself in more modest terms, and say that the psyche has awakened to spontaneous life.'[3]

In short, as Father Hostie points out, there has been a revaluation since the writing of *Psychology of the Unconscious* to allow for the importance of religion in the life of the individual as well as in the group.[4]

Whether the religious experience springs from sources outside

[1] *Psych. and Religion*, new ed. p. 8; old ed. p. 5.
[2] *Psych. Types*, p. 300.   [3] *Mod. Man*, p. 279.
[4] *Religion and the Psychology of Jung*, p. 148. London: Sheen & Ward, 1957

the total human psyche as well as outside the conscious ego is a problem which Jung often explains is not within his province. His main attitude is that the concern of the psychologist is solely with the effects of these experiences and with their origin so far as it is traceable in psychological terms, but that the concept of a divinity 'gives us the most appropriate expression for the peculiar way in which we experience the effects of the autonomous contents'.[1] In comparison with his attitude in *Psychology of the Unconscious*, where God is consistently regarded as a projection of man's own libido, he shows some ambivalence, writing in one place that 'It is not only immodest, it is intellectually immoral to make assertions that go beyond the reach of human cognition'[2] and yet in another, that although the picture which is presented when the unconscious has added its pieces to the puzzle of life may still be an imperfect one in the eyes of man, 'we may presume it to be satisfactory in the eyes of the unknown creator of the puzzle'.[3] But for the most part the transcendental element in Christianity is deprecated on two rather different grounds, its childishness and its remoteness. Under the first heading he writes that unlike the man of the East, who knows that redemption depends on the 'works' a person devotes to himself, we in the West are still so uneducated that we need laws from without and a taskmaster or Father above;[4] and under the second, that if a God is accepted who is absolute and beyond all human experience 'he leaves me cold. I do not affect him nor does he affect me. But if I know on the other hand that God is a mighty activity in my soul, at once I must concern myself with him'.[5] The Church, by making God transcendental, has become an instrument for protecting man from the religious or numinous experience, 'for it is written "it is terrible to fall into the hands of the living God"'. Although such protection has its value for the many, for the individual who is capable of the highest development, Christianity, like every completed form, tends to suppress the unconscious, offering in its stead 'stereotyped symbolical ideas'.[6]

Christianity is criticized also as having repressed man's natural instincts unduly; only a little more than a thousand years ago a race practising crude polytheism was brought into contact with a highly

---

[1] *Two Essays*, old ed. p. 267; new ed. p. 237.   [2] *Integ. of Person*, p. 16.
[3] *Ibid.*, p. 44.   [4] *Psych. Types*, p. 264.
[5] *Secret of the Golden Flower*, p. 129.   [6] *Psych. Types*, p. 70.

developed oriental religion which did not correspond to its own level. In order to accept it in some fashion instinctual life was repressed to such an extent that religious practice took on a brutal character, while the repressed elements vegetated unconsciously in their original barbarism. Thus the truth was lost sight of that religion is not a substitute for another side of life, but represents 'the integration of the self in the "fullness of life"'.[1] On the other hand, Jung expands an earlier suggestion[2] that the wisdom of the Church might be made use of in some way. Its truth may, he thinks, rightly call itself eternal, 'but its temporal garment must pay tribute to the evanescence of all earthly things and should take account of psychic changes'.[3] For instance, the Church has taught that 'Life demands for its consummation and fulfilment a balance between joy and suffering,[4] and the Christian doctrine of sacrifice can be interpreted as opening a door for new possibilities through liberation from old ties.[5] The hope of immortality has turned men's attention toward the future realization of ideas, instead of toward the past, as in the ancient world; and by giving each individual the dignity of an immortal soul—a privilege in earlier times reserved for the king—a step forward to consciousness was taken. Even now such a belief helps to avoid arrest and regression. Here, especially, Jung's regard for the *consensus gentium* can be seen: just as everybody demands salt, because of an instinctive need, although by far the greater portion of mankind does not know why the body needs it, so in the things of the psyche: 'A large majority of people have from time immemorial felt the need of believing in a continuance of life. The demands of therapy, therefore, do not lead us into any bypaths, but down the middle of the roadway trodden by human kind. And therefore we are thinking correctly in respect to the meaning of life, even though we do not understand what we think.'[6] Psychology itself rests on certain presuppositions of nearly two thousand years of Christian education. For instance, such a saying as, 'Judge not that ye be not judged', has created a will which strives toward a simple objectivity of judgment.[7] Another presupposition is found in the injunction, 'Know thyself': 'the acceptance of oneself is the essence of the moral problem and the epitome of a whole outlook

---

[1] *Integ. of Person.*, p. 187.   [2] *Psych. of the Unconsc.*, p. 45.
[3] *Practice of Psychotherapy*, p. 195.   [4] *Contemp. Events*, p. 42.
[5] *Psych. Types*, p. 25.   [6] *Mod. Man*, p. 129.   [7] *Contribs.*, p. 298.

upon life'.[1] The imitation of Christ, in the deepest and best under-standing of Christianity, is to be interpreted as a command to 'live our own proper lives as truly as he lived his in all its implications'.[2] Jung wishes his own description of the religious experience, 'as if the leadership of the affairs of life had gone over to an invisible centre', to be regarded as another formulation of 'the Kingdom of God is within you', or of the saying of the Apostle Paul, 'No longer do I live but Christ liveth in me.'[3]

There seems, then, in addition to an account of religious experi-ence which has something in common with Christian formulations, to be a value system of largely Christian origin. Further parallels for both can be found besides the ones that Jung himself has given, e.g. his comparison between Christian experience and individuation may be expanded by Evelyn Underhill's description of the mystical passivity as 'really a state of the most intense activity' in which 'the superficial self compels itself to be still, in order that it may liberate another more deep-seated power. . . . The surface must co-operate with the deeps, and at last merge with those deeps to produce that unification of consciousness upon high levels which alone can put a term to man's unrest.'[4] His belief in the art of letting things happen, and in the possibility of a new beginning at any stage, is not unlike the belief of the Christian that God speaks to the soul in His good time.[5] Tradition and historical continuity, and an attitude of cosmic or near-cosmic identification, as it might be called, ('In some way or other we are part of an all-embracing psychic life, of a single "greatest" man, to quote Swedenborg')[6] are also emphasized in Christian circles, and Jung's statement that 'by becoming conscious of my shadow I remember once more that I am a human being like any other' is, apart from the absence of the transcendental element, much the same as 'We are all sinners in God's sight'—in both, that is, an identification with the human community is sought in sinfulness as well as in good-feeling.

On the other hand, there are differences as well. Some of these are found in values. For example, Jung reacts to some extent against the

---

[1] *Mod. Man*, p. 271. [2] *Mod. Man*, p. 273.
[3] *Secret of the Golden Flower*, p. 132.
[4] *Mysticism*, p. 50; p. 68. London: Methuen, 1930.
[5] 'In some least expected moment, the common activities of life in progress, that Reality in Whom the mystics dwell slips through our closed doors, and suddenly we see It at our side.' Evelyn Underhill, *Mysticism*, p. 449.
[6] *Mod. Man*, p. 242.

Christian emphasis on fellowship, in favour of ideals of self-development—including 'widened or deepened consciousness'—saying that exclusive reliance on the principle of love is apt to bring about 'a collective culture . . . in which the individual threatens to be swallowed up, and individual values are depreciated on principle'.[1] Now an element of detachment is allowed for within the Christian tradition, e.g. in the contemplative orders of the Catholic Church, though perhaps less fully within the Protestant denominations. More divergent, perhaps, is a trend in Jung away from democracy. Although 'Every life is at bottom the realization of a whole',[2] the experiences with which Jung is most concerned seem to be comparatively rare. Those to whom they come are the creatively endowed exceptions. 'The vast majority need authority, guidance, law. . . . The Pauline overcoming of the law falls only to the man who knows how to put his soul in the place of conscience. Very few are capable of this.'[3] The Church, it is true, admits wide differences in capacity for spiritual experience; nevertheless, as part of its allegiance to the transcendental, it leaves initiative to God—individual creatures remain in some sense equal. In the practical sphere these differences may be overridden by Jung's insistence on commitment to life—commitment first to the tasks of growing up, securing a place in the community, and fulfilling 'the biological duty' of founding a new family, and commitment subsequently to the task of cultivating those aspects of the personality which have had to be left undeveloped owing to the earlier demands. Faith, love, hope and insight, he says, come through experience, the gaining of which is a venture which requires us to commit ourselves with our whole being.'[4] This term, although usually employed in such phrases as 'commitment to Christ/God/the doctrine of the Church', and the attitude implied, of individual decision, is of course greatly favoured within the Protestant denominations with which Jung will in practice have been most familiar. The detachment in his individuation process and in some measure the division of life into stages of social adaptation and self culture,[5] reflects the interest in Eastern writings which we saw to

[1] *Psych. Types*, p. 95.   [2] *Supra*, p. 103.
[3] *Two Essays*, new ed. p. 237; old ed. p. 267.   [4] *Mod. Man*, p. 261.
[5] See Zimmer, H., *Philosophies of India*, pp. 44–5. Briefly: the greater part of Indian philosophy proper is concerned with guiding the individual during the second, not the first, portion of his life. Not before but after one has accomplished the normal worldly aims of the individual career, after one's duties have been

be one element in his cultural background—as, more directly, do his introductions to several Eastern texts. The man who 'knows how to put his soul in the place of conscience' is reminiscent of that other nineteenth and early twentieth-century influence, Nietzsche with his doctrine of the Superman. Even so, it is probably fair to say that the values implicit in Jung's work are largely Christian in their origin.

The greatest difference between Jung and the Christian tradition is, clearly, that Jung is operating without the transcendental element. As David Cox points out, Christian faith is 'faith in a guide, who will lead one to the goal of life, whereas the faith for which Jung asks is faith that one will come to the goal without a guide, or . . . that there is a guide although one is not aware of being guided, and there is very little likeness between the two'.[1] Theologians, even those sympathetic toward Jung's work, are inevitably critical of his tendency to assimilate religious practice to psychotherapy. The priest's role, they insist, is entirely different from the therapist's. Whereas to Jung a great healing factor in psychotherapy is the doctor's personality, the Christian director does not offer himself as a support but points instead to Christ or God. And whereas the analyst is concerned with bringing to consciousness unconscious tendencies, for which the patient cannot be held responsible, the priest in the sacrament of confession mediates God's forgiveness of intentional conscious acts, of which the sinner has repented.[2]

These differences are unavoidable—as Jung points out, a psychologist as such cannot pronounce on the existence of the Deity. On the other hand, not only is it, as MacMurray states, 'high treason'[3] from the theologian's point of view 'to say you believe in God because it is helpful to believe in Him'—it may even be wondered whether, therapeutically, this type of attitude applied to any aspect of religious life is as helpful as Jung thinks. As another writer has suggested, 'We are faced by paradox: religion can be therapeutic only when it is not so regarded; when, instead, it is paid allegiance

---

served as a moral member and supporter of the family and community, one turns to the tasks of the final human adventure and practices 'a technique of transcending the senses in order to discover, know, and dwell at one with the timeless reality which underlies the dream of life in the world.'

[1] *Jung and St. Paul*, p. 244.

[2] White, *God and the Unconscious*, pp. 165–9; Hostie, *op. cit.*, pp. 164–5.

[3] Cited by Cattell, R., *Psychology and the Religious Quest*, p. 59. London: Nelson & Sons, 1938.

as a thing-in-itself'.[1] Nevertheless, radical though the difference may be in attitude to ultimate realities, from a psychological standpoint the similarities in teaching are such as to make very understandable Jung's report that many of his patients have come from the Church. An argument which may be brought against others besides Jung who have sought the essence of religion in numinous experience, is that such experience is no guarantee of religious activity nor is its absence incompatible with it. For instance, Father White, while agreeing with those theologians and anthropologists who find the primary religious experience in feelings of irrational awe and fascination, is not satisfied that they make up the most important components of religion. Jung's own work is full of examples which show that these feelings play a part not only in religion but also in magic, superstition, art, poetry, neurosis and especially in psychosis.[2] Even though the primitive experience may be vital in some of the cases with which Jung has been dealing, the confusion between what is prior in historical development and what is prior in importance, which Jung detected in Freud's conception of infantile sexuality, should not be carried over into the study of religious phenomena. Many religious people, White continues, will be dissatisfied with the small place granted to reason. The mystics themselves, along with their awareness of individual experience, have often stressed the value of religious activity carried out in a state of emotional aridity. The rational theist, whether Christian or otherwise, will strenuously deny that what he calls 'God' is an irrational fact or an emotionally stirring product of the unconscious, and will maintain, whatever Hume, Kant, or logical positivists may say, that although God transcends rational comprehension, conscious reasoning itself indicates that inquiry into his nature can be a rational procedure. Jung can be considered to show undue selectivity in ignoring these phenomena, and again in ignoring the empirical fact that to the respective devotees of Jahwe, Allah, Shiva and so forth, it is often the differences rather than the similarities which seem of paramount importance. Concerning White's last point, it could perhaps be argued that what people themselves take to be the most important aspects of their faith are not necessarily so from the psychological

---

[1] Green, Arnold W., 'Social Values and Psychotherapy.' *J. of Personality*, XIV, pp. 199–228 (p. 206.).
[2] *Soul and Pysche*, pp. 56 *et seq.*

standpoint but may be drawing to themselves affects displaced, or generalized, from other aspects. However, this suggestion does not dispose of the criticism, but if anything lends support to it, that Jung might have paid more attention to facts which he largely ignores. Father Hostie, in considering Jung's accounts of the history of religion, makes the same objection, that facts have been ignored. During Jung's own lifetime it has been increasingly realized by anthropologists that the old cultures had a far subtler idea of God than Tylor, Marrett and other nineteenth-century animists and pre-animists had thought. No one, therefore, can hope to discuss the origin, development and changes in these ideas 'without first making some sort of classification, based on scientific standards of a trust-worthy kind, of the various types of primitive'.[1] In short, theologians in their sphere, like psychologists in theirs, refer to what we have previously called a blanketing tendency in Jung's work. This may be found to some extent in other writers, but in Jung once more invades his own formulations. Thus Hostie points out that Jung refers in the same breath to 'metaphysical assertion or other pro-fessions of faith',[2] and concludes that 'he is really quite unable to see any difference between metaphysics, theology and faith. These three fields, so different in nature, are all put under the same single heading, "the religious point of view"'.[3] Another difficulty is a degree of indifference to objective truth. It is perhaps a little severe to say with Erich Fromm that 'In his eclectic admiration for any religion Jung has relinquished this search for the truth in his theory. Any system, if it is only nonrational, any myth or symbol, to him is of equal value',[4] or with Goldbrunner—otherwise an admirer of his work—that in Jung 'The absolutized Self revolves around itself in self-satisfied isolation'.[5] Nevertheless, it is extremely difficult, if not impossible, to ascertain how far Jung confines himself to state-ments of 'psychic truth' in accordance with an agnosticism concern-ing the nature of the outer world which he derives from Kant, and how far he slips over into allowing some of his conceptions a degree of objectivity in accordance with the view of commonsense. This is particularly noticeable in the *Answer to Job*, where, as Philp points out in a letter addressed to Jung, 'You continue to argue so strongly

[1] *Religion and the Psychology of Jung*, p. 127.
[2] *Psych. and Alchemy*, p. 14.   [3] *Op. cit.*, p. 157.
[4] *Man for Himself*, p. ix.   [5] *Individuation*, p. 200.

... that in the end we can only suppose you are concerned with the nature of the Godhead itself.'[1]

Generally speaking, however, Jung's reinterpretations of Christian dogma are remarkable for their humanism and agnosticism. In the 'Transformation Symbolism of the Mass'—while safeguarding himself, as it seems, with the words, 'Looked at from the psychological standpoint',—he regards the mass as 'the rite of the individuation process', i.e. 'the mystery of the Eucharist transforms the soul of the empirical man, who is only a part of himself, into his totality, symbolically expressed by Christ'.[2] The Trinity—again 'as a psychological symbol'—is taken to denote 'the homoousia or essential unity of a three-part process, to be thought of as a process of unconscious maturation'.[3] The Father denotes the unreflecting state of consciousness of the child, dependent on a definite ready-made pattern of existence which is set before it. The phase of the Son begins when the individual puts a reflective, rational consciousness in the place of the undifferentiated attitude, and in the third stage the new level of consciousness, the Son, recognizes that not it, but a higher authority, known, in projected form, as the Holy Ghost, is the source of insights and decisions.[4]

Most controversial of all are his views that man himself is a necessary agent in the redemption of God, and that the Divine Being should be thought of as a Quaternity and not a Trinity. In the *Answer to Job*, the Biblical accounts of God in his dealings with man are interpreted not as though *man's ideas* of God had undergone a process of moral development, but as though the conception were that the process of development had occurred within the nature of God himself. In the Book of Job, God, or Yahweh, figures as a superhuman being who is easily provoked. He is an antimony—a totality of inner opposites—omniscient and omnipotent, yet making pressing demands for praise and propitiation. Since he is everything in its totality he is, among other things, total justice and also its total opposite. A personality of this kind is lacking in self-reflection and has no insight into itself. Jung suggests that Yahweh's behaviour to Job may therefore be motivated by a secret resistance: 'Because of his littleness, puniness and defencelessness against the Almighty,

[1] *Jung and the Problem of Evil*, p. 70.
[2] *Psychology and Religion*, new ed. p. 273.   [3] *Ibid.*, p. 193.
[4] Cf. Hegel on the death, resurrection and exaltation of Christ, *supra*, p. 15.

he possesses . . . a somewhat keener consciousness. . . . Could a suspicion have grown up in God that man possesses an infinitely small yet more concentrated light than he, Yahweh, possesses ?'[1] Job, perhaps, came to realize God's inner antimony, i.e. that he is not human but in some respects less than human. In this discovery the creature surpasses the creator—man, in spite of his impotence, is raised up as a judge over God Himself, and in the Incarnation 'Yahweh must become man precisely because he has done man a wrong. . . . Because his creature has surpassed him he must regenerate himself.' The cause of the Incarnation, therefore, lies in Job's elevation, 'and its purpose is the differentiation of Yahweh's consciousness'.[2] This idea of the human assisting the redemption of the divine has a precursor in Jung's earlier citation from the German mystic, Angelus Silesius: '"I know that without me God can no moment live."'[3] It is found also in the operas of Wagner: Parsifal, bringing back the holy spear with which he cures Amfortas, the sick guardian of the Holy Grail, is hailed by a choir of angels singing, 'Redemption to the redeemer', for he has redeemed the sacred blood of Christ from the spell that was nullifying its operation.[4] A similar thought is apparently acceptable to the religious spirit of the East. To Western orthodoxy it is, of course, a serious heresy. In a work of non-theological nature this cannot be taken as a ground for automatic rejection, and a psychological meaning may perhaps be found, i.e. the conception seems rather like a poetic or semi-poetic expression of man's need to feel that his own efforts are a force for good in the universe. Nevertheless, it can be argued with Philp that this teaching of Jung's may be less constructive than he seems to think, for the assumption that there is a greater consciousness and more consistent purpose in man than God suggests that man has been thrown up by chance without conscious creation.[5]

Jung's substitution of a Quaternity for the Trinity is not without its difficulties. First, it is uncertain exactly which Quaternity he wishes to set up. Sometimes he repeats the idea, originally put forward in *Psychology of the Unconscious*,[6] that the Trinity is incomplete without the principle of evil. Sometimes it is the feminine principle which 'like the masculine, demands an equally personal

---

[1] *Psych. and Religion*, new ed. p. 375.   [2] *Ibid.*, p. 406.
[3] *Psych. Types*, p. 317.   [4] Zimmer, *op. cit.*, p. 233.
[5] *Op. cit.*, p. 55.   [6] *Supra*, p. 60.

representation'.[1] In order to maintain a fourfold structure he would seem to be confronted with the choice of eliminating one of the figures he has named or combining two. Usually he speaks of evil or of the feminine according to his context, but in one place he moves toward the second solution—saying that the recently declared dogma of the Bodily Assumption of Mary paves the way for her ultimate recognition as a goddess and 'At the same time, matter is included in the metaphysical realm, together with the corrupting principle of the cosmos, evil'.[2] Such an attempt to bring these two principles— both relatively unexplored in his work—into relation with each other is surely yet another illustration of Jung's blanketing propensity. What, then, can be said of the two Quaternities taken individually— that containing evil and that containing the principle of femininity?

The inclusion of evil, Jung's theological commentators have argued,[3] rests on a misunderstanding of its nature; since the time of the great Greek philosophers it has generally been held that evil as a force in its own right does not exist. Admittedly, evil actions, inclinations, people, etc. are very powerful and cannot be ignored. However, their badness consists not in the *possession* of some positive entity but in the *absence* of some positive entity which is accounted good. The conception of evil as *privatio boni* is undoubtedly a product of intellectual analysis and not of immediate sense experience, but if it is accepted evil or badness cannot possibly be something that can be added to something else to bring about completeness. 'Only the crudest picture-thinking can make it a "part" or a "side" of God.'[4] A similar argument, that Jung has concretized an image, is put forward against the inclusion of the feminine principle. To most instructed Christians, says Father White, the question will hardly seem a serious one.

'They have learned that God is pure spirit, without parts or passions, bodiless and neither male nor female. He is beyond all the opposites, including the opposite sexes. Although they address God as our Father,

---

[1] *Psych. and Religion*, new ed. pp. 465.   [2] *Ibid.*, p. 171.
[3] White, *Soul and Psyche*, p. 152 *et seq.* Hostie, *op. cit.*, p. 197; Philp, *op. cit.*, p. 38 *et seq.*
[4] Within Jung's own system or group of ideas, Father White suggests, the 'acceptance' or 'integration' of evil can quite well be met by the theory of *privatio boni*, since it seems to imply a recognition that good is contained in the 'shadow' and that what is bad about it is the privation it has suffered from the ego. From the psychological side it might be suggested Jung may also have it in mind that without some awareness of these privations called evil, the personality will lack a certain depth.

they understand the phrase as little more than a term of endearment. Indeed, leading theologians have taught them that this form of address is only an expression of their creatureliness before Almighty God, and not to be taken literally.'

The conceptualized dogma or doctrine, he adds, corrects and overcomes the limitations of the purely concrete image.[1] While recognizing certain needs which Jung seems to be trying to express through these additions, i.e. the need for acknowledging the 'wrath' as well as the 'love' of God, and for introducing a feminine figure into religion, he considers that these needs have long been met by the Church in its own tradition, and that to ignore this is a case of special pleading.

Turning to the question of a Quaternity in general, Father White notes that Jung's argument rests on his belief that the number four—which, of course, he uses in his psychological functions and finds in the mandala figures of his patients and the writings of the alchemists whom he cites so extensively as witnesses for the collective unconscious—expresses totality in an archetypal way. But, White asks, granted that four is found in many contexts—the four elements, the four cardinal virtues, etc., is it, after all, the only pattern? Divine beings, it would seem, are found far more often in triads or with threefold attributes in mythology than they are in quaternities; in view of this he thinks it somewhat surprising that Jung says repeatedly there is no empirical evidence to distinguish the symbol of the self, the human totality, from the symbol of the Deity. Furthermore, both White and Philp cast doubt on Jung's view that the number four was of paramount importance to the alchemists. The differentiation of the three from the four seems to have been of no less importance in their work, and there was no question for them, as for Jung, of expanding the three into the four. (One of their prescriptions ran: 'Make a round circle, and extract the quadrangle from this, and from the quadrangle the triangle.') In this criticism they are joined by a recent authority on the history of alchemy, E. J. Holmyard, who reports that according to his own reading of the evidence the number four was employed very little—three, five, and seven being more favoured.[2]

This brings us to a very wide problem—the use made by Jung of the sources which he cites so frequently, especially in his writings on

---

[1] *Soul and Psyche*, p. 119.   [2] Communication to Philp, *op. cit.*, pp. 74–5.

religion and its symbolism. While it is hardly possible to take this problem up at length, it does seem possible to point to various quotations which appear to have been interpreted in an unnecessarily complicated way. One illustration is his suggestion, in discussing the wisdom of the great religions, that the injunction, Not of this world, is to be interpreted as 'the inward subjective movement of the libido into the unconscious'. The general withdrawing and introversion of the libido, Jung continues, 'creates an unconscious libido concentration which is symbolized as a "treasure", as in the Parables of the "costly pearl" and the "treasure in the field"'.[1] A simpler interpretation would be that usually given, i.e. 'Not of this world' stands for a striving toward detachment and a permanent set of values against which the day-to-day activities of life can be measured. Again, the statement of an alchemistic writer, that the alchemistic work must be performed 'with the true imagination and not with the fantastic', and that the stone will be found 'when the search lies heavily upon the searcher' seems to Jung to indicate that 'the author is actually of the opinion that the essential secret of the art is concealed in the human spirit; that, as we would put it to-day, it is in the unconscious'.[2] It seems at least equally feasible to interpret the passage as meaning only that the writer deemed sincerity to be essential in the quest.

A reference which can readily be verified is that to the quaternity symbol in the Apocalypse. The final vision in the Apocalypse, which, as Jung says, is generally interpreted as referring to the relationship of Christ with the Church, has for him 'the meaning of a "uniting symbol" and is therefore a representation of perfection and wholeness: hence the quaternity which expresses itself in the city as a quadrangle. . . .'[3] But on turning to the Book of Revelation itself, many readers would conclude that, of the numbers mentioned, twelve, not four, is the one emphasized most strongly.[4] Jung's comments on the authorship of the Apocalypse may be queried also. On psychological grounds he identifies the John of the Apocalypse and the author of the Epistles of John ('One could hardly imagine a more suitable personality. . . . It was he who declared that God is light and that "in him is no darkness at all" . . . Under these circumstances a counterposition is bound to grow up in the uncon-

---

[1] *Psych. Types*, p. 309.
[2] *Integ of Person.*, p. 216.
[3] *Psych. and Religion*, new ed. p. 447.
[4] *Rev.*, XXI, 16–21.

scious . . .'[1]). But as is pointed out by a theological sympathizer—himself prepared to let such difficulties pass by lightly—'the proof of the unity of authorship depends on something more than psychological probability; language, style and thought-world have a great deal to do with it, and most of the people who study these things certainly would not agree with Jung on this point'.[2] In short, so far as we are able to review the matter, we cannot challenge the statement of Dom T. V. Moore, approaching Jung from a different background, that here and there are 'fragments of patristic literature interpreted in the light of Jung's own conceptions rather than in that of the context and in the light of the whole system of thought of the author quoted'.[3]

Nor do these textual distortions, if such they are, exhaust the cases of special pleading to be found in Jung. One example has been met in his underplaying of some aspects of the Church tradition when putting forward his theories of Quaternity. Something similar seems to be at work in his declarations that a Transcendental God leaves us cold and that Christianity tends to suppress the unconscious, together with the rather deprecating reference to the Protestant's 'unbearably sophisticated' I-You relationship to God. The onus of proof, surely, is on Jung in all these matters. Many Christians certainly appear to have united belief in a Transcendental God with the utmost devotion in religious life; in view of the large number of interpretations which have been given to the Gospel happenings it seems at least equally possible that they have acted as guides to the unconscious rather than suppressing factors; and it may be wondered whether, had Jung been less concerned with myth and symbolism, he might have welcomed the use by some Christian theologians of Martin Buber's 'I-Thou relationship' as a development within Christianity which minimized the father-child analogy that he himself regards as standing in the way of full maturity.

Reviewing what has so far been said, it seems doubtful—quite apart from any statements which give rise to difficulties within a purely Christian framework—whether the inexactitude and special pleading to be found in Jung's accounts of religion, together with the

[1] *Op. cit.*, p. 435.

[2] Evans, Erastus, 'An Assessment of Jung's "Answer to Job".' Guild of Pastoral Psychology. Lecture 78, 1954; p. 7.

[3] *The Nature and Treatment of Mental Disorders*, p. 64. London: Heinemann, 1944.

uncertainties in his treatment of science, noted previously, allow him to be considered fully successful in the task of reconciling the two disciplines. On the other hand, we may agree with Father White that Jung has been among the earliest psychologists to recognize the relevance of faith and religious practice to the needs and workings of the human psyche,[1] i.e. here, too, he has been something of a pioneer. The extent of his contributions may be clearer if, like the contributions in psychotherapy, they are seen in the light of some contemporary and later suggestions also, in the main, from psychology.

As might be expected from what has been seen of their work and antecedents, the writer with whom Jung probably has most in common is William James. There is in both the same quest for reconciliation of the old religious beliefs and the new scientific theories, the same turning to Christian sources in a universalistic rather than dogmatic spirit, and the same stress on the therapeutic value of religion. Religion, James writes, '*makes easy and felicitous what in any case is necessary;* and if it be the only agency that can accomplish this result, its vital importance as a human faculty stands vindicated beyond dispute. It becomes an essential organ of our life.'[2] Since nobody can know what the ultimate things are, Jung urges, 'We must, therefore, take them as we experience them. . . . Is there, as a matter of fact, any better truth about ultimate things than the one that helps you to live?'[3] In particular, both are concerned with experiences of personal religious life in which the individual's disharmonies are resolved and he seems to himself to be made anew. At the height of these experiences, James writes, he 'undoubtedly seems to himself a passive spectator or undergoer of an astounding process performed upon him from above'.[4] Or, as Jung says, *we* do not live the experience, it lives *us*. Both refer these experiences to the agency of the Unconscious. James proposes, 'as an hypothesis', that 'whatever it may be on its *farther* side, the "more" with which in religious experience we feel ourselves connected is on its *hither* side the subconscious continuation of our conscious life'.[5] Starting with a recognized psychological fact, he thinks, it is possible to preserve a contact with science which the ordinary theologian does

---

[1] *God and the Unconscious*, p. 69. [2] *Op. cit.*, pp. 51–2.
[3] *Psych. and Religion*, new ed. p. 105; old ed. pp. 113–14.
[4] *Op. cit.*, p. 226. [5] *Ibid.*, p. 512.

not have, while at the same time the theologian is vindicated in his contention that the religious man is moved by an external power, for it is one of the peculiarities of unconscious invasions that they suggest to the subject an external control. Jung, also, speaks of the Unconscious as containing 'the hidden treasure upon which mankind ever and anon has drawn'.[1] It is, he says elsewhere, 'as if the leadership of the affairs of life had gone over to an invisible centre'.[2]

On the other hand, there are some differences. While James acknowledges that in the spiritual realm, as in the physical, there are two ways in which inner unification may occur, one gradual, the other sudden, he himself is concerned mainly with the latter, and gives the impression that once the initial experience has occurred the personality is reorganized on a new and stable footing comparatively soon: 'a new perception, a sudden emotional shock . . . will make the whole fabric fall together'.[3] When ripe, 'the results hatch out, or burst into flower'.[4] Jung's individuation extends over a longer period; as we saw previously, the conscious personality is not changed or supplanted in a twinkling, but must work hard to assimilate unconscious contents.[5] This brings us to a second difference: James's conversion experience involves a full surrender, a giving up of oneself to an added dimension of emotion. Repeatedly he returns to this idea: 'the higher condition, having reached the due degree of energy, bursts through all barriers and sweeps in like a sudden flood'.[6] Again, 'Given a certain amount of love, indignation, generosity, magnanimity, admiration, loyalty, or enthusiasm of self-surrender, the result is always the same. That whole raft of cowardly obstructions . . . sinks away at once. . . . Set free of them, we float and soar and sing.'[7] And, 'If religion is to mean anything definite for us, it seems to me that we ought to take it as meaning . . . this enthusiastic temper of espousal'.[8] Jung by contrast is very much more cautious. Subjects producing the mandala symbolism, he warns us, are in danger of inflation and dissociation. The round or square enclosures, therefore, have the meaning of protective walls or a *vas hermeticum* to prevent an outburst and disintegration. They protect and isolate 'an inner content or process that should not become mixed with things outside'.[9] There is no place for floating,

---

[1] *Supra*, p. 85. [2] *Supra*, p. 198. [3] *Op. cit.*, p. 197.
[4] *Ibid.*, p. 230. [5] *Supra*, p. 97. [6] *Op. cit.*, p. 216.
[7] *Ibid.*, p. 266. [8] *Ibid.*, p. 48.
[9] *Psych. and Religion*, new ed. p. 95; old ed. p. 105.

soaring, singing, here. As a corollary to this, Jung's individuated personalities do not seem to have acquired, like James's converted souls, 'a new zest, which adds itself like a gift to life'.[1] They accept the universe and their place in it, as James would have them do, but they do so in a more detached and contemplative manner; indeed, we have already drawn attention to a tendency for the outer world, the universe, to be lost to view in Jung's work.

The difference in degree of relatedness to external objects is seen again in their attitude to the existence of a Deity. James plunges in with a statement which he describes as his own 'over-belief', admitting that it goes beyond the bounds of science, i.e. that

> 'just as our primary wide-awake consciousness throws open our senses to the touch of things material, so it is logically conceivable that *if there be* higher spiritual agencies that can directly touch us, the psychological condition of their doing so *might be* our possession of a subconscious region which alone should yield access to them. The hubbub of the waking life might close a door which in the dreamy Subliminal might remain ajar or open.'[2]

He is very forthright on the Transcendental issue. For naturalism, he says, the position of mankind is essentially that of a set of people living on a frozen lake, surrounded by cliffs over which there is no escape, and knowing that little by little the ice is melting and the inevitable day drawing near when the lot of all will be to drown. 'The merrier the skating, the warmer and more sparkling the sun by day, and the ruddier the bonfires at night, the more poignant the sadness with which one must take in the meaning of the total situation.'[3] Jung never speaks so bluntly. He is aware of the need for 'a supra-personal consciousness which is open to the sense of historical continuity'[4] but seeks it in the deeper strata of the psyche, the collective unconscious, stretching back to the prehistoric past. At times he appears to endow this concept with an aura of divinity; if it were permissible to personify it, we may recall, it might be described as 'a collective human being combining the characteristics of both sexes, transcending youth and age, birth and death. . . .'[5]

Another difference, stressed by a recent Jungian sympathizer, P. W. Martin,[6] is that James, living as he did in the years immediately preceding depth psychology, was dependent on recorded documents,

[1] *Op. cit.*, p. 485. [2] *Ibid.*, p. 242. [3] *Ibid.*, pp. 142–2.
[4] *Mod. Man*, p. 76. [5] *Supra*, p. 86. [6] *Experiment in Depth*, p. 199.

while Jung has developed the method of active imagination with patients consulting him personally over long periods. At the present time it does not seem that the field is sufficiently clarified for non-practitioners, at any rate, to judge whether Jung's studies of the dreams and artistic productions of his patients will yield material which can be presented in such a way as to throw light on questions concerning, for instance, the type of person most likely to undergo these integrative experiences, or the different types of integration which may come about, or whether, as Jung himself has said, 'It seems almost as if we were about to go on dreaming the century-old dream of alchemy, like the unconscious itself, and to continue piling new synonyms on the mountain of the old, only to know as much or as little about it in the end as did the ancients.'[1]

In spite of these differences Jung and James can be grouped together as thinkers who were strongly influenced by the Liberal Protestant tradition of the nineteenth and early twentieth centuries, with its emphasis on man's search for God and its willingness to re-interpret dogma. A small personal link between them is found in a letter which James wrote to Flournoy, shortly after Freud and Jung had lectured at Clark University: 'I went there for one day in order to see what Freud was like, and met also Yung'—sic—'of Zürich, who professed great esteem for you, and made a very pleasant impression.' I hope, James continues,

> 'that Freud and his pupils will push their ideas to the utmost limits, so that we may learn what they are. They can't fail to throw light on human nature; but I confess that he made on me personally the impression of a man obsessed with fixed ideas. . . . A newspaper report of the congress said that Freud had condemned the American religious therapy (which has such extensive results) as very "dangerous" because so "unscientific". Bah!'[2]

William James died in 1910. A comparison often made, which nonetheless may throw light on questions with which we are concerned, is again that between the work of Jung and Freud. Both, being immersed chiefly in the Judeo-Christian tradition, deal with the role of the parent-child relation in religious dogma. This is true for Jung especially in the intermediate period and the first half of his later period; for Freud it remained always a sufficient model.

[1] *Integ. of Person.*, p. 175.
[2] *Letters of William James*, Vol. II, pp. 327–8. Edited by his son, Henry James in Two Volumes. London: Longmans, Green & Co., 1920.

There is, however, a difference in their treatment. Jung, as we have seen, finds the transition from the real parents to God and to the Church a means of assisting the onward flow of life, weakening the actual ties and building other relationships in the place of the old; and although it is the task of modern man to take a further step toward maturity by outgrowing the symbolic ties in their turn, it is also possible for him to preserve the wisdom of the way of living associated with them. To Freud, the part played by religion in the building up of culture is derived from guilt-atoning sentiments: primitive man, after killing the primal father, or Old Man of the Horde, for the sake of access to his women, determined, in his reaction to the outrage once it was committed, to respect the father's will in future. Religious dogma is also wish-fulfilling: It would indeed be nice 'if there were a God, who was both Creator of the world and a benevolent providence, if there were a moral world order and a future life, but at the same time it is very odd that this is all just as we should wish it ourselves.'[1] Unlike Jung and James, he is strongly opposed to any extension or purification of the meaning of religious doctrines, declaring that 'Philosophers stretch the meaning of words until they retain scarcely anything of their original sense; by calling "God" some vague abstraction which they have created for themselves, they pose as deists, as believers.'[2] We will now, he says, after a similar attack, 'go back to the ordinary man and his religion—the only religion that ought to bear the name'.[3]

In the life of the individual, as in the history of the race, the need for religion is attributed to fear of the father—all the more so since the feeling is not simply carried on from childhood days but is perpetually kept alive by fear of what fate with its superior power will bring. Freud discusses the objection of a friend who had written that the ultimate source of religious sentiments consists, instead, of

'a peculiar feeling, which never leaves him personally, which he finds shared by many others, and which he may suppose millions more also experience. It is a feeling which he would like to call a sensation of "eternity", a feeling as of something limitless, unbounded, something "oceanic" . . . One may rightly call oneself religious on the ground of this oceanic feeling alone, even though one reject all beliefs and all illusions.'[4]

[1] *Future of an Illusion*, p. 58. London: Hogarth Press, 1949.   [2] *Ibid.*, p. 57.
[3] *Civilization and its Discontents*, p. 24. London Hogarth Press, 1930.
[4] *Ibid.*, p. 8.

While unable to discover this feeling in himself, Freud does not deny that it may be present in others. Its origin, he thinks, lies in the less sharply outlined nature of the infant's ego feeling. Only gradually does the infant learn to distinguish between the ego and the outer world; the ego feeling of the adult is only a shrunken vestige of a feeling which embraced the universe. This primary ego-feeling may be preserved in the minds of many people, to a greater or lesser extent, and may thus co-exist with the narrower, more sharply outlined ego feeling of maturity. He allows that connections might be traced with many obscure manifestations of mental life, such as trance and ecstasy, but it still seems to him 'incontrovertible' that the father sentiment is the basis of religion: 'I could not point to any need in childhood so strong as that for a father's protection.' I must again confess, he adds, 'that I find it very difficult to work with these intangible qualities' and 'am moved to exclaim, in the words of Schiller's diver, "Who breathes overhead in the rose-tinted light may be glad."'[1]

Freud's own account of the religious life is of course open to various criticisms. For instance, it has often been pointed out that the killing of the Old Man of the Horde and the guilt-reaction of the slayers is an hypothesis, without adequate anthropological backing, which involves him in the logical error of assuming the existence of the very social impulses which he is endeavouring to explain. There seems no necessary ground for restricting religion to that of 'the ordinary man', and it is entirely possible to hold that the primary ego feeling is a more overwhelming as well as an earlier experience than feelings toward the father, and that for this reason it forms the basis of religious feeling, upon which the later and more definite father-child pattern is imposed. Viewing his contributions not so much directly as in relation to the work of Jung, his attitude to the 'oceanic feeling' is of particular interest, since, although Jung does not use the term, his references to 'the numinous' with its awesome quality, and to the experience of oneness with humanity, indicate a strongly developed feeling of that kind.

There are other indications of Freud's preference for an attitude of limitation, or specificity, as it might be called, not unlike that suggested previously for the neo-analysts. Considering the precept of universal love—which, surely, has had its place in all the world

[1] *Ibid.*, pp. 21–2.

religions—he holds that a love which does not discriminate loses something of its value.

'My love seems to me a valuable thing that I have no right to throw away without reflection. It imposes obligations on me which I must be prepared to make sacrifices to fulfil. If I love someone, he must be worthy of it in some way or other. . . . But if he is a stranger to me and cannot attract me by any value he has in himself or any significance he may have already acquired in my emotional life, it will be hard for me to love him. I shall even be doing wrong if I do, for my love is valued as a privilege by all those belonging to me; it is an injustice to them if I put a stranger on a level with them. But if I am to love him (with that kind of universal love) simply because he, too, is a denizen of the earth, like an insect or an earthworm or a grass-snake, then I fear that but a small modicum of love will fall to his lot.'[1]

In addition to this greater *specificity* of affect, Freud has far more to say than Jung of aggression and hostility, as was seen to some extent in previous chapters. To tell the truth, he continues, this stranger has more claim to my hostility, even to my hatred.

'He does not seem to have the least trace of love for me, does not show me the slightest consideration. If it will do him any good, he has no hesitation in injuring me, never even asking himself whether the amount of advantage he gains by it bears any proportion to the amount of wrong done to me. What is more, he does not even need to get an advantage from it; if he can merely get a little pleasure out of it, he thinks nothing of jeering at me, insulting me, slandering me, showing his power over me; and the more secure he feels himself, or the more helpless I am, with so much more certainty can I expect this behaviour from him towards me.'[2]

Never before in any of my previous writings, he adds, 'have I had the feeling so strongly as I have now that what I am describing is common knowledge, that I am requisitioning paper and ink, and in due course the labour of compositors and printers, in order to expound things that in themselves are obvious'.[3]

Freud himself is not entirely without assumptions concerning the good life for human beings, but his chief proposals are a partial amelioration of unwelcome reality through the use of reason, and stoical acceptance of the rest. Whereas Jung holds that 'in the greatest and really decisive questions the reason proves inadequate',

[1] *Ibid.*, p. 81 *et seq.*   [2] *Ibid.*, p. 83.   [3] *Ibid.*, p. 94.

Freud writes that science has taught man much, and will increase his power still further.

> 'And as for the great necessities of fate, against which there is no remedy, these he will simply learn to endure with resignation. Of what use to him is the illusion of a kingdom on the moon, whose revenues have never yet been seen by anyone? As an honest crofter on this earth he will know how to cultivate his plot in a way which will support him.'[1]

The search for 'meaning' in life does not concern him greatly: 'It looks, on the contrary, as though one had a right to dismiss this question. . . . Nobody asks what is the purpose of the lives of animals.'[2] The argument that we should live 'as if' immortality or any other immemorial doctrine were true meets with the reply that it would be strange, certainly, 'if our poor, ignorant, enslaved ancestors had succeeded in solving all these difficult riddles of the universe'[3] and 'The man whose thinking is not influenced by the wiles of philosophy will never be able to accept it'.[4] Similarly there is no sense of man's continuity with Nature. Not only do human figures fill Freud's canvass—the non-human world is seen quite definitely as the enemy of man. With earthquakes, floods, disease and death 'nature rises up before us, sublime, pitiless, inexorable; thus she brings again to mind our weakness and helplessness, of which we thought the work of civilization had rid us.'[5] In short, while religion to Jung, in all its changing forms, is the means by which the essential harmony between man and the universe is brought within his understanding, to Freud it is the means by which he has endeavoured to conceal from himself its undifference or hostility.

Confronted with these attitudes in Freud we may again find it the more comprehensible that patients accustomed to a Christian outlook have been drawn to Jung's psychology, and that at times, perhaps, focusing on similarities rather than on differences, they have been able to substitute it for Christian doctrine.

However, as we have already seen in therapy, especially, the thinking of non-Jungian analysts does not stand exactly where Freud left it, and many psychoanalytically oriented writers have reached the same conclusion, that in addition to material needs man

---

[1] *Future of an Illusion*, p. 86. [2] *Civilization and its Discontents*, p. 26.
[3] *Future of an Illusion*, p. 58. [4] *Ibid.*, p. 50. [5] *Ibid.*, pp. 26–7.

has others which in the customary terminology are described as spiritual. Among the neo-analysts the writer who has explored these needs most fully is Erich Fromm. Unlike the rest of the animals, Fromm writes, man has lost his original harmony with nature—or, as Jung would say, his state of *participation mystique*—and has become a thinking being, asking such questions as why he is here and what is the purpose of his life. He tries to restore his unity and equilibrium by constructing an all-inclusive mental picture of the world which can serve him as a frame of reference enabling him to find an answer to the question where he stands and what he ought to do, and strives for relatedness in all spheres of his living—feeling and action equally with thought. But besides the need to be related man has the need to be himself. There is a tendency in all organisms to actualize potentialities: '*Existence and the unfolding of the specific powers of an organism are one and the same.*'[1] This means that 'The duty to be alive is the same as the duty to become oneself, to develop into the individual one potentially is.'[2] Under the conditions of the modern world great difficulty is experienced in satisfying either of these needs,[3] consequently there are many people for whom everything they do seems futile. The remedy lies in increasing insight into the problem, in tackling it with the aid of rational thought, and in understanding that the two needs are not contradictory but can be simultaneously fulfilled, since the only way of relating to the world which is permanently satisfying is that of 'productiveness', the use of one's powers.

'Man *produces things*, and in the process of creation he exercises his powers over matter. Man *comprehends the world*, mentally and emotionally, through love and through reason. His power of reason enables him to penetrate through the surface and to grasp the essence of his object by getting into active relation with it. His power of love enables him to break through the wall which separates him from another person and to comprehend him.'[4]

On the ethical side, in particular, many parallels can be found. Hadfield in the British eclectic school speaks of the organism as being impelled to the harmonious expression of all the vital forces towards a common purpose and end. It is this which urges us away from the mere expression of lusts and passions to the development of

---

[1] *Man for Himself*, pp. 19–20.   [2] *Ibid.*, p. 20.
[3] *Supra*, pp. 170–1.   [4] *Op. cit.*, p. 97.

character. 'So, throughout the whole realm of organic life, in biology, psychology, morality, and religion, the craving for fulfilment and the urge to completeness is the most potent force which drives us to live and strive with persistent energy, till the ultimate goal of self-realization is reached.'[1] Another member of the neo-analytical school, Angyal, believes that 'To make of one's life course a meaningful coherent whole, a work of art which one creates by living, seems to be the greatest concern of the person, although he may be only vaguely aware of such purpose'[2]—a statement almost identical with one by H. G. Baynes, in his Preface to the English Edition of *Psychological Types*, that the chief aim of the individual might be formulated as 'the effort to create out of oneself the most significant product of which one is capable'.[3] Goldstein's concept of self-actualization seems essentially the same.[4] Assumptions of this kind appear, indeed, to form a guiding philosophy for Western psychotherapy, traces of which, although often overlaid by other factors, are found even in the earlier psychoanalysts, as when Freud himself wrote of that great unity which we call the patient's ego fusing into one 'all the instinctual trends which before had been split off and barred away from it'[5] and Ernest Jones of the 'willing or even joyful acceptance of life, with all its visitations and chances, that distinguishes the free personality of one who is master of himself'.[6] Another psychoanalytical formulation on the side of values is Flugel's summing up of moral progress in terms of the transition from Egocentricity to Sociality (i.e. 'As we grow up, we become increasingly aware of the presence and claims of others'), from Unconscious to Conscious and from Autism to Realism, which are much the same, since consciousness is capable of a much more accurate and subtle appreciation of reality than the Unconscious; from Moral Inhibition, or relatively crude moral compulsion, to Spontaneous 'Goodness', or relatively spontaneous play of impulses which are conducive to harmonious social life; from Aggression to Tolerance and Love, from Fear to Security—freedom from irrational anxiety being perhaps the best single criterion of 'normality';

[1] *Op. cit.*, p. 65.   [2] *Op. cit.*, p. 364.   [3] *Psych. Types*, p. xx.
[4] Cf. Fromm-Reichmann, 'Notes on the Personal and Professional Requirements of a Psychotherapist.' *Psychiatry*, Vol. 12, No. 4, 1949; pp. 361-78.
[5] *Collected Papers*, Vol. II, p. 395.
[6] 'The Concept of a Normal Mind.' *Int. J. Psycho-Anal.*, Vol. 23, No. 1, 1942; p. 7.

from Heteronomy to Autonomy—'perhaps the most fundamental core of the total process of moral development'—through which the growing child substitutes his own moral judgment for that of the adults around him, gradually becoming more and more discriminating and reality adapted; and finally, the transition from Orectic (Moral) Judgment to Cognitive (Psychological) Judgment, or from aggression to understanding, which enables us to substitute more effective methods provided by knowledge and science for cruder procedures based on anger and moral condemnation.[1] These elements in the moral life form a kind of scale against which various elements in Jung may be compared. As with Flugel, the transition from Heteronomy to Autonomy ranks extremely high: the child emerges from a state of *participation mystique* with the parents into a state of *participation mystique* with the school, church, nation, and finally, if that is his destiny, to a state of autonomy which is intimately bound up with heightened consciousness; perhaps, however, in the stress which he lays on 'widened or deepened consciousness', and the making of decisions 'with full freedom and consciousness', Jung goes further than Flugel in making consciousness—i.e. reflective consciousness—to some extent a value in itself. The transition from Egocentricity to Sociality does not find so close a parallel, since the egocentricity of the child is not emphasized by Jung in the same way as his state of uncritical merging, and in his later years the individual, having played a part in society, is thought of as justified in paying attention to his own development. Nor is there a close parallel for the transition from Fear to Security, since, while Jung would acknowledge fear, like aggression, as an aspect of evil or 'the shadow side', he does not examine them in detail. In his attitude of 'unprejudiced objectivity' ('a kind of deep respect for facts and events and for the person who suffers from them') there may be a blend of two transitions, from Aggression to Tolerance and Love, and from Orectic to Cognitive Judgment, though the negative element that is moved away from might not be described so forcefully as 'aggression', nor, perhaps, would the 'deep respect for facts . . .' be considered quite so active as Flugel's 'more effective methods of knowledge and science'.

Similar differences—essentially a continuation of these noted in the previous chapter—are found between the work of Jung and

[1] *Man, Morals and Society*, pp. 242–54. London: Duckworth, 1945.

Fromm. For instance, it has been suggested that among the neo-analysts more activity, more immediate contact with the environment, is envisaged for the person who is in the process of achieving integration, but more independence of society in the making of ethical evaluations. This may be seen again in Fromm's productive living, which, as its name would indicate, is a means of actively relating oneself to the environment: through the exercise of his powers man produces things, he comprehends the world of people and ideas. Also, it is regarded by Fromm as something to be embarked on very early, while Jung confines individuation in the main to later life. As we saw, the possibility that the individual's best gifts may be largely destroyed by society's demands is not absolutely overlooked by Jung,[1] but it never becomes a central topic in his thinking. To Fromm, however, the person who is unable to live productively at an earlier stage 'deteriorates in his whole personality when his physical vigor, which had been the main spring of his activities, dries up'.[2] Jung's attitude, that adaptation must precede individuation, implies a greater respect for tradition.

Another illustration of his more activist approach is Fromm's attitude to death. To die, Fromm writes, is poignantly bitter. The difference between life and death is 'the most fundamental existential dichotomy'. 'All knowledge *about* death does not alter the fact that death is not a meaningful part of life and that there is nothing for us to do but to accept the fact of death; hence, as far as our life is concerned, defeat.'[3] To Jung, by contrast, 'Death is psychologically just as important as birth, and, like this, is an integral part of life.'[4] In other words, to Fromm it seems that the individual never ceases to strive for the fullest expression of potentialities, although some of these are forced to remain unrealized owing to the sheer limitation in the span of human life. Jung is more quietistic, nearer the attitude of 'Nunc dimittis'. (In the first half of life the will of the libido is for growth, 'in the second half of life it hints, softly at first, and then audibly, at its will for death'.[5]) The element of starkness, if such it may be called, in Fromm's attitude to death is found again in his attitude to the existence of a Deity. Whereas Jung seems at times to take refuge in a partial deification of the experience of humanity, Fromm openly declares there is only one solution to man's problem,

---

[1] *Supra*, p.159.   [2] *Man for Himself*, p. 163.   [3] *Ibid.*, pp. 41–2.
[4] *Secret of the Golden Flower*, p. 124.   [5] *Supra*, p. 69.

and that is 'to face the truth, to acknowledge his fundamental aloneness and solitude in a universe indifferent to his fate'.[1] That is, he accepts the predicament of naturalism as summed up by William James.

In Fromm's handling of religion and values, as in therapy, we find more use of rational analysis. One example is his discussion of faith and love. In the sphere of human relations, he points out, faith is an indispensable quality of any significant friendship or love. '"Having faith" in another person means to be certain of the reliability and unchangeability of his fundamental attitudes, of the core of his personality. . . . In the same sense we have faith in ourselves. . . . Another meaning of having faith in a person refers to the faith we have in the potentialities of others, of ourselves, and of mankind.'[2] The child's potentialities to love, to be happy, to use his reason, and more specific potentialities like artistic gifts, are seeds which grow if the proper conditions for their development are present, and without them can be stifled. One of the most important conditions is that the significant persons in the child's life have faith in his potentialities. Faith in others has its culmination in faith in mankind; it is based on the idea that man's potentialities are such as to be capable of building a social order governed by the principles of equality, justice, and love. This kind of faith may be contrasted with *irrational* faith, rooted in submission to a power which is felt to be overwhelmingly strong, omniscient and omnipotent. Humanistic faith is based on the opposite experience, i.e. awareness of the growth of our own potentialities, the strength of our own powers of love and reason. In a similar way, love is analysed as implying 'care, responsibility, respect and knowledge'. To love a person productively implies caring and feeling responsible for the growth and development of all his human powers; it means also being related to his human core—love for one individual, divorced from love for man, refers only to superficial and accidental qualities, and remains shallow. But without respect and knowledge, love deteriorates into domination and possessiveness. Respect denotes, in accordance with its root (*respicere*—to look at), the ability to see a person as he is, and this depends on knowledge.

If beside this analysis Jung's simpler statements are set, concerning the need of 'faith, hope, love and insight', we may see the advantage

---

[1] *Op. cit.* p. 44.,　　　　[2] *Op. cit.*, pp. 205 *et seq.*; pp. 98 *et seq.*

of rendering explicit what would otherwise remain implicit only. For those who are convinced already, or those who have lost interest in 'faith, hope, love and insight' largely through the traditional connection with dogmas which they are unable to accept, the simpler statements may suffice, and may even be preferred, but to many minds the working out of implications point by point is likely to increase their relevance in ordinary life. Another advantage in the explicit discrimination of different attitudes conventionally called 'faith' or 'love' is that the individual may be prevented from being confused by the one label and giving support in consequence to causes or doctrines from which he would really wish to turn away.

In addition to using this kind of analysis more fully in his own work, Fromm, unlike Jung, regards reason itself as the source of value judgments and the guiding force of the religious life. Valid ethical norms can be formed by man's reason and by it alone, he writes. The breakdown of eighteenth and nineteenth-century rationalism was due not to its belief in reason but to its unnecessarily narrow concepts, and not less but more reason will correct its errors. It is true that he speaks of 'the wondering, the marvelling, the becoming aware of life and of one's own existence, and . . . oneness not only in oneself, not only with one's fellow men, but with all life and beyond that, with the universe'.[1] Nevertheless, the wondering and the marvelling and the sense of oneness do not remain as a numinous experience but issue more specifically in a 'system of thought and action shared by a group which gives the individual a frame of orientation and an object of devotion'.[2] At the same time, the analysis of reason which Fromm gives may be another contribution which clarifies or supplements Jung's point of view. Beginning with a distinction between reason and intelligence, he notes that most of our thinking is concerned with achieving practical results, without inquiring into the validity of ends and premises or attempting to understand the nature of phenomena apart from their utilitarian value. It is this kind of thinking which he proposes to call intelligent. Reason, however, can be thought of as involving another dimension, that of depth. 'Its function is to know, to understand, to grasp, to relate oneself to things by comprehending them.' When thinking in this way the subject is not indifferent to his object—it is not experienced as something dead and divorced from himself—but is affected

[1] *Psychoanalysis and Religion*, pp. 99–100.   [2] *Ibid.*, p. 29.

by it. 'It is this very relationship between him and his object which stimulates his thinking in the first place.'[1]

If it is permissible to draw the two components together, this formulation would seem to do away with a difficulty which Jung himself deplores, namely, that 'One can, it is true, understand a great deal with the heart, but then the mind often finds it difficult to follow up with an intellectual formulation which gives suitable expression to what has been understood' and that 'There is also a form of understanding with the head, in particular that of the scientific mind, in which there is often too little room for the heart.'[2] Such a formulation could be of considerable significance, in removing from the sphere of the irrational the 'deeper', less clearly conscious mental activities which subserve the needs of the total organism, and reserving the term 'irrational' for outbursts in which some powerful emotional need secures its satisfaction without due regard for the wellbeing of the whole.

Having reviewed various expressions of the ethics of self-realization in the work of modern psychotherapists, we may wonder how far this type of theory—one of the great lines of thought in moral philosophy from Aristotle onwards—can meet the human situation. Clearly it is not to be equated with undisciplined indulgence, and to those who urge that even the disciplined search for self-expression can be selfish, it may be pointed out that the distinction between care for the self and care for others seems less valid than has often been supposed. That is, the man who respects himself and strives for the harmonious fulfilment of his powers is also the man who respects others and seeks to further *their* self-realization. Not the self-realizing personality, but the frustrated personality, is the one who frustrates others, who is selfish in the sense of greedily seizing upon anything which seems to be a satisfier. Or, as Jung writes, 'How can I love my neighbour, if I do not love myself? How can we be altruistic, if we do not treat ourselves decently?'[3] And if we agree with Murray that 'There are certain original (id born) moral conceptions derived from sensitiveness to pain, from empathy and love',[4] we may even include in the ethics of self-realization a suggestion

[1] *Man for Himself*, pp. 102–3.
[2] Cited by Jacobi, J., *Psychological Reflections*, p. 231.
[3] Cited by Jacobi, J., *Psychological Reflections*, p. 220.
[4] 'What Should Psychologists Do about Psychoanalysis?' *J. Abn. & Soc. Psychol.*, Vol. XXXV, 1940; p. 165.

made in criticism—that 'The highest ethical ideals man will ever be capable of will have had their origin, I think, in that first human being on earth who, having himself endured pain, understood the necessity of succouring his afflicted neighbour.'[1]

On the other hand, the world being the sort of place it is, with so many complex interactions between one person and another, it is difficult to see that *all* questions of how we ought to live and what we ought to do can be answered in terms of self-realization, according to any legitimate interpretation of the term. Take, for instance, the case of a man who decides that for the sake of his family he cannot afford to give up a distasteful job. While it is true that all things considered he prefers the course of action he has chosen, it would seem, in view of what is actually entailed, that to describe his choice as one of self-realization—i.e. 'realization of the higher self', is likely to cause a confusion of thought which could best be avoided by the introduction of a different concept, acceptance of moral obligation. But supposing this is granted, it still remains feasible to regard self-realization as the *basic* principle of ethical life, the application of which sometimes has to be curtailed by the individual on behalf of other people's claims to realization; attention then needs to be directed, in the political and economic fields, to minimizing those conditions in society which render choices of that kind unduly frequent, and, in any given case, to finding compensatory means of self-fulfilment. In Jung, more, possibly, than in the other writers, we have found that a good deal is said of obligations, in terms such as 'commitment to life', and 'fulfilment of biological duty', though once again his position is not developed in a detailed way, and there seems to be a theoretical over-simplification in his tendency to separate the two concepts by assigning them to different stages rather than to follow the interplay of both throughout the whole life span.

Reverting now to other aspects of Jung's contributions, we find that while no other writer in the psychological field has become so closely involved as Jung with Christian dogma, there is some indication that the increased attention paid by psychoanalysts to the synthesizing functions of the ego may lead to further studies of religious experience. Marjorie Brierley, using the division id, ego

---

[1] Kimmelman, G., Review of Fromm's *Man for Himself. J. Abn. & Soc. Psychol.*, Vol. XLIII, 1948; pp. 555-7.

and superego—partly, she explains, in order to avoid a flavour of super-naturalism associated with such terms as nature and spirit, and partly because discrimination between different types of integration is easier to make on a threefold basis than with pairs of opposites— postulates an 'integration of sanctity', with idealization of super-ego love and denigration of ego and id, including repudiation of aggression; and an integration which comes about through increase in ego-ability to tolerate psychological reality and accept with comparative serenity all the constituents of the personality. The former, she suggests, is very rare, and the lives of the saints are filled with accounts of id vengeance exacted in such forms as bodily ill-health and persecution by the devil. Psychoanalytical findings indicate that the latter—which might be called the humanistic integration— though the term is not actually used—is the high-road for the majority.[1] Jung's individuation process possibly contains elements of both: the assimilation of the shadow suggests the humanistic integration, the giving of leadership over to an invisible centre, the self, is perhaps nearer the integration of sanctity. In immediate therapeutic practice—even though in the long run, as with psychiatric diagnosis, some estimation of probabilities will be likely to prevent mistakes—the making of these differentiations may not be crucial provided patient and therapist accept what comes ('Each can take what he needs, in his own way and in his own language').[2] Theoretically, however, a division such as Brierley's may provide a starting point for research into what Jung himself has called 'an as yet very obscure field . . . much in need of exploration'.[3] Once again it looks as though the advantage, in terms of ability to clarify ideas and to develop them, may lie with a later writer, working independently.

There would seem to be one other aspect of Jung's teaching on modern man's dilemma and the importance of the collective unconscious which is clarified through the account of a later writer, this time in philosophy. Susanne Langer, in her *Philosophy in a New Key*, has much to say of the significance of symbols in our daily lives.[4] There are many symbols which carry with them different meanings, and these meanings have been integrated in such a way

---

[1] *Op. cit.*, pp. 180–293: 'Psycho-Analysis and Integrative Living.'
[2] *Two Essays*, new ed. p. 115.   [3] *Psych. and Alchemy*, p. 462.
[4] *Philosophy in a New Key*, pp. 284–94. London: Oxford University Press, 1951.

that all are apt to be invoked with any chosen one. A ship, for instance, is

'the image of precarious security in all surrounding danger, of progress toward a goal, of adventure between two points of rest, with the near, if dormant, connotation of safe imprisonment in the hold, as in the womb. Not improbably the similar form of a primitive boat and of the moon in its last quarter has served in past ages to reinforce such mythological values.'

Or, as Jung has put it,

'The symbol always covers a complicated situation which is so far beyond the grasp of language that it cannot be expressed at all in any unambiguous manner. Thus the grain and wine symbols have a fourfold layer of meaning: (1) as agricultural products; (2) as products requiring special processing (bread from grain, wine from grapes); (3) as expressions of psychological achievement (work, industry, patience, devotion, etc.) and of human vitality in general; (4) as manifestations of mana or of the vegetation daemon.'[1]

In this way, Langer continues, our lives are given 'a background of closely woven multiple meanings against which all conscious experiences and interpretations are measured . . . we respond to every new datum with a complex of mental functions'. Now man can adapt himself to anything his imagination can cope with, but he cannot deal with chaos. For this reason 'our most important assets are always the symbols of our general *orientation* in nature, on the earth, in society, and in what we are doing'. In modern times, human life is so changed and so diversified that people cannot share a few historic, 'charged' symbols with about the same wealth of meaning for them all, and the new forms have not yet acquired a 'rich, confused, historic accretion'. It may be that in the future an aeroplane may be a more powerful symbol than a ship, but for us it is too new— 'it does not sum up our past in guarantee of the present'. Or again as Jung has said, 'Man can live the most amazing things if they make sense to him. But the difficulty is to create that sense.'[2] Thus our general orientation is endangered, and with it our basic human freedom, which consists in 'opportunity to carry on our natural, impulsive, intelligent life, to realize plans, express ideas in action

---

[1] *Psych. and Religion*, new ed. p. 254.
[2] *Psych. and Religion*, new ed. p. 78.

or in symbolic formulation, see and hear and interpret all things that we encounter, without fear of confusion'. All the old symbols are gone, and thousands of average lives offer no new materials to a creative imagination. This, rather than physical want, is the starvation that threatens the modern worker, the tyranny of the machine. In Jung's more emotive terminology, What do factory workers and office employees know of the peasant's life with nature, 'of those grand moments when, as lord and fructifier of the earth, he drives his plough through the soil, and with a kingly gesture scatters the seed for the future harvest . . . ? From all this we city-dwellers, we modern machine minders, are far removed.'[1]

Such conditions lead to deep unrest: 'Numberless hybrid religions spring up, mysteries, causes, ideologies, all passionately embraced and badly argued. A vague longing for the old tribal unity makes nationalism look like salvation, and arouses the most fantastic bursts of chauvinism and self-righteousness, the wildest anthropological and historical legends'. Or, as Jung has it, 'the waters rise, and inundating catastrophes burst upon mankind'. It is not surprising, Langer adds, that philosophers should view these upheavals as reactions against the Age of Reason, but if symbol formation, not discursive reasoning, is accepted as the fundamental mark of rationality, they can be seen to be inspired, not merely by animal impulse, but by an attempt to satisfy the rational need of envisagement and understanding.

It is remarkable, as Murray Jackson comments,[2] that as late as a second edition in 1951 Langer does not include a single reference to Jung. A possible explanation is Jung's tendency, as we have noted,[3] to abandon in his work that habit of orderly and argued exposition which forms an accepted part of the rational approach.

[1] *Two Essays*, new ed. p. 255; old ed. p. 17.
[2] 'Jung's "archetype": clarity or confusion?' p. 83.
[3] *Supra*, p. 138.

Chapter IX

THE CHANGES IN JUNG'S WORK AND ITS APPEAL: SOME COGNITIVE AND EMOTIONAL FACTORS

We come now to fresh problems, namely, the reasons for the very marked changes in Jung's style of work from the early clinical and experimental investigations to the wider studies of religion, symbolism, and so forth in his later years; and for the appeal, and lack of appeal, which the later work has had. These two questions may not be entirely unrelated. For instance, one reason for the change of style may have been preoccupation with the needs of certain types of patient, while the expression given to this mentality may have been part of Jung's appeal. Beginning with the first question, however, we may recall Jung's statement, in the early days, that his thoughts had 'matured in almost daily intercourse with my venerable chief, Professor Bleuler', together with our own comments on the influence toward scientific studies which Bleuler probably exerted.[1] We may recall, too, the enthusiasm with which Jung threw himself for a period into the psychoanalytical movement, in spite, as it appears, of doubts which later came to light, his distress on finding that he had to withdraw his confidence in Freud,[2] and his turning back to the literary and philosophical works of his student reading. Already from this material it may be wondered whether a rather high degree of suggestibility has been characteristic of Jung's personality, and in this connection it may be worthwhile to take note of the controversy which arose during and after World War II, concerning Jung's relations with the Nazi movement.

The attackers in this argument are represented by S. S. Feldman,

[1] *Supra*, pp. 34–5.   [2] *Supra*, p. 81.

who, in a short article, 'Dr. C. G. Jung and National Socialism'[1] regards Jung as virtually a Nazi; and the defenders by Ernest Harms, who, in a long article, 'Carl Gustav Jung—Defender of Freud and the Jews',[2] insists that at all times Jung maintained his efforts to undermine Nazi domination of German psychiatric circles.

If the passages cited by Feldman are examined it will certainly be seen how close Jung can come to some portions of the Nazi ideology. For instance, in 1934 he wrote:

> '"the Aryan unconscious contains continuity and creative germs and has to live up to the task of its future. The young German race is still able to create new forms of culture, and this power, resting in the unconscious of every German individual, as a germ laden with energy, is able to kindle powerful fire. . . . The Jewish people, far more developed than others, does not bother with the unfolding of the tension of its future. The Aryan unconscious has a higher potential than the Jewish, and this is the advantage and also the disadvantage of a young people close to the barbarian . . . I warned the world of this and was therefore called an anti-semite. Freud is responsible for it. He and his Germanic followers could not understand the German psyche. Have they been taught a better lesson by the powerful National-socialism at which the whole world looks with admiration—a movement which pervades a whole people and is manifest in every German individual?"'

On V-E day, however,

> '"the German resembles a drunkard, awakening with a hangover, not knowing or not willing to know what he had done. He will try frantically to rehabilitate himself in the face of the world's accusations and hate— but that is not the right way. The only right way is his unconditional acknowledgement of guilt. . . . All, consciously or unconsciously, actively or passively, are concerned in the atrocities. They knew nothing of these things—yet they knew them."'

From this evidence the conclusion drawn by Feldman is one, in Freud's much earlier words, of unscrupulous self interest.[3] On the other hand, as Harms points out, anyone whose exclusive aim was to ingratiate himself with the Nazis would not have included, in his first book published after they had come to power, a study by a Jewish pupil, Dr. Hugo Rosenthal, on 'Typological Opposites in the History of the Jewish Religion'. Nor, we may add, would he have said in

[1] *Am. J. Psychiat.*, 102, 1945; p. 263.
[2] *Psychiatric Quarterly*, Vol. 20, No. 2, 1946; pp. 199-230.
[3] *Supra*, p. 80.

1941 that the aim of psychotherapy is 'to educate people towards independence and moral freedom' whereas in so far as the State is given pre-eminent value people have to be educated in accordance with its system 'even though they were thereby diverted from their own individual highest destiny'.[1] The situation becomes more understandable if Jung is seen not as essentially a Nazi or a fellow-traveller through motives of self-interest, but as a somewhat suggestible member of the German-speaking middle classes, having so much in common with the Nazis through their own tradition that they were, so to speak, betrayed from within. This interpretation finds some support, perhaps, in the colourful style of the passages which Feldman cites, and accords with Jung's own statement that he hesitated to condemn the rise of National Socialism partly because he thought the illness might contain its cure, and partly because Germany was 'our intellectual background to which we Swiss were bound by ties of blood, language and friendship'.[2] Among the common elements may be put this very idea of 'blood'—the exaltation of a supposedly biological unity, together with a yearning toward the superman, the man who, in Jung's words, 'knows how to put his soul in the place of conscience', and a looking toward the past, especially the past of the Teutonic peoples, as a source of inspiration in the style of the Romantics. ('Thundering and intoxicating, early Germanic history comes surging up . . .')[3]

With this evidence for suggestibility in other directions we may wonder what the effect is likely to have been in the therapeutic situation. One possibility is that the therapist's balance between identification and detachment may have veered rather far in the direction of the former. There is indeed a passage where we can almost watch this happening:

'Her eyes flash; an evil expression creeps into her face, the gleam of an unknown resistance never seen before. I am suddenly faced by the possibility of a painful misunderstanding. What is it? Disappointed love? Does she feel offended—depreciated? In her glance there lurks

---

[1] *Contemp. Events*, p. 29.   [2] *Ibid.*, p. 84.

[3] *Supra*, p. 86. To give another illustration: a statement that there is a need 'to liberate from the old documents of their ancestral past that power of old, that noble spirit which, unrecognized by us, is still sleeping in them' might easily form part of the same passage as Jung's reference to 'the old pagan in ourselves' who 'lies unconscious but living within us.' It comes, however, from the work of Friedrich Schlegel. (Cited by Wernaer, R. M., *Romanticism and the Romantic School in Germany*, p. 306. New York: Appleton & Co., 1910.)

something of the beast of prey, something really demoniacal. Is she a demon after all? Or am I the beast of prey, the demon, and is there sitting before me a terrified victim, trying to defend herself against my evil spells with the brute strength of despair? All this must surely be nonsense—fantastic delusion. What have I touched? What new chord is vibrating? Yet it is only a passing moment.'[1]

Furthermore, as we noted, it seems probable that patients who would be regarded as borderline schizophrenic have made up a fairly substantial proportion of Jung's analytical cases, or at any rate that such cases have impressed him strongly. This may not apply to all members of his school. Professor Meier reports, 'Personally, I have had a limited experience with the analytic treatment of schizophrenics'[2] and Dr. R. F. Hobson that 'Analytical psychologists have worked extensively with the milder depressive reactions occurring in middle life.'[3] However, as recently as 1960 there have come statements which suggest, pending the publication of empirical data, that a difference has existed between the Freudian and the Jungian school in this respect. The 'vast majority of people who may come to us for psychoanalysis are not psychotic', says D. W. Winnicott, 'and students must be taught first the analysis of non-psychotic cases'.[4] Analytical psychologists do not frequently come across clear-cut neurotic cases, says Ruth Strauss in the same symposium. 'This may well be due to the fact that borderline cases feel particularly attracted to analytical psychology.'[5] The benefits of psychotherapy for these patients have of course often been debated. Some workers are despondent, holding with Paul Hoch that nothing is more discouraging than the way in which years of therapeutic work can be wiped out within a few days, the patient being unable to maintain improvement independently.[6] Others, including Sullivan and his school, are more hopeful, believing that although their patients work out a style of living which does not correspond to the norms of an extraverted society, they are nonetheless able to maintain themselves in satisfying ways. Very possibly, as Sullivan suggests, the term schizophrenia is

---

[1] *Two Essays*, new ed., p. 90.   [2] *Jung and Analytical Psychology*, p. 69.
[3] 'Archetypal Themes in Depression.' *J. Analyt. Psychol.*, Vol. I, No. 1, pp. 33–47 (p. 33).
[4] 'Counter-transference.' *Brit. J. Med. Psychol.*, Vol. XXXIII, Pt. 1, 1960, pp. 17–21 (p. 19).
[5] 'Counter-transference.' *Brit. J. Med. Psychol.*, Vol. XXXIII, Pt. 1, 1960; pp. 23–7.
[6] Discussion of J. N. Rosen's paper, 'The Treatment of Schizophrenia by Direct Analytic Therapy.' *Psychiatric Quarterly*, Vol. 21, No. 1, 1947; pp. 28–31.

being used to cover at least two syndromes, one a slow organic deterioration which remains unaffected by analytical procedures, the other, a disorder of living which is sometimes reversible with their aid. However that may be, a point on which we found agreement earlier is the need, if such therapy is to be attempted, for a much fuller participation in the psychotic's inner world than is customary in neurotic cases. To this participation, by a therapist with a rather high degree of personal suggestibility, may perhaps be attributed the similarity between some of Jung's accounts of mental functioning and standard descriptions of early schizophrenic breakdown. Compare, in particular, the experiencing of the collective unconscious, which very often is accompanied by peculiar symptoms, such as 'dreams where the dreamer is flying through space like a comet, or thinks he is the earth, or the sun, or a star, or else is inordinately large or dwarfishly small; or has died, has come to a strange place . . .'[1] and the following account of the onset of a schizophrenic illness:

> 'An initial feeling of strangeness is rather common. In the words of one patient, the subject is often beset by a "flood of mental pictures as though an album within were unfolding itself". Elements of the unconscious come into awareness and are interpreted as manifestations of the supernatural, often with devastating impact. In the new world into which the patient is thrust previous principles and standards seem irrelevant. . . . To the individual the new experiences are so vivid that they seem to represent profound, new revelations. . . . In many of these patients the first experiences are followed by an acute sense of peril and fear of death.'[2]

Jung himself, we may remember, points to the analogy with mental illness, but makes the distinction that the experiencing of the collective unconscious leads in the end to greater health, though many clinicians would hesitate to make their diagnosis on the basis of therapeutic outcome. Similarly, Bleuler's account of the fragmentation of personality in schizophrenia may put us in mind of the Jungian figures: '*Single emotionally charged ideas or drives attain a certain degree of autonomy so that the personality falls to pieces. These fragments can exist side by side and alternately dominate the main part of the personality, the conscious part of the patient.*'[3] Some explanation of the feeling of having a second soul becomes a neces-

[1] *Supra*, p. 95.
[2] *Biology of Schizophrenia*, p. 85. New York: Norton, 1946.
[3] *Op. cit.*, p. 143. (Italicized in original.)

sity for the patient, and he concludes that he is possessed or hypnotically influenced. This may be compared too with the statement in Jung's later work that 'the psyche is not an indivisible unity, but a more or less divided totality'.[1]

There are several other indications of a schizoid influence. Very noticeable is a quality which might be called the *inwardness* of Jungian psychology—a neglect of the interaction between the individual and the social environment and a great deal of attention to avoidance of disintegration. In Jung's treatment of religion these qualities seem to be expressed in his undervaluation of the Transcendental element and the controlled nature of the individuation experience, during which, in contrast to James's converted souls who let go, who float and soar and sing, the subject is concerned with conscious assimilation of unconscious contents and produces symbols which provide protective walls against the danger of an outburst;[2] beside such statements may be placed the comment of a former schizophrenic patient that 'if you do really relax before you get to the bend in the road, then you can be quite certain that the total Unconscious will step up, finally and permanently, and will say, "Now I've got you!" and the job is done'.[3] A more specific illustration is Jung's account of *Einfühlung* and *Abstraktion* in *Psychological Types*, where he refers to the image in the case of the abstracting individual as 'representing a bulwark against the disintegrating effects of the unconsciously animated object', while 'for the feeling-into subject, the transference to the object is a defence against the disintegration caused by inner subjective factors'.[4] The ordinary person, it may be suggested, does not need to develop so much defence against disintegration. Or, as Heinz Werner says, 'In the schizophrenic the mental activity designed to restore the central focus of the personality is concerned solely with the ego,' whereas normal personality 'grows and becomes differentiated as against the growth and differentiation of the social world'.[5] Another conception, that of the psyche as consisting of paired opposites, may be in part derived from the same source, since a sharp line-up of opposing forces—good and evil, God and the devil—is a well-known characteristic of schizophrenic fantasy. It appears too that a rapid oscillation of opposites is experienced

[1] *Supra*, p. 94.   [2] *Supra*, p. 210.
[3] Howard-Ogdon, J. A., *Kingdom of the Lost*, p. 30. London: Bodley Head, 1947.   [4] *Psych. Types*, p. 369.
[5] *Comparative Psychology of Mental Development*, p. 467.

in their thinking: Bleuler cites the case of a philosophically educated catatonic who observed that '"When one expresses a thought, one always sees the counter-thought. This intensifies itself and becomes so rapid that one doesn't really know which was the first".'[1] A parallel can be found in Jung's statement that 'The structure of the psyche is in fact so radically contradictory or contrapuntal that one can scarcely make any psychological statement without immediately having to state the opposite.'[2]

It seems, too, that there may have been a psychotic influence on Jung's own style of writing. Turning back to his analysis of the thinking of his early dementia praecox patient,[3] we may find that her loose identifications, revealing, as Jung says, an inability to discriminate between one idea and another, are paralleled by identifications in his own later work such as that between 'society' and 'the State', or, more strikingly, the conclusion that since the body's carbon is simply carbon 'at bottom the psyche is simply "world"'.[4] Remembering that in the schizophrenic the concept basis or common link becomes vastly extended, so that everything may belong with everything else, we may wonder whether Jung's concept of determination by object or by subject may have been similarly widened—covering, as it has been seen to do, such diverse states of mind as, in the case of determination by the object', being unable to think something that would be displeasing to one's father and considering that one need not be ashamed of a thing if nobody knows about it.[5] Again, remembering that the schizophrenic has difficulty in maintaining a unitary set—so that a red object may be chosen, then another red object which happens to be rectangular, next a rectangular wooden block which in its turn may lead to the selection of a tool made partly of wood[6]—we may feel that Jung's progress from 'the personal' to 'the egocentric' and thence to 'the destructive' is rather similar.[7]

Finally, for both style and content Jung's work may be compared with the writing of an ex-patient, John Custance, who, in his book, *Wisdom, Madness and Folly*,[8] states that while he himself had been

---

[1] *Op. cit.*, p. 54.   [2] *Contemp. Events*, p. 37.
[3] *Supra*, p. 33.   [4] *Supra*, p. 89.   [5] *Supra*, p. 131.
[6] Rapaport, D., *et al.*, *Diagnostic Psychological Testing*, Vol. I, p. 404. Chicago: Year Book Publishers, 1946.
[7] *Supra*, p. 88.
[8] *Wisdom, Madness and Folly—the Philosophy of a Lunatic*. London: Victor Gollancz, 1951.

diagnosed as manic-depressive some of his thinking was not unlike that of others diagnosed as schizophrenic. Custance, like Jung, shows a proneness to loose identifications and to the grouping together of events whose similarities may seem to the reader less fundamental than their differences—in short, the same oversimplification of thinking. (For instance, the missing of a six-inch putt and the commission of a brutal murder are classified as essentially the same: 'they are more or less unpardonable errors for which I am responsible'.[1]) Similarities in content are: the vivid imagery which Custance reports, accompanied by a tendency to anthropomorphism, and the use of opposites, especially male and female, positive and negative ('The past is female, Negative . . . she must be wooed with effort and love, but once contact is made, she gives herself freely. . . . The future does not require to be wooed, like the past. On the contrary, it woos us.');[2] reliance on intuition rather than reason for regaining the truths of the Unconscious; and a readiness to accept explanation in terms of the archaic past. Under the last heading Custance writes of his interest in helping harlots—who formerly had concerned him not at all—that he associated this at the time with the recorded kindness of Christ toward sinners, but subsequent flights of ideas showed him that his state of mind had much more ancient associations, being in fact 'a regression to very ancient forms of orgiastic religion with which harlots, and ritual or religious prostitutes in particular, have been connected'.[3] And indeed Custance states that although he had never read Jung, he discovered later that his ideas 'correspond remarkably closely with those which seemed to be "revealed" to me',[4] while Jung in a recent translation[5] mentions the book by Custance as evidence that the events which he himself describes are not chimeras—without, apparently, realizing that it is his mode of ordering and explaining the occurrences reported which constitutes the main difficulty for psychologists of other schools.

Reviewing the development of Jung's ideas, it seems that the position may have been as follows. In the early days of his career there were no indications that he would become a theorist of note, as distinct from a clinician and experimentalist. He appeared, if anything, to have a descriptive rather than hypothesizing bent, to keep closely in touch with current psychological and biological conceptions,

---

[1] *Ibid.*, p. 126. [2] *Ibid.*, p. 177. [3] *Ibid.*, p. 49.
[4] *Ibid.*, p. 85. [5] *Archetypes and the Collective Unconscious*, p. 39.

and at times to show a slight weakness in his formulations, e.g. in the juxtaposition of his own ideas and Freud's,[1] and the tendency to stress first the similarities and then the differences between hysteria and dementia praecox.[2] First Bleuler, then Freud, exerted appreciable influence upon him, and then came a period of perplexity during which those influences were withdrawn and he turned back to the literary and philosophical reading of his student days. A few years later the catastrophe of the First World War occurred, bringing in its train moral and religious searchings among many educated people, or increasing those which had arisen in the nineteenth century. At the same time, working, so far as can be gathered, in relatively isolated circumstances, retired for many years even from the fairly quiet academic life of his Zürich environment, he was impressed by patients presenting psychotic symptoms, and participating in their experience more deeply than was customary. Under these circumstances it would not be surprising if some of his accounts of mental life were slightly generalized descriptions of happenings reported by such patients and others were derived largely from his reading. We may again mention, for instance, the use of the biological assumptions, Inheritance of Acquired Characters and Recapitulation, the borrowing of Levy Bruhl's concept of *participation mystique* to cover much of childhood, the tendency to equate childhood, primitive and psychotic thought and the interest in 'archaic experience', the use of the subject-object dichotomy and of opposites leading to synthesis, the picture of the Unconscious given by Carus and the *Elementargedanken* of Bastian, and even the pilgrimage theme, noted as a favourite one in German literature, which could well render the idea of encountering the figures of the collective unconscious more congenial. Now although it is true that all thinkers are dependent on what has gone before, the term, derivative, seems a possible one since relatively little independent development of these ideas is to be found in Jung's work, and indeed his mode of stating them is sometimes more obscure than the original, as in the case of the Recapitulation Theory.[3] Several of his accounts, i.e. of the unconscious, the subject-object dichotomy and the opposites in general, have of course been brought together also under the heading of a possible psychotic influence; what we may envisage is the converging of influences from two or more sources to produce the one effect.

[1] *Supra*, pp. 41.   [2] *Supra*, p. 79.   [3] *Supra*, p. 88.

Reverting to the first of these two sources, it would be understandable if a psychology which in some respects followed closely the lines of their own thinking had made an appeal to borderline psychotic patients. Besides the question of appeal there is the question of therapeutic value. As several writers have pointed out, the mentally disturbed patient may need to be provided with a schema for achieving the organization which he lacks, and since psychological events are many-sided, they can often be formulated in different ways with considerable justification for each. For some patients the very indefiniteness of Jungian theory, enabling the individual to choose what he needs for himself, may have advantages over a more rigid schema. Although we can agree that ultimately the establishing of abstract laws of mental functioning may be as important for psychotherapy as the establishing of a body of abstract physical principles has been in improving man's material well-being, it is nonetheless well recognized that theoretical and therapeutic inadequacies do not necessarily coincide, owing to the large number of factors at work in the concrete situation. It is even possible that therapeutically there may have been advantages in aspects of Jungian psychology which scientifically have drawbacks, e.g. the concept of the collective unconscious may have assisted the patient to achieve some measure of psychic distance from his experiences by pushing them back to a supposed source in the prehistoric past. Possibly also the references made to renewing contact with the experiences of the ancestors may have brought some of the subjective benefits of being linked with other people—mitigating the sense of being 'alone, alone, all, all alone, alone on a wide, wide sea' without placing too much strain on limited powers of social adaptation. Jung himself stresses the function of mythological interpretations in acting as a 'lifesaver' which 'guards against the dangerous isolation which everyone feels when confronted by an incomprehensible and irrational aspect of his personality',[1] and the same point is often made by his followers in discussions of their work. In other words, just as Klineberg—observing in Peking cases of mild schizophrenia which improved markedly when encouraged to develop an interest in Buddhistic literature— has suggested that many persons may be saved from the disease by finding this accepted outlet,[2] so we may suggest as well that the find-

[1] *Symbols of Transformation*, p. 442.
[2] Klineberg, O., *Social Psychology*, pp. 509–10. New York: Henry Holt, 1940.

ing of a shared expression in Jungian psychology may sometimes be helpful to patients of this type. Various attitudes which we have noted in Jung's writings may also be of particular relevance in dealing with the borderline psychotic. It is certainly not at all uncommon for schizophrenic patients to be highly sensitive about their own condition, and to have the feeling of experiencing something which was meant to be profoundly significant but which somehow misfired. Gerhard Adler, reporting the dreams of a schizophrenic, speaks of 'the agonizing nearness of rescue which nevertheless just does not "arrive".'[1] A patient, 'E. Dabney Hunter', writes:

> 'The self which one cannot be is ... sidetracked into that world which the analysts call fantasy—or escape from reality. But, as a patient, I continue to believe that this world, in its essence primitive and mystic, is a deeper and truer one than the normal level of superficial contact. It is difficult to reconcile this sort of internal reality with the reality of the outer world; the incoherent and seemingly irrelevant reality of poetry with the more rational experiment of prose. Both must hold their own truths and in time, one hopes they will merge. Illness, however, denies the perspective which makes the merging process bearable or complete.'[2]

In cases of this kind a reductive approach will need to be phrased in some such terms as trying to see *why* all this has not turned out to be so great as had been hoped. We have felt that Jung in his later work is not always sufficiently ready to press on to a reductive attack in any form. However, the tone of his statements, that the experience of the patient is very significant, with the warning that it is also a little dangerous and should be kept within bounds, and the expectation that with 'quiet waiting' and avoidance of too fixed a goal, the sought-for integration will emerge ('just the alarmingly chaotic . . . reaveals the deepest meaning' and '"rarely . . . people come to great things without they first go somewhat astray"')[3]—these attitudes are likely to have therapeutic value, in helping the patient to believe that, as 'Dabney Hunter' hopes, 'the sickness need not be wasted. As one discovers the courage to understand it, one sees that it is neither given up nor lost, but only transformed into something valuable. Thus the old fairy tales of dragon-princes in disguise seem to become real.'[4]

[1] *Studies in Analytical Psychology*, p. 39. London: Routledge & Kegan Paul, 1948.
[2] 'Subjective Difficulties Incident to the Acceptance of Psychoanalysis.' *Psychiatry*, Vol. 5, Nov. 1942; pp. 495-8 (p. 495).
[3] *Supra*, p. 130. [4] *Op. cit.*, p. 496.

Being ourselves fairly favourable in our attitude to Jungian therapy, we may in fairness add a less favourable interpretation by a neo-analytical writer, Clara Thompson. Thompson's 'chief overall criticism' is that it tends to take the patient away from reality, substituting a mystical, semi-religious fantasy life. It can be especially dangerous to psychotics, she thinks, in strengthening their tendency to confuse reality with autistic thinking. And in contemplating the experience of the race the patient's problem remains but thinking about something else has been substituted for it. This, she adds, 'is the classical mechanism of the obsessional neurosis'.[1]

At the present time we do not have sufficient empirical data to do more than make suggestions, though we may feel that in making her evaluation Thompson does not take account of Jung's insistence that the patients should continue with their daily work, i.e. in addition to participating in their fantasy he does endeavour in a practical way to point them toward the outer world. In swinging the balance between the positive and negative effects of this kind of treatment, the personality of the therapist can be expected to play a specially important part. A rather high degree of suggestibility, as postulated, would not by any means be incompatible with the capacity for *suggesting* much of a therapeutic nature ('You can exert no influence if you are not susceptible to influence'[2]), and Jung by all accounts has been endowed with a personality of exceptional impressiveness. Custance, for instance, writes of an interview with Jung that he was reminded of a great farming character in his district. 'The only word to describe him is massive; he is massive in stature and build, giving somehow a tremendous impression of massive solidity of character. . . . At once I had a feeling of complete confidence; here was a man, one felt, who would never let one down.'[3] With equal enthusiasm H. A. Murray reports that Jung was

'the first full-blooded, spherical—and Goethean, I should say—intelligence I had ever met, the man whom the judicious Prinzhorn called "the ripest fruit on the tree of psychoanalytical knowledge". We talked for hours, sailing down the lake and smoking before the hearth of his Faustian retreat. "The great flood-gates of the wonder-world swung open", and I saw things that my philosophy had never dreamt of. Within a

---

[1] *Psychoanalysis, its Evolution and Development*, pp. 168–9. London: George Allen & Unwin, 1952. [2] *Supra*, p. 145.
[3] *Adventure into the Unconscious*, p. 129. London: Christopher Johnson, 1954.

month a score of bi-horned problems were resolved, and I went off decided on depth psychology. I had *experienced* the unconscious— something not to be drawn out of books.'[1]

Even Freud, after the break, referred to Jung's 'exceptional talents ... and the impression of energy and assurance which his personality conveyed'.[2]

But the question of psychotic influence cannot be left without our making certain reservations. However much Jung's psychology may have been coloured by his contact with such patients, it is not, of course, to be dismissed as a psychology of schizophrenia only. On the theoretical side we have seen that other influences have combined to make it as it is. Therapeutically, much in Jung's work will have value for the non-psychotic also. To give an illustration: his use of the mechanism of cosmic identification ('In some way or other we are part of an all-embracing psychic life')[3] fits well the schizophrenic tendency to see everything as belonging with everything else, but is used by other people also ('Not as my sorrow, but as the sorrow of the world; not a personal isolating pain, but a pain without bitterness that unites all humanity. That this can help us needs no proof')[4] and may be responsible in part for that feeling of being ushered into a wider universe which several of Jung's followers have stressed.[5] Such a mechanism fits too the Idealistic philosophies, with their belief in the unreality of separateness. Nor do we wish to maintain that Jung and his followers are themselves schizophrenic; even a small amount of contact with psychotic patients is sufficient for their phraseology to be learnt and employed if, as occasionally happens, it expresses some experience in a brief and vivid way. And while in the present chapter we are chiefly concerned with factors which contribute to the distinctiveness of Jungian psychology, making it something different from anticipations pure and simple, it is highly relevant in estimating Jung's appeal to bear in mind the views which he shares with other deviants from the stricter psychoanalytical orthodoxy—the insights, extending even into Kleinian psychology, with which his work is shot through.

A further point. Supposing that a degree of schizophrenic influence can be demonstrated in Jung's work, this does not tell us anything

---

[1] 'What Should Psychologists Do About Psychoanalysis?' *J. Abn. & Soc. Psychol.*, Vol. XXXV, 1940; pp. 150–75 (p. 153).
[2] *Collected Papers*, Vol. I, p. 329.
[3] *Supra*, p. 198.   [4] *Contribs.*, pp. 108–9.   [5] *Supra*, p. x.

about the *value* of the experiences themselves. For workaday life the disadvantages of, for instance, being unable to make the commonly accepted differentiations, or to distinguish in the usual manner between objective and subjective reality, are obvious enough. Nevertheless, it might be, as William James suggests, and as some schizophrenics can be found to believe, that 'our normal waking consciousness, rational consciousness as we call it, is but one special type of consciousness, whilst all about it, parted from it by the filmiest of screens, there lie the potential forms of consciousness entirely different' and that 'No account of the universe in its totality can be final which leaves these other forms of consciousness quite disregarded.'[1] His own report on the effects of nitrous oxide intoxication is a well-known illustration. All the impressions in that state, he writes,

> 'converge towards a kind of insight to which I cannot help ascribing some metaphysical significance. The keynote of it is invariably a reconciliation. It is as if the opposites of the world, whose contradictoriness and conflict make all our difficulties and troubles, were melted into unity. Not only do they, as contrasted species, belong to one and the same genus, but *one of the species*, the nobler and better *one, is itself the genus, and so soaks up and absorbs its opposite into itself*. This is a dark saying, I know, when thus expressed in terms of common logic, but I cannot wholly escape from its authority. I feel as if it must mean something, something like what the hegelian philosophy means, if one could only lay hold of it more clearly.'[2]

Aldous Huxley, in more recent years, has written of his experiences during the schizophrenia-like condition produced by mescalin. Although it is the infinite significance of sensory experience that he emphasizes, rather than the ultimate reconciliation of opposites, his suggestions in some ways are similar to James's. Citing C. D. Broad, he thinks of so-called 'normal' consciousness as having been funnelled through the reducing valve of brain, nervous system and sense organs, which protect the organism from being overwhelmed by stimuli that have no relevance for the task of staying alive on the surface of the planet.

> 'Most people, most of the time, know only what comes through the reducing valve and is consecrated as genuinely real by the local language. Certain persons, however, seem to be born with a kind of bypass that

---

[1] *Op. cit.*, p. 388.   [2] *Op. cit.*, p. 388.

circumvents the reducing valve. In others temporary by-passes may be acquired either spontaneously, or as the result of deliberate "spiritual exercises", or though hypnosis, or by means of drugs. Through these permanent or temporary by-passes there flows, not indeed the perception "of everything that is happening everywhere in the universe" (for the by-pass does not abolish the reducing valve, which still excludes the total content of Mind at Large), but something more than, and above all something different from, the carefully selected utilitarian material which our narrowed, individual minds regard as a complete, or at least sufficient, picture of reality.'[1]

The schizophrenic can be thought of as a man who has lost the way back, who can no longer 'take refuge . . . in the home-made universe of common sense—the strictly human world of useful notions, shared symbols, and socially acceptable conventions'.[2] But no man who has had such experiences, Huxley declares, will ever be the same again. 'He will be wiser but less cocksure, happier but less self-satisfied, humbler in acknowledging his ignorance yet better equipped to understand the relationship of words to things, of systematic reasoning to the unfathomable Mystery which it tries, forever vainly, to comprehend.'[3]

Although our attention was first drawn to a psychotic element, it would seem from this that there may be some features distinguishing the Jungian mentality, as it might be called, from the accepted academic type, which, though they may occur in psychotic states, are not confined to them. One of these appears to be a strong interest in immediate experience. Even in the intermediate period Jung was found to say that while the scientific investigator draws up rules and categories, the physician would do well to 'put away his scholar's gown, bid farewell to his study, and wander with human heart through the world'.[4] Later he repeats that 'when we take a deep look into the psychology of actual cases . . . then we receive—to put it mildly—a lasting impression'.[5] Now as Ogden and Richards say, 'certain of these concrete, immediate, unintellectualized phases of life have in their own right a complexity and richness which no intellectual activities can equal'.[6] William James, similarly, writes: 'There is in the living act of perception always something that glimmers and twinkles and will not be caught, and for which reflec-

---

[1] *Doors of Perception*, p. 17. Chatto & Windus, 1941. [2] *Ibid.*, p. 44.
[3] *Ibid.*, p. 63. [4] *Supra*, p. 57. [5] *Contribs.*, p. 150.
[6] *The Meaning of Meaning*, p. 156. London: Kegan Paul, 1938.

tion comes too late.'[1] While for some persons an intense form of excitement may come from the logical operations of deduction and induction, others may find the tracing out of implications positively tedious and obtain from Jungian psychology the restoration of capacities which have been neglected. As Jung himself reports, 'to enter a realm of immediate experience is most stimulating for those who have done their utmost in the personal and rational spheres of life and yet have found no meaning and no satisfaction there. In this way, too, the matter-of-fact and the commonplace come to wear an altered countenance, and can even acquire a new glamour.'[2] Both types of experience, however, can be accompanied by a similar 'A-ah' reaction, and this, too, may have contributed to that confusion between artistic expression and theoretical formulation which has been noted in Jung's work.

It is not, one would imagine, simply the value of immediate experience which Jung is trying to teach, so much as the value of a certain attitude which may be taken toward it. This may be understood more fully from a passage which Evelyn Underhill has written on the state of contemplation. Take any object, she suggests, a picture, a statue, a tree, a distant hillside:

'Look, then, at this thing which you have chosen. Wilfully yet tranquilly refuse the messages which countless other aspects of the world are sending; and so concentrate your whole attention on this one act of loving sight that all other objects are excluded from the conscious field. . . . Almost at once, this new method of perception will reveal unsuspected qualities in the external world. . . . As you, with all your consciousness, lean out towards it, an answering current will meet yours. It seems as though the barrier between its life and your own, between subject and object, had melted away. You are merged with it, in an act of true communion: and you *know* the secret of its being deeply and unforgettably, yet in a way which you can never hope to express. Seen thus, a thistle has celestial qualities: a speckled hen a touch of the sublime.'[3]

In this is implied an attitude of aesthetic appreciation rather than manipulation, a belief, as 'Joanna Field' writes, that 'the act of welding, by means of words or shape or musical sound or colour— into some sort of tangible form—a single moment of raw lived experience, is action as real and effective, though not as obviously

---

[1] *Op. cit.*, p. 456.   [2] *Mod. Man*, p. 75.
[3] *Mysticism*, p. 301. London: Methuen, 1930.

so, as being able to order people about, break a sports record, be a social success. . . .'[1]

It is believable that those who value experience in this way will value also the imagery by which it is most vividly recalled, and certainly we have seen that the image is referred to often in Jung's writings. For instance, the archetypes express themselves in images, and in therapy we found that Jung relied less exclusively than Freud on the verbal material of his patients, and in general that Jung and Freud make decidedly different estimations of images and words. In one of the few passages where Jung speaks of himself he tells us that he once experienced a very violent earthquake; his first immediate feeling was that he 'no longer stood on the solid and familiar earth, but on the skin of a gigantic animal that was shuddering beneath me'. It was this image that impressed itself on him, he adds, not the physical fact.[2] Something more would seem to be involved than the mere possession of vivid visual imagery—there is also a spontaneous turning to it for the expression of affective life which does not always occur even when the visualizing capacity is present. (For instance, even persons who consider themselves able to visualize with fair success may report that they react to an earthquake by being *very much* aware of the physical fact, by kinaesthetic sensations of a bloodless, shaky type, and by a quick putting into words of the question, 'How long is this going to last?'). The same attitude to the image is found throughout the Jungian school; it is forcefully stated by Jacobi, who speaks of 'the often insurmountable difficulty of translating vision and experience into a conceptual language'[3] and cites a passage from Kerenyi: '"A torrent of mythological pictures streams out . . . that one does justice to not by interpretation and explanation but above all by letting it alone and allowing it to utter its own meaning."'[4] If, therefore, some of the assets and limitations of the image are considered, we may have a clearer impression of the assets and limitations of Jung's work.

Bartlett's discussion may be helpful here.[5] The image, like the word, is an instrument of the general function of dealing with objects

[1] *Experiment in Leisure*, p. 199.
[2] *Contribs.*, p. 114.
[3] *Complex/Archetype/Symbol*, p. 77. New York: Pantheon Books, 1959.
[4] *Ibid.*, p. 109.
[5] *Remembering*, Ch. XI, 'Images and their Functions,' pp. 215–26. Cambridge University Press, 1922.

at a distance—a sign indicating something which need not be perceptually present.

'By the aid of the image, and particularly of the visual image—for this, like the visual sense, is the best of all our distance mechanisms of its own type—a man can take out of its setting something that happened a year ago, reinstate it with much if not all of its individuality unimpaired, combine it with something that happened yesterday, and use them both to help him to solve a problem with which he is confronted to-day.'

Images are especially apt to be associated with specific emotional experiences and to emerge when personal interests or attitudes cross and combine. It does not seem fantastic to suppose that some people by temperament are peculiarly responsive to the subtle affective background of their interests.

'These are the people whose interests most readily flow and coalesce.... Others, however, are unable to combine realms of interest not conventionally put together, until some reason that can be formulated has been found by themselves or by some different person. The former forerun reasons, feeling a connection for which there is no good vocabulary. The latter must await analysis and logic.'

Because the image tends to retain its individualizing functions, or as we might say, to be more closely related to immediate experience, those people who are able to combine vivid images without waiting for formulated reasons will be the ones who deal chiefly with concrete representations, metaphor, practical problems. But for analysis and logic words are the necessary means, since they are able to 'indicate the qualitative and relational features of a situation in their *general* aspect just as directly as, and perhaps even more satisfactorily than, they can describe its peculiar individuality'. That is, thinking,

'in the proper psychological sense, is never the mere reinstatement of some suitable past situation produced by a crossing of interests, but is the utilization of the past in the solution of difficulties set by the present. Consequently it involves that amount of formulation which shows, at least in some degree, what is the nature of the relation between the instances used in the solution and the circumstances that set the problem.'

Susanne Langer, in making the same point, gives the following illustration: 'Consider the sentence, "Your chance of winning is one among a thousand of losing." Imagine a pictorial expression of this comparatively simple proposition! First, a symbol for "you, winning"; another for "you, losing," pictured a thousand times!' A thousand anythings is indeed far beyond apprehension on a basis of mere visual gestalt: 'to denote such a host of concepts and keep their relations to each other straight, we need a symbolism that can express both terms and relationships more economically.'[1]

The second advantage of words is that they are the most direct method of communicating meaning. The image, to be communicated, has itself to be expressed in words, and this is often very difficult, as the Jungians are aware. For discursive thinking, Langer adds, the sheer vividness of the image may be a handicap.

'A symbol which interests us *also* as an object is distracting. It does not convey its meaning without obstruction. For instance, if the word "plenty" were replaced by a succulent, ripe, real peach, few people could attend entirely to the mere concept of *quite enough* when confronted with such a symbol. . . . Peaches are too good to act as words; we are much too interested in peaches themselves. But little noises are ideal conveyors of concepts, for they give us nothing but their meaning. . . . Our conceptual activity seems to flow *through* them, rather than merely to accompany them, as it accompanies other experiences that we endow with significance.'[2]

With these points in mind we may turn back to Jung. In the first place, his style of writing becomes again more understandable, i.e. if language is often being used for the purpose of translating from images, the rather concrete and highly coloured nature of the passages noted earlier ('The virgin soil demands . . .', 'Thundering and intoxicating, early Germanic history comes surging up . . .')[3] is sufficiently explained. Secondly, concentration on the image, or on the experience immediately confronting him, may contribute to the contradictions in Jung's work—first one, then another, concrete instance being pictured, without the work of abstract co-ordination taking place. Thirdly, a certain lack of development in Jungian psychology may spring from the same source, since by development of thought is meant the very type of operation for which the image is least effective—the placing of material into logical categories of subordination, super-ordination and causation. In operating with images it is only too easy so to lose oneself in 'associative progression from picture resemblance to picture resemblance', as one writer

[1] *Op. cit.*, p. 74.   [2] *Ibid.*, p. 75.   [3] *Supra*, p. 86.

puts it, that the problems at issue really are not grasped.[1] This, may explain how it is that Jung, although speaking of individuation as 'an as yet very obscure field of research much in need of exploration',[2] has said also that 'It seems almost as if we were about to go on dreaming the century-old dream of alchemy, like the unconscious itself, and to continue piling new synonyms on the mountain of the old . . .'[3] and has doubted whether, in the last analysis, the human reason is a suitable instrument for the purpose. That is, he may have been inclined to attribute to reason limitations which are inherent in his own rather cumbrous symbolism but not in reason as such. It is possible, too, that when some form of explanation is unavoidable, those whose minds function in this way will be more likely than those whose thinking is carried out largely in words, to remain, as Jung himself appears to have done, rather closely attached to conceptions which are current in their milieu.

However, hampering though Jung's interest in the image may have been, both for the actual construction and development of a coherent theory of mind and for belief in the worthwhileness of making the attempt, therapeutically it may have had advantages. The image may be peculiarly fitted to sum up material on the threshold of consciousness, or again it may help to free more deeply unconscious material and to pave the way for full conscious understanding later on—a function which would accord with Bartlett's description of the image method as 'the method of brilliant discovery, whereby realms organized by interests usually kept apart are brought together'.[4] To give an illustration: Frances Wickes reports the case of a patient who consciously felt 'a rather sentimental pity' for his mother. Even though he resented her clinging ways, he never realized that they were power demands, but when he started to draw her picture it took the form of a catlike creature with embryonic legs and long arms reaching out with cat claws to hold him. 'Suddenly he felt an intuition of a reality hitherto unperceived.'[5] Another patient dreamt, '"I started to put on my street shoes but in one of them was a small green snake. . . . Suddenly I grew terrified; I knew that I could never go into the street and mingle with the crowd unless I could kill that snake."' Not satisfied that the Freudian

[1] P. Helwig (*Charakterologie*, 1936), cited by Spearman, C. 'German Science of Character.' *Character and Personality*, Vol. 6, 1937–8; pp. 36–50.
[2] *Supra*, p. 225. [3] *Integ. of Person.*, p. 175.
[4] *Op. cit.*, p. 226. [5] *The Inner World of Man*, pp. 263–4.

emphasis on abnormal fear of sexuality was appropriate in this case, the therapist asked the patient to keep the image in mind and see if any associations arose spontaneously. One day a vivid association did arise. The patient saw the coat of arms which used to hang in the front hall of her family home, and realized that the snake in her dream was exactly like a snake in the coat of arms. She then remembered how carefully her mother had always chosen her playmates, exhorting her to remember her ancestors and never to demean herself in any way. Therefore, when she was beginning to long for a life of her own, 'the unconscious presented this picture which said, "Your greatest peril is symbolized by your own coat of arms. Until you can overcome this sense of the importance of your ancestors, you cannot go down into the street and mingle with all kinds of people and meet the common experiences of life."' If this patient had been told, 'You are a snob, you care more about family position than personal worth', she would have denied it indignantly. 'But when her own dream of the snake was associated with the ancestral coat of arms and with her own childhood and had showed her how these attitudes had grown up in her without her knowledge, then she could not repudiate the meaning.'[1]

It may be that a softening effect is achieved through the dreamer's interest in the images in and for themselves—in fact, through one of the very peculiarities which are disadvantageous when transferred to writing which is expected to be systematic. That is, the dream or fantasy unfolds like a panorama, and the dreamer, while interested, feels less personally implicated, perhaps less guilt-laden, than in the experiences and conflicts of waking life from which they may have sprung. Admittedly, images can be harsh enough and terrifying enough at times. Even so, there seems to be a difference between experiencing, for instance, the insights given above in images, and expressing them in words. Some individuals, to be sure, are capable of accepting such insights direct in verbal form. One wonders, though, whether in that way there is a loss—whether a preliminary statement in images may have its value in preserving certain rather elusive qualities of personality. H. G. Baynes describes fantasy as 'nature's means of protecting the immature mind against the shocks of the real'.[2] Reflecting along these lines, one may think that to use almost exclusively the medium of words, or to proceed too rapidly

[1] *Ibid.*, pp. 25–6.   [2] *Analytical Psychology and the English Mind*, p. 224.

to the work of translation, is liable to produce an effect on the personality almost as though the natural covering of an animal or plant had been torn away and a second, harder covering were grown in its place. Something rather similar is suggested by Marion Milner, i.e. that the substitute satisfaction of fantasy life has been over-stressed by the Freudians, and that 'When the urgency of the need for immediate magical satisfaction of the wish is not too great, the conjured-up wish fulfilment does seem to function as a kind of experimental rather than magical action'. Through providing a basis for knowing our own deepest feeling experiences, 'internal object fantasies', or images representing internal happenings, give 'a means by which we can continue assimilating, reflecting upon, developing our past experience'. They are 'the vehicle by which the psyche can carry on its relation to its first loves, developing and enriching this throughout life and long after these loved people no longer exist in the external world; and this continuous development itself enriches and enlarges the boundaries of the ego'.[1]

In *An Experiment in Leisure*, Marion Milner—now known to be the 'Joanna Field' of this and other books—describes more simply and at greater length the role of images in her own experience, as we noted in part while referring previously to alchemistic symbols. Only by a process of 'image-finding', she declares, was it possible for her to 'come closer in touch with the movement of life' and at the same time to live more reasonably. ('By living more reasonably I meant, a little less liable to strive for incompatible ends, less liable to impose un-necessary duties upon myself and then be miserable about it, less liable to look round for other people of whom I could say that all my inadequacies were their fault, less liable to that most uncomfort-able state of wanting to grab other people's successes for oneself.'[2]) Neither bald fact nor abstractions helped her to think about her life. The bald fact, 'he said this and she said that', was too unrelated —it did not give the real meaning of the happening and so make her wiser for the future. Nor was it helpful to talk about castration complexes, overcompensations, and so forth, for although, in-

---

[1] 'Some Aspects of Phantasy in Relation to General Psychology.' *Int. J. Psycho-Anal.*, Vol. XXVI, 1945; pp. 143–52. Freud himself in one place (*Ego and the Id*, p. 23) acknowledges that it is possible for thought processes to become conscious through a reversion to visual residues, and adds that for many persons this seems to be a favourite method. However, presumably because of his own orientation toward the word, he does not expand this idea.

[2] *Op. cit.*, p. 222.

tellectually, she could recognize the truth of such ideas, they 'seemed somehow to put out the living glow of experience so that there was nothing there to explain'. Instead, 'To wait quietly and watch for images, for those pictures and metaphors that the mind itself threw up, this seemed to be the way that understanding grew'. The assumption has often been made, she continues, that the transition from passion to reason can be accomplished in a single bound. 'It seemed obvious to me now, that there must be a mediator between them; then I discovered that Jung had said, of the mythological type of image, that it has the capacity to reconcile idea with feeling.'

The finding of images became possible only through 'non-action', 'plunging into the void', 'wiping out of oneself', 'repeated giving up of every kind of purpose', and 'willingness to recognize that the moment of blankness and extinction was the moment of incipient fruitfulness, the moment without which the invisible forces within could not do their work'.[1] This is similar to a point suggested by passages in Jung, i.e. that the balance aimed at between 'the conscious' and 'the unconscious', or between rationality and emotion—not that one would wish to identify the two entirely—differs somewhat from that which Freud envisaged ('Where id was, there shall ego be') or that which is fairly common in academic and related circles, where direct rational control is often relied on rather heavily. It is as though there were a partial giving in, letting the affect flow through one's being more diffusely and with less organization. 'It is far better,' Jung says, 'to admit the affect and submit to its violence than to try to escape it by all sorts of intellectual tricks.'[2] Or again, as we have noted elsewhere,[3] 'If we picture the conscious mind, with the ego as its centre, as being opposed to the unconscious, and if we now add to our mental picture the process of assimilating the unconscious, we can think of this assimilation as a kind of approximation of conscious and unconscious. . . .' Such a state is reminiscent of the Eastern mind as Jung describes it, 'less egocentric, as if its contents were more loosely connected with the subject, and as if greater stress were laid on mental states which include a depotentiated ego'.[4] These descriptions can be summed up, perhaps, as indicating an attitude of 'constructive passivity' toward unconscious processes, as toward immediate experiences in the previous passages.

---

[1] *Ibid.*, p. 205.   [2] *Psych. and Religion*, p. 366.
[3] *Supra*, p. 97.   [4] *Psych. and Religion*, p. 485.

At the same time—while we may hesitate to interrupt our more positive discussion—it may be that in therapy itself so heavy a reliance upon imagery is not entirely free from drawbacks. In discussing the religious aspect of Jung's work we felt that had Jung been less concerned with myth and symbolism he might not have considered the 'I-Thou' relationship so unbearably sophisticated. In therapy, similarly, the Jungian concentration upon images may be a handicap in, for instance, working out the exact relevance of affective experiences for the patient's interpersonal relationships. In this sphere, more probably than most, the image is indeed 'the method of brilliant discovery', but unless followed by considerable analysis of the relational type, for which words are the necessary instruments, much of its impact may be lost. There may, too, be some danger of confusing mode of expression with underlying capacities, i.e. so attuned may the analyst become to affective life expressed in visual imagery, that he may be prone to underestimate affective life which flows through other channels. We do not wish to maintain that this will always happen in a Jungian analysis, but we believe it can do. For these reasons there would seem much to be said for regarding the image as a valuable adjunct to, rather than the main vehicle of, the analytic process. 'Let us not despise the use of words in psychotherapy.'

Nevertheless, reviewing the qualities which have been suggested as forming part of a 'Jungian mentality'—interest in immediate experience, including an aesthetic—and indeed almost a religious—contemplation, expressiveness through the image, in particular the visual image, and a more receptive attitude to processes at work outside the ego-structure, together with the approach to the patient outlined previously, it may be thought that the Jungians have been in psychotherapy the main exponents of the view that just as the love of the beauty of crystals, the contemplation of their order, internal structure and inter-relations has played a large part in the development of mineralogy, so 'one of the chief guides in looking at a personality is *appreciation*'.[1] People will vary in the extent to which lack of such appreciation leads them to feel, in the words of William James, 'menaced and negated in the springs of our innermost life'[2] but some may feel this strongly. It may be this more than anything else which lies behind Jung's injunction to 'Learn your theories as

[1] Murphy, Gardner, *Personality*, p. 13.   [2] *Op. cit.*, p. 10.

Chapter X

JUNGIAN PSYCHOLOGY AND ITS APPEAL: THE SOCIAL BACKGROUND

There remains for consideration a further possibility, namely, that Jung's work has been a good cultural fit—using 'culture' in the wider, anthropological sense to denote a total way of life—for groups to which the work of Freud, again on cultural grounds, could not gain such ready access.

Indications of a difference in background between the Jungian and the Freudian schools have been found already,[1] and there are other pointers in the same direction. A. A. Roback, himself of Jewish origin, declares: 'the facts in the case are correct, *viz.*, Jewish patients and Jewish practitioners play a predominant part in psychoanalysis'.[2] Indeed, he continues,

'I should venture to state that the particulars contained in the hundreds of psychoanalytic articles regarding Jewish idiosyncrasies and peculiarities are of inestimable value both as literature and psychology; and it would not be presumptuous to predict that these studies will be greatly prized by the future Jewish historian, who will seek to reconstruct our age in the light of these intimate details.'[3]

For the Jungian school in general, as distinct from Jung himself, no statement quite so clear-cut appears to have been made, and indeed we noted that analytic psychology does contain within its

[1] *Supra,* pp. 44–5.
[2] *Jewish Influence in Modern Thought,* p. 174. Camb., Mass.: Sci-Art Publishers, 1929.
[3] Among the Jewish practitioners whom Roback mentions are: Adler and Stekel, Fritz Wittels, Hans Sachs, Karl Abraham, Max Eitingon, Ernst Simmel, Franz Alexander, Paul Schilder, Melanie Klein, Barbara Low, Sandor Ferenczi, Otto Rank, Paul Federn and Theodor Reik. Even Ernest Jones, after describing himself as the only Gentile in the circle, adds that coming of an oppressed race—the Welsh—he found it easy to identify with the Jewish outlook. (*Sigmund Freud,* Vol. II, p. 183.)

ranks some Jewish members.[1] Nevertheless, the information that many of his patients have come from the Church, as well as his preoccupation with Christian dogma, gives a sufficient inkling of the groups with which he has largely been in touch.

Although Jung refers to the importance of the personal equation in the making, and still more in the presentation and interpretation, of observations, he does not seem, apart from the two statements cited,[2] to have paid much attention to his social background—there was, presumably, no need for him to do so. From Freud's writings, on the other hand, it is clear that the Jewish problem was often in his thoughts. In addition to the personal references[3] he writes in more general terms of Judaism as made up of '"many dark emotional forces, all the more potent for being so hard to grasp in words, as well as the clear consciousness of an inner identity, the intimacy that comes from the same psychic structure"'[4]—though his only suggestion as to its influence on his actual work is that non-acceptance at the University gave him early familiarity with the fate of being in the opposition and laid the foundation for an independent outlook.

Roback, among the earlier analysts and commentators, suggested that the habit of causal analysis is especially congenial to the Jewish mind, and that some aspects of Freud's work—the stress laid on male and female and the exploitation of all sorts of symbols to suit a particular conjecture—have their counterparts in Cabbalistic writings.[5] Suttie, a few years later, referred to the influence of the materialistic and aggressive character of modern society in leading the Freudians to assume that the root motive of human life is the advantage of the individual, and as we saw in discussing the Oedipus complex, described Freud's own antecedents as lying in 'perhaps the most patriarchal of all cultures'.[6] At about the same time Crichton Miller declared, 'there is great significance in the fact that Freud is a Jew and Jung a Teuton',[7] but such expansion of this idea as he gave was couched in rather vague and racialistic terms.* More recently Erich Fromm has drawn attention to a connection between psycho-

---

[1] *Supra*, p. 80.   [2] *Supra*, p. 1.   [3] *Supra*, p. 44.
[4] 'On Being of the B'Nai Brith,' cited by Puner, H. L., *Freud, His Life and His Mind*, p. 126. Grey Walls Press, 1942.
[5] *Op. cit.*, p. 161.   [6] *Supra*, p. 169.   [7] *Op. cit.*, pp. 182-3.
* 'To the Jew, with all his heritage of injustice and inferiority, any philosophy which exculpates will be acceptable. . . . . In racial psychology the polar opposite of the Jew is the Teuton with all his power sense, his thrust and executive ability, to say nothing of his Hapsburg sense of superiority. . . .'

analysis and the life of the urban middle class in Western Europe,[1] and the same influences are discussed by David Riesman in more detail.[2] The Cabbalistic theme has been taken up again by David Bakan.[3] For the Jungian school, once more, less material is available, but a piece of indirect social history exists in an account by Baynes of his own adaptation of Jungian psychology to the needs of English patients. From these and other sources a reconstruction can be made of the two ways of life suggested—the Jungians having been identified with those sections of the European middle class which traditionally since medieval times have occupied positions in Church, school and University, and the Freudians with Jewish people in particular and with those sections which have been engaged more fully than the traditionalist groups in capitalist enterprise. The Jungian or traditionalist background will be taken first, as being, in Western Europe, the older of the two.

Like other periods, but more perhaps than most, the Middle Ages was one in which a wide gap existed between concept and actuality. On the one hand, a magnificent theory of unity under Church and Holy Roman Empire, on the other, lawlessness and barbarity, roads unsafe for travel and one city at war against its neighbour. Of the concepts themselves, R. H. Tawney's judgment is, that they took the primary social facts of exploitation and serfdom and gave them ethical meaning, since nothing, to that age, could be treated as alien to religion.[4] Nevertheless, in theory, and to some extent in practice, medieval society was an organic unity in which each individual had his place—lord, knight, monk, serf, etc.—with certain rights and duties appertaining to it. His function was to fill that place, not only for his own benefit but also for the common good. While some avenues for promotion existed, expecially in the Church, a man was not normally expected to advance; in so far as he did, the advance itself was patterned as the acquiring of another place in the social hierarchy, carrying with it a new set of rights and obligations to which the private pursuit of wealth and power was at any rate in part

---

[1] *Fear of Freedom*, pp. 8 *et seq.* See also, 'The Social Philosophy of "Will Therapy".' *Psychiatry*, Vol. 2, 1939; pp. 229–37.

[2] 'Themes of Work and Play in the Structure of Freud's Thought' and 'Authority and Liberty in the Structure of Freud's Thought.' *Psychiatry*, Vol. 13, 1950; pp. 1–16 and 167–87.

[3] *Sigmund Freud and the Jewish Mystical Tradition*. New Jersey: Van Nostrand Co., 1958.

[4] *Religion and the Rise of Capitalism*, p. 22. London: John Murray, 1936.

subordinated. Exceptions naturally existed—greed and ambition do not suddenly come into being a few centuries further on; we may recall, for instance, some of the abbots of large monasteries, with their general-like marshalling of manpower and resources, and no doubt a strong element of authoritarianism. Nevertheless, the exceptions *were* exceptions, and to a considerable extent continued, themselves, to think in the categories given. As Tawney puts it, 'Society was interpreted, . . . not as the expression of economic self-interest, but as held together by a system of mutual, though varying, obligations.'[1] Toward the large-scale means of profit—trade and money-lending—there was a strong feeling of disapproval and suspicion. Medieval economy was mainly a subsistence economy, geared to the production of such goods as were required for use, and to the giving and receiving of a fair exchange (or 'just price') for the labour entailed, in order that the producer might maintain whatever position he was entitled to by custom. Within the classes the theory was equality; all trades were organized into guilds, one of whose functions was the regulation of opportunity in accordance with this principle. Middlemen, those who merely sold the goods of others without participating in any form of production, were thought to contribute nothing 'real', and therefore to be social parasites. Such an economy —its essential features are not found only in the European Middle Ages—is closely tied to the country, to farming and allied pursuits. The tempo of life is slower than in more urbanized societies—fewer and less diversified experiences, fewer and less diversified contacts, are encountered in the same span of time. Aspects of life not controlled by man—movements of the heavenly bodies, changing of the seasons, tempest, drought, birth, death—are more often present to awareness. Among the human contacts made, a large proportion are of the face-to-face variety, where the individual is known to those with whom he deals sufficiently well to be perceived by them, and also by himself, as 'ABC, fulfilling such and such a function', rather than 'a seller', or 'a buyer', and nothing more. That is, there is more likelihood of being experienced by others, and experiencing oneself as a 'Thou' rather than an 'It'—a subject rather than an object. Similarly, much of the individual's training for his function in society is carried on in a direct, personal way, often in the home, otherwise through relationships such as master and apprentice, which are closely

[1] *Ibid.*, p. 24.

modelled on the parent-child relationship. The sense of rootedness is strong; while groups of wanderers can be found—students, friars and minstrels in the Middle Ages—these groups might be said to have wandering as one aspect of their role. Otherwise it was as rare in medieval times for a man to change his town or village as to change his social rank—more often he held the land his father held before him, and many, of course, were 'bound' to the land. In a society of this type the past with its accumulated traditions is something greatly to respect—something very near, virtually, indeed, a part of the present. It is, in short, a comparatively static society, for which the maintenance of what has always existed is the keynote, not striving toward the new. Behind the medieval society itself, with its visible, structured unity and attempts at unity, was conceived to lie an overriding purpose or meaning, the Will of God for His Creation, which the outward arrangements were interpreted as serving.

But even in the Middle Ages this rather simple economy did not suffice in all respects. Two characteristic medieval activities, fighting and building, both of which involved the large-scale movement of personnel and raw materials, could not be carried on without more ready money and a more complex financial organization. There was also a strong demand for commodities which could not be produced in Europe itself—spices of all kinds, silks and precious stones. The function of supplying these needs—important to the society, yet forbidden to its members or at least regarded with disapprobation—was therefore permitted to an element which lived in the society without in the normal sense being of it, viz. the Jews.

Long before the Middle Ages Jews were active traders. Their own historians[1] state that most of the Jews who came to Western and Central Europe did not come direct from Palestine but were descended from families which had dwelt for centuries in countries possessing highly developed economic systems, such as Babylonia, Egypt and Roman Italy. From the fifth century to the seventh, trade in Western Europe was largely in the hands of 'Syrian' traders, who must have included a substantial proportion of Jews, since the language which they used was closely allied to that in which Rabbinical correspondence was carried on; and in legal documents of

[1] See, for instance, Roth, C., *A Short History of the Jewish People*. London: MacMillan & Co., 1936, and Ruppin, A., *The Jewish Fate and Future*. London: MacMillan & Co., 1940.

the ninth century the terms Jew and merchant were used almost inter-changeably. In the tenth century, when the Italian Republics began to take over trading to the Orient, and at the same time the Church set its face more firmly against the lending of money at interest, banking became the Jews' special field, and here, as in trading, their widely scattered connections stood them in good stead. With this background, cut off from the Church on religious grounds, and in consequence denied membership of guilds and the right of owning land, the Jews naturally came to represent, as Ruppin says, 'the principle of free competition and the pursuit of profit, within an economic system bound up with the common ownership of the soil or with guild regulations or monopolies'.[1] The Church itself could not do without them, e.g. Aaron of Lincoln, the great Jewish financier of the twelfth century, assisted in the construction of no fewer than nine Cistercian monasteries, as well as the abbey of St. Albans, and the Crusades were made possible partly by the Jews' financial aid.

With the discovery of the New World, such independent and experienced entrepreneurs were naturally in a stronger position for reaching out to the new trading opportunities than were the conser-vative medieval corporations, limited by their close ties with the particular regions whose trade they had secured in the past—and indeed, by their whole outlook, tending as it did in the direction of maintenance rather than expansion. By the seventeenth century, according to the same historians, trade in sugar, tobacco and similar commodities was to a large extent in Jewish hands. However, it was the nineteenth century, with the final ending of the guild system during the Industrial Revolution and the vast expansion of markets over-seas, which gave the fullest opportunity. The whole of the Jews' past history, Ruppin declares, had prepared them for it—their attunement to the tempo and pattern of city life their freedom from deep attach-ments and consequent adaptability. 'The Jews' commercial activities lost their exceptional character, and their social position in the business world became normalized. In banking, commerce, and industry, they advanced rapidly and in many cases attained pros-perity and wealth.'[2]

An impression can be formed of the type of personality which this second economic set-up will develop in contrast to the first. Clearly

[1] *Op. cit.*, p. 120.   [2] *Ibid.*, p. 126.

it will be more individualistic, less concerned with a network of rights and obligations, and motivated by desire for personal gain and for expansion rather than preservation of the duly constituted order, hence living in a time-dimension of 'present-cum-future' rather than 'present-laden-with-the-past' or 'past-bearing-on-the-present'—in short, dynamic, not static, in its outlook. Dwelling for the most part in cities, it will deal with many and diversified contacts in a short span of time; these brief and usually transitory contacts will be viewed not as slowly developing wholes, or ends in themselves, but more directly in terms of relevance to the purpose in hand, buying and selling and the rendering of instrumental services. Needing to move readily from place to place it will, as Ruppin says, be less deeply rooted in attachments but will possess the capacity for rapid adjustment and the taking of initiative in the midst of strange peoples and surroundings. In this more complicated life a greater need of rational planning will arise—things will not continue of themselves, as in the simpler, stabler system. At the same time, the greater remoteness from those realities not made by man will diminish the sense of awe in the face of the universe—the city-dweller with his crowded days does not live constantly in the shadow of the unfathomable—and the viewing of life as a succession of relatively disconnected situations will tend to produce a cast of mind which is not only more inclined to doubt the existence of an all-pervading cosmic purpose, but also less interested 'one way or the other'.

The equating of Jews and capitalism, non-Jews and the feudal components in European life, is of course too simple. By the Renaissance and Reformation periods, and to some extent before, under the influence of the Crusading movements, some non-Jews also were finding the medieval structure too narrow and were reaching out to greater opportunities. During and after the Reformation the Calvinistic or Reformed Churches, especially, numbered among their adherents many merchants and industrialists; the works of Weber and of Tawney following Weber, together with Fromm's analysis from the psychological standpoint, have made the modern reader aware of a connection between the individualism of the new economic order and the emphasis on the individual soul, the individual decision, combined with the contradictory sense of man's powerlessness, in the Protestant theology. However, as is pointed out by Tawney, the connection between even the Reformed Churches and capitalism is not the whole truth about their ethos. After the shattering of the unity of the medieval Church, each of the denominations which emerged tried, so far as it could, to perpetuate the Church as a civilization. In the Reformed Churches themselves the medieval outlook was far from being submerged; there survived, not only the belief in the visible human order as part of the ordained cosmic order, but also, at least within the group itself in relation to its members, the conception of a community in which each one had his place. Besides the more radical Churches another type came into being—the Anglican and Lutheran—which remained in closer association with the feudal elements while these were reorganized in the interests of the nation state. Among such elements—the landed gentry, the Army, the University, the personnel of the Church itself, all those components of the medieval structure which were furthest removed from the distribution of commodities—much of the older outlook has remained, in spite of many blends; and one of these blends, though not of course the only one, has been a claim for individual development, less in the economic sphere than along intellectual and emotional lines, i.e. the more abstract kind of Liberalism. Generally speaking, however, the medieval components of European society, originally rather static, have gradually been driven back, first by the capitalist expansion, then by the continuous growth of working-class movements and of State authority.

With this picture in mind it may be possible to show that although Jung repudiates the paternalistic aspects of medieval life as childish and sets his face against an ascetic or life-denying element in medieval values,[1] his outlook to a large extent is that of the feudal or medieval remnant, as indeed he himself has said of his background.[2] For the time being certain attitudes and theories will be cited, leaving therapy until more has been said of Freud as well.

The acceptance of a role-conscious attitude can be seen in Jung's descriptions of the persona ('Society expects, and indeed must expect, every individual to play the part assigned to him as perfectly as possible. . . .')[3] The specialization of functions in his later theory of psychological types would seem to reflect the habits of a society where the individual is expected to identify himself with one major set of

[1] Cf. *Psych. of the Unconsc.*, p. 189: 'The medieval ideal of life for the sake of death needs gradually to be replaced by a natural conception. . . .'
[2] *Supra*, p. 1: they 'belonged to the later part of the Middle Ages'.
[3] *Supra*, p. 94.

tasks and to perform them well.[1] The conservatism of this section can be seen in Jung's attitude to education—only after the norms of society have been learnt, we may remember, can individuality be cultivated[2]—and in his belief, on the whole, that individuation does not result in alienation from society. The same respect for tradition is seen in his willingness to take the *consensus gentium* as a serious argument, e.g. in his statements on immortality.[3] Perhaps, too, the less actively striving formulations of Freudian concepts[4] may take their colouring from this slower-moving way of life. The sense of mystery, of 'only the un-understandable' having 'significance,' may arise in part from the greater nearness of the elemental forces. Here Jung's idealization of country life may be recalled,[5] or, more matter-of-factly, his lament that 'The educated public, the flower of our present civilization, has detached itself from its roots, and is about to lose its connection with the earth.'[6] Again the search for 'meaning' is suggestive of a society like that described, where human life and the cosmic order are conceived to be linked together by eternal purpose.

Less directly traceable to the medieval foundations, but characteristic of the traditionalist middle classes as they had developed during the late nineteenth and early twentieth centuries, is the family set-up assumed in Jung's work. His attitude to the thinking capacity of woman in general and his description of the animus-ridden woman in particular[7] expresses the outlook of a group in which comparatively little was expected of a woman along those lines and the opportunities open even to women of ability were not always adequate to render them well-trained in logical discussion. Very similar is his view that woman's world, 'outside her husband, terminates in a sort of cosmic mist'[8] and that it 'fits in with her nature to remain in the background as an independently willing and responsible ego, in order not to hinder the man, but rather to invite him to make real his aims with respect to herself'.[9] There can be little doubt that the ability to live in the background and to identify herself strongly with her

---

[1] This may reflect especially the habits of the German, or German-speaking, middle class, which would seem to be rather more occupational in outlook, with fewer leisure-class attributes, than its English counterpart. (Cf. E. Kohn-Bramsted, *Aristocracy and the Middle Classes in Germany*, p. 29. London: P. S. King & Son, Ltd., 1937: 'The noble can strive for the harmonious cultivation of all his powers, whilst the commoner must concentrate on a one-sided cultivation of individual function.')

[2] *Supra*, p. 159.   [3] *Supra*, p. 197.   [4] *Supra*, p. 42.
[5] *Supra*, p. 227.   [6] *Psych. and Religion*, new ed. p. 78; old ed. p. 95.
[7] *Supra*, p. 96.   [8] *Two Essays*, new ed. p. 208.   [9] *Contribs.*, p. 168.

husband's interests were two of the main desiderata for the woman of Jung's social group and generation. The professional set-up of the period may be reflected in the stages of life: after striving very hard in a limited number of directions and leaving other potentialities uncared for, the individual gains an assured position or the means of retiring from professional activities, so that if he wishes he can turn attention to self-culture. Both professional and family set-ups may be seen in Jung's reference to the anima-induced moods of the husband: 'Take, for instance, the "spotless" man of honour and public benefactor, whose tantrums and explosive moodiness terrify his wife and children.'[1] That is, in a society where heavy demands are made by the profession, the home not infrequently includes among its functions that of being a permissible place for the release of any tensions. And indeed, Jung gives us such a view directly, saying elsewhere that

> 'Great numbers of men of the educated classes are obliged to move in two, for the most part totally different, milieux—viz. in the family and domestic circles and in the world of affairs. These two totally different environments demand two totally different attitudes. . . . The domestic character is, as a rule, more the product of the subject's *laissez-aller* indolence and emotional demands.'[2]

If, now, we note some of the areas of strain and maladjustment in the traditionalist system during the last two generations, we may understand, at least at the more superficial level, the problems that Jung is likely to have been meeting in his patients.

Ideally, perhaps, a survey should begin with childhood. Child-rearing customs, being among the relatively hidden aspects of behaviour, are less readily outlined without specific observation than are adult situations. Nevertheless, it can be said that the child of the rather old-fashioned middle classes will have been born into a family which might be described as intermediate in type between the city suburban family, with the two parents and their children housed independently and largely cut off from other relatives, and the extended rural-familistic group in which several generations live together side by side. That is, the core of the family will be the parents and children, with other figures—grandparents, uncles, aunts, cousins—incorporated on a semi-permanent or sometimes permanent basis, the whole being somewhat patriarchal in its

[1] *Two Essays*, new ed. p. 198.   [2] *Psych. Types*, p. 589.

governance. While discipline has often been strict, and sheer authoritarianism by no means absent, the impression in the main, aimed at by the parent and received by the child, has probably been one of training for the role, for fitting into the organized and meaningful structure—a creative rather than a soul-destroying obedience, as many modern psychotherapists would view it. It may be speculated that such an upbringing would give a better foundation for that wider integration of the personality which Jung envisages after the role function has been fulfilled, than would be provided by a family organization which was more rigidly authoritarian. At the same time, there has probably been a preference for keeping the child *as* a child. 'Being-a-child' might almost be said to constitute a role in itself, so that relationships with elders have in effect a double aspect—that of learning future roles, and that of fulfilling the role of child in the present. In this concept, being-a-child, ideas of innocence and spontaneity have been included, and a degree of immaturity has rather been encouraged, in the form, for instance, of belief in Santa Claus and the treatment of animals and dolls as human beings. Jung's comments on the child as having no problems of his own, on his spontaneity, and on the anthropomorphic nature of his thinking,[1] are perhaps connected with these cultural trends.

As we know, it is the adult with whom Jung for the most part is concerned. Turning, therefore, to some of the problems with which the adult is confronted, we may note that the professional life of the European middle classes is in its own way apt to be exacting. This holds good both for the profession itself and for its training—many other capacities, many other inclinations must often be sacrificed. Even if the profession proves unsatisfying, the individual still has to put a large proportion of his energies into it in order to live at all, at the level to which he is accustomed—and in a highly stratified society there is little real possibility of adjustment at any other level, once the path has been chosen. The choice itself in many cases has been less the decision of the individual than the outcome of family expectations and connections. There is also a close interaction between professional and private life; the burden is seldom laid down after a given hour but remains—with varying degrees of consciousness, admittedly, but never far from the surface. In innumerable encounters there is the professional role to sustain; if a member of this group learns,

[1] *Supra*, p. 104.

for instance, that a colleague has been charged with dangerous driving, the reaction is not simply, 'Poor So-and-So, how unfortunate!' but 'Poor So-and-So, how unfortunate for a man in our position!' Even in his private relationships the individual is sustaining a complicated system. Let us imagine the case of a Warden in a Hall of Residence, who invites his cousin, living in unattractive digs, to spend the Easter holidays with him. It is not only a wish to see his cousin that motivates the invitation—there is also the desirability of doing the right thing by one's family. In short, this may be a culture which is more prone than some to rather subtle blends of self-interest and natural proclivities, or self-interest and helpfulness to others, or of all three together. By every right-thinking individual the component of self-interest will be nicely subordinated to other considerations, and this too entails a further effort. (For instance, a man is at liberty to choose his friends, and wife, with some eye to personal advancement—the son-in-law of the Director has not been uncommon—but the fulfilling of responsibilities as friend or husband requires also the giving of sincere affection.)

Now if all goes reasonably well—if the personality is naturally robust, if there is a good fit between the roles played in society and the underlying capacities, the individual of this background is perhaps more contented than many; the feeling of belonging to an integrated whole is more strengthening than exhausting, and the innumerable commitments and responsibilities, wholeheartedly identified with, impart 'meaning' to his life.

But if something goes wrong—if the personality is not so robust to begin with, if the roles which the individual has taken upon himself, well-nigh irrevocably, are not suited to him, or if he finds himself in situations where the patterns of thought and conduct learnt so carefully can no longer be applied, a condition of world-weariness may set in, or alternatively, if there is still some time to live but less than formerly, the individual's feeling of being inextricably caught may find expression in some violent outburst. Such cases will come readily to mind, especially perhaps to those familiar with the pre-war generations. For instance, a man who had wished to enter the Church felt himself forced on the death of his father to take over the management of a family business. In middle life he developed a passion for farming, about which he knew nothing, and eventually lost everything in a series of unlucky enterprises. Another had taken a medical degree in the days when this was customary for students interested in natural history; he succeeded in building up a flourishing practice but retired at the age of fifty-five on the ground that his health would not stand the strain—lingering on for thirty years in a state described by those who knew him well as sheer neurotic funk. A third had wished to become a medical missionary, the theological interest being, apparently, the main one. At the end of the medical course this man, like the first, was left with dependants. He, too, carried on till middle life, retiring early in a state of mild collapse. Both declared that if there had been any other form of work that they could do they would have done it—a remark which illustrates the position of this specialized class. Obviously these are anecdotal cases only, in which the deeper causes of malaise could not be examined. They are, however, the kind of anecdotes found in Jung himself. Consider, for instance, the case of the manufacturer who, having worked his way to a high level of attainment and success, 'began to remember a certain phase of his youth when he took great pleasure in art. He felt the necessity of returning to these pursuits and began to make artistic patterns for the wares he manufactured. The result was that no one wanted to buy these artistic products and the man became bankrupt after a few years.'[1] Much the same is the case of the hardened old general who dreamt of a major, looking like himself when young, who was able to give a definition of 'the beautiful' which the general himself would have given if he could.[2] Cases of straight-out exhaustion are recorded, as well as those of suppressed potentialities. For example, one patient consulted Jung because he suffered from the symptoms of mountain sickness.

'He had had an unusually successful career, and had risen, with the help of ambition, industry and native talent from a humble origin as the son of a poor peasant. Step by step he had climbed, attaining at last an important post that offered him every opportunity for further social advancement. He had actually reached a place in life from which he could have begun his ascent into the upper regions, when suddenly his neurosis intervened.'

Dissatisfied with Jung's interpretation, he 'tried to exploit the professional openings that tempted his ambition and ran . . . violently off the track'.[3]

---

[1] *Contribs.*, p. 43.
[2] *Ibid.*, pp. 358–9; new ed. *Development of Personality*, p. 102.
[3] *Mod. Man*, pp. 3–5. See also the novel, *Buddenbrooks*, by Thomas Mann.

From another source, a post-war survey of the English middle classes, comes a similar picture. The English Civil Servant, according to the writers of this report, is apt in middle life to be 'just a little tired'. Forty to forty-five hours' brain work a week, they continue, can be extremely exhausting, if the work carries heavy responsibilities and requires close attention to detail and a wide grasp of general issues at the same time. They suggest too that the very intensive and arduous training of these men, although enabling them to do their jobs exceptionally well in their prime, tends to diminish their reserves of vitality and nervous energy comparatively soon. 'As a result, they are apt to find themselves, from early middle age onwards, always a little below par, so that their work becomes more and more of an effort and their interest in it less and less fresh.'[1] To this there seems a parallel in Jung's own statement that during the second half of life 'Consciousness still presses forward, in obedience, as it were to its own inertia, but the unconscious lags behind, because the strength and inner will-power needed for further expansion have been sapped'.[2] An additional factor making for exhaustion in this group is that if the energies of the dominant member of the household are beginning to flag, if for any reason problems of adaptation are too great, then others are called upon to supplement, and to supplement, not by striking out on independent paths, but by a slow draining of their own resources along existing channels. This has been one of the worst features from the woman's point of view. Jung does not come to grips with the last factor in those terms, but we may recall that he speaks of the wife's being compelled to 'reflect the shadow-side' of the husband. ('I once made the acquaintance of a very venerable personage. . . . Then, on the fourth day, his wife came to consult me. . . .')[3]

Summing up, it might be suggested that this is a culture which has worked such mechanisms as introjection and identification exceptionally hard, and that these mechanisms are more exhausting than some, especially if the impact of work and other obligations makes itself felt beyond a certain point, as under present-day conditions it very often will. It may be partly for this reason that Jung has stressed the constructive possibilities of temporary re-

[1] Lewis, R. and Maude, A., *The English Middle Classes*, p. 114. London: Phoenix House, 1949.
[2] *Contribs.*, p. 194; *Development of Personality*, p. 194.   [3] *Supra*, p. 96.

gression, of *reculer pour mieux sauter*, i.e. the individual who uses introjection or identification heavily may have a special need for periods of recuperation. Furthermore, to such a culture, making heavy demands, and more liable than some to dam up by pressure in youth the sources from which greater energy might come, the decline of religious belief may be especially serious, since the personality can no longer feel itself sustained by some force outside the system but related to it. In addition to those with direct personality problems, people can be found who to all intents and purposes are functioning well enough in their particular sphere, but cannot altogether shut out from their minds some inkling of industrial conditions, mining discontents, etc. But it is by no means easy for the average individual in the more sheltered sections of the middle class to know what to do about such matters. For one thing, he is divided within his own mind—he wants a better world for all, but does not want to jeopardize the only way of life he knows. At the same time, he may develop a suspicion that such a mode of life, at once sheltered and exacting, is causing him to miss important life experiences, or alternatively, he may rebel inwardly against the expedients of 'selling oneself' to which, in our very mixed society, he may be driven. Here, perhaps, are further reasons for the appeal of the collective unconscious. To be told that even now it is possible to regain the wisdom of the ancestors and to make contact with 'the old pagan within ourselves'—this may be a welcome message for any so perplexed.[1] A somewhat gloomy picture has been painted, since the aim has been to bring to light some causes of breakdown in this particular division of society, in so far as they take on a colouring from the social setting. In contrasting the Jungian and the Freudian backgrounds there will be opportunities for noting its less unfavourable features, though first it may be useful to turn to the confirmation of these connections in H. G. Baynes's essay.[2]

Beginning with a reference to the idea of the gentleman as 'a psychic potential of untold efficacy', Baynes writes that 'To be worthy of the spiritual lineage of this aristocratic idea a man must actively

[1] There is sometimes a tendency among persons from these social groups to locate the source of needed vitality or simplicity in the Dominions. They recognize the unlikelihood that they will ever go there—they would, in fact, be among those least fitted for life in countries where robustness of physique and outlook counts for much—but it seems to comfort them to think of such places as existing, even though far out of reach.

[2] *Analytical Psychology and the English Mind*, pp. 34 *et seq.*

create an attitude that extends service and gentleness to all, as though everyone and every creature were his kin'—a statement which suggests that the European traditionalist system with its heavy responsibilities and its predominance of face-to-face contacts is not unlike an extended and modified rural familistic system. The ethical principle of fair-play, Baynes continues, has become the generally accepted criterion. 'In fact, the gentleman's code of the public schools and universities is based solely on this idea.' It is perhaps significant to find him saying that 'Considering the nature of their subject-matter Jung's writings are widely read in England.' It is the 'cultured mind' (in contrast to the 'merely educated') which feels the attraction; by comparison the ideas of Freud and Adler have excited very little positive interest outside the medical and educational professions, 'though in the case of some of Freud's later writings a deep repugnance has not been lacking'. Several applications of Jung's theories are suggested. The idea of accepting and honouring the self 'comes into direct succession to the idea of fealty to the king; the idea of accepting and re-instating unconscious functions and elements that have been suppressed by an exclusively social adaptation is seen as a new extension of the principle of fair-play; the gradual unfolding of the process of individuation in the autonomous life of the psyche means a deeper and more intimate realization of the concept of evolution' and 'the idea of relating to the anima, and, through the anima, to the denizens of the unconscious is cogent to the English mind under the aspect of the knightly quest'. In short, 'the hospitality already accorded to, and waiting for, the fundamental conceptions of Jung in the aristocratic interior of English culture is ensured by the fact that the principles which govern Jung's conceptions are already rooted in the Englishman's basic philosophy'.

Returning now to the background of Freud and his followers, we will realize that although the Jews have so far been spoken of without a definition, the problem, What constitutes a Jew? cannot be avoided altogether. The racial criterion, which is often loosely employed, really has to be discarded. Throughout Western European history the Jews seem to have included two ethnic types, one long-headed, with oval face, fine features, straight or slightly waving hair and rather fragile build, the other round-headed, with coarse features, including the so-called Jewish nose, kinky hair and stocky build.

In addition, sufficient intermarriage has taken place over the generations, especially in more recent times, to produce a number of
individuals calling themselves Jews and considered Jews by others
who are, nevertheless, indistinguishable physically from the surrounding population, especially in the Mediterranean countries,
where the physical characteristics are not in any case so very different.
(For instance, an unpublished study by Boaz is reported in which
forty per cent of the Italians at a New York college were taken to
be Jews, and the same percentage of Jews were judged to be Italians.)
The value of religion as a distinguishing mark is also rather limited,
since many individuals who, again, consider themselves Jews and
are considered such by others, are at the same time rationalists or
agnostics and may even have been brought up without synagogue
affiliation.

Another suggestion is that a Jew is a member of a particular culture or sub-culture maintaining itself in independence or semi-
independence of the cultures or sub-cultures by which it is surrounded. This criterion too is not without its difficulties. Scattered
as it is through many countries, with differing degrees of contact
between itself and the human environment around it, anything which
can be described as a Jewish culture or sub-culture certainly shows
variations. That was so even in the Middle Ages, e.g. according to
Roth[1] the severe Gothic of the oldest German synagogues is a
striking contrast to the flowing Arabesques of Toledo, and Hebrew
codices were illuminated in the same manner—perhaps even by the
same artists—as the missals of the Church. How much more important will such contacts have become during and after the emancipation of the nineteenth century. Everywhere a fringe exists. In the
mixed marriages which have been increasingly common, all kinds
of compromise will occur between the two extremes of the Jewish
member who aspires by virtue of the marriage to be fully accepted
into the group of the non-Jewish partner, and the Jewish member
who expects the non-Jewish partner to make a good integration
with his own community. The children of such marriages will
sometimes marry back into Jewry, sometimes marry those in like
case with themselves, and sometimes become absorbed by marriage
into the Gentile population. Perhaps, however, it is the frequency

---

[1] *Cambridge Medieval History*, Vol. VII, Ch. XXII, 'The Jews in the Middle
Ages,' pp. 632–63.

with which even the third or fourth generation retains some characteristics which seem to be not quite those of the surrounding group, and keeps up some slight connection with other Jewish families, that justifies, as much as anything else, the conception of a Jewish mentality and way of life.

On the religious side the fullest suggestions have been made in Bakan's book, which adds appreciably to Roback's hints some thirty years ago on the affinities between Freud and the Cabbalistic writings. Bakan refers to the two major currents in Jewish religious thought since the Dispersion, the mystical and the rabbinical, with their different answers to the question: Why does God chastise his chosen people?—the rabbinical seeking the explanation in their defection from the law and urging redoubled efforts to observe it, the mystical emphasizing their lack of understanding of God's message— and sees in the psychoanalytical method of free association a parallel to the Cabbalistic method of taking a passage out of its context and giving associative material to it. He thinks that the place of sexuality is similar in psychoanalytical theory and the Cabbalistic tradition, i.e. in both marital sexuality is used as a symbol of creativity—a complex metaphor in which all human strivings are somehow involved; characteristic of the Cabbala, too, is the thought that the prepubertal stages are dominated by impulses ordinarily considered unhealthy and immoral.[1]

In family relationships Bakan among others suggests that owing to the Jewish endogamous tendency and the habit, especially in Eastern Europe, of living in small communities, incest problems have been extremely important. Within this framework it is likely that the mother-son relationship has been especially accentuated, as Suttie believed. 'It seems to us,' Landes and Zborowski report in their paper on the Eastern European Jewish family, 'that though the marital obligations are fulfilled with the husband, the romance exists with the son.'[2] From the observations of ordinary life the present writer has felt that there existed a tendency—at any rate among the Jewish middle-class families of Western Europe—to treat their children rather more like miniature adults, although in a

[1] In Freud's private fantasy system, so to speak, the influence of the Jewish Messianic tradition is clear from his identification with such heroes as Moses and Joseph.

[2] 'Hypotheses Concerning the Eastern European Jewish Family.' *Pyschiatry*, Vol. 13, No. 4, 1950; pp. 447–64 (p. 453).

playful spirit, than is common in middle-class non-Jewish households. A similar point is made by a Jewish writer for his people in general: the Jew, 'as his existence depended upon prompt and adequate responses . . . matured early, and having missed his childhood, lived an abnormal adult life'.[1] This may have contributed to a tendency on Freud's part to attribute rather definite motives to the infant, e.g. it soils itself *in order to annoy* the mother; it may explain also why, as Makhdum comments,[2] there seems to be no place for the childlike in Freud's conception but only for the infantile.

However, just as in the survey of the Jungian group attention was concentrated mainly on the adult, functioning within his framework of rights and obligations, so now the aspects of the Freudian background to which most attention will be given are, its connection with the capitalist order or in wider terms its long association with urban environments, and its familiarity with persecution. Some of the characteristics springing from the former set of circumstances have already been suggested—the individualism; the striving and dynamic outlook, together with a relative lack of respect for tradition; the experience of brief and diversified contacts viewed as means to an end; the capacity for rapid adaptation; the reliance on rational planning and absence of a strongly developed sense of the mysterious or of cosmic purpose. Such trends can certainly be found in Freud. For instance, the child 'loves himself first and only later learns to love others and to sacrifice something of his own ego to them. . . .'[3] The more striving and active quality of his formulations of repression in comparison with Jung's has been noted, and the lack of respect for tradition was seen in his denial of any argument from the *consensus gentium* ('It would be strange if our poor, ignorant enslaved ancestors had succeeded in solving all these difficult riddles. . . .'[4]) While the element of rationality in psychoanalysis is well-known, its effects can be seen in more detail through some of the previous contrasts between Jung and Freud. The difference in their basic attitudes is plainly stated, in Freud's belief that 'man is not entirely without means of assistance; since the time of the deluge science has taught him much' and in Jung's doubt whether 'in the greatest and really decisive questions' reason has ever been adequate.

---

[1] Review of E. Friedman, *The Jewish Mind in the Making*, *J. Ment. Sci.*, Vol. 70, 1924, pp. 651–2.
[2] *Op. cit.*, p. 9.   [3] *Supra*, p. 54.   [4] *Supra*, p. 216.

Freud's work was seen, also, to have a note of limitation and specificity about it—the direct opposite of the wide identifications in the
work of Jung. For instance, instead of becoming one with all
humanity, Freud regards his love as 'a valuable thing that I have no
right to throw away without reflection . . .'[1] This specificity suggests
the customs of a contract-forming society in which responsibilities
must be sharply laid down. The absence of awe and wonder in his
psychology has been seen in his repudiation of the *ozeanisches*
Gefühl and his search for the origin of religion in the emotions—again
more specific in their type—of the Oedipal situation; the disbelief
in any cosmic purpose is expressed partly in his view of Nature as
essentially hostile or indifferent, and more directly in his statement
that 'It looks . . . as though one had a right to dismiss this question.
. . . Nobody asks what is the purpose of the lives of animals.'[2]

Other effects on personal relationships will be discussed in comparison of the Jungian and the Freudian therapy, but one or two
points are sufficiently independent of therapy to be included now.
For instance, Erich Fromm points out that in capitalist society each
person works for himself, at his own risk, not primarily in co-
operation with others, but he has to enter into economic relations
with other people for the purposes of buying and selling. And in
Freud the individual appears fully equipped with biologically determined drives which must be satisfied; in order to satisfy them he
enters into relations with other 'objects'. That is, the field of human
relations as Freud sees it is similar to the market: 'it is an exchange
of satisfaction of biologically given needs, in which the relationship
to the other individual is always a means to an end but never an end
in itself'.[3]

David Riesman stresses the capitalist-determined attitude to work
in Freud, as well as the attitude to persons. Only in our Western
industrial culture, he believes, does work have the features Freud
attaches to it, of being sharply set off against love, against pleasure,
against consumption. He suggests that this attitude has had a profound influence on the psychoanalytic method, leading Freud to
assume as a matter of course that any answer to which one came
without arduous toil must be wrong, and that the more far-fetched a
solution, the more probable was its correctness. Since work is unnatural to man, the baroque imagery of dreams 'must hide some-

[1] *Supra*, p. 215.   [2] *Supra*, p. 216.   [3] *Fear of Freedom*, p. 9.

thing, must cover up a most forbidden thought'. To the capitalist outlook Riesman attributes also the Freudian assumption that nothing new happens in the course of development which leads men to desire activity for its own sake, and that children do not naturally want to grow up but must be 'forcibly socialized, forcibly adpated to reality'.

A minor point revealing the influence of the market can be found in a paper on transcience, where Freud disputes the view that the impermanence of the beautiful involves any diminution in its worth 'On the contrary, an increase! Transcience value is scarcity value in time. Limitation in the possibility of an enjoyment raises the value of the enjoyment.'[1] Again, there is a slight difference in Freud's attitude to women which suggests, in comparison with Jung, the background of a competitive and urbanized society. Whereas in Jung 'it fits in with her nature to remain in the background as an independently willing and responsible ego', in Freud the patient endeavours 'to re-assure herself of her irresistibility, to destroy the physician's authority by bringing him down to the level of a lover'.[2] Such points make it probable that the influence of capitalism on Freud's outlook has not been negligible. However, the second factor—life situation as a persecuted people—seems to be significant as well.

From one point of view the Jewish culture, in so far as it can be described as such, may be regarded as having evolved in order to enable as many of its members as possible to survive under conditions from which a certain amount of strain is seldom absent, and which may at any time develop into an extreme emergency. Accounts of the more dramatic experiences have been written by Jewish people themselves. For instance, Elie Cohen, describing his first days in a concentration camp, speaks of a condition of acute depersonalization as he watched a man being beaten to death. 'My reaction to this, I observed, was an apparent splitting of my personality. I felt as if I did not belong, as if the business did not concern me; as if "I were looking at things through a peephole".'[3] Professor Bruno Bettelheim writes in almost identical terms:

> 'He'—the writer—'has no doubt that he was able to endure the transportation, and all that followed, because right from the beginning he

[1] 'On Transcience.' *Collected Papers*, Vol. V, pp. 79–83 (p. 80).
[2] *Collected Papers*, Vol. II, p. 381.
[3] Cohen, Elie A., *Human Behaviour in the Concentration Camp*. W. W. Norton, 1953, p. 116.

became convinced that these horrible and degrading experiences some-how did not happen to "him" as a subject, but only to "him" as an object. . . . All the thoughts and emotions which the author had during the transportation were extremely detached. It was as if he watched things happening in which he only vaguely participated. Later he learned that many prisoners had developed this same feeling of detachment, as if what happened really did not matter to oneself.'[1]

These feelings persisted throughout the time spent in camp. Cohen speaks also of the egotism produced by the imminence of death. During the first day in Auschwitz his sole object was to contact the physician and nursing staff of the prisoners' hospital in order to learn how to be allowed to join the medical attendants. 'The interests of my fellow prisoners I did not consider at all.' On the other hand, another writer, Bondy, gives a brief example of what could sometimes be achieved by *group* egotism. From the beginning, a group of twenty agricultural trainees and their director, interned in a concentration camp, set themselves the task of bringing the entire group out of the camp without loss of life or breakdown of nerves. Over an admittedly short period of about six weeks before they were released, they succeeded. 'Every one from this special group came out alive, with-out having suffered serious illness or loss of sanity. . . . But all this could only be won at the cost of periodically abandoning specific moral principles which were of extreme importance to them.'[2]

An account of a different type of experience is given by a young Frenchman of Jewish descent, who reports the day-to-day difficulties encountered under an assumed name during the German Occupation. First he chose and had inscribed on his false papers the name, Gilbert Olivier, 'simply because I thought it pretty'. Presently he realized the inadvisability of having a name on his identity card with initials quite different from those on his linen, and fixed himself up with the name, Lucien Didier. Even so, quickness of wit was continually needed in manipulating the past—if one element was suppressed all kinds of complications followed. 'I could not be, for example, a Doctor of Laws, because my thesis is catalogued in all the university libraries of France. But what was Lucien Didier doing in 1936 while Didier Lazard was writing his thesis?' Awkward situations often arose

[1] Bettelheim, B., 'Individual and Mass Behavior in Extreme Situations.' *J. Abn. & Soc. Psychol.*, Vol. XXVIII, 1943; pp. 417–52.
[2] Bondy, Curt, 'Problems of Internment Camps.' *J. Abnorm. Soc. Psychol.*, Vol. XXXVIII, pp. 459–75.

through the widespread human desire to establish connecting links; in one district where he lived quietly for some time he found people trying to connect him with a schoolteacher nearby who was also called Didier. '"But he is almost as tall you you",' they would say. '"Ah, but he is stouter"' said I.' 'To control oneself ceaselessly, to master one's words, never to say anything which will provoke a question to which one is unable to answer—at first these are an effort, then they become a habit.... One can never be natural. If he lets himself go he feels that he might betray himself.'[1]

A psychoanalytical writer, Erwin Stengel, makes two points about an experience which will often have followed the more extreme misfortunes, namely, learning a new language. For one thing, he thinks, our relations to an object change when that object obtains a new name. 'This can be proved by the strange feeling we experience if one of our friends changes his name and assumes a new foreign name which has no relation to his old one. It seems as if his new name forces us to renew our libidinal relations to him. We feel an initial resistance against objects which we are compelled to denote by new names.'[2] Now whether the learning of new names for objects is invariably accompanied by a feeling of resistance is rather doubtful. On the contrary, for those whose tutors take pride in their progress, who meet congenial companions and look forward to travelling abroad, it is possible to recapture in the learning of a new language something of the triumph which may be found in the small child who is just making the acquaintance of his own. But in circumstances of forced migration, where the understanding of the new language takes on an urgency for daily work and a foreign accent is a source of humiliation and anxiety, i.e. in the circumstances under which many Jewish people will have learnt new languages, often late in life, a feeling of resistance is not at all surprising.

Stengel's other suggestion is that during the learning of the new language a disturbance in visual imagery occurs. Whereas words in the native language call up a picture of a simple, lifeless pattern, the corresponding words in the foreign language call up the images of living actions, i.e. the images following the word in the foreign language are more primitive and concrete. For instance, 'the word

[1] 'Two Years Under a False Name.' *J. Abnorm. Soc. Psychol.*, Vol. XLI, 1946; pp 161–8.
[2] 'On Learning a New Language.' *Int. J. Psycho-Anal.*, Vol. XX, 1939; pp. 471–9 (p. 474).

"slaughter house", spoken in the native language, may produce the picture of a house, but in the new language the picture of the act of slaughtering an animal'.[1] He adds that this peculiarity of the images is only temporary and disappears at an early stage, especially if the new language is being learnt in the foreign country itself, but that something similar remains—a feeling of uncertainty, often, as to whether a word is being used in its literal meaning or only figuratively.

Looking over these reports, it may be wondered what the effects are likely to be, of regarding oneself for longish periods as 'object' rather than as 'subject'; of reaching, more than incidentally, a stage of affect where one begins to be protected by the feeling of unreality; of constantly relying on one's wits to surmount a sudden difficulty; of having to adapt to new surroundings against one's inclinations. Accepting the view that attitude to self and attitude to others are essentially the same, the first experience might be expected to reinforce the 'It' rather than 'Thou' attitude of the urban trader; from the second might be expected an approach which was sensitive perceptually but comparatively uninvolved, noting the progress of emotional events almost like the working out of a problem in geometry—an attitude closely allied to the first, and, also, to the habit of quick, rational thinking in stress situations. The latter in its turn could reinforce the tendency to rational planning and organization which was noted previously as needed by the successful entrepreneur. The fourth experience, enforced adaptation, would be likely to coalesce with the general effects of the urban environment in rendering contacts superficial, laying stress on the appearance of adaptation rather than the reality, and, perhaps most important of all, imparting to the personality a degree of 'resistance' very different from the effortless merging in the environment of those who are secure in belonging to one place. Whatever the effects, it is not merely the experiences of isolated individuals which we are considering, but the experiences of a group, i.e. the reactions of the individual are supported by the reactions of his close associates and by social habits developed through past centuries. (For instance, the Marranos, or New Christians, in the Iberian peninsula underwent experiences comparable to those of Didier Lazard over a period of several generations.) Nor should too much emphasis be laid on the more

[1] *Ibid.*, p. 473.

dramatic episodes. In what for the Jew is ordinary life—say in Great Britain or the U.S.A.—the existence of a mild in-group/out-group situation means the existence of a large class of persons, non-Jews, from whom psychic distance may, if counteracting factors do not intervene, increase the 'objects' tendency; it means also that in many encounters an attempt at conscious working-out will have to take the place of participation in social customs learnt unconsciously from childhood. Not, of course, that these qualities can be ascribed to Jews and Jews alone, or to Jews inherently. As Ruppin remarks of urbanization, if this development should continue, qualities at present regarded as predominantly Jewish will become more and more widespread, and the same could be said of membership of a minority or persecuted group.

Some of those characteristics of Freudian writing which Riesman attributes to the influence of the capitalist order could be attributed equally to the latter set of factors. For instance, the assumption that dreams and other symbolic presentations cover 'a most forbidden thought' seems to reflect as well the attitude of a people which can never afford to take things at their face value, never afford to trust, but must always beware of the trap hidden beneath the fair promise, always look for the nigger in the woodpile. Again, Freud's assumption that the child is reluctant to grow up, expressed, for instance, in his view that no matter how much the infant has had, he will leave his mother's breast with the feeling that it was too little and the time too short, might be thought of as indicating some disturbance for which Stengel's description of 'resistance to objects' could be relevant. Statements of this kind have been made by other analysts. One of these declares that the fully-analysed patient is left with a sense of resentment at being deprived of the old infantile pleasures: 'Not even the analyst can with impunity lay hands on the infantile elements in the human psyche.'[1] Another reports that 'just when analysis is crowned with success, the patients often shed tears and reproach us more or less vehemently, according to their character, with depriving them of everything—leaving them nothing at all. . . . Once the neurosis is gone, there is no way of sulking at life, one can no longer snap one's fingers at it and its demands, nor revolt against the laws of society, of life and of love, and without feeling responsible or blame-

---

[1] Bergler, E., 'Therapeutic Results of Psycho-Analysis.' *Int. J. Psycho-Anal.*. Vol. XVIII, pp. 146–60 (p. 158).

worthy for one's attitude'.[1] Once more, the attitudes depicted might be expected to arise more frequently in a life situation of inescapable chronic stress and insecurity than in a stabilized environment. Or at least, one pattern of response occurring rather readily might be a *basic* resistance, which the individual knows he cannot afford in the interests of self-preservation, and a rather frantic, restless compensation for it. In a stabilized environment, failure of the tendency toward growth may take the form of inertia and complacency, a resting on one's oars rather than an active resistance to demands. The 'revolt against demands' leads us to the charge of a-morality, not to say immorality, which has sometimes been raised against the psychoanalytical movement—nor would it be surprising if, in a world that tended to be hostile, 'the laws of society, of life and of love' sometimes seemed more like restrictions arbitrarily imposed than paths laid down by earlier generations for the purpose of ultimate fulfilment. In addition to the bias of nineteenth-century science, exposure to extreme situations and the difference in moral standards observed between one country and another, may have contributed to that absence of interest in values as a means of personality orientation of which the Jungians and others have complained.

A related point may be that the individual in Freud appears to possess not only a high degree of resistance to the demands of socialization in general, but an inordinate desire for pleasure in particular. Others besides Freud have made use of the pleasure principle. What is found especially in Freud is the note of immoderation. The child, he has said, 'knows no *enough* and insatiably demands the repetition of whatever has pleased it or tasted good to it'[2]—learning to practise moderation, to be modest and resigned, only through culture and education. It may be that when the long-term goals are more difficult to attain, and more uncertain when they are attained, the tendency is greater to snatch at pleasure, any pleasure that comes along, pleasure in and for itself—restrictions seeming to the individual concerned to spring from external limitation rather than from the needs of the organism functioning as a whole. Or perhaps any goal, under the conditions outlined, acquires an intense motivating force, but the overtones of experience, as they

---

[1] LaForgue, R., 'Resistances at Conclusion of Analytic Treatment.' *Int. J. Psycho-Anal.*, Vol. XV, pp. 419–34 (p. 433–4).
[2] *Supra*, p. 52.

might be called, are rather lacking, since the more diffuse giving of oneself to the environment, which leads to a greater richness of association, can seldom come about. An illustration in Freud's writings is the statement that in non-neurotic females the wish for a penis 'changes into the wish for a man, accepting the man as an appendage, as it were, of the penis'.[1] Another effect which might be attributed to lack of overtones is an absence of discrimination between one area of experience and another, a bringing of everything down to the one level, as in the declaration that 'a physician can always do harm if he is clumsy or unscrupulous, no more and no less in probing into the sexual life of his patients than in other directions'.[2] Closely connected may be a rather clear-cut attitude toward the past. A flatly dropping-out habit is one of the commonest reactions which Freud records of himself. For instance, he writes of Breuer that 'The development of psycho-analysis afterwards cost me his friendship. It was not easy for me to pay such a price, but I could not escape it';[3] of Adler, that his ' "Individual Psychology" is now one of the many psychological movements adverse to psycho-analysis; its further development is no concern of ours';[4] and of a certain book on the electrical treatment of nervous diseases: 'The realization that the work of the greatest name in German neuro-pathology had no more relation to reality than some "Egyptian" dream book, such as is sold in cheap book-shops, was painful, but it helped to rid me of another shred of the innocent faith in authority from which I was not yet free.'[5] No attempt is made to carry these people along with him in the community of scholars, and the same is true of a somewhat more general attitude, that those who seek something other than the scientific *Weltanschauung* 'may look for it where they can find it. We shall not blame them for doing so; but we cannot help them and cannot change our own way of thinking on their account.'[6] In Freudian theory itself the assumption seems to be either that the individual is unhealthily fixated to the past or that the past has dropped out of his life, i.e. if he is not in the grip of a repetition-compulsion,

'Reality passes its verdict—that the object no longer exists—upon each single one of the memories and hopes through which the libido was

---

[1] *Collected Papers*, Vol. II, p. 167. [2] *Collected Papers*, Vol. I, p. 222.
[3] *Autobiographical Study*, p. 33. [4] *Collected Papers*, Vol. I, p. 340.
[5] *Autobiographical Study*, p. 27. [6] *New Introd. Lectures*, p. 233.

attached to the lost object, and the ego, confronted as it were with the decision whether it will share this fate, is persuaded by the sum of its narcissistic satisfactions in being alive to sever its attachment to the non-existent object.'[1]

The past does not figure in psychoanalysis as a constant source of self-renewal, and in this respect, too, may be revealed the outlook of a people which has suffered violent breaks of continuity and has had to take up the threads of life in new environments, not willingly, but through external circumstance. As Jung has said, without reference to this special problem, 'though I do violence to myself and succeed in my efforts to tear down those threads, . . . I suffer grave damage to all those feelings that clothe the hard rock-bottom of naked reality as with a rich covering of living bloom.'[2]

A feature of those breaks which may have had some influence on psychoanalytical terminology is the learning of new languages as described by Stengel. Stengel has spoken of a feeling of uncertainty as to whether a word is being used literally or only figuratively. Now sometimes it is found, in the incidents of daily life as well as in the work of Freud, that a certain literalness of interpretation occurs, in spite of, or rather, intermingled with, the theoretical formulations of this gifted people. In Freud, for instance, it is always the penis *as such* which the little girl envies, not the penis taken as a symbol of the boy's total position in a patriarchal society. Possibly the confusions concerning the narrow-broad connotation of sexuality have been affected by some such habit of thought. It may be wondered whether, just as Jung's psychology could have a rather intoxicating effect on those with a latent tendency to picture-thinking, so the work of Freud, with its blend of subtlety and literalness, would make a particular appeal to fellow Jews. We may recall Freud's own reference to 'racial relationship'[3] and the difference between Jung's reaction and Hanns Sachs' to their first reading of the *Interpretation of Dreams*: all Jung could do was to put the book aside for the time being, while Sachs felt that he had found the one thing worth while for him to live for.[4] Often the literalism is combined with an emphasis on trauma—castration threats or sexual assaults. This applies especially to Freud's early work, but even in his later writings the tendency is found, i.e. in the postulated murder of the Old Man of the Tribe;

[1] *Collected Papers*, Vol. IV, p. 166.   [2] *Psych. Types*, p. 49.
[3] *Supra*, p. 44.   [4] *Supra*, p. 6.

and here, also, may be reflected the experience of a people on whom traumatic happenings have had an exceptionally strong impact.

By implication it has been suggested that the traditionalist assumption will be that things are what they are until proved otherwise; that the traditionalist patient may not be suffering from quite the same type of resistance to following the stages on life's way; that the search for pleasure is less actively present to awareness and that restrictions are less apt to be thought of as springing from external sources only; that values are used more deliberately as a means of unifying the personality; that the past receives less drastic treatment; that literal formulations are less favoured; and that traumatic experience is thought to play a smaller part in personality formation than the long-continued influence of the whole environment. It is, in fact, this contrasted set of attitudes which can be discovered in the work of Jung. His respect for the past has been seen already; the assumption that things are what they are until proved otherwise may contribute to his view of the symbol as the best means of expression for something not yet understood, and the dream as endeavouring to communicate the inner condition of the dreamer; inertia, rather than fixation to infantile pleasures, is his main explanation of neurotic disorder in so far as he turns to the past, and emphasis on values and a philosophy of life becomes, if anything, increasingly dominant in his work. A lack of interest in literal interpretations runs through the whole of the later work and was noted in the summary of his early paper on the 'Significance of the Father', where psycho-sexuality seemed to have been linked almost too readily to general issues, without exploration of the intervening territory.[1] There are also many passages which reveal the importance to Jung of steady growth and development rather than traumatic experience; he speaks, for instance, of 'the continuity of the living process' and of psychotherapy in general and analysis in particular as 'a procedure that breaks into a purposeful and continuous development, now here and now there'.[2] Possibly, too, Freud's use of the single dream as the unit of study and Jung's use of the dream series[3] may reflect the discreteness of many situations in the one social background and the relative continuity of the other; Jung's reliance on time as a healing factor again points to a greater stability of background and a slower pace of life.

[1] *Supra*, p. 40.　　　[2] *Mod. Man.*, p. 31.　　　[3] *Supra*, p. 148.

So far attention has been concentrated mainly upon culturally influenced attitudes as affecting theory, but these impressions can be amplified from the writings of Jung and Freud on therapy.[1] It will be remembered that for Freud the psychoanalytical situation requires the existence of a 'superior' and 'inferior', whereas in Jung 'the man in the patient confronts the man in the doctor upon equal terms'. It may be suggested that the world with which Jung has been associated is not primarily an authoritarian world, but one in which the feeling-tone for the most part is that of freely accepted membership in a society where controlling figures are thought of as 'first among equals' rather than bosses in the straight-out sense. Freud was also found to speak of the *struggle* between patient and physician. Elsewhere he compares his patients to the opponents of psychoanalysis: in both the same resistances are found, but 'with patients one was in a position to bring pressure to bear on them, so as to induce them to realize their resistances and overcome them'.[2] Again, 'all accidental occurrences arising during the treatment are made use of by the patient to interfere with it, anything which could distract him or deter him from it . . . indeed, he even converts every improvement in his condition into a motive for slackening his efforts'[3] and it may at times be convenient to say something which will cause him to fall into a trap. To Jung, on the other hand, what is needed is 'a mutual agreement which is the fruit of joint reflection'. He is inclined to take deep-seated resistances seriously, for the doctor 'can hardly know better than the nature and will to live of the patient' and 'would do better to take the fact as an indication of his own growing inability to understand the situation'.

Here, obviously, is an atmosphere of much closer and readier co-operation. The assumption again is that things are what they are until proved otherwise, i.e. that the patient's desire to be cured can be taken as the reason for the relationship; there is no sign of Freud's attempt to catch the patient out. It may be wondered—as, indeed, on the theoretical side, with the Jungian and the Freudian conceptions of a Death Instinct[4] and later with the Id and the collective unconscious[5]—whether the anxiety and insecurity postulated as components of the psychoanalytical background may engender an

---

[1] For citations, unless otherwise stated, see *supra*, Ch. VI, pp. 141–60.
[2] *Introd. Lectures*, p. 246.   [3] *Collected Papers*, Vol. I, p. 306.
[4] *Supra*, p. 74.   [5] *Supra*, p. 106.

amount of hostility which is not found in happier life circumstances; at any rate, there is general recognition that aggression, whether directly expressed or displaced, is one common response to frustration. In Jung's handling of resistance, the assumption that the patient may have a quite legitimate objection which it is part of the doctor's job to understand, suggests that there may easily be cultural differences in the extent to which blame will be laid upon others or the self. Readiness to accept the blame oneself would seem to fit the attitude of the traditionalist toward the taking of responsibilities. Particularly in a situation like that of patient and physician, the physician, though not perhaps regarding himself as the superior in an authoritarian sense, will regard himself as the superior in normality and psychic strength. Therefore, in accordance with mutual aid—the weak in this society being able to draw on the resources of the strong until such time as they are ready to take over for themselves—it would hardly be felt suitable for the physician to be too hasty in putting a further burden on the patient. (It may be that the blaming of oneself first rather than the other person is a more feasible method of adjustment when the disturbance or misunderstanding can be set against the background of a society which by and large is felt to operate in everybody's favour. If in a more permanently stressful situation largely beyond his own control the individual took quite so much unto himself, his ego might be in danger of succumbing.)

Other reservations may be recalled in the Freudian approach to the patient. The patient is looking for substitutive gratifications, and while a certain amount must be permitted to him, 'it is not good to let it become too much. . . . It is expedient to deny him precisely those satisfactions which he desires most intensely and expresses most importunately.' Aside from the circumstance that the Jungian patient seems less intense and importunate in his demands to begin with—a difference which may be linked with the slower tempo and greater basic security of the life he ordinarily leads or is perhaps conceived by Jung to lead—there is again a more limited liability flavour about Freud, very different from the all-in relationship of 'a trustworthy man . . . at hand, lending moral aid'.

The same passage brings to light another aspect. It is *expedient*, Freud says, to deny that which is desired. Beside this statement may be put one by Theodor Reik on the silence of the analyst. At first, Reik says, this silence has a comforting, calming effect, signifying that the analyst is taking an interest in the patient, but gradually it becomes more and more uncomfortable, and the patient feels that it is a punishment and a withdrawal of love. Thereupon 'the compulsion to confess is set in motion. . . . Sometimes the impression produced by this silence . . . is so powerful that the patient implores: "Please, do say something," or "Please, speak to me."'[1] Rather similar in tone is a statement by Ignacio Matte Blanco that there exists an optimum point of anxiety in which the circumstances are most favourable for therapeutic change. 'It is important from this point of view to keep an eye on the amount of anxiety present—when it is too much to relieve it, and to arouse it deliberately when it is too little, as is often the case in some obsessive structures.'[2] There are really two points here. First, it is implied that some degree of anxiety other than the minimum is likely to be the optimum for treatment, whereas in Jung the assumption seems to be that optimum and minimum will coincide. ('Someone whom the patient trusts reaches out a hand. . . .') This may arise from a difference in the tension level, or perhaps from a difference in the kind of response given to threat and to permissiveness. It is not impossible that those who themselves have undergone, or whose relatives and friends have undergone, the experiences described by Cohen and Bettelheim, and who in any case have been under the necessity of developing a certain degree of imperviousness to social snubs, may do best with an approach which is rather less permissive than that favoured by those from a more settled group where responsiveness to some quite small rebuke seems often rather high. Such an impression is reinforced by the reference to setting in motion 'the compulsion to confess'. Those from the Jungian, or traditionalist, background, will, I think, object to the suggestion that something can be dragged out of the patient, in some degree involuntarily. Secondly, Freud in his passage says, 'It is expedient . . .' and Blanco, 'It is important to arouse deliberately . . .'. Not only is the thought of deliberately evoking painful effect unappealing to this group; the conception of standing essentially outside a relationship of this sort while one manipulates it for an end—even though the end be the patient's recovery—may be considered out of harmony with that element of

[1] Cited by Bergler, E., 'Psycho-Analysis of the Uncanny.' *Int. J. Psycho-Anal.*, Vol. XV, pp. 215–44 (pp. 231–2).
[2] 'Some Reflections on Psycho-Dynamics.' *Int. J. Psycho-Anal.*, Vol. XXI, 1940; pp. 253–79 (p. 269).

the 'personal within the framework of the impersonal professional treatment' which is the rule with Jung.

In addition to the strict limitation of affective involvement, the interest of the Freudian analyst in his patient seems of a more segmental type. In general, says Helene Deutsch,

'we refuse to take an interest in the patient's case in so far as it regards his purely intellectual preoccupations, and consider it as a resistance when he seeks to guide the analysis in this direction. In matters of the intellect we are interested in his disturbances only in so far as they hide an inhibition or a symptom. His sublimations, so long as they are successful, lie outside our interests.'[1]

Once more, it seems likely that as one aspect of the 'whole person' relationship, the traditionalist group will feel that anything which concerns the consulting partner sufficiently, anything which he thinks to be relevant to his personality, is of interest to the other partner also—indeed, the other person *must* take notice of it, otherwise he will not be able to play his own part in the relationship, i.e. it is implied that everything in a personality is tied up with everything else, so that if the diseased components are dealt with in a rather isolated manner, less will be achieved. Furthermore, the unspoken argument would run, who knows what clues may be discovered if we take our time and avoid having set ideas?

This raises a further question, i.e. the approach of 'knowing essentially what you're going to find before you start', may not be considered satisfactory by this group. Not that the Jungian school ignores in practice the existence of resemblances and uniformities— see, for instance, the attention paid to psychological types—nor that the Freudians would deny the existence of individual differences. Nevertheless, as we have noted,[2] Freud's closely woven body of doctrine has been regarded by his followers as covering, if not the whole truth about human nature, at any rate by far the greater portion of the truth. Those like our postulated traditionalist patient or practitioner, for whom psychoanalytical terminology is not a perfect fit, may be troubled by a conviction that other, more meaningful or 'real' aspects of experience are passed over. In illustration a paper on 'English Manners', by a recognized psychoanalyst, may

[1] 'A Discussion of Certain Forms of Resistance.' *Int. J. Psycho-Anal.*, Vol. XX, 1939; pp. 72–83 (p. 76). [2] *Supra*, p. 79.

be cited. The writer reports the story of a friend who went to visit a famous British scientist. 'My friend expected the scientist to be a man from whose lips would come very deep remarks,' but in summing up the afternoon 'could only remember that the eminent scientist had enlarged at great length upon his garden, had spent a good deal of his time teasing and playing with his dog, and, after tea, had sunk comfortably into his chair in an attitude of abandonment and reverie, sucking at his pipe with every sign of enjoyment.' Connecting pipe-smoking with the oral-sucking period, the writer continues with the suggestion that the English preparation of roast beef, in very thin slices, 'points to a particularly strong repression of cannibalistic impulses'. That may indeed be so, but outside the framework of psychoanalytical theory is the possibility that some sections of the English middle class have worked out a way of life that accords well with the probable laws of learning and creative activity—intense mental exertion followed by periods of relaxation in which very little is done to impede unconscious integrative processes—to say nothing of a practical application of the projective principle, observing and evaluating the guest in a relatively unstructured situation.[1] Some reaction of this sort exists within the Jungian school. Jung himself declares, 'One always knows beforehand where the whole matter will finally emerge'[2] and adds elsewhere that 'this superior knowing in advance undermines the patient's independence of mind, a most precious quality that should on no account be injured'.[3] Baynes charges the Freudian school with being insufficiently curious about individual and typological variations to modify their psychological conceptions,[4] and E. A. Bennet has spoken similarly of the 'preconceived notions' of Freudian analysis.[5]

Some of these points can be brought together under H. H. Anderson's formulation, dominative vs. integrative relationships, best known to readers in this country from the summary by Harding.[6] The dominative person, Harding writes, is one who knows what he believes and what he wants and has no intention of changing because

---

[1] The reference to this paper is included in the Bibliography.
[2] *Contribs.*, p. 289.   [3] *Development of Personality*, p. 94.
[4] *Analytical Psychology and the English Mind*, p. 127.
[5] 'Psychotherapeutic Method.' R.M.P.A. lecture, Nov. 2, 1953.
[6] Harding, D. W., *The Impulse to Dominate*, pp. 23 *et seq.* London: Allen & Unwin, 1953.

he meets someone who thinks differently. He proceeds with only one intention, that of securing other people's agreement and support. The integrative person, on the other hand, is aiming at 'a fully reciprocal social process by which people are each modified and something new, unpredictable, and different from both of them emerges'. He expresses his contribution more tentatively and offers it with the feeling that 'though he would like the other to agree, it is much more important that this other person should test it thoroughly to the full extent of his capacity, and in the light of his own information and his own scale of values'. The explanation of these differences in Freud and Jung may be that, as Anderson and others have pointed out, resistance and submission are both fear responses. Therefore it would not be surprising if the member of the more anxiety-ridden group was less able to make the response of ' "an individual so unconcerned with his own security that he is not afraid to change or give up his present status" '.

To take up a rather different point, it may be wondered whether, therapeutically, the members of the traditionalist group gain as much from the rational working through of problems as the Freudians are inclined to assume for all above a certain level of intelligence. As mentioned earlier, both the urban trader and the member of a minority group have more occasion than the traditionalist to employ rational analysis in their daily lives, and it would be understandable if a psychiatry or psychotherapy arising in that background reflected such a habit of mind along with other habits. In traditionalist circles, however, there even seems to be a partial taboo on the application of rational analysis to human relationships, a feeling that it encroaches too much upon privacy, is too much bound up with the acquisition of instrumental or manipulative knowledge, and as such does not harmonize with an approach to personality which is perhaps more contemplative and aesthetic. Such an attitude has its own limitations and advantages. It might be argued that interpersonal relations which are governed by it sometimes remain at an unnecessarily rudimentary level, and that in the political and economic spheres the absence of the rationalist's thrust forward into specificities, and the contentment with general maxims on the part of the average member of this group, has contributed to the inability of traditionalist culture to stem the tide of capitalism. On the other hand, in minor disturbances, perhaps too in those major disturbances about which comparatively little has so far been discovered, there may be value in a 'letting-be' which gives the personality opportunities for righting itself in its own time and with its own resources. But whatever the pros and cons, if the traditionalist groups have been keeping afloat without much analysis of interpersonal relations, it is believable that the patient from such groups will not take kindly to it unless it is blended, in a way that seems to him appropriate, with those aids in living to which he is accustomed.

Looking back, that is exactly what we found ourselves suggesting for the work of Jung—that what he sought was a blend of rational analysis with other factors.[1] Now it rather seems—possibly, in the first instance, as a result of the more direct living with one's work in the craftsman's and the countryman's existence, and the personal associations in the training—that learning by example is almost important in this group as rational analysis of a situation is for the other, and this also has been seen in Jung. In order to assist a cure, we may remember, the doctor must *be* the man through whom he wishes to influence others, and the patient 'suns himself, as it were, in the analyst's commonsense, poise, and normality'. More general indications are given in the statements that 'with talk you get nowhere' and that 'Every educator . . . should constantly ask himself whether he is actually fulfilling his teachings in his own person and in his own life, to the best of his knowledge and with a clear conscience.'[2] In so far as rational analysis is used, therefore, the physician will need to pattern the situation in such a way that he as well as the patient is involved, not only, or perhaps not even primarily, as an individual, but as a member of that wider whole to which they both belong. As Jung expresses it, the holding back of a secret cuts the patient off from intercourse with the rest of mankind, and through confession the patient throws himself into the arms of humanity represented by the physician, 'freed at last from the burden of moral exile'. Furthermore, a large amount of time and energy will have

---

[1] *Supra*, p. 151.

[2] *Development of Personality*, p. 140. Cf. the statement of a former Headmaster of Harrow, that even though the teacher's business in the classroom is to teach the Rule of Three, 'it makes a lot of difference what sort of man he is, whether he knows his boys, and for what values he stands, and if he is a good enough man to stand for the values that are right and the boys know it and feel it, he will impart, not only the Rule of Three more efficiently but he will impart other things that are of far more value.' Norwood, C., *The English Tradition of Education*. London: John Murray, 1929, p. 58.

been spent by this group in expressing difficult matters with the utmost possible delicacy—a concept made up, probably, of assumptions noted previously—that 'wounds are not to be multiplied beyond necessity', that the patient has as good a chance of being right about his own condition and requirements as the physician or advisor, that the matter under review must not be dealt with too strictly in isolation from other, more healthy, aspects of the personality, and that contrary to Freud's opinion that no more and no less harm may be done by a clumsy probing in one direction than in another, there are gradations of experience, i.e. like the physical organism itself the personality has some components which need to be handled with more care than others.

Several of these attitudes can be illustrated from the case material. In the first place there is the case of Jung's Anna and Freud's little Hans.[1] The more active, striving qualities of Hans and his parents seem to us now an expression of the greater need for taking the initiative on the part of an urban and uprooted people, the traditionalist being able more easily to sit back in his appointed place and avoid any forcing of an issue. The literalism, too, of Freud's account—the child's observation of basins filled with blood and water in the confinement-room, together with the explanation later given to the child, that babies were 'brought into the world by being pressed out . . . like lumf, and this involves a great deal of pain'—may be taken as an indication of the greater starkness of outlook, with fewer overtones or 'wrappings', of a persecuted people, when compared with the explanation in terms of earth and seed in Jung. The accounts by Jung and Freud of their patients with mistresses[2] have already been cited as illustrating the difference in emphasis on values and rational analysis respectively; there is in Freud's account as well ('he felt the need of detaching himself . . . he wanted to be free, to lead his own life . . . and . . . was able with the help of analysis to make a love choice outside the magic circle within which he had been spell-bound') something of that flatly dropping-out quality to which reference has been made in this chapter.

To sum up, it is suggested that the attitudes we have described, arising in part at any rate from two different ways of life, cover some portion of what is meant by the statement, often made by his supporters, that Jung is more spiritual than Freud; perhaps in

[1] *Supra*. pp. 42-3.   [2] *Supra*, pp. 154–5.

barest outline they can be stated as the sense of belonging to a meaningful and worthwhile whole, and the habit of treating individuals
as ends in themselves.

The argument having been stated, one or two provisos should be
added. In the first place, we do not wish to reduce the whole of
Jungian and Freudian psychology to origins in social background;
our intention is the more limited one of pointing out ways in which
the cultural component may have caused both Jung and Freud to
perceive or to emphasize some facts and to be less aware of others.
In dealing with the cultural component itself it is possible to over-
simplify. In addition to overlapping, there may well be counter-
balancing factors within the groups themselves, e.g. in Jewish life
the extensive use, as it seems, of the parent-child relationship. (As
Pryns Hopkins says of Freud, 'My own impression on the few
occasions of my contact with him was, I am sure, felt by many others
—it was that of a supremely wise and kindly fatherliness.')[1] As in
the previous chapter, there are, of course, two problems—the
appeal of Jungian psychology and the influences which have gone to
make it at the outset, and it may be that we are on safer ground in
dealing with the latter, since in the sorting-out of patient and physician not only a selection process but also an element of chance will
enter. However, a clue to the relevance of cultural factors in therapy
as well can be found in a number of accounts from the patient's
point of view. While no such accounts appear to have been written
for the Jungian school, for psychoanalysis several have been brought
together in a Symposium, 'Psycho-Analysis as Seen by Analysed
Psychologists'.[2] It so happens that the psychologists participating
were American, and, therefore, that a third group is being introduced
with features of its own, but although this seems at first sight not to
be ideal, there are, as it turns out, certain compensations.

One contributor, Edwin Boring, goes so far as to say, 'The first
analyst I saw repelled me'; another, H. A. Murray, does not
use that term, but speaks of 'the oppressive bias, obvious to so
many, that runs through the entire Freudian system—a bias which
seriously distorts truth and annuls, in some cases, the therapeutic
benefits of the procedure'.[3] A subsidiary contributor opens his
account by reporting that after consulting two analysts, neither of

---

[1] 'Sigmund Freud.' *Character & Personality*, VIII, pp. 163–9.
[2] *J. Abn. & Soc. Psychol.*, XXXV, 1940.   [3] *Ibid.*, p. 167.

whom impressed him favourably, he met one who seemed to be a person for whom he could feel some respect and warmth.[1] Boring, the only one who gives specific grounds for his reaction, refers to a matter which has partially escaped our notice, namely, payment of the fee. His first analyst seemed to him too mercenary. 'He had not talked half an hour before he explained that, were I to miss any conferences I should have to pay just the same. I know, of course, the reason for that rule; yet he seemed to be thinking less about my health than about his own pocket-book.' Then Boring met Dr. Hanns Sachs and liked him at once. ('He reminded me of Titchener, whose image has always dominated my professional life.') Speaking of this analysis he adds, 'The expense seemed to me to play the role that was expected of it. The analysand is supposed to make a sacrifice in order to obtain the analysis; this sacrifice secures his serious co-operation.'[2] Boring's statement seems to stand midway between that of his first analyst and the attitude which may be postulated for the old-style traditionalist. That is, while he objects to having financial arrangements brought forward rather early, as the traditionalist patient also would, he does not challenge the whole psychoanalytical outlook on the question of expense, but is willing to accept it. Now the traditionalist, of course, expects to pay. But he may expect to pay on different grounds, expressing the matter rather in the following terms: 'Those who are capable of rendering exacting professional services are entitled to a position of esteem in the community, and should be so rewarded that they can sustain this position in a fitting manner,' i.e. he is more likely to think in terms of the old medieval ideas of the just price and payment according to the requirements of one's station. Or again, the Jungian analyst, too, may introduce the idea of sacrifice, and the patient may accept it, but stress will be laid chiefly on the necessity of making a sacrifice—which in the analytical situation will take the form in part of a financial sacrifice—if anything valuable is to be achieved. Any suggestion that monetary considerations will influence the revelation of one's inmost thoughts, that 'Because you are paying, therefore you will tell me about yourself more readily,' brings into association two aspects of life, the financial and the spiritual, which

---

[1] Wood, Austin B., 'Another Psychologist Analysed.' *J. Abn. & Soc. Psychol.*, XXXVI, 1941, pp. 87–90.
[2] *J. Abn. & Soc. Psychol.*, XXXV, 1940; p. 6.

in the thinking of this group—following, perhaps, the medieval objection to the trader—have been divorced so far as possible—it may be, indeed, too much. We may recall, too, that there is some reason to suppose Jung's own attitude in financial matters to be different from that commonly accepted among psychoanalysts: if the sittings are spaced out, he writes, and the intervals filled in with the patient's own work, the treatment becomes financially more endurable.[1] This may link up with another point, i.e. that in this group a minimal degree of anxiety seems, in general, to be considered the optimum for treatment.

Two points raised previously—the 'limited liability' nature of the analyst's interest, and his readiness to blame the patient—receive in one of these articles some corroboration. It happened occasionally, one analysand relates, that after a childhood experience had been recounted by him, the analyst would make an interpretation with which he disagreed. This disagreement usually arose out of the fact that the analyst had an urban European background while his own was that of a small American village in the Middle West.

> 'I am certain that he no more understood the cultural pattern and its attendant emotional tone than I would have understood his account of his boyhood in Europe if he had recounted it to me. This fact constituted a problem to me. I must attempt to report so he would understand and so I would not create misapprehension and misunderstanding. The next hour I would be more precise in reporting, and he would sigh and say, "You hate me today for what I said yesterday and so are showing resistance. Don't be so precise. Let your thoughts go as they will."'

Landis, like Boring in respect of payment, takes up an intermediate attitude. He notes the difficulty with good humour, and essentially lines himself up with the analyst's position. 'Of course he was right. The purpose of the analysis was to help me understand something about myself, not for me to educate him about Ohio.'[2] That is, there seems to be in these writers a trend of the kind anticipated by Ruppin, when he says that should human life develop further in the direction of urbanization, certain qualities which at present are considered to be predominantly Jewish will become to an increasing extent general qualities of mankind. The old-style traditionalist would, more probably, have held to the opinion that to stick too

---

[1] *Supra*, p. 149.   [2] *J. Abn. & Soc. Psychol.*, XXXV, pp. 17–28.

closely to the purpose in situations such as these is to run the risk of losing it.

It seems likely, therefore, that one of the influences on Jung's psychology has been the way of living of the traditionalist groups, and that even bearing in mind provisos concerning the absence of hard and fast boundaries, the purely personal equation, and the element of chance, this kind of harmony has been one source of its appeal. Two further considerations may be urged. First, cultural resistance may be more difficult for both patient and analyst to cope with than individual resistance. In the latter sphere the individual stands largely on his own feet, and is dealing with material of which he is not infrequently ashamed; in the former, he has the backing of those influences in his past life with which he has identified as right and proper, and is therefore more likely to have confidence in his own judgment as against the analyst's. Secondly, the traditionalist groups, in some of their divisions at any rate, are inclined to set store by conformity to rather intricate patterns of behaviour, and so might be more inclined than some to seek a therapist from their own setting. Here, too, may be one source of the bitterness and misinterpretation which have characterized the relations of the two schools with one another. Culture conflict of the subtler type brings problems of its own—it is just in those circumstances, where the language and the visible structure of life is the same in its broad outlines, but the attitudes which modify it diverge in many ways—in other words, when both sides are slightly 'off the beam' for one another without quite realizing what each other's background situation is, that recriminations and misinterpretations are likely to occur. Especially in the early days of psychoanalysis the cultural component might play an important part in binding its adherents together, almost usurping the role of a strong professional tradition, while at a later period it would no longer be needed to the same extent. Something of the sort is implied in Suttie's statement, twenty years ago, that 'Psychoanalysis in fact is losing much that made it obnoxious to European philosophy, good sense and good feeling.'[1]

Another point to be considered is the position of the neo-analysts. Have they not put forward, independently of Jung, many of the same ideas, and yet, is their background not similar, in many

[1] *Op. cit.*, p. 12.

instances, to that of orthodox analysis? However, when the matter is examined, the neo-analysts may be found to confirm the present conclusions rather than disprove them. In the first place, even dating the beginnings of the movement at about 1933, that still gives Jung a lead of twenty years—just the sort of time lag which might be expected if cultural factors were in operation. Very often also, as we saw, the similarity between Jung and the later writers remains, after all, a similarity, not an identity, of outlook.[1] The differences will be recalled as well—the contrast between Horney's 'middle class neurotic of Western civilization', characterized by great potential hostility and acquisitiveness, and Jung's patient with his search for meaning; the much more detailed analysis of present-day conditions, given by Fromm and Horney revealing a first-hand knowledge which Jung, with his simpler lament that 'The educated public . . . has lifted itself up from its roots and is about to lose its connection with the earth,' seems not to possess; the more active, rationalistic, and at the same time more suspicious, approach to the patient of Horney and Fromm-Reichmann; the willingness to *manipulate* the relationship shown especially in the citation from Alexander and French; the tendency for the neo-analyst to think of the patient's best abilities as being stifled by society, compared with Jung's greater identification, on the whole, with the values of society; and in religion the starker approach of Erich Fromm, in particular, to man's place in the universe and the ending of his life. Even the suggestions made by Fromm-Reichmann about the conflicts of the analyst—the danger that he will be afraid of appearing ridiculous in the eyes of his colleagues or subordinates, and will become pre-occupied with the idea that his patients have to get well for the sake of his reputation—indicate a more competitive and anxiety-ridden way of life than that of 'the trustworthy man reaching out a hand . . .'. In short, in the case of Jung, what we seem to be confronted with is a simple cultural expressiveness; in the case of the later writers there is something more like a cultural transcendence which at some points retains the influence of the way of life which it transcends. So far as they go, the clues that can be gathered from the early British eclectics reinforce the argument by revealing a background similar to Jung's, though with the addition of a certain militancy—a 'taboo on tenderness' and 'fighting ahead'—more characteristic,

[1] *Supra*, pp. 180–6.

probably, of the English than the Continental middle classes. That is, the world of McDougall, Rivers, Hadfield, seemed more stable and secure than the world depicted by the early Freudians or the neo-analysts, with less facility in verbal manipulations, a more trusting relationship between patient and physician, and conflicts centred at least as much around fulfilment of commitments as around enhancement of personal prestige.[1] In a similarity of social background also may be found the common source which we were inclined to postulate for the attitudes apparently worked out independently by Jung and Prinzhorn.[2] Even the 'very pleasant impression' which William James reported after meeting Jung, his uncertainty concerning Freud, and his 'Bah!' to some of his pronouncements,[3] adds to the picture of Jung as expressing very fully the outlook of the academic and ecclesiastical classes of Western Europe and to some extent its offshoots.

After seeing something in this chapter of the place of cultural factors in the work of Jung and paying attention previously to possible factors of mentality, is it feasible to suggest a link between the two, i.e. do these social groups contain large numbers of individuals with a trend toward the 'Jungian mentality', and are there any aspects of the present situation which might accentuate that trend? Several features of the traditionalist way of life can be suggested as likely to suit individuals of a rather sensitive and 'introverted' nature, the more extreme cases of which might fall into the category of Fromm-Reichmann's 'schizophrenia as a way of living'—the slower tempo, giving more opportunity for working out their own methods of adjustment, the highly developed role system which, provided that it does not tax the energies too much, acts as a mediating agency between the individual and the outer world, and values such as reserve and dignity. The lesser need for rational and specific thinking in a secure and long-continued social setting has been noted; it is probable that such a setting would favour the development of that attitude of contemplation urged by Evelyn Underhill rather than one of manipulative skill. If an environment does suit a certain type, the likelihood is that the type will be found in it quite frequently, similar individuals from other environments gravitating to it, and individuals with more drive in other directions moving off. In this way might be explained the

---

[1] *Supra*, pp. 187–8.   [2] *Supra*, pp. 189–91.   [3] *Supra*, p. 212.

exceptions in the Jungian school especially: remembering in particular the mysticism of the influential, though not dominant, Chassidic sect within the Jewish faith, it can well be imagined that its adherents will sometimes be drawn in the direction of Jung rather than of Freud. For this reason it may be surmised that of the two sets of influence it is the factors of mentality which are the more significant.[1]

To reconstruct one possible 'Jungian situation': it will be recalled that the medieval elements in European life have been steadily declining, and that the First World War was an additional blow to old-established ways. Hence Jung in his work as a therapist will have been faced with the problem of enabling patients who had grown up in a more traditionalist environment to retain or to regain their mental balance in a world where many of the old landmarks had been, or were being, submerged. This problem may have been accentuated by the lack of adaptability of the traditionalist personality, as though flexibility and verve are largely lost in the learning of a set of complicated rules, so that the rules are clung to as long as life itself remains. Provided the rules still apply, the individual functions in a manner satisfying to himself and to society. If for any reason they cease to apply, he is in danger of being stranded. Furthermore, fully two thirds of Jung's patients, as he tells us, were over thirty-five—in the biological sense, too, beyond the most adaptable period of their lives.

As the literature of these and later years attests, not many new patterns of creative living were available. Liberalism, which might have appealed, was sharing the general decline. Communism would have little to offer to this type of patient, with its authoritarianism, regimentation and disrespect for bourgeoisie—not, indeed, that the Jungian patient shows much leaning toward political life. The Church, which clearly interested him a good deal more, had on the whole failed, as he realized, to keep pace with modern thought and living—hence his search in the therapy and theory of the Jungian school for some meaning in life other than 'blank resignation and mournful retrospect'.

[1] In this connection may be cited, with permission, the verbal report of a psychologist undergoing Jungian analysis, that while the cultural factors drew him toward the Jungian movement, his relative lack of interest in 'image-finding' as a means of expressing emotional experience seemed to him to limit the benefit he gained.

Returning briefly to the theoretical side, we will recall that Jung seems to have been prevented by several factors from expressing his ideas more clearly. Two of these can, perhaps, be attributed in part to social background—the habit of following wherever the patient led, resulting at times in over-identification with the patient's productions; and a reluctance, on grounds of delicacy, to publish personal material, which may have brought about an increased emphasis on the 'collective' contents.

Considered in the broadest terms, there would seem to be something almost symbolic about the obscurities of Jung—a typifying, that is, of the relative helplessness of a stabler, more slow-moving, less word-minded group when confronted with a way of life which is less deeply rooted, more aggressive, more rapid in its manipulation of things and human beings, having less to give in terms of fundamental needs for security and love, but geared to a short-term success.

CONCLUSION

We are now ready to review those aspects of Jung's psychology which have concerned us in this study.

Taking as our starting-point the problem posed by the widely differing estimations of his work and the changes in its style, we saw Jung at the outset of his career as the inheritor of many trends in nineteenth-century thought.[1] In psychiatry itself there was the German classificatory and descriptive work, associated especially with Kraepelin, and the more psychologically oriented schools which had grown up in France; Freud's early work, published in the last five years of the century, had not yet attracted the attention of the learned world. Behind psychiatry lay the natural sciences, especially the biological sciences, which through the accepted methods of rigorous observation and, where possible, experiment had made remarkable strides in the preceding generations. In addition to these were the humanistic disciplines—archaeology, throwing fresh light on the ancient Greek and Hebrew civilizations from which much of European civilization had itself arisen; history and anthropology, immersed, like evolutionary biology, in the search for origins and the reconstruction of the primal state of man; Liberal theology, with its attempts to reinterpret Christian dogma in accordance with the new discoveries; philosophy, with the great systems of Kant, Fichte, Hegel, and the less systematized work of Schelling, in the early part of the century, and a more definite foreshadowing of the concept of the Unconscious by Schopenhauer, Von Hartmann and Nietzsche in the later years. Running through much of this work on the humanistic side was a strong influence from Romanticism.

We then turned to the development of Jung's own work.[1] His first psychiatric study ('On So-Called Occult Phenomena'), written

---

[1] Chapter I, 'The Historical Background,' pp. 1–20.
[1] Chapter II, 'The Early Work,' pp. 21–45.

in 1900 as an M.D. dissertation, combined the French work on dual personality with an hypothesis of his own, influenced by the philosophical theory of Unconscious Will, that the second personality represented an attempt of the patient's future personality to break through into consciousness; references were included to Freud's *Interpretation of Dreams*, which had appeared in that year, but it was clear that Jung had not assimilated the Freudian concepts of conflict and repression so fully as Janet's concept of dissociation owing to psychopathic deficit. Under Professor Bleuler at the Burghöltzli Hospital and Zürich University he was brought more closely into touch with the academic psychiatry of the day, and much of his Word Association work reflects that influence. At the same time he came independently on disturbances of association under emotional stress which pointed toward the work of Freud. During this period also he analysed the delusions of a chronic case of schizophrenia or dementia praecox with the help of the Freudian method of free association and in essentially Freudian terms, and shortly afterwards, in 1907, he became, as it seemed, a full disciple of Freud. Although, in both the papers and the biographical material of these years, there were small indications that he may not have accepted the Freudian point of view so fully as has often been supposed,[1] it might on the whole have been imagined that his future role would be that of expositor and experimentalist within the Freudian movement —a link, as Freud had hoped, between psychoanalysis and the academic world. Comparatively little in these studies, rather descriptive in type, related carefully to existing thought and at times showing a tendency to set earlier concepts of his own beside the Freudian concepts without a full co-ordination, suggested a bent toward theoretical psychology, and several of the differences between his views at this stage and those which he put forward subsequently were quite marked—in particular, he showed a relative lack of interest in symbolic thought, and a search for explanatory connections only in the life of the individual himself. There was some reason to think the relationships of the period were rather complicated. Toward the end a slight note of disparagement entered into Jung's references to Blueler, while at the same time tension seemed to have existed between Jung and the Viennese followers of Freud, if not between Jung and Freud themselves.

[1] See *supra*, pp. 40–1.

The next few years brought many changes.[1] Between 1912 and 1915 Jung put forward his main criticisms of the Freudian position—his preference for thinking in terms of a fund of general psychic energy rather than a bundle of impulses organized into the adult sexual drive, aim-inhibited according to the dictates of society, etc.; his emphasis on problems of the present situation and the future in the genesis of mental illness rather than the childhood constellation of the Oedipus complex, conflict and repression, which, again, he only partially accepted; his belief that social and self-restraining impulses form part of man's innate equipment and that a religious outlook, broadly considered, is essential to health; and his conception of the patient-physician relationship as one which exists primarily in its own right, with fewer repetitions and sexual features than have been attributed to it in the Freudian theory of the transference. His previous view of unconscious processes as compensatory and prospective was reaffirmed, coupled now with an increased regard for symbols, largely visual symbols, which, he held, were not predominantly signs or symptoms of repressed material but analogies for general concepts not yet fully grasped. *Psychology of the Unconscious* paved the way for the later theory of the collective unconscious by postulating a layer of unconscious thought common to the individual and the race, and using the symbols of many different ages and places to elucidate the fantasies of a patient whom Jung himself had not actually seen. Throughout this work, indeed, the emphasis had moved from the individual case to 'that wider relation which reveals each neurotic conflict to be involved with human fate as a whole'.[2] Its main theme could be taken as the universal struggle of the human being toward independent life against the backward pull of the mother, interpreted not primarily as a sexual object but as the giver of all, the guardian of the paradisical state of early infancy—the first formulation in depth psychology, it would seem, of the Good and Bad Mother. As with the occasional juxtaposition in his previous papers, however, it was not always clear how much of the Freudian connotation was still being retained, e.g. in the use of such a term as incest. His theory of desexualization of libido in the course of history, besides being an attempt to reconcile his own and Freudian views, was one example of the way in which he too was influenced by the nineteenth-century search for origins.

[1] Chapter III, 'The Intermediate Period,' pp. 46–81.   [2] *Supra*, p. 61.

While the religious question was not yet central to Jung's thinking, *Psychology of the Unconscious* had the further interest of indicating, e.g. in the statements that 'In the Deity man honours his own libido', and 'I think belief should be replaced by understanding',[1] the humanism and subjectivism apparent equally in Jung's later writings. A further contribution in this period was the outline of his theory of psychological types—the introvert who gives his fundamental interest to his own subjective processes, and the extravert, whose energies turn primarily toward the outer world. These years were regarded as intermediate ones not only on account of their subject-matter, giving the germs of ideas which were afterwards expanded, but also on account of their style, which showed traces of the later involvements but still seemed clearer than it afterwards became, and their aim, which was not yet predominantly therapeutic. Jung's distinction was noted between the responsibilities of the scientist and the therapist—interest in rules and categories and the search for truth belonging to the former, interest in immediate experience and practical helpfulness belonging to the latter. The question was raised of the necessity for the break between the Zürich and Vienna schools. The answer seemed to depend in part upon the breadth or narrowness of the construction placed on the psychoanalytical movement, and since Freud's construction was of the narrower variety, it was difficult to see that Jung could have continued to function as a member of the International Association. Indeed, even with a more liberal interpretation, it was difficult to see that a worker who, like Jung, was comparatively uninterested in early developmental processes could have remained active in a group which believed, as did the Freudians, that the study of these processes added a third set of causes to those of heredity and precipitating stress which had already been acknowledged. In these happenings there was again the element of personal strain, followed by a dropping-out reaction on the part of Freud and a feeling of loss and bewilderment in Jung.[2]

Without making a sharp sub-division of the third period, from the publication of *Two Essays on Analytical Psychology* onwards, we noted that the first part, roughly from 1916 to 1930, was given mainly to psychotherapy and concepts of mind arising out of it, and that in the second part, from about 1930 to the present day,

---

[1] *Supra*, p. 59; p. 63.   [2] *Supra*, p. 81.

problems of religion came especially to the fore, with the work on alchemy and Eastern texts, and latterly on Christian dogma.

In introducing the period we paid some attention to stylistic peculiarities which were apt to impart a haze to the later writing, at least when theory was discussed, together with Jung's distinction, not unlike that of the intermediate period, between knowledge, which involved the laying down of general laws, and the understanding of the individual. While in his previous writings we thought we could detect a descriptive rather than hypothesizing bent, in this period we found him clearly doubting the feasibility of tracing cause and effect in mental life, and doubting, indeed, the adequacy of rational analysis to the human situation as a whole.[1] We then turned to Jung's main postulates concerning mental structure and function —the collective unconscious, that substratum of unconscious mental life which he took to be common to mankind; the archetypes, or recurrent patterns of apprehension and behaviour of the collective unconscious—chiefly in Jung's work the former; the figures of the unconscious, or personified archetypes, entering more consistently than the others into the structure of the personality; and an extended form of his earlier theory of psychological types.[2] For the collective unconscious and the archetypes two main types of statement were found—those referring, for example, to 'the sediment of all the experience of the universe', which seemed to imply the Inheritance of Acquired Characters, and those referring to 'a potential system of psychic functions' only.[3] Since Jung has repudiated the first meaning, particularly in the new edition, we confined attention mainly to the second, though in view of the indefiniteness of many of his statements we did not think that he could be entirely absolved from the charge of out-of-date biology. For psychological types we noted the addition of four functions to the introverted and extraverted attitudes— thinking, feeling, sensation and intuition. In stating these concepts it became necessary to introduce Jung's further concept of individuation, or the coming into being of the self, representing integrative processes largely within the adult personality—a concept intimately bound up with his therapeutic and religious teachings.

Turning in Chapter V[4] to further discussion of mental structure

[1] *Supra*, pp. 83–6.
[2] Chapter IV, 'Jung's Later Concepts of Mind: Exposition.' pp. 82–107.
[3] *Supra*, p. 91.
[4] Chapter V, 'Jung's Later Concepts of Mind: Discussion,' pp. 108–40.

and functioning, we suggested that the inclusiveness of the term, Collective Unconscious, might lead to a neglect of problems, a failure, for instance, to inquire into the variations shown by a phenomenon or the conditions under which it showed itself. Jung's treatment of some of the archetypes seemed to us to give support to this suggestion, e.g. we doubted whether, in his derivation of the theory of conservation of energy and primitive ideas of spirit from the same archetypal form, he had done justice to the significance for human thought of the differences between them. Particularly noticeable was the omission of cultural differences; while similarities of myth and symbol undoubtedly occur, we felt there was an echo of the earlier nineteenth-century anthropology in his habit of comparing myths and symbols in isolation from the cultures of which they were components. The same argument could be applied to his assumption of identity or very great similarity between childhood, primitive and psychotic thinking, even though it seemed clear that some kind of non-logical, affectively determined thought existed, such as Jung, and Freud with his primary and secondary processes, had described. The possibility was admitted by more than one writer outside the Jungian school that this form of thinking, manifestly inferior to logical thinking in reality testing, had, nevertheless, constructive and recuperative functions of its own. We then examined the argument that unconscious symbolism of the type assumed by Jung was really dependent on a conscious choice, and suggested that while Jung had sometimes been inclined to bypass evidence of conscious awareness on the one side and Freudian symbol-formation on the other, there might be further aspects of the symbol which were equally unknown to the patient and therefore equally in need of investigation by special means. Considering the archetypal figures, we thought that although his treatment was handicapped by neglect of developmental factors, Jung had anticipated the internal object theories of the Kleinian school. It seemed probable too that besides this core of meaning in the concept of the collective unconscious and the archetypes, there were various accretions which might make an appeal in some quarters, e.g. Jung in endeavouring to break away from the narrowness of the individual analytical relationship may have sought a biological cum historical solution according to the pattern of his early training rather than a social one such as might now be provided in group psychotherapy. The charge of being excessively molar could also be brought against Jung's handling of mental energy, the opposites and psychological types, especially the formulation, 'determination by object or by subject',[1] and it seemed a further weakness that attempts to introduce precision, notably in psychological types, had come from other schools. For reasons such as these we proposed to think of Jung as a pre-scientific writer rather than as scientific, but wished at the same time to search for value of a different kind which his contributions might possess.

This was found to a large extent in his teachings on psycho-therapy,[2] e.g. in the co-operative atmosphere of his patient-physician relationship, where 'the man in the patient confronts the man in the doctor upon equal terms',[3] which was compared with Freud's more authoritarian attitude of 'inferior' and 'superior'. Jung's accounts of the therapeutic situation were analysed in terms of the factors to which he attributed a cure; it seemed that he was relying less on rational analysis and more on social linking-up, identification with the therapist, and moral or religious values than was customary in the Freudian school. The goal of therapy—individuation—usually seemed to involve the assimilation of archetypal contents, but there was also a transformation which came about through the patient-physician relationship—in the meeting of the two personalities 'both are transformed'[4]—and it was even allowed that any life, being at bottom the realization of a whole, could be called individuation. The lack of co-ordination between these accounts had been mentioned previously[5] as something of a drawback, but by and large Jung appeared to have in mind the development of a type of personality which maintained toward its own experiences a balance between participation and detachment similar to that taken by the physician to the experience of his patients. There was reason to think that he had given attention to groups of patients with which orthodox psychoanalysis, in past years at any rate, had been less concerned— borderline psychotics on the one hand and cases of character disturbance on the other, i.e. 'those suffering from no clinically definable neurosis'.[6]

In the chapter following[7] we discovered many parallels between

---

[1] *Supra*, pp. 131.
[2] Chapter VI, 'The Jungian Therapy and Related Insights,' pp. 141–60.
[3] *Supra*, p. 144.　　[4] *Supra*, p. 145.　　[5] *Supra*, p. 103.　　[6] *Supra*, p. 149.
[7] Chapter VII, 'Jung's Critique of Freud and Psychotherapy: Discussion,' pp. 305–61.

Jung's critique of Freud and psychotherapy and those of later writers—the eclectic British school of Rivers and McDougall, the neo-analysts in the U.S.A., and indeed a number of analysts at the present time who would be accounted full members of psycho-analytical societies. These parallels, e.g. lesser regard for the sexual and repetitive components in the patient-physician relationship and willingness to admit questions of moral value into psychotherapy, could be expected, independently of the truth or falsehood of the views put forward, to have significance as one source of Jung's appeal: if until comparatively recent years leading exponents of such views were less common, individuals inclined to them might have been drawn the more readily toward Jung. In considering ways of making the evidence for and against clinical opinions more precise, we inquired into Jung's distinction between knowledge and under-standing, and in view of the guidance which the therapist could gain even from the knowledge of different emotional constellations—deprived patients, overprotected patients, and so forth—which we have already, we thought that knowledge was more important as a basis for understanding than Jung in some of his written statements seemed to allow.[1] In a subsidiary part of the discussion we noted some of the differences as well as similarities between Jung and later writers; reviewing the neo-analysts, especially, with their greater stress on rational planning and their concern with aggression, we saw that the world pictures which they and Jung presented were far from being identical.

In a chapter on Jung's handling of religion[2] we found that his earlier insistence on the therapeutic value of a *Weltanschauung*, together with his profound concern over the turmoil of the last two generations, had led him increasingly to seek a remedy for the loss of belief in the old religious forms. In the manner of the nineteenth-century Liberal theologians he found the essence of religion in the experience of the individual, particularly in the experience, which, following the slightly later theologian, Rudolf Otto, he described as 'numinous', of being seized and controlled by powerful factors outside the conscious will which ultimately, with the co-operation of consciousness, led to greater integration. Such experiences, occurring in his patients at the present time, and expressed often in mandala

[1] *Supra*, p. 57; p. 84.
[2] Chapter VIII, 'Some Notes on Religion in the Work of Jung,' pp. 192–227.

P.J.—11*

symbols, were compared to the Christian account, 'No longer do I live but Christ liveth in me.'[1] For our own part we tended to feel that Jung's account of religion was incomplete in undervaluing the Transcendental element,[2] in being apt, like that of some other humanistic writers, to lose sight of the fact that the therapeutic value of religion is something of a by-product, depending on religion's being regarded first as a thing in itself,[3] in ignoring other facts, such as the importance which the mystics themselves attached to religious activity unaccompanied by any emotionally toned experience,[4] and engaging in some amount of special pleading. (We wondered, for instance, whether, if Jung had been less concerned with the importance of myth and symbolism, he might have been less deprecating toward the Protestants' 'unbearably sophisticated I-You relationship' to God, and have seen this instead as a development within Christianity which endeavoured to minimize the father-child analogy that he himself regarded as standing in the way of full maturity.) Particularly in discussing Jung's reinterpretations of Christian dogma, we felt that the blanketing tendency in his accounts of the Collective Unconscious was encountered again in his theological ideas. For instance, in substituting a Quaternity for the Trinity he inclined sometimes toward inclusion of the feminine principle and sometimes toward inclusion of the principle of evil, and in one place[5] he even seemed to attempt to combine them. By theologians, we noted, the interpretation of evil as a positive principle instead of a *privatio boni* had in any case been strongly attacked as unduly concretistic, and the same objection had been raised to his inclusion of femininity in the Godhead, or strictly, man's conception of the Godhead, which in pure doctrine is held to be beyond both male and female. In general the evidence for substituting any Quaternity for the Trinity as the most adequate expression of man's conception of the Deity did not seem as strong as Jung had supposed,[6] and other examples were given of quotations which he appeared to have incorporated more in the light of his own requirements than in the light of the original.[7] In short, and bearing in mind at the same time our preference already stated for regarding him as a pre-scientific rather than a scientific writer, we felt that Jung had only

[1] *Supra*, p. 198.   [2] *Supra*, p. 200; p. 208.   [3] *Supra*, p. 201.
[4] *Supra*, p. 200.   [5] *Supra*, p. 205.   [6] *Supra*, p. 206.
[7] *Supra*, pp. 207–8.

partially succeeded in reconciling science and religion, as has some-times been claimed on his behalf.[1] We thought, nevertheless, that the similarities between the states of mind which he described and those described by Christian writers, and, still more, the similarity of values despite some further influence from Eastern sources, could well give his work an attraction for 'Christian unbelievers'. This seemed all the more likely to have happened since William James, whose approach through the extreme left wing of Protestant theology had much in common with his own, had died in 1910, and Freud on his side was so uncompromisingly opposed to the religious quest.[2]

Continuing the comparisons of the previous chapter, we found that in values, as distinct from archetypal and dogmatic aspects, there was much in common also between the outlook of Jung and that of later writers in depth psychology who had concerned themselves with problems of religion, among whom we cited Erich Fromm, J. C. Flugel and Marjorie Brierley.[3] The values of self-realization which they shared appeared to form an ethical basis for Western psycho-therapy, but to need some reinforcement by the principle of moral obligation, which Jung tacitly supplied in writing of 'commitment'; on the other hand, it seemed to be an advantage in the accounts of the later writers that reason, rather than numinous experience, was regarded as the guiding factor in religious life. Various additional differences, such as the more active note in Fromm's productive living, and his attitude toward death as something 'poignantly bitter' rather than, as in Jung, a part of life itself, reinforced our impression of a somewhat different world picture among the neo-analysts. Finally, Jung's account of the religious significance of symbolism seemed to be clarified through the independent account of a later writer, Susanne Langer, in philosophy,[4] who stressed the disorienta-tion which results when our lives are no longer lived against a closely woven background of meaning. Once again, Langer's description of symbol formation as essentially a rational activity of mind seemed to us a safeguard which Jung, with his narrower conception of reason, might not always possess.

We came, lastly, to a third set of problems—the reasons for the changes in Jung's style of work and for the appeal which his psycho-logy has made in some quarters and its absence of appeal in others,

[1] *Supra*, p. xiv.   [2] *Supra*, pp. 213–6.   [3] *Supra*, pp. 217–25.
[4] *Supra*, pp. 225–7.

in so far as this had not been accounted for above.[1] As we looked back on the years spent with Bleuler, in an atmosphere of academic and scientific work, the enthusiastic contact with the Freudian movement, coupled with increasing doubts, and the uncertainty when that contact could no longer be sustained, it seemed possible that Jung was, if anything, almost too receptive to influences from his intellectual and emotional environment, and this impression was reinforced by his comments at different stages of the Nazi movement.[2] We noted that from about 1909 onwards he had turned again to the German philosophers, anthropologists and others of his student days, and that through the catastrophe of the First World War his attention was drawn further toward the problem of *Weltanschauung* in the modern world. At the same time, as we have said, it appeared from his own references that his therapeutic practice brought him into contact with a proportion of patients who would be regarded as borderline psychotics, and it could be shown that their experience made a strong impression on him, so that some of his accounts, for instance, that of experiencing the collective unconscious,[3] were reminiscent of their own reports. It seemed likely that a psychology geared closely to the mentality of a particular type of patient would make an appeal in that direction, though we recognized the further problem of the *value* of the experience in question; to some writers, William James, and more recently Aldous Huxley, the psychotic-like experiences produced by certain drugs, at any rate, had a value in bringing with them a sense of ultimate reconciliation or infinite significance. Nor did we wish to sum up the later work of Jung simply as a psychology of borderline psychosis. There seemed to be other characteristics, not necessarily tied to such illness, which, while they might not assist in theoretical clarification, were nevertheless an important part of life, and which were expressed in Jungian psychology more fully than in others: interest in immediate experience and in its contemplation and recall through imagery, a tendency also to use images to make contact with and assimilate emotion, and along with this an attitude of constructive passivity, so to speak, in which the ego is less tightly organized than is necessary in conscious reasoning. It was to patients with these potentialities that Jungian therapy

---

[1] Chapter IX, 'The Changes in Jung's Work and its Appeal—Some Cognitive and Emotional Factors,' pp. 228–52.
[2] *Supra*, p. 229.   [3] *Supra*, p. 232.

seemed likely to have much to offer. In theoretical development, however, Jung's orientation toward the image could be a handicap, since by development of thought is meant the placing of material into logical categories of subordination, superordination, causation and so forth—all those operations for which images are least effective. Even in therapy itself, the image might need to be supplemented by more verbal analysis of its impact upon relationships, etc. than is apparent in Jung's work. Nevertheless, turning to some of the attitudes in Jungian therapy, e.g. 'just the alarmingly chaotic . . . reveals the deepest meaning' and '"rarely . . . people come to great things without they first go somewhat astray",'[1] we thought that Jung may have been the chief exponent of the importance of *appreciation* of personality in psychotherapy, and suggested that if it is not always easy for the verbally minded to find words with which to express this point of view, how much more inclined may the less verbally minded have been to accept Jung's psychology as it was, without analysis into its components. And to all this must be added the effect of Jung's own personality, which has, undoubtedly, been capable of evoking affection and respect in high degree.

Another possibility was that Jung's work had been a good cultural fit for groups in which the work of Freud, again for cultural reasons, did not gain a ready hearing.[2] Remembering the initial difference in their background—Jung having his origins in a family which 'belonged to the later part of the Middle Ages',[3] Freud 'as a Jew who has never sought to hide the fact that he is a Jew',[4] we were able to build up a picture of the two contrasting ways of life—the one with a strong sense of community and predominance of face-to-face contacts, close connection with the soil and relatively slow tempo; the other highly urbanized and more individualistic, with less security, a more rapid tempo and greater dependence upon rational planning. Both in theory and in therapy the influence of these two ways of life was seen, e.g. in the more active quality of Freud's formulations of repression and the 'limited liability' flavour of his relations with the patient, contrasted with Jung's statements about the 'purposeful and continuous development of the living process' and his attitude that no longer does the patient stand alone, 'but someone whom he trusts reaches out a

---

[1] *Supra*, p. 150.
[2] Chapter X, 'Jungian Psychology and its Appeal: the Social Background,' pp. 253–97.   [3] *Supra*, p. 1.   [4] *Supra*, p. 44.

hand, lending him moral strength'.[1] It seemed probable, too, that many of the differences between Jung and the later neo-analytical writers had sprung from the same source—the greater reliance on rational planning again, and their awareness of insecurities. It was suggested that factors of this kind, recognized, but only vaguely,[2] contributed to the strain in relationships between the Vienna and the Zürich schools, and that especially in the early days cultural or sub-cultural similarities may have been important in binding the adherents of Freud or Jung together. More tentatively, we wondered whether two factors which may have played a part in Jung's emphasis on the Collective, rather than the Personal, Unconscious were culturally derived, or partially so, namely, willingness to follow wherever the patient led, resulting, at times, in over-identification with the patient's productions, and reluctance, on grounds of delicacy, to publish personal material. Viewing the situation very broadly, we felt there was something almost symbolic in the obscurities of Jung, recalling the relative helplessness of a more slow-moving, less word-minded group confronted with a way of life less deeply rooted, more aggressive and rapid in manipulation of the environment, with less to give in terms of security and love, but able more readily to achieve short-term success.

It remains to ask, What is Jung's place in the history of psychology, and what part can we expect his work to play in future? Any suggestions can be only tentative, all the more so since we are still so close to Jung at present. Through his early work he will, of course, be remembered as the first investigator to bring together psychoanalysis and the experimental method, to apply psychoanalysis to a study of psychotic symptoms, and, a few years afterwards, to state a number of objections to the outlook and doctrines of the psychoanalytical movement which have at least been felt quite widely. In his later work he can perhaps best be regarded as a writer, of a type commoner in the German-speaking areas than the English, who lived 'always on the borderline of poetry and science' in the region, as Theodor Merz described it years ago, 'where scientific and philosophical forms and methods avail little or nothing, but which is nevertheless the spontaneous and creative source out of which all other mental efforts flow'.[3] Some of his theoretical and practical anticipations have been

---

[1] *Supra*, p. 144.   [2] *Supra*, p. 44; p. 254.
[3] *Op. cit.*, Vol. IV, p. 40; p. 95.

seen, and there may well be others. In the future much, inevitably, will depend on the work of his successors. In the practical sphere it would seem most probable that the schools of depth psychology with their different traditions will continue, in somewhat the same way that, no matter how unified knowledge or belief may become, such foundations as Oxford or Cambridge or the major denominations within the Christian Church are likely to maintain their independent life. On the theoretical side we have seen indications in recent years, especially in the work of the British analytical psychologists, that gaps and confusions are being dealt with and that the Jungian school may contribute to a greater extent than formerly to the development of a shared set of hypotheses concerning personality in all its aspects.

But whatever the final estimation of Jung's work may be, there is perhaps no better way of summing up than to add his own words:

'I do not forget that my voice is but one voice, my experience a mere drop in the sea, my knowledge no greater than the visual field in a microscope, my mind's eye a mirror that reflects a small corner of the world, and my ideas—a subjective confession.'[1]

[1] *Mod. Man*, p. 254.

BIBLIOGRAPHY

ADLER, A. *Practice and Theory of Individual Psychology.* 1925. London: Kegan Paul.

ADLER, A. *Understanding Human Nature.* 1927. London: George Allen & Unwin.

ADLER, G. *Studies in Analytical Psychology.* 1948. London: Routledge & Kegan Paul.

ALEXANDER, F. *Psychoanalysis and Psychotherapy.* 1957. London: Allen & Unwin.

ALEXANDER, F. and FRENCH, T. *Psychoanalytic Therapy.* 1946. New York: Ronald Press Co.

ALLPORT, G. W. *The Individual and His Religion.* 1951. London: Constable.

ANGYAL, A. *Foundations for a Science of Personality.* 1941. New York: Commonwealth Fund.

BACH, H. J. 'C. G. Jung on "Synchronicity".' 1953. Guild of Pastoral Psychology. Lecture No. 77.

BAKAN, D. *Sigmund Freud and the Jewish Mystical Tradition.* 1958. New Jersey: D. Van Nostrand Co.

BARTLETT, F. C. *Remembering.* 1932. Cambridge University Press.

BAYNES, H. G. *Analytical Psychology and the English Mind.* 1950. London: Methuen.

BAYNES, H. G. *Mythology of the Soul.* 1949. London: Methuen.

BERGLER, E. 'Psycho-Analysis of the Uncanny.' 1934. *Int. J. Psycho-Anal.* XV, pp. 215–44.

BERGLER, E. 'Therapeutic Results of Psycho-Analysis.' 1937. *Int. J. Psycho-Anal,,* XVIII, p. 146-60.

BETTELHEIM, BRUNO. 'Individual and Mass Behaviour in Extreme Situations.' 1943. *J. Abnorm. Soc. Psychol.,* XXXVIII, pp. 417–52.

BLANCO, I. M. 'A Psycho-Analytic Comment on English Manners.' 1941. *Psychiatry,* IV, pp. 189–99.

BLANCO, I. M. 'Some Reflections on Psycho-Dynamics.' 1940. *Int. J. Psycho-Anal.,* XXI, pp. 253–79.

BLUELER, E. *Dementia Praecox.* 1950. New York: International Universities Press.

BONDY, C. 'Problems of Internment Camps.' 1943. *J. Abnorm. Soc. Psychol.,* XXXVIII, pp. 453–75.

BORING, E. G. 'Was This Analysis A Success?' 1940. *J. Abnorm. Soc. Psychol.,* XXXV, pp. 4–10.

BRIERLEY, M. Review of Jacobi's *Psychology of C. G. Jung.* 1943. *Int. J. Psycho-Anal.,* XXIV, pp. 81–4.

BRIERLEY, M. Review of Jung's *Integration of the Personality.* 1941. *Int. J. Psycho-Anal.* XXII, pp. 172–4.

312

BRIERLEY, M. *Trends in Psycho-Analysis.* 1951. London: Hogarth Press.
BROWN, W. *Psychology and Psychotherapy.* 1920. London: Edward Arnold.
BURROW, T. *Social Basis of Consciousness.* 1927. New York: Harcourt, Brace & Co.

CASEY, R. P. 'Transient Cults.' 1941. *Psychiatry*, IV, pp. 525–34.
CHASE, H. W. 'Consciousness and the Unconscious.' 1917. *Psychol. Bull.*
CHASE, STUART. *The Tyranny of Words.* 1939. London: Methuen.
COHEN, E. A. *Human Behaviour in the Concentration Camp.* 1953. Norton.
COX, D. *Jung and St. Paul.* 1959. London: Longmans, Green & Co.
CRAWSHAY-WILLIAMS, R. *The Comforts of Unreason.* 1947. London: Kegan Paul.
CRICHTON MILLER, H. *Psycho-Analysis and its Derivatives.* 1945. London: Oxford University Press.
CUSTANCE, J. *Adventure into the Unconscious.* 1954. London: Christopher Johnson.
CUSTANCE, J. *Wisdom, Madness and Folly.* 1951. London: Gollancz.

D'ARCY, M. C. *The Mind and Heart of Love.* 1946. London: Faber & Faber.
DAVIE, T. M. 'Jung's Theory of Psychological Types.' 1933. *J. of Mental Sci.*, LXXIX, **325**, pp. 247–85.
DE BEER, G. R. *Embryos and Ancestors.* 1940. Oxford: Clarendon Press.
DE SANCTIS, S. 'The Psychophysiology of the Dream.' 1933–4. *Character and Personality*, **2**, pp. 269–87.
DEUTSCH, H. 'A Discussion of Certain Forms of Resistance.' 1939. *Int. J. Psycho-Anal.*, XX, pp. 72–83.

EISSLER, K. R. 'Remarks on the Psycho-Analysis of Schizophrenia.' 1951. *Int. J. Psycho-Anal.*, XXXII, pp. 140–56.
EVANS, ERASTUS. 'An Assessment of Jung's "Answer to Job".' 1954. Guild of Pastoral Psychology. Guild Lecture No. 78.
EYSENCK, H. J. *The Structure of Human Personality.* 1953. London: Methuen.

FAIRBAIRN, W. R. D. 'Freud, the Psycho-Analytic Method and Mental Health.' 1957. *Brit. J. Med. Psychol.*, XXX, **2**, pp. 53–62.
FAIRBAIRN, W. R. D. 'Observations in Defence of the Object Relations Theory of the Personality.' 1955. *Brit. J. Med. Psychol.* XXVIII, **2 & 3**, pp. 144–56.
FAIRBAIRN, W. R. D. *Psycho-Analytic Studies of the Personality.* 1952. London: Tavistock Publications.
FARRELL, B. A. 'The Scientific Testing of Psycho-Analytic Findings and Theory.' 1951. *Brit. J. Med. Psychol.*, XXIV, **1**, pp. 35–41.
FEDERN, P. 'The Analysis of Psychotics.' 1934. *Int. J. Psycho-Anal.*, XV, 1934, pp. 209–14.
FELDMAN, S. S. 'Dr. C. G. Jung and National Socialism.' 1945. *Am. J. Psychiat.*, **102**, p. 263.
FERENCZI, S. 'Confusion of Tongues Between the Adult and the Child.' 1949. *Int. J. Psycho-Anal.*, XXX, pp. 225–30.
'FIELD, JOANNA'. *An Experiment in Leisure.* 1937. London: Chatto & Windus.
FINKELSTEIN, L. (ed.). *The Jews.* 1949. New York: Harper.
FLEMING, G. U. T. H. (ed.). *Recent Progress in Psychiatry.* 1950. London: J. & A. Churchill.

FLUGEL, J. C. *Man, Morals and Society.* 1945. London: Duckworth.

FORDHAM, F. 'Dr. Jung on Life and Death.' *The Listener.* Oct. 29, 1959. pp. 722–5.

FORDHAM, F. *An Introduction to Jung's Psychology.* 1953. London: Penguin Books.

FORDHAM, M. 'Counter-Transference.' 1960. *Brit. J. Med. Psychol.,* XXXIII, **1**, pp. 1–8.

FORDHAM, M. 'The Evolution of Jung's Researches.' 1956. *Brit. J. Med. Psychol.* XXIX, pp. 3–19.

FORDHAM, M. *The Life of Childhood.* 1944. London: Kegan Paul.

FORDHAM, M. 'Professor C. G. Jung.' 1945. *Brit. J. Med. Psychol.,* XX, pp. 221–35.

FREUD, S. *Autobiographical Study.* 1935. London: Hogarth Press.

FREUD, S. *Beyond the Pleasure Principle.* 1948. London: Hogarth Press.

FREUD, S. *Civilization and its Discontents.* 1930. London: Hogarth Press.

FREUD, S. *Collected Papers,* Vols. I–V. 1933. London: Hogarth Press.

FREUD, S. *The Ego and the Id.* 1949. London: Hogarth Press.

FREUD, S. *The Future of an Illusion.* 1949. London: Hogarth Press.

FREUD, S. *The Interpretation of Dreams.* 1920. London: George Allen & Unwin.

FREUD, S. *Introductory Lectures on Psycho-Analysis.* 1922. London: George Allen & Unwin.

FREUD, S. *New Introductory Lectures on Psycho-Analysis.* 1949. London: Hogarth Press.

FREUD, S. 'An Outline of Psycho-Analysis.' 1940. *Int. J. Psycho-Anal.,* XXI, pp. 27–84.

FREUD, S. *Three Contributions to the Theory of Sexuality.* 1918. New York: Nervous and Mental Diseases Publishing Company.

FREUD, S. *Totem and Taboo.* 1950. London: Routledge & Kegan Paul.

FREY, L. 'The Beginnings of Depth Psychology from Mesmer to Freud.' Unpublished Essay.

FROMM, E. *The Forgotten Language.* 1952. London: Gollancz.

FROMM, E. *Man for Himself.* 1947. New York: Rinehart.

FROMM, E. *Psychoanalysis and Religion.* 1950. Newhaven: Yale University Press.

FROMM, E. 'The Social Philosophy of "Will Therapy".' *Psychiatry.* 1939. II, pp. 229–37.

FROMM-REICHMANN, F. 'Notes on the Development of Treatment of Schizophrenics by Psychoanalytic Psychotherapy.' 1948. *Psychiatry,* XI, pp. 263–74.

FROMM-REICHMANN, F. 'Personal and Professional Requirements of a Psychotherapist.' 1949. *Psychiatry,* XII, pp. 361–78.

FROMM-REICHMANN, F. *Principles of Intensive Psychotherapy.* 1953. London: Allen & Unwin.

FROMM-REICHMANN, F. 'Recent Advances in Psychoanalytic Therapy.' 1941. *Psychiatry,* IV, **2**, pp. 161–4.

FROMM-REICHMANN, F. 'Remarks on the Philosophy of Mental Disorder.' 1946. *Psychiatry,* IX, **4**, pp. 294–308.

GLOVER, E. *Freud or Jung.* 1950. London: Allen & Unwin.

GOLDBRUNNER, J. *Individuation.* 1955. London: Hollis & Carter.

GREEN, A. 'Social Values and Psychotherapy.' *J. Pers.,* XIV, pp. 199–228.

GROTJAHN, M. 'Some Features Common to Psychotherapy of Psychotic Patients and Children.' 1938. *Psychiatry,* I, **3**, pp. 317–22.

HADFIELD, J. A. *Psychology and Morals*. 1923. London: Methuen.

HALLOWELL, A. IRVING. 'The Child, the Savage, and Human Experience.' *Proc. of the 6th Institute on the Exceptional Child*. Oct. 1939.

HARDING, D. W. *The Impulse to Dominate*. 1941. London: Allen & Unwin.

HARMS, E. 'Carl Gustav Jung—Defender of Freud and the Jews.' 1946. *Psychiatric Quarterly*, **20**, 2; pp. 199-230.

HEPBURN, R. W. 'Poetry and Religious Belief.' Ch. of MacIntyre, A. (ed.) *Metaphysical Beliefs*. 1952. London: S.C.M. Press, pp. 85–166.

HOBSON, R. F. 'Archetypal Themes in Depression.' 1956. *J. Analyt. Psychol.*, I, **1**, pp. 33–47.

HOPKINS, PRYNS. 'Sigmund Freud.' 1939. *Character and Personality*. VIII, pp. 163–69.

HORNEY, K. *The Neurotic Personality of Our Time*. 1937. London: Kegan Paul.

HORNEY, K. *New Ways in Psychoanalysis*. 1947. London: Kegan Paul.

HOSKINS, R. G. *The Biology of Schizophrenia*. 1946. Norton Chapman.

HOSTIE, R. *Religion and the Psychology of Jung*. 1957. London: Sheen & Ward.

HOWARD-OGDON, J. A. *Kingdom of the Lost*. 1947. London: Bodley Head.

'HUNTER, E. DABNEY'. 'Subjective Difficulties Incident to the Acceptance of Psychoanalysis.' 1942. *Psychiatry*, V, **4**, pp. 495–8.

HUXLEY, A. *The Doors of Perception*. 1954. Chatto & Windus.

JACKSON MURRAY. 'Jung's "Archetypes" and Psychiatry.' *J. Ment, Sci.*, CVI, **445**, 1960; pp. 1518-26.

JACKSON, MURRAY. 'Jung's "archetype": clarity or confusion?' 1960. *Brit. J. Med. Psychol*. XXXIII, 2, pp. 83–94.

JACOBI, J. *Complex/Archetype/Symbol*. 1959. New York: Pantheon Books.

JACOBI, J. *Psychological Reflections—An Anthology of the Writings of C. G. Jung*. 1953. London: Routledge & Kegan Paul.

JACOBI, J. *The Psychology of C. G. Jung*. 1942. London: Kegan Paul.

JACOBI, J. *Two Essays on Freud and Jung*. 1958. Zürich: Privately printed for the Students' Association, C. G. Jung Institute.

JAMES, E. O. *The Beginnings of Religion*. 1949. London: Hutchinson's University Library.

JAMES, HENRY (ed.). *The Letters of William James*. 1920. London: Longmans, Green & Co.

JAMES, WILLIAM. *Varieties of Religious Experience*. 1902. London: Longmans, Green & Co.

JANET, P. *Psychological Healing*. 1925. London: Allen & Unwin.

JONES, E. Business Report of the Central Executive. 1934. *Int. J. Psycho-Anal.*, XV, 4, pp. 510–17.

JONES, E. 'The Concept of a Normal Mind.' 1942. *Int. J. Psycho-Anal.*, XXIII, **1**, pp. 1–8.

JONES, E. *Free Associations*. 1959. London: Hogarth Press.

JONES, E. 'How Can Civilization Be Saved?' *Int. J. Psycho-Anal.*, XXIV, 1943, pp. 1–7.

JONES, E. Obituary of Karl Abraham. 1926. *Int. J. Psycho-Anal.*, VII.

JONES, E. *Papers on Psycho-Analysis*. 1920. London: Ballière, Tindall & Cox.

JONES, E. *Presidential Report, 16th International Psychoanalytical Congress*. *Int. J. Psycho-Anal.*, XX, **3**.

JONES, E. *Sigmund Freud, His Life and Work*. Vols. I–III, 1953-7. London: Hogarth Press.

JUNG, C. G. *Aion.* 1959. London: Routledge & Kegan Paul.

JUNG, C. G. *Answer to Job.* 1954. London: Routledge & Kegan Paul.

JUNG, C. G. *Archetypes and the Collective Unconscious.* 1958. London: Routledge & Kegan Paul.

JUNG, C. G. *Collected Papers on Analytical Psychology.* 1934. London: Ballière, Tindall & Cox.

JUNG, C. G. *Contributions to Analytical Psychology.* 1945. London: Kegan Paul.

JUNG, C. G. *Development of Personality.* 1954. London: Routledge & Kegan Paul.

JUNG, C. G. *Essays on Contemporary Events.* 1947. London: Kegan Paul.

JUNG, C. G. *The Integration of the Personality.* 1940. London: Kegan Paul.

JUNG, C. G. *Modern Man in Search of a Soul.* 1934. London: Kegan Paul.

JUNG, C. G. *Practice of Psychotherapy.* 1954. London: Routledge & Kegan Paul.

JUNG, C. G. *Psychiatric Studies.* 1957. London: Routlege & Kegan Paul.

JUNG, C. G. *Psychology and Alchemy.* 1955. London: Routledge & Kegan Paul.

JUNG, C. G. *Psychology and Religion.* 1938. New Haven: Yale University Press.

JUNG, C. G. *Psychology and Religion.* 1958. New York: Pantheon Books.

JUNG, C. G. *Psychology of Dementia Praecox.* 1936. New York: Nervous & Mental Disease Monographs.

JUNG, C. G. *Psychological Types.* 1949. London: Routledge & Kegan Paul.

JUNG, C. G. *Psychology of the Unconscious.* 1944. London: Kegan Paul.

JUNG, C. G. *The Secret of the Golden Flower.* 1931. London: Kegan Paul.

JUNG, C. G. *Studies in Word Association.* 1918. London: Heinemann.

JUNG, C. G. 'The Symbolic Life.' (1939). Guild of Pastoral Psychology. Guild Lecture No. 80, 1954.

JUNG, C. G. *Symbols of Transformation.* 1957. London: Routledge & Kegan Paul.

JUNG, C. G. *Theory of Psychoanalysis.* 1915. New York: Journal of Nervous & Mental Disease Publishing Co.

JUNG, C. G. *Two Essays on Analytical Psychology.* 1928. London: Ballière, Tindall & Cox.

JUNG, C. G. *Two Essays on Analytical Psychology.* 1953. London: Routledge & Kegan Paul.

JUNG, C. G. *The Undiscovered Self.* 1958. London: Routledge & Kegan Paul.

JUNG, C. G. and PAULI, W. *The Interpretation of Nature and the Psyche.* 1955. New York: Pantheon Books.

KASANIN, J. S. (ed.). *Language and Thought in Schizophrenia.* 1946. Berkeley: University of California Press.

KIMMELMAN, G. Review of Erich Fromm's *Man for Himself.* 1947. *J. Abnorm. Soc. Psychol.*, XLIII, pp. 555–7.

KLINEBERG, O. *Social Psychology.* 1940. New York: Henry Holt.

KOHN-BRAMSTEDT, E. *Aristocracy and the Middle Classes in Germany.* 1937. London: P. S. King & Son.

LAFORGUE, R. 'Resistances at Conclusion of Analytic Treatment.' 1934. *Int. J. Psycho-Anal.*, XV, **4**, pp. 419–34.

LANDES, R. and ZBOROWSKI, M. 'Hypotheses Concerning the Eastern European Jewish Family.' 1950. *Psychiatry*, XIII, **4**, pp. 447–64.

LANDIS, C. 'Psychoanalytic Phenomena.' 1940. *J. Abnorm. Soc. Pyschol.*, XXXV, pp. 17–28.

LANGER, S. K. *Philosophy in a New Key*. 1951. London: Oxford University Press.

LASKI, H. J. *The Rise of European Liberalism*. 1936. London: Allen & Unwin.

LAYARD, J. W. *The Lady of the Hare*. 1944. London: Faber & Faber.

LAYARD, J. W. *Stone Men of Malekula*. 1942. London: Chatto & Windus.

LAZARD, D. 'Two Years Under a False Name.' 1946. *J. Abnorm. Soc. Psychol.*, XLI, pp. 161–8.

LEVY, E. 'Some Aspects of the Schizophrenic Formal Disturbance of Thought.' 1943. *Psychiatry*, VI, 1, pp. 55–69.

MACALPINE, I. and HUNTER, R. A. 'Observations on the Psycho-Analytic Theory of Psychoses.' 1954. *Brit. J. Med. Psychol.*, XXVII, 4, pp. 175–92.

MCDOUGALL, W. *The Energies of Men*. 1932. London: Methuen.

MCDOUGALL, W. *An Outline of Abnormal Psychology*. 1926. London: Methuen.

MACKINTOSH, H. R. *Types of Modern Theology*. 1937. London: Nisbet.

MAKHDUM, MOHAMMAD A. 'A Comparative Study of Freudian and Jungian Methods of Analysis.' 1952. Unpublished Ph.D. Thesis, Univ. of London.

MARTIN, P. W. *Experiment in Depth*. 1955. London: Routledge & Kegan Paul.

MEAD, G. H. *Movements of Thought in the Nineteenth Century*. 1936. Chicago, Illinois: University of Chicago Press.

MEIER, C. A. 'C. G. Jung's Contributions to the Theory and Therapy of Schizophrenia.' 1957. *Congress Report of IInd International Congress for Psychiatry*, Zürich.

MEIER, C. A. *Jung and Analytical Psychology*. 1959. Department of Psychology, Andover Newton Theological School. Newton Centre, Massachusetts.

MERZ, J. T. History of European Thought in the Nineteenth Century. (4 Vols.) 1914. Blackwood.

METMAN, P. 'Analysis of a Schizophrenic Man.' 1951. *Brit. J. Med. Psychol.*, XXIV, 1, pp. 55–63.

MILNER, M. 'Some Aspects of Phantasy in Relation to General Psychology.' *Int. J. Psycho-Anal.*, 1945, XXVI, pp. 143–52.

MOORE, T. V. *The Nature and Treatment of Mental Disorders*. 1944. London: Heinemann.

MULLAHY, P. (ed.). *The Contributions of Harry Stack Sullivan*. 1952. New York: Hermitage Press.

MULLAHY, P. *Oedipus Myth and Complex*. 1948. New York: Hermitage Press.

MUNROE, RUTH L. *Schools of Psychoanalytic Thought*. 1957. London: Hutchinson Medical Publications.

MURCHISON, C. (ed.). *Handbook of Child Psychology*. 1931. Worcester, Mass.: Clark University Press.

MURPHY, G. *Personality*—A Biosocial Approach to Origins and Structure. 1947. New York: Harper.

MURRAY, H. A. *Explorations in Personality*. 1938. New York: Oxford University Press.

MURRAY, H. A. 'What Should Psychologists Do About Psycho-Analysis?' 1940. *J. Abnorm. Soc. Psychol.*, XXXV, pp. 150–75.

MYERS, F. W. H. *Human Personality and its Survival of Bodily Death*. 1918. London: Longmans, Green & Co.

NEUMANN, E. *The Great Mother*. 1955. New York: Pantheon Books.

NEUMANN, E. *The Origins and Development of Consciousness*. 1954. London: Routledge & Kegan Paul.

NEUMANN, E. 'The Significance of the Genetic Aspect for Analytical Psychology.' 1959. *J. Analyt. Psychol.*, IV, **2**, pp. 125–37.

NICOLE, J. E. Review of Jung's 'Modern Man in Search of a Soul.' 1934. *J. Ment. Sci.*, LXXX, 331, pp. 718–20.

NORWOOD, C. *The English Tradition of Education.* 1929. London: John Murray.

OBERNDORF, C. P. 'Forty Years of Psycho-Analytic Psychiatry.' 1949. *Int. J. Psycho-Anal.*, XXX, **3**, pp. 153–61.

OERI, A. 'Ein Paar Jugend-erinnerung.' in *Die Kulturelle Bedeutung des Komplexen Psychologie.* 1935. Berlin: Verlag von Julius Springer. pp. 524–8.

OGDEN, C. K. and RICHARDS, I. A. *The Meaning of Meaning.* 1938. London: Kegan Paul.

PENNIMAN, T. K. *A Hundred Years of Anthropology.* 1935. London: Duckworth.

PETERS, R. S. (ed.). *Brett's History of Psychology.* 1952. London: Allen & Unwin.

PHILP, H. L. *Jung and the Problem of Evil.* 1958. London: Rockliff.

PLAUT, A. 'Aspects of Consciousness.' 1959. *Brit. J. Med. Psychol.*, XXXII, **4**, pp. 239–48.

PLAUT, A. 'Hungry Patients: Reflections on Ego Structure.' 1959. *J. Analyt. Psychol.*, IV, **2**.

PRINZHORN, H. *Psychotherapy.* 1932. London: Jonathan Cape.

PROGOFF, I. *Jung's Psychology and its Social Meaning.* 1953. London: Routledge & Kegan Paul.

PUMPIAN-MINDLIN, E. (ed.). *Psychoanalysis as Science.* 1952. Stanford University Press, Stanford, Calif.

PUNER, H. L. *Freud, His Life and His Mind.* 1949. London: Grey Walls Press.

RAPAPORT, D., *et al. Diagnostic Psychological Testing.* 1946. Chicago: Year Book Publishers.

REDLICH, H. *et al.* 'Social Structure and Psychiatric Disorders.' 1953. *Am. J. Psychiat.*, 109, pp. 729–34.

RICKMAN, J. 'Reflections on the Function and Organization of a Psycho-Analytical Society.' *Int. J. Psycho-Anal.*, 1951, XXXII, **3**, pp. 218–37.

RIEFF, P. *Freud—the Mind of the Moralist.* 1959. London: Gollancz.

RIESMAN, D. 'Authority and Liberty in the Structure of Freud's Thought.' 1950. *Psychiatry*, XIII, **2**, pp. 167–87.

RIESMAN, D. 'Themes of Work and Play in the Structure of Freud's Thought.' 1950. *Psychiatry*, XIII, **1**, pp. 1–16.

RIVERS, W. H. R. *Conflict and Dream.* 1923. London: Kegan Paul.

RIVERS, W. H. R. *Instinct and the Unconscious.* 1924. London: Cambridge University Press.

ROBACK, A. A. *Jewish Influence in Modern Thought.* 1929. Camb., Mass., Sci-Art Publishers.

ROBACK, A. A. 'Race and Mode of Expression: A Preliminary Investigation in Collective Personality.' 1935. *Character and Personality*, IV, pp. 53–60.

ROSEN, J. N. 'The Treatment of Schizophrenia by Direct Analytic Therapy.' 1947. *Psychiatric Quarterly*, 11, **1**, pp 28-31.

ROSENZWEIG, S. 'A Dynamic Interpretation of Psycho-Therapy Oriented Towards Research.' 1938. *Psychiatry*, I, **4**, pp. 521–26.

ROSENZWEIG, S. Review of Jung's 'Integration of the Personality.' 1940. *J. Abnorm. Soc. Psychol.*, XXXV, pp. 579–82.

ROTH, C. 'The Jews in the Middle Ages.' *Cambridge Medieval History*, Vol. VII, Chapter XXII.

ROTH, C. *A Short History of the Jewish People.* 1936. London: MacMillan.

RUPPIN, A. *The Jewish Fate and Future.* 1940. London: MacMillan.

RUSSELL, B. *History of Western Philosophy.* 1946. London: Allen & Unwin.

SACHS, H. *Freud, Master and Friend.* 1945. London: Imago Publishing Co.

SCHAER, H. *Religion and the Cure of Souls in Jung's Psychology.* 1951. London: Routledge.

SCHEINFELD, A. *Women and Men.* 1947. London: Chatto & Windus.

SHERIF, M. *An Outline of Social Psychology.* 1948. New York: Harper.

SILBERER, H. *Problems of Mysticism and its Symbolism.* 1917. New York.

SPEARMAN, C. 'German Science of Character.' 1937–8. *Character and Personality.* VI, pp. 36–50.

SPINKS, A. G. S. 'Archetypes and Apocalypse: a study of apocalyptic literature from the standpoint of Jungian Psychology.' 1946. Unpublished Ph.D. thesis, University of London.

STENGEL, E. 'On Learning a New Language.' 1939. *Int. J. Psycho-Anal.*, XX, pp. 471–79.

STENGEL, E. 'The Scientific Testing of Psychoanalytical Findings and Theory.' *Brit. J. Med. Psychol.* 1951. XXIV, **1**, pp. 26–34.

STRAUSS, R. 'Counter-Transference.' 1960. *Brit. J. Med. Psychol.*, XXXIII, **1**, pp. 23–7.

SULLIVAN, H. S. *Conceptions of Modern Psychiatry.* 1945. Washington: Wm. Alanson White Foundation.

SULLIVAN, H. S. *The Psychiatric Interview.* 1954. New York: Norton.

SULLIVAN, H. S. *Interpersonal Theory of Psychiatry.* 1952. New York: Norton.

SULLIVAN, H. S. 'Therapeutic Investigations in Schizophrenia.' 1947. *Psychiatry*, X, **2**, pp. 121–5.

SUTTIE, I. D. *Origins of Love and Hate.* 1935. London: Kegan Paul.

TABOR, E. *The Cliff's Edge—Songs of a Psychotic.* 1951. London: Sheed & Ward.

TAWNEY, R. H. *Religion and the Rise of Capitalism.* 1936. London: John Murray.

THOMPSON, C. *Psychoanalysis, Its Evolution and Development.* 1952. London: Allen & Unwin.

THOMPSON, C. 'Ferenczi's Contribution to Psychoanalysis.' 1944. *Psychiatry*, VII, **3**, pp. 243–52.

THOMPSON, C. Review of Jung's 'Modern Man in Search of a Soul.' *Int. J. Psycho-Anal.*, 1934, XV, **3**, pp. 349–51.

THOMPSON, J. A. 'Science.' *Encyclopaedia of Religion and Ethics.* Vol. 11, pp. 252–61.

THOULESS, R. H. 'Methodology and Research in Psycho-Pathology.' 1951. *Brit. J. Med. Psychol.*, XXIV, **1**, pp. 8–12.

UNDERHILL, Evelyn. *Mysticism.* 1930. London: Methuen.

VERNON, P. E. 'The American *vs.* the German Methods of Approach to the Study of Temperament and Personality.' 1933. *Brit. J. Psychol.*, pp. 156–77.

WERNAER, R. M. *Romanticism and the Romantic School in Germany*. 1910. New York: Appleton.

WERNER, H. *Comparative Psychology of Mental Development*. 1940. Harper.

WHITE, VICTOR. *God and the Unconscious*. 1952. London: Harvill Press.

WHITE, VICTOR. *Soul and Psyche*. 1960. London: Harvill Press.

WICKES, FRANCES, G. *The Inner World of Man*. 1938. New York: Henry Holt.

WINDELBAND, W. *A History of Philosophy*. 1931. New York: MacMillan.

WINNICOTT, D. W. 'Counter-Transference.' 1960. *Brit. J. Med. Psychol.*, XXXIII, **1**, pp. 17–21.

WINNICOTT, D. W. 'Hate in the Counter-Transference.' 1949. *Int. J. Psycho-Anal.*, XXX, **2**, pp. 69–74.

WOOD, A. B. 'Another Psychologist Analysed.' 1941. *J. Abnorm. Soc. Psychol.*, XXXVI, pp. 87–90.

ZILBOORG, G. *A History of Medical Psychology*. 1941. New York: Norton.

ZIMMER, H. *Philosophies of India*. 1951. New York: Pantheon Books.

INDEX OF NAMES

321

INDEX OF SUBJECTS